Learning Python for Forensics
Second Edition

Leverage the power of Python in forensic investigations

Preston Miller
Chapin Bryce

BIRMINGHAM - MUMBAI

Learning Python for Forensics
Second Edition

Commissioning Editor: Gebin George
Acquisition Editor: Joshua Nadar
Content Development Editor: Chris D'cruz
Technical Editor: Dinesh Pawar
Copy Editor: Safis Editing
Project Coordinator: Namrata Swetta
Proofreader: Safis Editing
Indexer: Rekha Nair
Graphics: Tom Scaria
Production Coordinator: Nilesh Mohite

First published: May 2016
Second edition: January 2019

Production reference: 1310119

Published by Packt Publishing Ltd.
Livery Place
35 Livery Street
Birmingham
B3 2PB, UK.

ISBN 978-1-78934-169-0

www.packtpub.com

Mapt

Contributors

About the authors

Preston Miller is a consultant at an internationally recognized risk management firm. Preston holds an undergraduate degree from Vassar College and a master's degree in digital forensics from Marshall University. While at Marshall, Preston unanimously received the prestigious J. Edgar Hoover Foundation's scientific scholarship. Preston is a published author, recently of *Python Digital Forensics Cookbook*, which won the Forensic 4:cast Digital Forensics Book of the Year award in 2018. Preston is a member of the GIAC advisory board and holds multiple industry-recognized certifications in his field.

To my grandfather, who taught me the value of hard work, dedication, and the pursuit of excellence, without whose love and support I would not be the person I am today.

Chapin Bryce is a consultant at a global firm that is a leader in digital forensics and incident response investigations. After graduating from Champlain College with a bachelor's degree in computer and digital forensics, Chapin dove into the field of digital forensics and incident response joining the GIAC advisory board and earning four GIAC certifications: GCIH, GCFE, GCFA, and GNFA. As a member of multiple ongoing research and development projects, he has authored several books and articles in professional and academic publications, including *Python Digital Forensics Cookbook* (Forensic 4:Cast Digital Forensics Book of the Year, 2018), *Learning Python for Forensics, First Edition*, and *Digital Forensic Magazine*.

To Alexa, who I hope will learn Python in the near future.

About the reviewer

Marek Chmel is an IT consultant and trainer with more than 10 years' experience. He is a frequent speaker, focusing on Microsoft SQL Server, Azure, and security topics. Marek writes for Microsoft's TechnetCZSK blog and has been an MVP: Data Platform since 2012. He has earned numerous certifications, including MCSE: Data Management and Analytics, EC Council Certified Ethical Hacker, and several eLearnSecurity certifications.

Marek earned his MSc (business and informatics) degree from Nottingham Trent University. He started his career as a trainer for Microsoft server courses. Later, he joined AT&T as a principal database administrator specializing in MSSQL Server, data platforms, and machine learning.

Packt is searching for authors like you

If you're interested in becoming an author for Packt, please visit `authors.packtpub.com` and apply today. We have worked with thousands of developers and tech professionals, just like you, to help them share their insight with the global tech community. You can make a general application, apply for a specific hot topic that we are recruiting an author for, or submit your own idea.

Table of Contents

Preface

At the outset of writing *Learning Python for Forensics*, we had one goal: to teach the use of Python for forensics in such a way that readers with little to no programming experience could follow along immediately and develop practical code for use in casework. That's not to say that this book is intended for the Python neophyte; throughout, we ease the reader into progressively more challenging code and end by incorporating many of the scripts in previous chapters into a forensic framework. This book makes a few assumptions about the reader's programming experience, and where it does, there will often be a detailed explanation with examples and a list of resources to help bridge the gap in knowledge.

The majority of the book will focus on developing code for various forensic artifacts; however, the first two chapters will teach the basics of the language. This will level the playing field for readers of all skill levels. We intend for the complete Python novice to be able to develop forensically sound and relevant scripts by the end of this book.

Much like in the real world, code development will follow a modular design. Initially, a script might be written one way before rewritten in another to show off the advantages (or disadvantages) of various techniques. Immersing you in this fashion will help build and strengthen the neural links required to retain the process of script design. To allow Python development to become second nature, please retype the exercises shown throughout the chapters for yourself to practice and learn common Python tropes. Never be afraid to modify the code, you will not break anything (except maybe your version of the script) and will have a better understanding of the inner workings of the code as a result.

Who this book is for

If you are a forensics student, hobbyist, or professional that is seeking to increase your understanding of forensics through the use of a programming language, then this book is for you.

You are not required to have previous experience of programming to learn and master the content within this book. This material, created by forensic professionals, was written with a unique perspective to help examiners learn programming.

What this book covers

`Chapter 1`, *Now for Something Completely Different*, is an introduction to common Python objects, built-in functions, and tropes. We will also cover basic programming concepts.

`Chapter 2`, *Python Fundamentals*, is a continuation of the basics learned in the previous chapter and the development of our first forensic script.

`Chapter 3`, *Parsing Text Files*, discusses a basic setup API log parser to identify first use times for USB devices and introduce the iterative development cycle.

`Chapter 4`, *Working with Serialized Data Structures*, shows how serialized data structures such as JSON files can be used to store or retrieve data in Python. We will parse JSON-formatted data from the Bitcoin blockchain containing transaction details.

`Chapter 5`, *Databases in Python*, shows how databases can be used to store and retrieve data via Python. We will use two different database modules to demonstrate different versions of a script that creates an active file listing with a database backend.

`Chapter 6`, *Extracting Artifacts from Binary Files*, is an introduction to the struct module, which will become every examiner's friend. We use the struct module to parse binary data into Python objects from a forensically-relevant source. We will parse the UserAssist key in the registry for user application execution artifacts.

`Chapter 7`, *Fuzzy Hashing*, explores how ssdeep compatible hashes are generated and how to use the pre-built ssdeep module to perform similarity analysis.

`Chapter 8`, *The Media Age*, helps us understand embedded metadata and parse them from forensic sources. In this chapter, we introduce and design an embedded metadata framework in Python.

`Chapter 9`, *Uncovering Time*, provides the first look at the development of the GUI with Python to decode commonly encountered timestamps. This is our introduction to GUI and Python class development.

`Chapter 10`, *Rapidly Triage Systems*, shows how you can use Python to collect volatile and other useful information from popular operating systems. This includes an introduction to a very powerful Windows-specific Python API.

`Chapter 11`, *Parsing Outlook PST Containers*, demonstrates how to read, index, and report on the contents of an Outlook PST container.

`Chapter 12`, *Recovering Deleted Database Records*, introduces SQLite Write-Ahead Logs and how to extract data, including deleted data, from these files.

`Chapter 13`, *Coming Full Circle*, is an aggregation of scripts written in previous chapters into a forensic framework. We explore concepts and methods for designing these larger projects.

To get the most out of this book

To follow along with the examples in this book, you will need the following:

- A computer with an internet connection
- Python 2.7.15 or Python 3.7.1
- Optionally, an IDE for Python

In addition to these requirements, you will need to install various third-party modules that we will make use of in our code. We will indicate which modules need to be installed, the correct version, and, often, how to install them.

Download the example code files

You can download the example code files for this book from your account at `www.packt.com`. If you purchased this book elsewhere, you can visit `www.packt.com/support` and register to have the files emailed directly to you.

You can download the code files by following these steps:

1. Log in or register at `www.packt.com`.
2. Select the **SUPPORT** tab.
3. Click on **Code Downloads & Errata**.
4. Enter the name of the book in the **Search** box and follow the onscreen instructions.

Once the file is downloaded, please make sure that you unzip or extract the folder using the latest version of:

- 7-Zip/WinRAR for Windows
- Keka/Zipeg/iZip/UnRarX for Mac
- 7-Zip/PeaZip for Linux

The code bundle for the book is also hosted on GitHub at `https://github.com/PacktPublishing/Learning-Python-for-Forensics-Second-Edition`. In case there's an update to the code, it will be updated on the existing GitHub repository.

We also have other code bundles from our rich catalog of books and videos available at `https://github.com/PacktPublishing/`. Check them out!

Download the color images

We also provide a PDF file that has color images of the screenshots/diagrams used in this book. You can download it here: `https://www.packtpub.com/sites/default/files/downloads/9781789341690_ColorImages.pdf`.

Conventions used

There are a number of text conventions used throughout this book.

`CodeInText`: Indicates code words in text, database table names, folder names, filenames, file extensions, pathnames, dummy URLs, user input, and Twitter handles. Here is an example: "This chapter outlines the basics of Python, from `Hello World` to core scripting concepts."

A block of code is set as follows:

```
# open the database
    # read from the database using the sqlite3 library
    #     store in variable called records
    for record in records:
        # process database records here
```

Any command-line input or output is written as follows:

```
>>> type('what am I?')
<class 'str'>
```

Bold: Indicates a new term, an important word, or words that you see onscreen. For example, words in menus or dialog boxes appear in the text like this. Here is an example: "Select **System info** from the **Administration** panel."

Warnings or important notes appear like this.

Tips and tricks appear like this.

Get in touch

Feedback from our readers is always welcome.

General feedback: If you have questions about any aspect of this book, mention the book title in the subject of your message and email us at `customercare@packtpub.com`.

Errata: Although we have taken every care to ensure the accuracy of our content, mistakes do happen. If you have found a mistake in this book, we would be grateful if you would report this to us. Please visit `www.packt.com/submit-errata`, selecting your book, clicking on the Errata Submission Form link, and entering the details.

Piracy: If you come across any illegal copies of our works in any form on the Internet, we would be grateful if you would provide us with the location address or website name. Please contact us at `copyright@packt.com` with a link to the material.

If you are interested in becoming an author: If there is a topic that you have expertise in and you are interested in either writing or contributing to a book, please visit `authors.packtpub.com`.

Reviews

Please leave a review. Once you have read and used this book, why not leave a review on the site that you purchased it from? Potential readers can then see and use your unbiased opinion to make purchase decisions, we at Packt can understand what you think about our products, and our authors can see your feedback on their book. Thank you!

For more information about Packt, please visit `packt.com`.

1

Now for Something Completely Different

This book presents Python as a necessary tool to optimize digital forensic analysis—written from an examiner's perspective. In the first two chapters, we introduce the basics of Python in preparation for the remainder of this book, where we will develop scripts to accomplish forensic tasks. While focused on the use of the language as a tool, we will also explore the advantages of Python and how they allow many individuals in the field to create solutions for complex forensic challenges. Like Monty Python, Python's namesake, the next 12 chapters aim to present *something completely different*.

In this fast-paced field, a scripting language provides flexible problem solving in an automated fashion, allowing the examiner additional time to investigate other artifacts that, due to time constraints, may not have been analyzed as thoroughly otherwise. Admittedly, Python may not always be the right tool to complete the task at hand, but it is an invaluable tool to add to anyone's DFIR arsenal. Should you undertake the task of mastering Python, it will more than pay off the time investment as you will increase your analysis capabilities many fold and greatly diversify your skill set. This chapter outlines the basics of Python, from `Hello World` to core scripting concepts.

This chapter will cover the following topics:

- An introduction to Python and healthy development practices
- Basic programming concepts
- Manipulating and storing objects in Python
- Creating simple conditionals, loops, and functions

When to use Python

Python is a powerful forensic tool. However, before deciding to develop a script, it is important to consider the type of analysis that's required and the project timeline. In the examples that follow, we will outline situations where Python is invaluable and, conversely, when it is not worth the development effort. Though rapid development makes it easy to deploy a solution in a tough situation, Python is not always the best tool to implement. If a tool exists that performs the task at hand, and is available, it may be the more appropriate method for analysis.

Python is a preferred programming language for forensics due to its ease of use, library support, detailed documentation, and interoperability among operating systems. There are two main types of programming languages: those that are interpreted and those that are compiled. Compiling code allows the programming language to be converted into machine language. This lower-level language is more efficient for the computer to interpret. Interpreted languages are not as fast as compiled languages at runtime, but do not require compilation, which can take some time. Because Python is an interpreted language, we can make modifications to our code and immediately run and view the results. With a compiled language, we would have to wait for our code to re-compile before viewing the effect of our modifications. For this reason, Python may not run as quickly as a compiled language, but allows for rapid prototyping.

An incident response case presents an excellent example of when to use Python in a real-life setting. For example, let's consider that a client calls, panicked, reporting a data breach and is unsure of how many files were exfiltrated over the past 24 hours from their file server. Once on site, you are instructed to perform the fastest count of files accessed in the past 24 hours as this count, and the list of compromised files, will determine the course of action.

Python fits this bill quite nicely here. Armed with just a laptop, you can open a text editor and begin writing a solution. Python can be built and designed without the need for a fancy editor or toolset. The build process of your script may look like this, with each step building upon the previous one:

1. Make the script read a single file's last accessed timestamp
2. Write a loop that steps through directories and subdirectories
3. Test each file to see if that timestamp is from the past 24 hours
4. If it has been accessed within 24 hours, then create a list of affected files to display file paths and access times

The process here would result in a script that recurses over the entire server and output files found with a last accessed time in the past 24 hours for manual review. This script will likely be approximately 20 lines of code and have required 10 minutes, or less, for an intermediate scripter to develop and validate—it is apparent this would be more efficient than manually reviewing timestamps on the filesystem.

Before deploying any developed code, it is imperative that you validate its capability first. As Python is not a compiled language, we can easily run the script after adding new lines of code to ensure we haven't broken anything. This approach is known as **test-then-code**, a method commonly used in script development. Any software, regardless of who wrote it, should be scrutinized and evaluated to ensure accuracy and precision. Validation ensures that the code is operating properly, and although more time-consuming, provides reliable results that are capable of withstanding the courtroom, an important aspect in forensics.

A situation where Python may not be the best tool is for general case analysis. If you are handed a hard drive and asked to find evidence without additional insight, then a pre-existing tool will be the better solution. Python is invaluable for targeted solutions, such as analyzing a given file type and creating a metadata report. Developing a custom all-in-one solution for a given filesystem requires too much time to create when other tools, both paid and free, exist that support such generic analysis.

Python is useful in pre-processing automation. If you find yourself repeating the same tasks for each piece of evidence, it may be worthwhile to develop a system that automates those steps. A great example of suites that perform such analysis is ManTech's analysis and triage system (mantaray: `http://github.com/mantarayforensics`), which leverages a series of tools to create general reports that can speed up analysis when there is no scope of what data may exist.

When considering whether to commit resources to develop Python scripts, either on the fly or for larger projects, it is important to consider what solutions already exist, the time available to create a solution, and the time saved through automation. Despite best intentions, the development of solutions can go on for much longer than initially conceived without a strong design plan.

Development life cycle

The development cycle involves at least five steps:

- Identify
- Plan

- Program
- Validate
- Bugs

The first step is self-explanatory; before you develop, you must identify the problem that needs to be solved. Planning is perhaps the most crucial step in the development cycle:

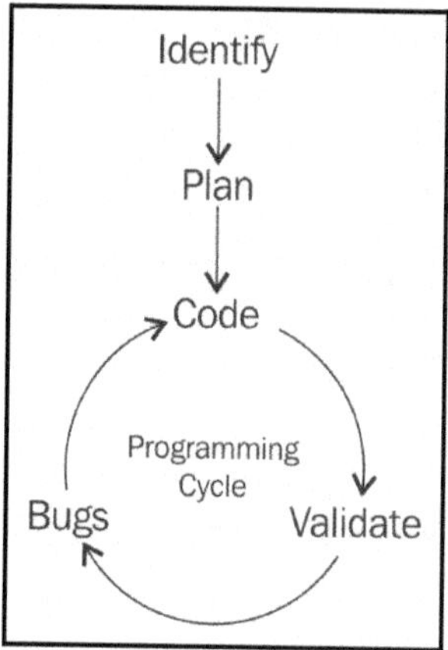

Good planning will help later by decreasing the amount of code required and the number of bugs. Planning becomes even more vital during the learning process. A forensic programmer must begin to answer the following questions: how will data be ingested, what Python data types are most appropriate, are third-party libraries necessary, and how will the results be displayed to the examiner? In the beginning, just as if we were writing a term paper, it is a good idea to write, or draw, an outline of your program. As you become more proficient in Python, planning will become second nature, but initially, it is recommended to create an outline or write pseudocode.

Pseudocode is an informal way of writing code before filling in the details with actual code. Pseudocode can represent the bare bones of the program, such as defining pertinent variables and functions while describing how they will all fit together within the script's framework. Pseudocode for a function might look like this:

```
# open the database
  # read from the database using the sqlite3 library
  # store in variable called records
  for record in records:
    # process database records here
```

After identifying and planning, the next three steps make up the largest part of the development cycle. Once your program has been sufficiently planned, it is time to start writing code! Once the code is written, break in your new program with as much test data as possible. Especially in forensics, it is critical to thoroughly test your code instead of relying on the results of one example. Without comprehensive debugging, the code can crash when it encounters something unexpected, or, even worse, it could provide the examiner with false information and lead them down the wrong path. After the code has been tested, it is time to release it and prepare for bug reports. We are not talking about insects here! Despite a programmer's best efforts, there will always be bugs in the code. Bugs have a nasty way of multiplying even as you squash one, perpetually causing the programming cycle to begin repeatedly.

Getting started

Before we get started, it is necessary that you install Python on your machine. It is important to understand that, at the time of writing this book, there are two supported versions of Python: Python 2 and 3. We will use both Python 2 and 3 to develop our solutions. Historically, many of the useful third-party forensic libraries were developed for Python 2. At this point, most libraries are compatible with Python 3, which has superior Unicode handling, a major headache in Python 2, among a number of other improvements. All of the code in this book has been tested with the latest appropriate versions of Python 2 (v. 2.7.15) or 3 (v. 3.7.1). In some cases, our code is compatible with both Python 2 and 3, or only works with one of the two. Each chapter will describe what version of Python is required to run the code.

Additionally, we recommend using an **integrated development environment**, or **IDE**, such as JetBrain's PyCharm. An IDE will highlight errors and offer suggestions that help streamline the development process and promote best practices when writing code. In the case that the installation of an IDE is not available, a simple text editor will work. We recommend an application such as Notepad++, Sublime Text, or Visual Studio Code. For those who are command line orientated, an editor such as vim or nano will work as well.

With Python installed, let's open the interactive prompt by typing `python` into your Command Prompt or Terminal. We will begin by introducing some built-in functions for use in troubleshooting. The first line of defense when confused by any object or function discussed in this book, or found in the wild, is the `type()`, `dir()`, and `help()` built-in functions. We realize we have not yet introduced common data types and so the following code might appear confusing.

However, that is exactly the point of this exercise. During development, you will encounter data types you are unfamiliar with or be unsure what methods exist to interact with the object. These three functions help solve those issues. We will introduce the fundamental data types later in this chapter.

The `type()` function, when supplied with an object, will return its `__name__` attribute, providing type identifying information about the object. The `dir()` function, when supplied with a string representing the name of an object, will return its attributes, showing the available options of the functions and parameters belonging to the object. The `help()` function can be used to display the specifics of these methods through its **docstrings**. Docstrings are nothing more than descriptions of a function that detail the inputs, outputs, and how to use the function.

Let's look at the `str`, or string, object as an example of these three functions. In the following example, passing a series of characters surrounded by single quotes to the `type()` function results in a type of `str`, or string.

When we show examples where our typed input follows the >>> symbol, this indicates that you should type these statements in the Python interactive prompt. The Python interactive prompt can be accessed by typing `python` in the Command Prompt.

These basic functions behave similarly in both Python 2 and 3. Unless otherwise stated, these function calls and their output are executed with Python 3.7.1. Please note, however, that the purposes of these built-in functions largely remain the same and have similar outputs between Python versions.

Here is an example:

```
>>> type('what am I?')
<class 'str'>
```

If we pass in an object to the `dir()` function, such as `str`, we can see its methods and attributes. Let's say that we want to know what one of these functions, `title()`, does. We can use the `help()` function specifying the object and its function as the input.

The output of the function tells us no input is required, the output is a string object, and that the function capitalized the first character of every word. Let's use the `title` method on the `what am I?` string:

```
>>> dir(str)
['__add__', '__class__', '__contains__', '__delattr__',
'__doc__', '__eq__',
...
'swapcase', 'title', 'translate', 'upper', 'zfill']

>>> help(str.title)
Help on method_descriptor:

title(...)
    S.title() -> str

    Return a titlecased version of S, i.e. words start with title case
characters, all remaining cased characters have lower case.

>>> 'what am I?'.title()
'What Am I?'
```

Next, type `number = 5`. Now we have created a variable, called `number`, that has the numerical value of `5`. Using `type()` on that object indicates that `5` is an `int`, or integer. Going through the same procedure as before, we can see a series of available attributes and functions for the integer object. With the `help()` function, we can check what the `__add__()` function does for our `number` object. From the following output, we can see that this function is equivalent to using the `+` symbol on two values:

```
>>> number = 5
>>> type(number)
<class 'int'>

>>> dir(number)
>>> ['__abs__', '__add__', __and__', '__class__', '__cmp__', '__coerce__',
...
'denominator', 'imag', 'numerator', 'real']

>>> help(number.__add__)
__add__(...)
x.__add__(y) <==> x+y
```

Let's compare the difference between the `__add__()` function and the + symbol to verify our assumption. Using both methods to add `3` to our `number` object results in a returned value of `8`, as expected. Unfortunately, we've also broken a best practice rule illustrating this example:

```
>>> number.__add__(3)
8
>>> number + 3
8
```

Notice how some methods, such as `__add__()`, have double leading and trailing underscores. These are referred to as magic methods, and are methods the Python interpreter calls and should not be called by the programmer. These magic methods are instead called indirectly by the user. For example, the integer `__add__()` magic method is called when using the + symbol between two numbers. Following the previous example, you should never run `number.__add__(3)` instead of `number + 3`.

This rule is broken in a few cases, which we will cover throughout this book, though unless the documentation recommends using a magic method, it is best to avoid them.

Python, like any other programming language, has a specific syntax. Compared to other common programming languages, Python is rather English-like and can be read fairly easily in scripts. This feature has attracted many, including the forensics community, to use this language. Even though Python's language is easy to read, it is not to be underestimated as it is powerful and supports common programming paradigms.

Most programmers start with a simple `Hello World` script, a test that proves they are able to execute code and print the famous message into the console window. With Python, the code to print this statement is a single line, as seen here, written on the first line of a file:

```
001 print("Hello World!")
```

Please note that when discussing the code in a script, as opposed to code in the interactive prompt, line numbers, starting at **001**, are shown for reference purposes only. Please do not include these line numbers in your script. The code for this script and all scripts can be downloaded at `https://packtpub.com/books/content/support`.

Save this line of code in a file called `hello.py`. To run this script, we call Python and the name of the script. If you are using Python 3, the message `Hello World!` should be displayed in your Terminal:

```
(py3.7.1) C:\book\chapters\chapter_01>python hello.py
Hello World!

(py3.7.1) C:\book\chapters\chapter_01>
```

Let's discuss why this simple script will not execute successfully in some versions of Python 2.

The omnipresent print() function

Printing in Python is a very common technique as it allows the developer to display text to the console as the script executes. While there are many differences between Python 2 and 3, the way printing is called is the most obvious change, and is the reason why our previous example primarily only works with Python 3 as it is currently written. With Python 3, `print` became a function rather than a statement, as was the case with older versions of Python 2. Let's revisit our previous script and see a slight difference.

Note the following for Python 3:

```
print("Hello World!")
```

Note the following for Python 2:

```
print "Hello World!"
```

The difference is seemingly minor. In Python 2, where `print` is a statement, you do not need to wrap what is being printed in parentheses. It would be disingenuous to say the difference is just semantics; however, for now just understand that `print` is written in two different ways, depending on the version of Python being used. The ramifications of this minor change mean that legacy Python 2 scripts that use `print` as a statement cannot be executed by Python 3.

Where possible, our scripts will be written to be compatible with both versions of Python. This goal, while seemingly impossible due to the difference in `print`, can be accomplished by importing a special Python library, called `__future__`, and changing the `print` statement to a function. To do this, we need to import the `print` function from the `__future__` library and then write all `print` commands as `function`.

The following script executes in both Python 2 and 3:

```
from __future__ import print_function
print("Hello World!")
```

```
(py3.7.1) C:\book\chapters\chapter_01>python hello_v2.py
Hello World!

(py2.7.15) C:\book\chapters\chapter_01>python hello_v2.py
Hello World!
```

In the previous screenshot, you can see the result of this script in Python 2.7.15 and Python 3.7.1.

Standard data types

With our first script complete, it is time to understand the basic data types of Python. These data types are similar to those found in other programming languages, but are invoked with a simple syntax, which is described in the following table and sections. For a full list of standard data types available in Python, visit the official documentation at `https://docs.python.org/3/library/stdtypes.html`:

Data Type	Description	Example
`Str`	String	`str(), "Hello", 'Hello'`
`Unicode`	Unicode characters	`unicode(),u'hello',"world".encode('utf-8')`
`Int`	Integer	`int(),1,55`
`Float`	Decimal precision integers	`float(),1.0,.032`
`Bool`	Boolean values	`bool(),True,False`
`List`	List of elements	`list(), [3, 'asd', True, 3]`
`Dictionary`	Set of key:value pairs used to structure data	`dict(),{'element': 'Mn', 'Atomic Number': 25, 'Atomic Mass': 54.938}`
`Set`	List of unique elements	`set(), [3, 4, 'hello']`
`Tuple`	Organized list of elements	`tuple(), (2, 'Hello World!', 55.6, ['element1'])`
`File`	A file object	`open('write_output.txt', 'w')`

We are about to dive into the usage of data types in Python, and recommend that you repeat this section as needed to help with comprehension. While reading through how data types are handled is important, please be at a computer where you can run Python when you work through it the first few times. We invite you to explore the data type further in your interpreter and test them to see what they are capable of.

You will find that most of our scripts can be accomplished using only the standard data types Python offers. Before we take a look at one of the most common data types, strings, we will introduce comments.

Something that is always said, and can never be said enough, is to comment your code. In Python, comments are formed by any line beginning with the pound, or more recently known as the hashtag, # symbol. When Python encounters this symbol, it skips the remainder of the line and proceeds to the next line. For comments that span multiple lines, we can use three single or double quotes to mark the beginning and end of the comments rather than using a single pound symbol for every line. What follows are examples of types of comments in a file called `comments.py`. When running this script, we should only see `10` printed to the console as all comments are ignored:

```
# This is a comment
print(5 + 5) # This is an inline comment.
# Everything to the right of the # symbol
# does not get executed
"""We can use three quotes to create
multi-line comments."""
```

The output is as follows:

```
(py3.7.1) C:\book\chapters\chapter_01>python comments.py
10
```

When this code is executed, we only see the preceding at the console.

Strings and Unicode

Strings are a data type that contain any character, including alphanumeric characters, symbols, Unicode, and other codecs. With the vast amount of information that can be stored as a string, it is no surprise they are one of the most common data types. Examples of areas where strings are found include reading arguments at the command line, user input, data from files, and outputting data. To begin, let us look at how we can define a string in Python.

There are three ways to create a string: with single quotes, double quotes, or with the built-in `str()` constructor method. Note that there is no difference between single- and double-quoted strings. Having multiple ways to create a string is advantageous, as it allows us to differentiate between intentional quotes within a string. For example, in the `'I hate when people use "air-quotes"!'` string, we use the single quotes to demarcate the beginning and end of the main string. The double quotes inside the string will not cause any issues with the Python interpreter. Let's verify with the `type()` function that both single and double quotes create the same type of object:

```
>>> type('Hello World!')
<class 'str'>
>>> type("Foo Bar 1234")
<class 'str'>
```

As we saw with comments, a block string can be defined by three single or double quotes to create multi-line strings. The only difference is whether we do something with the block-quoted value or not:

```
>>> """This is also a string"""
This is also a string
>>> '''it
 can span
 several lines'''
it\ncan span\nseveral lines
```

The `\n` character in the returned line signifies a line feed or a new line. The output in the interpreter displays these newline characters as `\n`, though when fed into a file or console, a new line is created. The `\n` character is one of the common escape characters in Python. Escape characters are denoted by a backslash following a specific character. Other common escape characters include `\t` for horizontal tabs, `\r` for carriage returns, `\'`, `\"`, and `\\` for literal single quotes, double quotes, and backslashes, among others. Literal characters allow us to use these characters without unintentionally using their special meaning in Python's context.

We can also use the add (`+`) or multiply (`*`) operators with strings. The add operator is used to concatenate strings together, and the multiply operator will repeat the provided string values:

```
>>> 'Hello' + ' ' + 'World'
Hello World
>>> "Are we there yet? " * 3
Are we there yet? Are we there yet? Are we there yet?
```

Let's look at some common functions we use with strings. We can remove characters from the beginning or end of a string using the `strip()` function. The `strip()` function requires the character we want to remove as its input, otherwise it will replace whitespace by default. Similarly, the `replace()` function takes two inputs the character to replace and what to replace it with. The major difference between these two functions is that `strip()` only looks at the beginning and end of a string:

```
# This will remove colon (`:`) from the beginning and end of the line
>>> ':HelloWorld:'.strip(':')
HelloWorld


# This will remove the colon (`:`) from the line and place a
# space (` `) in it's place
>>> 'Hello:World'.replace(':', ' ')
Hello World
```

We can check if a character or characters are in a string using the `in` statement. Or, we can be more specific, and check if a string `startswith()` or `endswith()` a specific character(s) instead (you know a language is easy to understand when you can create sensible sentences out of functions). These methods return `True` or `False` Boolean objects:

```
>>> 'a' in 'Chapter 2'
True
>>> 'Chapter 1'.startswith('Chapter')
True
>>> 'Chapter 1'.endswith('1')
True
```

We can quickly split a string into a list based on some delimiter. This can be helpful to quickly convert data separated by a delimiter into a list. For example, **comma-separated values** (**CSV**) data is separated by commas and could be split on that value:

```
>>> print("Hello, World!".split(','))
["Hello", " World!"]
```

Formatting parameters can be used on strings to manipulate them and convert them based on provided values. With the `.format()` function, we can insert values into strings, pad numbers, and display patterns with simple formatting. This chapter will highlight a few examples of the `.format()` method, and we will introduce more complex features of it throughout this book. The `.format()` method replaces curly brackets with the provided values in order.

This is the most basic operation for inserting values into a string dynamically:

```
>>> "{} {} {} {}".format("Formatted", "strings", "are", "easy!")
'Formatted strings are easy!'
```

Our second example displays some of the expressions we can use to manipulate a string. Inside the curly brackets, we place a colon, which indicates that we are going to specify a format for interpretation. Following this colon, we specify that there should be at least six characters printed. If the supplied input is not six characters long, we prepend zeroes to the beginning of the input. Lastly, the `d` character specifies that the input will be a base 10 decimal:

```
>>> "{:06d}".format(42)
'000042'
```

Our last example demonstrates how we can easily print a string of `20` equal signs by stating that our fill character is the equals symbol, followed by the caret (to center the symbols in the output), and the number of times to repeat the symbol. By providing this format string, we can quickly create visual separators in our outputs:

```
>>> "{:=^20}".format('')
'===================='
```

While we will introduce more advanced features of the `.format()` method, the site `https://pyformat.info/` is a great resource for learning more about the capabilities of Python's string formatting.

Integers and floats

The integer is another valuable data type that is frequently used—an integer is any whole positive or negative number. The float data type is similar, but allows us to use numbers requiring decimal-level precision. With integers and floats, we can use standard mathematical operations, such as: `+`, `-`, `*`, and `/`. These operations return slightly different results based on the object's type (for example, `integer` or `float`).

An integer uses whole numbers and rounding, for example dividing two integers will result in another whole number integer. However, by using one float in the equation, even one that has the same value as the integer will result in a float; for example, `3/2=1` and `3/2.0=1.5` in Python. The following are examples of integer and float operations:

```
>>> type(1010)
<class 'int'>
```

```
>>> 127*66
8382
>>> 66/10
6
>>> 10 * (10 - 8)
20
```

We can use `**` to raise an integer by a power. For example, in the following section, we raise `11` by the power of `2`. In programming, it can be helpful to determine the numerator resulting from the division between two integers. For this, we use the modulus or percent (`%`) symbol. With Python, negative numbers are those with a dash character (`-`) preceding the value. We can use the built-in `abs()` function to get the absolute value of an integer or float:

```
>>> 11**2
121
>>> 11 % 2 # 11 divided by 2 is 5.5 or 5 with a remainder of 1
1
>>> abs(-3)
3
```

A float is defined by any number with a decimal. Floats follow the same rules and operations as we saw with integers, with the exception of the division behavior described previously:

```
>>> type(0.123)
<class 'float'>
>>> 1.23 * 5.23
6.4329
>>> 27/8.0
3.375
```

Boolean and none

The integers `0` and `1` can also represent Boolean values in Python. These values are the Boolean `False` or `True` objects, respectively. To define a Boolean, we can use the `bool()` constructor statement. These data types are used extensively in program logic to evaluate statements for conditionals, as covered later in this chapter.

Another built-in data type is the null type, which is defined by the keyword `None`. When used, it represents an empty object, and when evaluated will return `False`. This is helpful when initializing a variable that may use several data types throughout execution. By assigning a null value, the variable remains sanitized until reassigned:

```
>>> bool(0)
False
>>> bool(1)
True
>>> None
>>>
```

Structured data types

There are several data types that are more complex and allow us to create structures of raw data. This includes lists, dictionaries, sets, and tuples. Most of these structures are comprised of the previously mentioned data types. These structures are very useful in creating powerful units of values, allowing raw data to be stored in a manageable manner.

Lists

Lists are a series of ordered elements. Lists support any data type as an element and will maintain the order of data as it is appended to the list. Elements can be called by position or a loop can be used to step through each item. In Python, unlike other languages, printing a list takes one line. In languages like Java or C++, it can take three or more lines to print a list. Lists in Python can be as long as needed and can expand or contract on the fly, another feature uncommon in other languages.

We can create lists by using brackets with elements separated by commas. Or, we can use the `list()` class constructor with an iterable object. List elements can be accessed by index where `0` is the first element. To access an element by position, we place the desired index in brackets following the list object. Rather than needing to know how long a list is (which can be accomplished with the `len()` function), we can use negative index numbers to access list elements in reference to the end (that is, `-3` would retrieve the third to last element):

```
>>> type(['element1', 2, 6.0, True, None, 234])
<class 'list'>
>>> list((4, 'element 2', None, False, .2))
[4, 'element 2', None, False, 0.2]
>>> len([0,1,2,3,4,5,6])
7
>>> ['hello_world', 'foo bar'][0]
```

```
hello_world
>>> ['hello_world', 'foo_bar'][-1]
foo_bar
```

We can add, remove, or check if a value is in a list using a couple of different functions. The `append()` method adds data to the end of the list. Alternatively, the `insert()` method allows us to specify an index when adding data to the list. For example, we can add the string `fish` to the beginning, or `0` index, of our list:

```
>>> ['cat', 'dog'].append('fish')
# The list becomes: ['cat', 'dog', 'fish']
>>> ['cat', 'dog'].insert(0, 'fish')
# The list becomes: ['fish', 'cat', 'dog']
```

The `pop()` and `remove()` functions delete data from a list either by index or by a specific object, respectively. If an index is not supplied with the `pop()` function, the last element in the list is popped. Note that the `remove()` function only gets rid of the first instance of the supplied object in the list:

```
>>> [0, 1, 2].pop()
2
# The list is now [0, 1]

>>> [3, 4, 5].pop(1)
4
# The list is now [3, 5]
>>> [1, 1, 2, 3].remove(1)
# The list becomes: [1, 2, 3]
```

We can use the `in` statement to check if some object is in the list. The `count()` function tells us how many instances of an object are in the list:

```
>>> 'cat' in ['mountain lion', 'ox', 'cat']
True
>>> ['fish', 920.5, 3, 5, 3].count(3)
2
```

If we want to access a subset of elements, we can use list slice notation. Other objects, such as strings, also support this same slice notation to obtain a subset of data. Slice notation has the following format, where `a` is our list or string object:

```
a[x:y:z]
```

In the preceding example, `x` represents the start of the slice, `y` represents the end of the slice, and `z` represents the step of the slice. Note that each segment is separated by colons and enclosed in square brackets. A negative step is a quick way to reverse the contents of an object that supports slice notation and would be triggered by a negative number as `z`. Each of these arguments is optional. In the first example, our slice returns the second element and up to, but not including, the fifth element in the list. Using just one of these slice elements returns a list containing everything from the second index forward or everything up to the fifth index:

```
>>> [0,1,2,3,4,5,6][2:5]
[2, 3, 4]
>>> [0,1,2,3,4,5,6][2:]
[2, 3, 4, 5, 6]
>>> [0,1,2,3,4,5,6][:5]
[0, 1, 2, 3, 4]
```

Using the third slice element, we can skip every other element or simply reverse the list with a negative one. We can use a combination of these slice elements to specify how to carve a subset of data from the list:

```
>>> [0,1,2,3,4,5,6][::2]
[0, 2, 4, 6]
>>> [0,1,2,3,4,5,6][::-1]
[6, 5, 4, 3, 2, 1, 0]
```

Dictionaries

Dictionaries, otherwise known as `dict`, are another common Python data container. Unlike lists, this object does not add data in a linear fashion. Instead, data is stored as key and value pairs, where you can create and name unique keys to act as an index for stored values. It is important to note that, in Python 2, dictionaries do not preserve the order in which items are added to it. This is no longer true as of Python 3.6.5, though in general, we should not rely on the `dict()` object maintaining order for us. These objects are used heavily in forensic scripting, as they allow us to store data by name in a single object; otherwise, we may be left assigning a lot of new variables. By storing data in dictionaries, it is possible to have one variable contain very structured data.

We can define a dictionary by using curly braces ({ }), where each key and value pair is delimited by a colon. Additionally, we can use the dict() class constructor to instantiate dictionary objects. Calling a value from a dictionary is accomplished by specifying the key in brackets following the dictionary object. If we supply a key that does not exist, we will receive a KeyError (notice that we have assigned our dictionary to a variable, a). While we have not introduced variables at this point, it is necessary to highlight some of the functions that are specific to dictionaries:

```
>>> type({'Key Lime Pie': 1, 'Blueberry Pie': 2})
<class 'dict'>
>>> dict((['key_1', 'value_1'],['key_2', 'value_2']))
{'key_1': 'value_1', 'key_2': 'value_2'}
>>> a = {'key1': 123, 'key2': 456}
>>> a['key1']
123
```

We can add or modify the value of a preexisting key in a dictionary by specifying a key and setting it equal to another object. We can remove objects using the pop() function, similar to the list pop() function, to remove an item in a dictionary by specifying its key instead of an index:

```
>>> a['key3'] = 789
>>> a
{'key1': 123, 'key2': 456, 'key3': 789}
>>> a.pop('key1')
123
>>> a
{'key2': 456, 'key3': 789}
```

The keys() and values() functions return a list of keys and values in the dictionary. We can use the items() function to return a list of tuples containing each key and value pair. These three functions are often used for conditionals and loops:

```
>>> a.keys()
dict_keys(['key2', 'key3'])
>>> a.values()
dict_values([456, 789])
>>> a.items()
dict_items([('key3', 789), ('key2', 456)])
```

Sets and tuples

Sets are similar to lists in that they contain a list of elements, though they must be unique items. With this, the elements must be immutable, meaning that the value must remain constant. For this, sets are best used on integers, strings, Boolean, floats, and tuples as elements. Sets do not index the elements, and therefore we cannot access the elements by their location in the `set`. Instead, we can access and remove elements through the use of the `pop()` method mentioned for the list method. Tuples are also similar to lists, though they are immutable. Built using parenthesis in lieu of brackets, elements do not have to be unique and of any data type:

```
>>> type(set([1, 4, 'asd', True]))
<class 'set'>
>>> g = set(["element1", "element2"])
>>> g
{'element1', 'element2'}
>>> g.pop()
'element2'
>>> g
{'element1'}
>>> tuple('foo')
('f', 'o' , 'o')
>>> ('b', 'a', 'r')
('b', 'a', 'r')
>>> ('Chapter1', 22)[0]
Chapter1
>>> ('Foo', 'Bar')[-1]
Bar
```

The important difference between a tuple and a list is that a tuple is immutable. This means that we cannot change a tuple object. Instead, we must replace the object completely or cast it to a list, which is mutable. This casting process is described in the next section. Replacing an object is very slow since the operation to add a value to a tuple is `tuple = tuple + ('New value',)`, noting that the trailing comma is required to denote that this addition is a tuple.

Data type conversions

In some situations, the initial data type might not be the desired data type and needs to be changed while preserving its content. For example, when a user inputs arguments from the command line, they are commonly captured as strings and sometimes that user input needs to be, for example, an integer. We would need to use the integer class constructor to convert that string object before processing the data. Imagine we have a simple script that returns the square of a user-supplied integer; we would need to first convert the user input to an integer prior to squaring the input. One of the most common ways to convert data types is to wrap the variable or string with the constructor method, as shown here, for each of the data types:

```
>>> int('123456') # The string 123456
123456 # Is now the integer 123456
>>> str(45) # The integer 45
'45' # Is now the string 45
>>> float('37.5') # The string 37.5
37.5 # Is now the float 37.5
```

Invalid conversions, for example, converting the letter `'a'` to an integer, will raise a `ValueError`. This error will state that the specified value cannot be converted to the desired type. In this case, we would want to use the built-in `ord()` method, which converts a character to its integer equivalent based on the ASCII value. In other scenarios, we may need to use other methods to convert between data types. The following is a table of common built-in data type conversion methods we can utilize for most scenarios:

Method	Description
`str()`, `int()`, `float()`, `dict()`, `list()`, `set()`, `tuple()`	Class constructor methods
`hex()`, `oct()`	Converts an integer into a base 16 (hex) or base 8 (octal) representation
`chr()`, `unichr()`	Converts an integer into an ASCII or Unicode character
`ord()`	Converts a character into an integer

We can also interchange the type or ordered collections found in our list, set, and tuple types. Since sets have requirements for what data may be inserted, we generally do not cast anything to a set. It is more common, instead, to case a set to a list so that we can access values by position:

```
>>> tuple_1 = (0, 1, 2, 3, 3)
>>> tuple_1
```

```
(0, 1, 2, 3, 3)
>>> set_1 = set(tuple_1)
>>> set_1
{0, 1, 2, 3}
>>> list_1 = list(tuple_1)
>>> list_1
[0, 1, 2, 3, 3]
>>> list_2 = list(set_1)
>>> list_2
[0, 1, 2, 3]
```

Files

We will often create file objects to read or write data from a file. File objects can be created using the built-in `open()` method. The `open()` function takes two arguments, the name of the file and the mode. These modes dictate how we can interact with the file object. The mode argument is optional, and if left blank defaults to read-only. The following table illustrates the different file modes available for use:

File Mode	Description
`r`	Opens the file for read-only mode (default). *This does not offer forensic write protection! Please always use a certified process to protect evidence from modification.*
`w`	Creates, or overwrites the file if it exists, for writing.
`a`	Creates a file if it doesn't exist for writing. If the file does exist, the file pointer is placed at the end of the file to append writes to the file.
`rb`, `wb`, or `ab`	Opens the file for reading or writing in binary mode.
`r+`, `rb+`, `w+`, `wb+`, `a+`, or `ab+`	Opens the file for reading and writing in either standard or binary mode. If the file does not exist, the `w` or `a` modes create the file.

Most often, we will use read and write in standard or binary mode. Let's take a look at a few examples and some of the common functions we might use. For this section, we will create a text file called `file.txt` with the following content:

```
This is a simple test for file manipulation.
We will often find ourselves interacting with file objects.
It pays to get comfortable with these objects.
```

In the following example, we open a file object that exists, `file.txt`, and assign it to a variable, `in_file`. Since we do not supply a file mode, it is opened in read-only mode by default. We can use the `read()` method to read all lines as a continuous string. The `readline()` method can be used to read individual lines as a string. Alternatively, the `readlines()` method creates a string for each line and stores it in a list. These functions take an optional argument, specifying the size of bytes to read.

The `readline()` and `readlines()` functions use the `\n` or `\r` newline characters to segment the lines of a file. This is good for most files, though may not always work based on your input data. As an example, CSV files with multiple lines in a single cell would not display properly with this type of file-reading interface.

Python keeps track of where we currently are in the file. To illustrate the examples we've described, we need to use the `seek()` operation to bring us back to the start of the file before we run our next example. The `seek()` operation accepts a number and will navigate to that decimal character offset within the file. For example, if we tried to use the `read()` method before seeking back to the start, our next print function (showcasing the `readline()` method) would not return anything. This is because the cursor would be at the end of the file as a result of the `read()` function:

```
>>> in_file = open('file.txt')
>>> print(in_file.read())
This is a simple test for file manipulation.
We will often find ourselves interacting with file objects.
It pays to get comfortable with these objects.
>>> in_file.seek(0)
>>> print(in_file.readline())
This is a simple test for file manipulation.
>>> in_file.seek(0)
>>> print(in_file.readlines())
['This is a simple test for file manipulation.\n', 'We will often find
ourselves interacting with file objects.\n', 'It pays to get comfortable
with these objects.']
```

In a similar fashion, we can create, or open and overwrite, an existing file using the `w` file mode. We can use the `write()` function to write an individual string or the `writelines()` method to write any iterable object to the file. The `writelines()` function essentially calls the `write()` method for each element of the iterable object.

For example, this is tantamount to calling `write()` on each element of a list:

```
>>> out_file = open('output.txt', 'w')
>>> out_file.write('Hello output!')
>>> data = ['falken', 124, 'joshua']
>>> out_file.writelines(data)
```

Python does a great job of closing connections to a file object automatically. However, best practice dictates that we should use the `flush()` and `close()` methods after we finish writing data to a file. The `flush()` method writes any data remaining in a buffer to the file, and the `close()` function closes our connection to the file object:

```
>>> out_file.flush()
>>> out_file.close()
```

Variables

We can assign values to variables using the data types we just covered. By assigning values to variables, we can refer to that value, which could be a large 100-element list, by its variable name. This not only saves the programmer from re-typing out the value over and over again, but helps enhance the readability of the code and allows us to change the values of a variable over time. Throughout this chapter, we have already assigned objects to variables using the = sign. Variable names can technically be anything, although we recommend the following guidelines:

- Variable names should be short and descriptive of the stored content or purpose.
- Begin with a letter or underscore.
- Constant variables should be denoted by capitalized words.
- Dynamic variables should be lowercase words separated by underscores.
- Never be one of the following or any Python-reserved name: `input`, `output`, `tmp`, `temp`, `in`, `for`, `next`, `file`, `True`, `False`, `None`, `str`, `int`, `list`.
- Never include a space in a variable name. Python thinks two variables are being defined and will raise a syntax error. Use underscores to separate words.

Generally, programmers use memorable and descriptive names that indicate the data they hold. For example, in a script that prompts for the phone number of the user, the variable should be `phone_number`, which clearly indicates the purpose and contents of this variable. Another popular naming style is `CamelCase`, where every word is capitalized. This naming convention is often used in conjunction with class names (more on those later in this book).

A variable assignment allows the value to be modified as the script runs. The general rule of thumb is to assign a value to a variable if it will be used again. Let's practice by creating variables and assigning them data types we have just learned about. While this is simple, we recommend following along in the interactive prompt to get in the habit of assigning variables. In the first example here, we assign a string to a variable before printing the variable:

```
>>> print(hello_world)
Hello World!
```

The second example introduces some new operators. First, we assign the integer, `5`, to the variable, `our_number`. Then, we use the plus-gets (+=) as a built-in shorthand for `our_number = our_number + 20`. In addition to plus-gets, there is minus-gets (-=), multiply-gets (*=), and divide-gets (/=):

```
>>> our_number = 5
>>> our_number += 20
>>> print(our_number)
25
```

In the following code block, we assign a series of variables before printing them. The data types used for our variables are `string`, `integer`, `float`, `list`, and `Boolean`, respectively:

```
>>> BOOK_TITLE = 'Learning Python for Forensics'
>>> edition = 2
>>> python2_version = 2.7.15
>>> python3_version = 3.7.1
>>> AUTHOR_NAMES = ['Preston Miller', 'Chapin Bryce']
>>> is_written_in_english = True
>>> print(BOOK_TITLE)
'Learning Python for Forensics'
>>> print(AUTHOR_NAMES)
['Preston Miller', 'Chapin Bryce']
>>> print(edition)
1
>>> print(python2_version)
2.7.15
>>> print(is_written_in_english)
True
```

Notice the `BOOK_TITLE` and `AUTHOR_NAMES` variables. When a variable is static, for instance, non-changing throughout the execution of a script, it is referred to as a constant variable. Unlike other programming languages, there is not a built-in method for protecting constants from being overwritten, so we use naming conventions to assist in reminding us not to replace the value. While some variables such as the edition of the book, language, or version of Python might change, the title and authors should be constants (we hope). If there is ever confusion when it comes to naming and styling conventions in Python, try running the following statement in an interpreter:

```
>>> import this
```

As we saw previously, we can use the `split()` method on a string to convert it into a list. We can also convert a list into a string using the `join()` method. This method follows a string containing the desired common denominator and the list as its only argument. In the following example, we are taking list containing two strings and joining them into one string, where the elements are separated by a comma:

```
>>> print(', '.join(["Hello", "World!"]))
Hello, World!
```

Understanding scripting flow logic

Flow control logic allows us to create dynamic operations by specifying different routes of program execution based upon a series of circumstances. In any script worth its salt, some manner of flow control is present. For example, flow logic would be required to create a dynamic script that returns different results based on options selected by the user. In Python, there are two basic sets of flow logic: conditionals and loops.

Flow operators are frequently accompanied by flow logic. These operators can be strung together to create more complicated logic. The following table represents a *truth table* and illustrates the value of various flow operators based on the *A* or *B* variable Boolean state:

A	**B**	**A and B**	**A or B**	**not A**	**not B**
F	F	F	F	T	T
T	F	F	T	F	T
F	T	F	T	T	F
T	T	T	T	F	F

The logical `AND` and `OR` operators are the third and fourth columns in the table. Both *A* and *B* must be `True` for the `AND` operator to return `True`. Only one of the variables needs to be `True` for the `OR` operator to be `True`. The `not` operator simply switches the Boolean value of the variable to its opposite (for example, `True` becomes `False` and vice versa).

Mastering conditionals and loops will take our scripts to another level. At its core, flow logic relies on only two values, `True` or `False`. As noted earlier, in Python, these are represented by the Boolean `True` and `False` data types.

Conditionals

When a script hits a conditional, it's much like standing at a fork in the road. Depending on some factor, say a more promising horizon, you may decide to go east over west. Computer logic is less arbitrary in that if something is true the script proceeds one way, and if it is false then it will go another. These junctions are critical; if the program decides to go off the path we've developed for it, we'll be in serious trouble.

There are three statements that are used to form a conditional block: `if`, `elif`, and `else`. The conditional block refers to the conditional statements, their flow logic, and code. A conditional block starts with an `if` statement followed by flow logic, a colon, and indented line(s) of code. If the flow logic evaluates to `True`, then the indented code following the `if` statement will be executed. If it does not evaluate to `True`, the **Python virtual machine** (**PVM**) will skip those lines of code and go to the next line on the same level of indentation as the `if` statement. This is usually a corresponding `elif` (else-if) or `else` statement.

Indentation is very important in Python. It is used to demarcate code to be executed within a conditional statement or loop. A standard of four spaces for indentation is used in this book, though you may encounter code that uses a two-space indentation or uses tab characters. While all three of these practices are allowed in Python, four spaces are preferred and easier to read.

In a conditional block, once one of the statements evaluates to `True`, the code is executed and the PVM exits the block without evaluating the other statements.

```
# Conditional Block Pseudocode
if [logic]:
    # Line(s) of indented code to execute if logic evaluates to True.
elif [logic]:
    # Line(s) of indented code to execute if the 'if'
    # statement is false and this logic is True.
else:
```

```
    # Line(s) of code to catch all other possibilities if
    # the 'if' and 'elif' statements are all False.
```

Until we define functions, we will stick to simple `if` statement examples:

```
>>> a = 5
>>> b = 22
>>> a > 0
True
>>> a > b
False
>>> if a > 0:
...     print(str(a) + ' is greater than zero!')
...
5 is greater than zero!
>>> if a >= b:
...     print(str(a) + ' beats ' + str(b))
...
>>>
```

Notice how when the flow logic evaluates to `True`, then the code indented following the `if` statement is executed. When it evaluates to `False`, the code is skipped. Typically, when the `if` statement is false, you will have a secondary statement, such as an `elif` or `else` to catch other possibilities, such as when `a` is less than or equal to `b`. However, it is important to note that we can just use an `if` statement without any `elif` or `else` statements.

The difference between `if` and `elif` is subtle. We can only functionally notice a difference when we use multiple `if` statements. The `elif` statement allows for a second condition to be evaluated in the case that the first isn't successful. A second `if` statement will be evaluated regardless of the outcome of the first `if` statement.

The `else` statement does not require any flow logic and can be treated as a catch-all case for any remaining or unaccounted for case. This does not mean, however, errors will not occur when the code in the `else` statement is executed. Do not rely on `else` statements to handle errors.

Conditional statements can be made more comprehensive by using the logical `and` or `or` operators. These allow for more complex logic in a single conditional statement:

```
>>> a = 5
>>> b = 22
>>> if a > 4 and a < b:
...     print('Both statements must be true to print this')
...
Both statements must be true to print this
>>> if a > 10 or a < b:
```

```
...     print('One of these statements must be true to print this')
...
Only one of these statements must be true to print this
```

The following table can be helpful to understand how common operators work:

Operator	Description	Example	Evaluation
<, >	less than, greater than	`8 < 3`	`False`
<=, >=	less than equal to, greater than equal to	`5 =< 5`	`True`
`==, !=`	equal to, not equal to	`2 != 3`	`True`
`not`	switches Boolean value	`not True`	`False`

Loops

Loops provide another method of flow control, and are suited to perform iterative tasks. A loop will repeat inclusive code until the provided condition is no longer `True` or an exit signal is provided. There are two kinds of loops: `for` and `while`. For most iterative tasks, a `for` loop will be the best option to use.

The for loop

`for` loops are the most common and, in most cases, the preferred method to perform a task over and over again. Imagine a factory line; for each object on the conveyor belt, a `for` loop could be used to perform some task on it, such as placing a label on the object. In this manner, multiple `for` loops can come together in the form of an assembly line, processing each object, until they are ready to be presented to the user.

Much like the rest of Python, the `for` loop is very simple syntactically, yet powerful. In some languages, a `for` loop needs to be initialized, have a counter of sorts, and a termination case. Python's `for` loop is much more dynamic and handles these tasks on its own. These loops contain indented code that is executed line by line. If the object being iterated over still has elements (for example, more items to process) at the end of the indented block, the PVM will position itself at the beginning of the loop and repeat the code again.

The `for` loop syntax will specify the object to iterate over and what to call each of the elements within the object. Note that the object must be iterable. For example, `lists`, `sets`, `tuples`, and `strings` are iterable, but an integer is not. In the following example, we can see how a `for` loop treats strings and lists and helps us iterate over each element in iterable objects:

```
>>> for character in 'Python':
...     print(character)
...
P
y
t
h
o
n
>>> cars = ['Volkswagon', 'Audi', 'BMW']
>>> for car in cars:
...     print(car)
...
Volkswagon
Audi
BMW
```

There are additional, more advanced, ways to call a `for` loop. The `enumerate()` function can be used to start an index. This comes in handy when you need to keep track of the index of the current loop. Indexes are incremented at the beginning of the loop. The first object has an index of `0`, the second has an index of `1`, and so on. The `range()` function can execute a loop a certain number of times and provide an index:

```
>>> numbers = [5, 25, 35]
>>> for i, x in enumerate(numbers):
...     print('Item', i, 'from the list is:', x)
...
Item 0 from the list is: 5
Item 1 from the list is: 25
Item 2 from the list is: 35
>>> for x in range(0, 100):
...     print(x)
0
1
# continues to print 0 to 100 (omitted in an effort to save trees)
```

The while loop

`while` loops are not encountered as frequently in Python. A `while` loop executes as long as a statement is true. The simplest `while` loop would be a `while True` statement. This kind of loop would execute forever since the Boolean object `True` is always `True` and so the indented code would continually execute.

If you are not careful, you can inadvertently create an infinite loop, which will wreak havoc on your script's intended functionality. It is imperative to utilize conditionals to cover all your bases such as `if`, `elif`, and `else` statements. If you fail to do so, your script can enter an unaccounted situation and crash. This is not to say that `while` loops are not worth using. `while` loops are quite powerful and have their own place in Python:

```
>>> guess = 0
>>> answer = 42
>>> while True:
...     if guess == answer:
...         print('You've found the answer to this loop: ' + str(answer))
...         break
...     else:
...         print(guess, 'is not the answer.')
...         guess += 1
```

The `break`, `continue`, and `pass` statements are used in conjunction with `for` and `while` loops to create more dynamic loops. The `break` escapes from the current loop, while the `continue` statement causes the PVM to begin executing code at the beginning of the loop, skipping any indented code following the `continue` statement. The `pass` statement literally does nothing and acts as a placeholder. If you're feeling brave or bored, or worse, both, remove the `break` statement from the previous example and note what happens.

Functions

Functions are the first step to creating more complex Python code. At a high level, they are containers of Python code that can be bundled together into a callable block. A simple model function requires a single input, performs an operation on the provided data, and returns a single output. However, this quickly becomes more complicated as functions can run without inputs or optional inputs or do not need to return an output at all.

Functions are an integral component of any programming language and have already been encountered many times in this chapter. For example, the append from `list.append()` is a function that requires input to add to a list. Once a function is created, you can invoke it by its name and pass any required inputs.

When it comes to writing functions, more is better. It is much easier to handle and troubleshoot a bug in a program with many small functions than one big function. Smaller functions make your code more readable and make it easier to find troublesome logic. That being said, functions should contain code for a singular purpose, such as accessing a certain key in a registry file. There is no need to create functions for each line of code in your script. Consider using functions as logical blocks of code. Sometimes that is three lines, sometimes that is 50 lines; what's important is that the purpose and operation of the functional unit of code is clear.

The function syntax starts with a definition, `def`, followed by the name of the function, any inputs in parenthesis, and a colon. Following this format are indented lines of code that will run when the function is called. Optionally, a function may have a return statement to pass information back to the instance where it was called from:

```
>>> def simple_function():
...     print('I am a simple function')
...
>>> simple_function()
I am a simple function
```

In the example we've just seen, we've created a function named `simple_function()` that takes no inputs. This function does not return anything and instead prints a string. Let's take a look at more complicated examples.

Our first function, `square()`, takes one input and squares it. As this function returns a value, we catch it by assigning it to a variable when invoking the function. This variable, `squared_number`, will be equal to the returned value of the function. While this is a very succinct function, it is very easily broken if given the wrong input. Give the square function some other data type, such as a string, and you will receive a `TypeError`:

```
>>> def square(x):
...     return x**2
...
>>> squared_number = square(4)
>>> print(squared_number)
16
```

Our second function, even_or_odd, is slightly more advanced. This function first checks if it is passed an input that is of type integer. If not, it returns immediately, which causes the function to exit. If it is an integer, it performs some logic that displays to the user whether the integer is even or odd. Notice that when we try to give the function the string, '5', not to be confused with the integer, 5, it returns nothing, whereas in the square function, which lacks any input validation checks, this would have caused an error:

```
>>> def even_or_odd(value):
...     if isinstance(value, int):
...         if value % 2 == 0:
...             print('This number is even.')
...         else:
...             print('This number is odd.')
...     else:
...         return
...
>>> values = [1, 3, 4, 6, '5']
>>> for value in values:
...     even_or_odd(value)
...
This number is odd.
This number is odd.
This number is even.
This number is even.
```

Aspiring developers should get in the habit of writing functions. As always, functions should be well-commented to help explain their purpose. Functions will be used throughout this book, especially as we begin to develop our forensic scripts.

Summary

This chapter has covered a wide range of introductory content that provides a foundation to be built upon throughout the duration of this book; by the end, you will become well-versed in Python development. These topics have been handpicked as the most important items to comprise a basic understanding of the language as we move forward. We have covered data types, what they are and when they are used, variable naming and the associated rules and guidelines, logic and operations to manipulate and make decisions based on values, and conditions and loops that provide a sequential organization for our scripts and form the baseline of everything we develop. The code for this project can be downloaded from GitHub or Packt, as described in the *Preface*.

Please consider re-reading this chapter and working through the examples multiple times to help with comprehension. Just like anything else, learning a new language requires a lot of practice.

Through these features alone, we can create basic scripts. Python is a very powerful and complex language belying its simplistic syntax. In the next chapter, we will explore more complex foundational items and continue expanding upon knowledge established in this chapter, prior to moving on to real-world examples.

2
Python Fundamentals

We have explored the basic concepts behind Python and fundamental elements used to construct scripts. We will now build a series of scripts throughout this book using the data types and built-in functions that we have discussed in the first chapter. Before we begin developing scripts, let's walk through some additional important features of the Python language, building upon our existing knowledge.

In this chapter, we will explore more advanced features that we will utilize when building our forensic Python scripts. This includes complex data types and functions, creating our first script, handling errors, using libraries, interacting with the user, and some best practices for development. After completing this chapter, we will be ready to dive into real-world examples featuring the utility of Python in forensic casework.

This chapter will cover the following topics:

- Advanced features, including iterators and `datetime` objects
- Installing and using modules
- Error handling with `try`, `except`, and `raise` statements
- Sanity checking and accessing user-supplied data
- Creating forensic scripts to find USB vendor and product information

Advanced data types and functions

This section highlights two common features, iterators and `datetime` objects, of Python that we will frequently encounter in forensic scripts. Therefore, we will introduce these objects and functionality in more detail.

Iterators

You previously learned about several iterable objects, such as `lists`, `sets`, and `tuples`. In Python, a data type is considered an iterator if an `__iter__` method is defined or if elements can be accessed in a sequenced manner. These three data types (that is, `lists`, `sets`, and `tuples`) allow us to iterate through their contents in a simple and efficient manner. For this reason, we often use these data types when iterating through the lines in a file or through file entries within a directory listing, or when trying to identify a file based on a series of file signatures.

The `iter` data type allows us to step through data in a manner that doesn't preserve the initial object. This seems undesirable; however, when working with large sets or on machines with limited resources, it is very useful. This is due to the resource allocation associated with the `iter` data type, where only active data is stored in memory. This preserves memory allocation when stepping through every line of a 3 GB file by feeding one line at a time and preventing massive memory consumption while still handling each line in order.

The code block mentioned here steps through the basic usage of iterables. We use the `next()` function on an iterable to retrieve the next element. Once an object is accessed using `next()`, it is no longer available in `iter()`, as the cursor has moved past the element. If we have reached the end of the iterable object, we will receive `StopIteration` for any additional `next()` method calls. This exception allows us to gracefully exit loops with an iterator and alerts us to when we are out of content to read from the iterator:

```
>>> y = iter([1, 2, 3])
>>> next(y)
1
>>> next(y)
2
>>> next(y)
3
>>> next(y)
Traceback (most recent call last):
 File "<stdin>", line 1, in <module>
StopIteration
```

In Python 2.7, you can use the `obj.next()` method call to get the same output as the preceding example via use of the `next()` function. For simplicity and uniformity, Python 3 renamed `obj.next()` to `obj.__next__()` and encourages the use of the `next()` function. With this, it is recommended to use `next(y)`, as shown previously, in place of `y.next()` or `y.__next__()`.

The `reversed()` built-in function can be used to create a reversed iterator. In the following example, we reverse a list and retrieve the following object from the iterator using the `next()` function:

```
>>> j = reversed([7, 8, 9])
>>> next(j)
9
>>> next(j)
8
>>> next(j)
7
>>> next(j)
Traceback (most recent call last):
  File "<stdin>", line 1, in <module>
StopIteration
```

By implementing generators, we can further take advantage of the `iter` data type. Generators are a special type of function that produces iterator objects. Generators are similar to functions, as those discussed in `Chapter 1`, *Now for Something Completely Different*—though, instead of returning objects, they `yield` iterators. Generators are best used with large datasets that would consume vast quantities of memory, similar to the use case of the `iter` data type.

The code block mentioned here shows the implementation of a generator. In the `file_sigs()` function, we create a list of tuples stored in the `sigs` variable. We then loop through each element in `sigs` and yield a `tuple` data type. This creates a generator, allowing us to use the `next()` function to retrieve each tuple individually and limit the generators' memory impact. See the following code:

```
>>> def file_sigs():
...     sigs = [('jpeg', 'FF D8 FF E0'),
...             ('png', '89 50 4E 47 0D 0A 1A 0A'),
...             ('gif', '47 49 46 38 37 61')]
...     for s in sigs:
...         yield s

>>> fs = file_sigs()
>>> next(fs)
('jpeg', 'FF D8 FF E0')
>>> next(fs)
('png', '89 50 4E 47 0D 0A 1A 0A')
>>> next(fs)
('gif', '47 49 46 38 37 61')
```

You can find additional file signatures at `http://www.garykessler.net/library/file_sigs.html`.

datetime objects

Investigators are often asked to determine when a file was deleted, when a text message was read, or the correct order for a sequence of events. Consequently, a great deal of analysis revolves around timestamps and other temporal artifacts. Understanding time can help us piece together the puzzle and further understand the context surrounding an artifact. For this, and many other reasons, let's practice handling timestamps using the `datetime` module.

Python's `datetime` module supports the interpretation and formatting of timestamps. This module has many features, most notably getting the current time, determining the change (or delta) between two timestamps, and converting common timestamp formats into a human readable date. The `datetime.datetime()` method creates a `datetime` object and accepts the year, month, day, and optionally hour, minute, second, millisecond, and time zone arguments. The `timedelta()` method shows the difference between two `datetime` objects by storing the difference in days, seconds, and microseconds.

First, we need to import the `datetime` library so that we can use functions from the module. We can see the current date with the `datetime.now()` method. This creates a `datetime` object, which we then manipulate. For instance, let's create a `timedelta` object by subtracting two `datetime` objects, separated by a few seconds. We can add or subtract the `timedelta` object to or from our `right_now` variable to generate another `datetime` object:

```
>>> import datetime
>>> right_now = datetime.datetime.now()
>>> right_now
datetime.datetime(2018, 6, 30, 7, 48, 31, 576151)

>>> # Subtract time
>>> delta = datetime.datetime.now() - right_now
>>> delta
datetime.timedelta(0, 16, 303831)

>>> # Add datetime to time delta to produce second time
>>> right_now + delta
datetime.datetime(2018, 6, 30, 7, 48, 47, 879982)
```

The output may vary, as you are running these commands at a different time than when they were for this book.

Another highly used application of the `datetime` module is `strftime()`, which allows `datetime` objects to be converted into custom-formatted strings. This function takes a string format as its input. This format string is made up of special characters beginning with the percentage sign. The following table illustrates examples of the formatters we can use with the `strftime()` function:

Description	Formatter
Year (YYYY)	`%Y`
Month (MM)	`%m`
Day (DD)	`%d`
24 hour (HH)	`%H`
12 hour (HH)	`%I`
Minute (MM)	`%M`
Second (SS)	`%S`
Microseconds (SSSSSS)	`%f`
Timezone (Z)	`%z`
AM/PM	`%p`

You can find additional timestamp formatting information at `http://strftime.org/` or via the official documentation: `https://docs.python.org/3/library/datetime.html#strftime-and-strptime-behavior`.

In addition, the `strptime()` function, which we do not showcase here, can be used for the reverse process. The `strptime()` function will take a string containing a date and time and convert it into a `datetime` object using the formatting string. We can also interpret epoch time (also called Unix or POSIX time), represented as an integer, into a UTC `datetime` object:

```
>>> epoch_timestamp = 874281600
>>> datetime_timestamp =
datetime.datetime.utcfromtimestamp(epoch_timestamp)
```

We can print this new object and it will be automatically converted into a string representing the `datetime` object. However, let's pretend that we do not like to separate our date by hyphens. Instead, we can use the `strftime()` method to display the date with forward slashes or using any of the defined formatters. Lastly, the `datetime` library has a few pre-built formatters such as `isoformat()`, which we can use to easily produce a standard timestamp format:

```
>>> from __future__ import print_function
>>> print(datetime_timestamp)
1997-09-15 00:00:00
>>> print(datetime_timestamp.strftime('%m/%d/%Y %H:%M:%S'))
09/15/1997 00:00:00
>>> print(datetime_timestamp.strftime('%A %B %d, %Y at %I:%M:%S %p'))
Monday September 15, 1997 at 12:00:00 AM
>>> print(datetime_timestamp.isoformat())
1997-09-15T00:00:00
```

As a note, we have imported `print_function` into our interpreter to allow us to print these date values in both Python 2 and Python 3.

The `datetime` library alleviates a great deal of stress involved in handling date and time values in Python. This module is also well-suited for processing time formats that are often encountered during investigations.

Libraries

Libraries, or modules, expedite the development process, making it easier to focus on the intended purpose of our script rather than developing everything from scratch. External libraries can save large amounts of developing time and, if we're being honest, they are often more accurate and efficient than any code we, as developers, can cobble together during investigations. There are two categories of libraries: standard and third-party. Standard libraries are distributed with every installation of Python and carry commonly used code that's supported by the Python Software Foundation. The number and names of the standard libraries vary between Python versions, especially as you move between Python 2 and Python 3. We will do our best to call out when a library is imported or used differently between Python 2 and 3. In the other category, third-party libraries introduce new code, add or improve functionality to the standard Python installation, and allow for the community to contribute modules.

Installing third-party libraries

We know that we do not need to install standard modules because they come with Python, but what about third-party modules? The Python Package Index is a great place to start looking for third-party libraries. This can be found at `https://pypi.org/`. This service allows tools, such as `pip`, to install packages automatically. If an internet connection is not available or the package is not found on PyPi, a `setup.py` file can usually be used to install the module manually. The examples of using `pip` and `setup.py` are shown later. Tools such as `pip` are very convenient as they handle the installation of dependencies, check whether items are already installed, and suggest upgrades if an older version is installed. An internet connection is required to check for online resources, such as dependencies and newer versions of a module; however, `pip` can also be used to install code on an offline machine.

These commands are run in the Terminal or Command Prompt, not the Python interpreter. Please note that in the example mentioned below, full paths may be necessary if your Python executable is not included in the current environment's `PATH` variable. `pip` may need to be run from an elevated console, either using `sudo` or an elevated Windows Command Prompt. Full documentation for `pip` can be found at `http://pip.pypa.io/en/stable/reference/pip/`:

```
$ pip install python-registry==1.0.4
Collecting python-registry
Collecting enum34 (from python-registry)
  Using cached
https://files.pythonhosted.org/packages/af/42/cb9355df32c69b553e72a2e28daee
25d1611d2c0d9c272aa1d34204205b2/enum34-1.1.6-py3-none-any.whl
Installing collected packages: enum34, python-registry
Successfully installed enum34-1.1.6 python-registry-1.0.4

$ pip install yarp==1.0.17
https://github.com/msuhanov/yarp/archive/1.0.17.tar.gz
Collecting https://github.com/msuhanov/yarp/archive/1.0.17.tar.gz
  Downloading https://github.com/msuhanov/yarp/archive/1.0.17.tar.gz
     \ 716kB 12.8MB/s
Building wheels for collected packages: yarp
  Running setup.py bdist_wheel for yarp ... done
  Stored in directory: C:\USERS\...\APPDATA\LOCAL\TEMP\pip-ephem-wheel-
cache-78qdzfmy\wheels\........
Successfully built yarp
Installing collected packages: yarp
Successfully installed yarp-1.0.17
```

Libraries in this book

In this book, we use many third-party libraries that can be installed with `pip` or the `setup.py` method. However, not all third-party modules can be installed so easily and sometimes require you to search the internet. As you may have noted in the previous code block, some third-party modules, such as the `yarp` module, are hosted on source code management systems such as GitHub. GitHub and other SCM services allow us to access publicly available code and view changes made to it over time. Alternatively, Python code can sometimes be found on a blog or a self-hosted website. In this book, we will provide instructions on how to install any third-party modules that we use.

Python packages

A Python package is a directory containing Python modules and a `__init__.py` file. When we import a package, the `__init__.py` code is executed. This file contains the imports and code that's required to run other modules in the package. These packages can be nested within subdirectories. For example, the `__init__.py` file can contain `import` statements that bring in each Python file in the directory and all of the available classes or functions when the folder is imported. The following is an example directory structure and below that is the `__init__.py` file, which shows us how the two interact when imported. The last line in the following code block imports all specified items in the subdirectory's `__init__.py` file.

The hypothetical folder structure is as follows:

```
| -- packageName/
    | -- __init__.py
    | -- script1.py
    | -- script2.py
    | -- subDirectory/
        | -- __init__.py
        | -- script3.py
        | -- script4.py
```

The top-level `__init__.py` file's contents is as follows:

```
from script1 import *
from script2 import function_name
from subDirectory import *
```

The code mentioned below executes the `__init__` script we mentioned previously, and it will import all functions from `script1.py`, only `function_name` from `script2.py`, and any additional specifications from `subDirectory/__init__.py`:

```
import packageName
```

Classes and object-oriented programming

Python supports **object-oriented programming** (**OOP**) using the built-in class keyword. Object-oriented programming allows advanced programming techniques and sustainable code that supports better software development. Because OOP is not commonly used in scripting and is above the introductory level, this book will implement OOP and some of its features in later chapters after we master the basic features of Python. What's important to keep in mind is almost everything in Python, including classes, functions, and variables, are objects. Classes are useful in a variety of situations, allowing us to design our own objects to interact with data in a custom manner.

Let's look at the `datetime` module for an example of how we will interact with classes and their methods. This library contains several classes, such as `datetime`, `timedelta`, and `tzinfo`. Each of these classes handles different functionality associated with timestamps. The most commonly used is the `datetime` class, which can be confusing as it is a member of the `datetime` module. This class is used to represent dates as Python objects. The two other mentioned classes support the `datetime` class by allowing dates to be added or subtracted, through the `timedelta` class, and time zones represented through the `tzinfo` class.

Focusing on the `datetime.datetime` class, we will look at how we can use this object to create multiple instances of dates and extract data from them. To begin, as seen in the following code block, we must import our printing statement and this library to access the `datetime` module's classes and methods. Next, we pass arguments to the `datetime` class and assign the `datetime` object to `date_1`. Our `date_1` variable contains the value to represent April Fool's Day, 2018. Since we did not specify a time value when initiating the class, the value will reflect midnight, down to the millisecond. As we can see, like functions, classes too can have arguments. Additionally, a class can contain their own functions, commonly called methods. An example of a method is the call to `now()`, allowing us to gather the current timestamp for our local machine and store the value as `date_2`. These methods allow us to manipulate data that's specific to the defined instance of the class. We can see the contents of our two date objects by printing them in the interactive prompt:

```
>>> from __future__ import print_function
>>> import datetime
```

```
>>> date_1 = datetime.datetime(2018,04,01)
>>> date_2 = datetime.datetime.now()
>>> print(date_1, " | ", date_2)
2018-04-01 00:00:00.000  |  2018-04-01 15:56:10.012915
```

We can access the properties of our date objects by calling specific class attributes. These attributes are usually leveraged by code within the class to process the data, though we can also use these attributes to our advantage. For example, the hour or year attributes allow us to extract the hour or the year from our date objects. Though this may seem simple, it becomes more helpful in other modules when accessing the parsed or extracted data from the class instance:

```
>>> date_2.hour
15
>>> date_1.year
2018
```

As mentioned previously, we can always run the `dir()` and `help()` functions to provide context on what methods and attributes are available for a given object. If we run the following code, we can see that we can extract the weekday or format the date using the ISO format. These methods provide additional information about our `datetime` objects and allow us to take full advantage of what the class object has to offer:

```
>>> dir(date_1)
['__add__', '__class__', '__delattr__', '__doc__', '__eq__', '__format__',
'__ge__', '__getattribute__', '__gt__', '__hash__', '__init__', '__le__',
'__lt__', '__ne__', '__new__', '__radd__', '__reduce__', '__reduce_ex__',
'__repr__', '__rsub__', '__setattr__', '__sizeof__', '__str__', '__sub__',
'__subclasshook__', 'astime zone', 'combine', 'ctime', 'date', 'day',
'dst', 'fromordinal', 'fromtimestamp', 'hour', 'isocalendar', 'isoformat',
'isoweekday', 'max', 'microsecond', 'min', 'minute', 'month', 'now',
'replace', 'resolution', 'second', 'strftime', 'strptime', 'time',
'timetuple', 'timetz', 'today', 'toordinal', 'tzinfo', 'tzname',
'utcfromtimestamp', 'utcnow', 'utcoffset', 'utctimetuple', 'weekday',
'year']
>>> date_1.weekday()
4
>>> date_2.isoformat()
2016-04-01T15:56:10.012915
```

Try and except

The try and except syntax is used to catch and safely handle errors that are encountered during runtime. As a new developer, you'll eventually become accustomed to having people telling you that your scripts don't work. In Python, we use the `try` and `except` blocks to stop preventable errors from crashing our code. Please use the `try` and `except` blocks in moderation. Don't use them as if they were band-aids to plug up holes in a sinking ship—instead, reconsider your original design and contemplate modifying the logic to better prevent errors. One great way to help with this is to provide instructions for use through command-line arguments, documentation, or otherwise. Using these correctly will enhance the stability of your program. However, improper usage will not add any stability and can mask underlying issues in your code. A good practice is to use as few lines of code within a `try` and `except` block as possible; this way, the error handling is focused and addressed properly.

For example, say we have some code that performs a mathematical calculation on two numerical variables. If we anticipate that a user may accidentally enter non-integer or float values, we may want to wrap a `try` and `except` around the calculation to catch any `TypeError` exceptions that may arise. When we catch the error, we can try and convert the variables to integers with the class constructor method before entering the `try` and `except` block again. If successful, we have saved our code from a preventable crash and maintained specificity to prevent our program from accepting dictionary input, for example. In the case of receiving a dictionary object, we would want the script to crash and present debug information to the user.

Any line that has a reasonable chance of generating an error should be handled by its own try and except block with a solution for that specific line to ensure that we are properly handling the specific error. There are a few variations of the `try` and `except` block. In short, there are catch-all, catch-as-variable, and catch-specific types of blocks. The following pseudocode shows examples of how the blocks are formed:

```
# Basic try and except -- catch-all
try:
    # Line(s) of code
except:
    # Line(s) of error-handling code

# Catch-As-Variable
try:
    # Line(s) of code
except TypeError as e:
    print(e.message)
    # Line(s) of error-handling code
```

```
# Catch-Specific
try:
    # Line(s) of code
except ValueError:
    # Line(s) of error-handling code for ValueError exceptions
```

The catch-all or bare except will catch any error. **This is often regarded as a poor coding practice as it can lead to undesired program behaviors.** Catching an exception as a variable is useful in a variety of situations. The error message of the exception stored in `e` can be printed or written to a log by calling `e.message`—this can be particularly useful when an error occurs within a large multi-module program. In addition, the built-in `isinstance()` function can be used to determine the type of error.

For support in both Python 2 and Python 3, please use the `except Exception as error` syntax as described previously, as opposed to the `except Exception, error` syntax supported by Python 2.

In the example that we'll look at next, we define two functions: `give_error()` and `error_handler()`. The `give_error()` function tries to append `5` to the `my_list` variable. This variable has not yet been instantiated and will generate a `NameError` instance. In the except clause, we are catching a base `Exception` and storing it in the `e` variable. We then pass this exception object to our `error_handler()` function, which we define later.

The `error_handler()` function takes an exception object as its input. It checks whether the error is an instance of `NameError` or `TypeError`, or it passes otherwise. Based on the type of exception, it will print out the exception type and error message:

```
>>> from __future__ import print_function
>>> def give_error():
...     try:
...         my_list.append(5)
...     except Exception as e:
...         error_handler(e)
...
>>> def error_handler(error):
...     if isinstance(error, NameError):
...         print('NameError:', error.message)
...     elif isinstance(error, TypeError):
...         print('TypeError:', error.message)
...     else:
...         pass
...
>>> give_error()
NameError: global name 'my_list' is not defined
```

Finally, the catch-specific try and except block can be used to catch individual exceptions and has targeted error-handling code for that specific error. A scenario that might require a catch-specific try and except block is working with an object, such as a list or dictionary, which may or may not be instantiated at that point in the program.

In the following example, the results list does not exist when it is called in the function. Fortunately, we wrapped the append operation in a `try` and `except` to catch the `NameError` exceptions. When we catch this exception, we first instantiate the results list as an empty list and then append the appropriate data before returning the list. Here is the example:

```
>>> def double_data(data):
...     for x in data:
...         double_data = x*2
...         try:
...             # The results list does not exist the first time
...             # we try to append to it
...             results.append(double_data)
...         except NameError:
...             results = []
...             results.append(double_data)
...     return results
...
>>> my_results = doubleData(['a', 'b', 'c'])
>>> print my_results
['aa', 'bb', 'cc']
```

For (hopefully) obvious reasons, the previous code sample is intended to show the handling of exceptions. We should always be sure to initiate variables before usage.

The raise function

As our code can generate its own exceptions during execution, we can also manually trigger an exception to occur with the built-in `raise()` function. The `raise()` method is often used to raise an exception to the function that called it. While this may seem unnecessary, in larger programs, this can actually be quite useful.

Imagine a function, `function_b()`, which receives parsed data in the form of a packet from `function_a()`. Our `function_b()` function does some further processing on the packet and then calls `function_c()` to continue to process the packet. If `function_c()` raises an exception back to `function_b()`, we might design some logic to alert the user of the malformed packet instead of trying to process it and producing faulty results. The following is some pseudocode representing such a scenario:

```
import module

def main():
    function_a(data)

def function_a(data_in):
    try:
        # parse data into packet
        function_b(parsed_packet)
    except Exception as e:
        if isinstance(e, ErrorA):
            # Address this type of error
            function_b(fixed_packet)
        [etc.]

def function_b(packet):
    # Process packet and store in processed_packet variable
    try:
        module.function_c(processed_packet)
    except SomeError:
        # Error testing logic
        if type 1 error:
            raise ErrorA()
        elif type 2 error:
            raise ErrorB()
        [etc.]

if __name__ == '__main__':
    main()
```

In addition, raising custom or built-in exceptions can be useful when dealing with exceptions that Python doesn't recognize on its own. Let's revisit the example of the malformed packet. When the second function received the raised error, we might design some logic that tests some possible sources of error. Depending on those results, we might raise different exceptions back to the calling function, `function_a()`.

When raising a built-in exception, make sure to use an exception that most closely matches the error. For example, if the error revolves around an index issue, use the `IndexError` exception. When raising an exception, we should pass in a string containing a description of the error. This string should be descriptive and help the developer identify the issue, unlike the following string that's used. The adage *do what we say, not what we do* applies here, as we are simply demonstrating functionality:

```
>>> def raise_error():
...     raise TypeError('This is a TypeError')
...
>>> raise_error()
Traceback (most recent call last):
  File "<stdin>", line 1, in <module>
  File "<stdin>", line 2, in raise_error
TypeError: This is a TypeError
```

Creating our first script – unix_converter.py

Our first script will perform a common timestamp conversion that will prove useful throughout this book. Named `unix_converter.py`, this script converts Unix timestamps into a human readable date and time value. Unix timestamps are generally formatted as an integer representing the number of seconds since `1970-01-01 00:00:00`.

On line one, we provide a brief description of our script to the users, allowing them to quickly understand the intentions and uses of the script. Following this are import statements on lines two through four. These imports likely look familiar, providing support (in order) for printing information in Python 2 and 3, interpreting timestamp data, and accessing information about the version of Python used. The `sys` library is then used on lines 6 through 12 to check what version of Python was used to call the script to properly handle accepting user input. Python 2 uses the `raw_input` function to accept data at the Terminal for the user, while Python 3 implements the `input` function. This `if/elif/else` statement is then concluded with `NotImplementedError` for other (future) versions of Python not specified. To make things easier, we built this conditional in a manner that you can easily plug into your code. See the following for the described code:

```
001 """Script to convert Unix timestamps."""
002 from __future__ import print_function
003 import datetime
004 import sys
005
006 if sys.version_info[0] == 3:
007     get_input = input
008 elif sys.version_info[0] == 2:
```

```
    get_input = raw_input
else:
    raise NotImplementedError(
        "Unsupported version of Python used.")
```

After an omitted license statement (please see the source code for the MIT license information), we provide additional script information for reference by the user and to standardize our script implementation. We then move to the `main()` function, which prompts the user for a timestamp to convert and then prints the results of the transformed timestamp from our `Unix_converter()` function. To break apart line 49 a little more, let's start at the innermost component, the `get_input()` function call. This function is supplied with a string that will be displayed to the user in front of the buffer allowing user input. This `get_input()` function returns a string value of the data entered into the console by the user, although we need to convert this value into an integer. We use the `int` class to initialize an integer value that we then store in the `unix_ts` variable.

Applying concepts
How could we redesign line 49 to better handle the user input and any exceptions that may arise when accepting this data?
Hint
It may take more than one line.

```
042 __authors__ = ["Chapin Bryce", "Preston Miller"]
043 __date__ = 20181027
044 __description__ = """Convert Unix formatted timestamps (seconds
045     since Epoch [1970-01-01 00:00:00]) to human readable."""
046
047
048 def main():
049     unix_ts = int(get_input('Unix timestamp to convert:\n>> '))
050     print(unix_converter(unix_ts))
```

On line 50 in the previous code block, we call the `unix_converter()` function, providing the integer input from the user. This function then, as defined on line 53 in the following code, calls the `datetime` module and uses the `utcfromtimestamp()` method to read the integer as a `datetime` object. We are using the `utcfromtimestamp()` method here instead of the similarly named `fromtimestamp()` method, as the `utcfromtimestamp()` version does not apply time zone modifications to the provided data and leaves the timestamp in the original time zone. This returned `datetime` object is then converted into a human-readable string using the `strftime()` method and the resulting string is returned to the calling function, which ultimately prints this value to the console:

```
053 def unix_converter(timestamp):
054     date_ts = datetime.datetime.utcfromtimestamp(timestamp)
```

```
055     return date_ts.strftime('%m/%d/%Y %I:%M:%S %p')p')
```

Our script is concluded with two lines of code, as shown in the following snippet, which will become very frequent in the conclusions of our scripts. The first of these lines, on line 57, is a conditional that's used to check whether the script was executed as a script instead of imported as a module. This allows us to change the functionality of our code based on how it is used. In an example, a console version of our code should, generally, accept command-line arguments while a version used as a library will not need to prompt the user for those details as the calling script may only use a subset of functions within this code. This means that line 58 is the only logic we want to execute if this code is called at the command line, which starts the `main()` function. If this script is imported as a module to another script, nothing will occur as we have no further logic to run on import. If it is imported, we will be able to use the functions without worrying about other calls occurring on import:

```
057 if __name__ == '__main__':
058     main()
```

We can now execute this script by calling `unix_converter.py` at the command line. This script ran, as shown in the following screenshot, until it required input from the user. Once the value was entered, the script continued execution and printed the converted timestamp to the console:

```
(py3.7.1) C:\book\chapters\chapter_02>python unix_converter.py
Unix timestamp to convert:
>> 1525780110
05/08/2018 11:48:30 AM
```

User input

Allowing user input enhances the dynamic nature of a program. It is a good practice to query the user for file paths or values rather than explicitly writing this information into the code file. Therefore, if the user wants to use the same program on a separate file, they can simply provide a different path, rather than editing the source code. In most programs, users supply input and output locations or identify which optional features or modules should be used at runtime.

User input can be supplied when the program is first called or during runtime as an argument. For most projects, it is recommended to use command-line arguments because asking the user for input during runtime halts the program execution while waiting for the input.

Using the raw input method and the system module – user_input.py

Both `input()` and `sys.argv` represent basic methods of obtaining input from users. Be cognizant of the fact that both of these methods return string objects, as previously discussed for the Python 2 `raw_input()` and Python 3 `input()` functions. We can simply convert the string into the required data type using the appropriate class constructor.

The `input()` function is similar to asking someone a question and waiting for their reply. During this time, the program's execution thread halts until a reply is received. We define a function later that queries the user for a number and returns the squared value. As seen in our first script, when converting Unix timestamps, we have to wait for the user to provide a value before the script can continue. While this wasn't an issue in that very short script, larger code bases or long-running scripts should avoid this delay.

Arguments supplied at the command line are stored in the `sys.argv` list. As with any list, these arguments can be accessed with an index, which starts at zero. The first element is the name of the script, while any element after that represents a space-separated user-supplied input. We need to import the `sys` module to access this list.

On line 39, we copy the arguments from the `sys.argv` list into a temporary list variable named `args`. This is preferred because, on line 41, we remove the first element after printing it. For the remaining items in the `args` list, we use a `for` loop and wrap our list with the built-in `enumerate()` function. This gives us a counter for our loop, `i`, to count the number of loop iterations or arguments used in this case. On lines 43 and 44, we print out each argument and its position and data type. We have the following code:

```
001 """Replicate user input in the console."""
002 from __future__ import print_function
003 import sys
...
033 __authors__ = ["Chapin Bryce", "Preston Miller"]
034 __date__ = 20181027
035 __description__ = "Replicate user input in the console"
036
037
038 def main():
039     args = sys.argv
040     print('Script:', args[0])
041     args.pop(0)
042     for i, argument in enumerate(sys.argv):
043         print('Argument {}: {}'.format(i, argument))
044         print('Type: {}'.format(type(argument)))
```

```

if __name__ == '__main__':
    main()
```

After saving this file as `user_input.py`, we can call it at the command line and pass in our arguments.

As you can see in the following example, arguments are space delimited, therefore an argument with spaces needs to be wrapped with quotes. It is also clear in the following example that all argument values from `sys.argv` are stored as string values. The `input()` function also interprets all input as string values:

```
(py3.7.1) C:\book\chapters\chapter_02>python user_input.py hello world "what's new?"
Script: user_input.py
Argument 0: hello
Type: <class 'str'>
Argument 1: world
Type: <class 'str'>
Argument 2: what's new?
Type: <class 'str'>
```

For smaller programs that do not have many command-line options, the `sys.argv` list is a quick and easy way to obtain user input without blocking script execution.

File paths that contain a space should be double-quoted. For example, `sys.argv` would split `C:/Users/LPF/misc/my books` into `C:/Users/LPF/misc/my` and `books`. This would result in an `IOError` exception when trying to interact with this directory in a script. Additionally, watch for file paths containing the backslash character `\`; we need to escape this character to prevent our command line Terminal and our code from misunderstanding the input. This character is escaped by using a second backslash, like so: `\\`.

Understanding Argparse – argument_parser.py

Argparse is a module in the standard library and will be used throughout this book as a means of obtaining user input. Argparse can help develop more complicated command-line interfaces. By default, `argparse` creates a `-h` switch or a help switch to display help and usage information for the scripts. In this section, we will build a sample `argparse` implementation that has required, optional, and default arguments.

We import the `argparse` module, following our usual `print_function` and script description. We then specify our usual script header details as `__author__`, `__date__`, and `__description__` as we will be using all three in our `argparse` implementation. On line 38, we then define an overly simple `main()` function to print the parsed argument information, as we don't have any plans for this script other than to show off some neat user argument handling. To accomplish that goal, we first need to initiate our `ArgumentParser` class instance, as shown on lines 43 through 48. Notice how we only implement this if the script is called from the command line with the conditional on line 42.

On line 43, we initialize `ArgumentParser` with three optional arguments. The first is the description of the script, which we will read in from the `__description__` variable that was previously set. The second argument is the epilog or details provided at the end of the help section. This can be any arbitrary text, as can the description field, though we chose to use this to provide authorship and version information. For getting started, using date values as a version number is helpful for user reference and prevents complications with numbering schemes. The last optional argument is a formatter specification, instructing our argument parser to display any default values set by the script so that the user can know whether options will be set if they do not modify them through an argument. It is highly recommended to include this as a force of habit:

```
001 """Sample argparse example."""
002 from __future__ import print_function
003 import argparse
...
033 __authors__ = ["Chapin Bryce", "Preston Miller"]
034 __date__ = 20181027
035 __description__ = "Argparse command-line parser sample"
036
037
038 def main(args):
039     print(args)
040
041
042 if __name__ == '__main__':
043     parser = argparse.ArgumentParser(
044         description=__description__,
045         epilog='Built by {}. Version {}'.format(
046         ", ".join(__authors__), __date__),
047         formatter_class=argparse.ArgumentDefaultsHelpFormatter
048     )
```

We can now leverage our newly instantiated parser object to add an argument specification. To start, let's discuss some healthy practices for required and optional arguments. Argparse, by default, uses the presence of one or two dashes prior to an argument name to note whether the argument should be considered optional or not. If the argument specification has a leading dash, it will be considered both optional and non-positional; the inverse, a lack of a leading dash, will instruct argparse to interpret an argument as required and positional.

Use the following as an example; in this script, the `timezone` and `input_file` arguments are required and must be provided in that order. Additionally, the arguments for these two items do not require an argument specifier; instead, `argparse` will look for an unpaired value to assign to the `timezone` argument and then look for a second unpaired value to assign to the `input_file` argument. Inversely, the `--source`, `--file-type`, `-h` (or `--help`), and `-l` (or `--log`) arguments are non-positional and can be provided in any order as long as the appropriate value is immediately following, that is, paired with, with the argument specifier.

To make things a little more complex, but more customizable, we can require non-positional arguments. This has an advantage, as we can now allow the user to enter the arguments in an arbitrary order, though as a disadvantage it requires additional typing for fields that are required for the script to operate. You'll notice in the following code that the `--source` argument on the second line does not have square brackets surrounding the value. This is argparse's (subtle) way of indicating that this is a required non-positional argument. It can be tricky for a user to understand this at first glance, though argparse will halt the execution of the script and alert the user if the argument is missing from the provided arguments. You may want to use non-positional required arguments in your scripts or avoid them all together—it is up to you as the developer to find the most comfortable and fitting interface for your users:

```
$ python argument_parser.py --help
usage: argument_parser.py [-h] --source SOURCE [-l LOG]
 [--file-type {E01,RAW,Ex01}]
 timezone input_file

Argparse command-line parser sample

positional arguments:
 timezone timezone to apply
 input_file

optional arguments:
 -h, --help show this help message and exit
 --source SOURCE source information (default: None)
 -l LOG, --log LOG Path to log file (default: None)
```

```
  --file-type {E01,RAW,Ex01}

Built by Chapin Bryce, Preston Miller. Version 20181027
```

Mini-tangent aside, let's start adding arguments to the parser object we initiated. We will start with one of the positional arguments we previously discussed. The `timezone` argument is defined using the `add_argument()` method, allowing us to provide a string representing the argument name and optional parameters for additional detail. On line 51, we simply offer helpful information to provide context to how this argument should be used:

```
050     # Add positional required arguments
051     parser.add_argument('timezone', help='timezone to apply')
```

The next argument we add, on line 54, is the non-positional required argument previously discussed. Notice how we use the `required=True` statement to indicate that, regardless of the leading dashes, this argument is required for execution:

```
053     # Add non-positional required argument
054     parser.add_argument('--source',
055         help='source information', required=True)
```

We now add our first non-positional and optional argument for the log file. Here, we are providing two options for how the user can specify the argument, `-l` or `--log`. This is recommended for common arguments, as it provides the frequent user shorthand and the novice user context for argument use:

```
057     # Add optional arguments, allowing shorthand argument
058     parser.add_argument('-l', '--log', help='Path to log file')
```

Not all arguments need to accept a value; in some instances, we just need a Boolean answer from the argument. Additionally, we may want to allow the argument to be specified multiple times or have custom functionality when called. To support this, the `argparse` library allows for the use of actions. The actions we will commonly use in this book are demonstrated as follows.

The first action that is handy is `store_true` and is the opposite of `store_false`. These are handy for getting information on enabling or disabling functionality in your script. As shown in the following code block on lines 61 through 64, we can see the action parameter being used to specify whether `True` or `False` should be stored as a result of the argument. In this case, this is duplicative, and one of these two arguments could be used to determine whether the email in this example should be sent. Additional actions are available, such as `append`, as shown on line 66 and 67, where each instance of an email address, in this example, will be added to a list that we can iterate through and use.

The last action example in the following code is used to count the number of times an argument is called. We see this implementation primarily for increasing verbosity or debugging messages, though it can be used elsewhere in the same fashion:

```
# Using actions
parser.add_argument('--no-email',
    help='disable emails', action="store_false")
parser.add_argument('--send-email',
    help='enable emails', action="store_true")
# Append values for each argument instance.
parser.add_argument('--emails',
    help='email addresses to notify', action="append")
# Count the number of instances. i.e. -vvv
parser.add_argument('-v', help='add verbosity', action='count')
```

The `default` keyword dictates the default value of an argument. We can also use the `type` keyword to store our argument as a certain object. Instead of being stuck with strings as our only input, we can now store the input directly as the desired object, such as an integer, and remove the need for user input conversions from our scripts:

```
# Defaults
parser.add_argument('--length', default=55, type=int)
parser.add_argument('--name', default='Alfred', type=str)
```

Argparse can be used to directly open a file for reading or writing. On line 76, we open the required argument, `input_file`, in reading mode. By passing this file object into our main script, we can immediately begin to process our data of interest. This is repeated on the next line to handle opening a file for writing:

```
075    # Handling Files
076    parser.add_argument('input_file', type=argparse.FileType('r'))
077    parser.add_argument('output_file', type=argparse.FileType('w'))
```

The last keyword we will discuss is `choices`, which takes a list of case-sensitive options that the user can select from. When the user calls this argument, they must then provide one of the valid options. For example, `--file-type RAW` would set the `file-type` argument to the RAW choice, as follows:

```
# Allow only specified choices
parser.add_argument('--file-type',
    choices=['E01', 'RAW', 'Ex01'])
```

Finally, once we have added all of our desired arguments to our `parser`, we can parse the arguments. On line 84, we call the `parse_args()` function, which creates a `Namespace` object. To access, for example, the length argument that we created on line 72, we need to call the `Namespace` object such as `arguments.length`. On line 85, we pass our arguments into our `main()` function, which prints out all of the arguments in the `Namespace` object. We have the following code:

```
083     # Parsing arguments into objects
084     arguments = parser.parse_args()
085     main(arguments)
```

These `Namespace` objects may be reassigned to variables for easier recall.

With the basics of the `argparse` module behind us, we can now build simple and more advanced command-line arguments for our scripts. Therefore, this module is used extensively to provide command-line arguments for most of the code we will build. When running the following code with the `--help` switch, we should see our series of required and optional arguments for the script:

```
(py3.7.1) C:\book\chapters\chapter_02>python argument_parser.py --help
usage: argument_parser.py [-h] --source SOURCE [-l LOG] [--no-email]
                          [--send-email] [--emails EMAILS] [-v]
                          [--length LENGTH] [--name NAME]
                          [--file-type {E01,RAW,Ex01}]
                          timezone input_file output_file

Argparse command-line parser sample

positional arguments:
  timezone              timezone to apply
  input_file
  output_file

optional arguments:
  -h, --help            show this help message and exit
  --source SOURCE       source information (default: None)
  -l LOG, --log LOG     Path to log file (default: None)
  --no-email            disable emails (default: True)
  --send-email          enable emails (default: False)
  --emails EMAILS       email addresses to notify (default: None)
  -v                    add verbosity (default: None)
  --length LENGTH
  --name NAME
  --file-type {E01,RAW,Ex01}

Built by Chapin Bryce, Preston Miller. Version 20181027
```

Forensic scripting best practices

Forensic best practices play a big part in what we do and, traditionally, refer to handling or acquiring evidence. However, we've designated some forensic best practices of our own when it comes to programming, as follows:

- Do not modify the original data you're working with
- Work on copies of the original data
- Comment code
- Validate your program's results (and other application results)
- Maintain extensive logging
- Return output in an easy-to-analyze format (your users will thank you)

The golden rule of forensics is: strongly avoid modification of the original data. Work on a verified forensic copy whenever possible. However, this may not be an option for other disciplines, such as for incident responders where the parameters and scope varies. As always, this varies on the case and circumstances, but please keep in mind the ramifications of working on live systems or with original data.

In these cases, it is important to consider what the code does and how it might interact with the system at runtime. What kind of footprint does the code leave behind? Could it inadvertently destroy artifacts or references to them? Has the program been validated in similar conditions to ensure that it operates properly? These are the kinds of considerations that are necessary when it comes to running a program on a live system.

We've touched on commenting code before, but it cannot hurt to overstate its value. Soon, we will create our first forensic script, `usb_lookup.py`, which is a little over 90 lines of code. Imagine being handed the code without any explanation or comments. It might take a few minutes to read and understand what it does exactly, even for an experienced developer. Now, imagine a large project's source code that has thousands of lines of code—it should be apparent how valuable comments are, not just for the developer but also those who examine the code afterwards.

Validation essentially comes down to knowing the code's behavior. Obviously, bugs are going to be discovered and addressed. However, bugs have a way of frequently turning up and are ultimately unavoidable as it is impossible to test against all possible situations during development. Instead, what can be established is an understanding of the behavior of the code in a variety of environments and situations. Mastering the behavior of your code is important, not only to be able to determine if the code is up for the task at hand but also when asked to explain its function and inner workings in a courtroom.

Logging can help keep track of any potential errors during runtime and act as an audit-chain of sorts for what the program did and when. Python supplies a robust logging module in the standard library, unsurprisingly named `logging`. We will use this module and its various options throughout this book.

The purpose of our scripts is to automate some of the tedious repetitive tasks in forensics and supply analysts with actionable knowledge. Oftentimes, the latter refers to storing data in a format that is easily manipulated. In most cases, a CSV file is the simplest way to achieve this so that it can be opened with a variety of different text or workbook editors. We will use the `csv` module in many of our programs.

Developing our first forensic script – usb_lookup.py

Now that we've gotten our feet wet writing our first Python script, let's write our first forensic script. During forensic investigations, it is not uncommon to see references to external devices by their **vendor identifier** (**VID**) and **product identifier** (**PID**) values; these values are represented by four hexadecimal characters. In cases where the vendor and product name are not identified, the examiner must look up this information. One such location for this information is the following web page: `http://linux-usb.org/usb.ids`. For example, on this web page, we can see that a Kingston DataTraveler G3 has a VID of 0951 and a PID of 1643. We will use this data source when attempting to identify vendor and product names by using the defined identifiers.

First, let's look at the data source we're going to be parsing. A hypothetical sample illustrating the structure of our data source is mentioned later. There are USB vendors and, for each vendor, a set of USB products. Each vendor or product has four-digit hexadecimal characters and a name. What separates vendor and product lines are tabs because products are tabbed over once under their parent vendor. As a forensic developer, you will come to love patterns and data structures, as it is a happy day when data follows a strict set of rules. Because of this, we will be able to preserve the relationship between the vendor and its products in a simple manner. Here is the afore-mentioned hypothetical sample:

```
0001 Vendor Name
    0001 Product Name 1
    0002 Product Name 2
    ...
    000N Product Name N
```

This script, named `usb_lookup.py`, takes a `VID` and `PID` that's supplied by the user and returns the appropriate vendor and product names. Our program uses the `urlopen` method from the `urllib` module to download the `usb.ids` database to memory and create a dictionary of VIDs and their products. Since this is one of the libraries that changed between versions 2 and 3 of Python, we have introduced some logic in a `try` and `except` block to ensure we are able to call the `urlopen` method without issue, as shown in the following code. We also import the `argparse` module to allow us to accept `VID` and `PID` information from the user:

```
"""Script to lookup USB vendor and product values."""
from __future__ import print_function
try:
    from urllib2 import urlopen
except ImportError:
    from urllib.request import urlopen
import argparse
```

If a vendor and product combination is not found, error handling will inform the user of any partial results and exit the program gracefully.

The `main()` function contains the logic to download the `usb.ids` file, store it in memory, and create the USB dictionary. The structure of the USB dictionary is somewhat complex and involves mapping a `VID` to a list, containing the name of the vendor as the first element, and a product dictionary as the second element. This product dictionary maps PIDs to their names. The following is an example of the USB dictionary containing two vendors, `VendorId_1` and `VendorId_2`, each mapped to a list containing the vendor name, and a dictionary for any product ID and name pairs:

```
usbs = {
    VendorId_1: [
        VendorName_1,
        {ProductId_1: ProductName_1,
         ProductId_2: ProductName_2,
         ProductId_N: ProductName_N}
    ], VendorId_2: [
        VendorName_2,
        {ProductId_1: ProductName_1}
    ], ...
}
```

It may be tempting to just search for `VID` and `PID` in the lines and return the names rather than creating this dictionary that links vendors to their products. However, products can share the same ID across different vendors, which could result in mistakenly returning a product from a different vendor. With our previous data structure, we can be sure that the product belongs to the associated vendor.

Once the USB dictionary has been created, the `search_key()` function is responsible for querying the dictionary for a match. It first assigns the user-supplied two arguments, `VID` and `PID`, before continuing with the execution of the script. Next, it searches for a `VID` match in the outermost dictionary. If `VID` is found, the innermost dictionary is searched for the responsive `PID`. If both are found, the resolved names are printed to the console. Lastly, starting at line 81, we define our arguments for the user to provide the `VID` and `PID` values before calling the `main()` function:

```
042 def main():
...
065 def search_key():
...
080 if __name__ == '__main__':
081     parser = argparse.ArgumentParser(
082         description=__description__,
083         epilog='Built by {}. Version {}'.format(
084             ", ".join(__authors__), __date__),
085         formatter_class=argparse.ArgumentDefaultsHelpFormatter
086     )
087     parser.add_argument('vid', help="VID value")
088     parser.add_argument('pid', help="PID value")
089     args = parser.parse_args()
090     main(args.vid, args.pid)
```

For larger scripts, such as this, it is helpful to view a diagram that illustrates how these functions are connected together. Fortunately, a library named `code2flow`, available on GitHub (`https://github.com/scottrogowski/code2flow.git`), exists to automate this process for us. The following schematic illustrates the flow from the `main()` function to the `search_key()` function. There are other libraries that can create similar flow charts. However, this library does a great job of creating a simple and easy to understand flowchart:

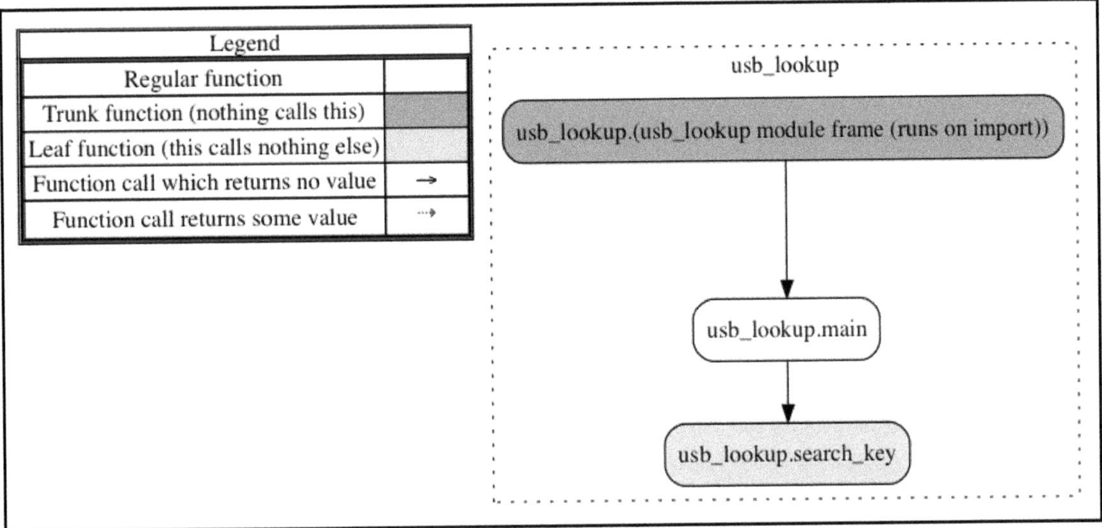

Understanding the main() function

Let's start by examining the `main()` function, which is called on line 90, as seen in the previous code block. This function, on line 42, requires the `vid` and `pid` information supplied by the user's arguments for resolution in the `usb.ids` database. On lines 43 through 46, we create our initial variables. The `url` variable stores the URL containing the USB data source. We use the `urlopen()` function from the `urllib` module to create a list of strings from our online source. We will use a lot of string operations, such as `startswith()`, `isalnum()`, `islower()`, and `count()`, to parse the `usb.ids` file structure and store the parsed data in the `usbs` dictionary. The `curr_id` variable, defined as an empty string on line 46, will be used to keep track of which vendor we are currently processing in our script:

```
042 def main(vid, pid):
043     url = 'http://www.linux-usb.org/usb.ids'
044     usbs = {}
045     usb_file = urlopen(url)
046     curr_id = ''
```

An important concept in Python string manipulation is encoding. This is one of the most common issues when writing Python 2 and Python 3 compatible code. The following `for` loop on line 48 starts iterating over each line in the file, providing the line for review. For Python 3 support, we have to check whether the line variable is an instance of bytes, a raw data type that (in this case) is holding encoded string data. If this is the case, we must decode it using the `decode()` method and provide the proper encoding—`latin-1` in this instance, as seen on line 50. Python 2 reads data from files as strings and therefore will not enter this conditional, so we can move forward with parsing the line:

```
048     for line in usb_file:
049         if isinstance(line, bytes):
050             line = line.decode('latin-1')
```

Our next conditional checks for commented lines in the `usb.ids` file, skipping any blank lines (only containing a newline or tab character) and any comment lines starting with a pound character. To check for comment lines, we can use the `startswith()` string method to check whether the provided string, of one or more characters, is the same as the line we are checking. To simplify our code, we also leveraged the `in` statement, which allows us to handle an `or`-like comparison of equality for the line. This is a handy shortcut you will see in a variety of scripts. If either of these conditions is true, we will use the continue statement as seen on line 52 to step into the next loop iteration:

```
051         if line.startswith('#') or line in ('\n', '\t'):
052             continue
```

The second half of our conditional handles additional validation of the line format. We want to confirm that the line we are inspecting matches the format of a vendor line, so we can include our vendor-related parsing code within it. To do this, we check to make sure the line does not start with a tab character and the first character is alphanumeric with the `isalnum()` call:

```
053         else:
054             if not(line.startswith('\t')) and line[0].isalnum():
```

Knowing that the line passed our check for confirming it is a vendor informational line, we can start extracting the needed values and fill out our data structure. On line 55, we extract our two values from the line, `uid` and `name`, by stripping the line and using the `split()` method. The `split()` method is using two parameters here, one for the character to split on and the second for the number of times to split. In this case, we are splitting on a space character and only splitting after finding the first space.

This is useful, as our vendor name may contain a space in it and we want to keep those details together. Since we anticipate two values returning, we can use the assignment seen on line 55 to simultaneously populate the `uid` and `name` variables with the correct values, though this can lead to errors if the `split()` method only returns one object. In this instance, we know our data source and have validated that this should always return two values, though this is a great spot to add a try-except block in your version of the code to handle any errors that may arise.

We then assign the `uid` variable to the `curr_id` value for use while parsing `PID` details on line 56. Finally, on line 57, we add this information to our data structure, `usbs`. Since the `usbs` structure is a dictionary, we assign the VID's `uid` value as the key and set up our list with the `VID` common name as the first element and an empty dictionary for product details as a second. On line 57, we ensure that the vendor name does not have any unwanted whitespace characters on it by calling the `strip()` method on the string:

```
055             uid, name = line.strip().split(' ', 1)
056             curr_id = uid
057             usbs[uid] = [name.strip(), {}]
```

Now that we have processed the vendor data pattern, let's turn our attention to the product data pattern. First, we will use an `elif` conditional to check that the line does start with a tab character and, using the `count()` method, ensure that it is the only tab character in the line. On line 59, we make a familiar call to strip and split the line into our required values. On line 60, we then add the product information to our data structure. As a quick refresher, `usbs` is a dictionary, where the keys are VIDs. Within a VID's value is a list where element zero is the vendor name and element one is the dictionary to store PID details. As expected, we will use the `uid` value as the key for the product details and assign the product name to the `PID` key. Notice how we use the `curr_id` value from the prior vendor line to ensure we are correlating the VIDs and PIDs properly:

```
058         elif line.startswith('\t') and line.count('\t') == 1:
059             uid, name = line.strip().split(' ', 1)
060             usbs[curr_id][1][uid] = name.strip()
```

The previous lines then repeat in a `for` loop until the end of the file is reached, parsing out the vendor and product details and adding them into the `usbs` dictionary.

We are almost there—the last part of our `main()` function is a call to the `search_key()` function, which takes the user-supplied `vid` and `pid` information, along with our newly built `usbs` dictionary for lookup. Notice how this call is indented with four spaces, placing it outside of the `for` loop and allowing us to only call this method one time, once the `usbs` lookup dictionary is complete:

```
062     search_key(vid, pid, usbs)
```

This takes care of the logic in the `main()` function. Now, let's take a look at the `search_key()` function to determine how we will lookup our VID and PID values.

Interpreting the search_key() function

The `search_key()` function, originally called on line 62 of the `main()` function, is where we search for the user-supplied vendor and product IDs, and display the resolved results to the user. In addition, all of our error handling logic is contained within this function.

Let's practice accessing nested lists or dictionaries. We discussed this in the `main()` function; however, it pays to actually practice rather than take our word for it. Accessing nested structures requires us to use multiple indices rather than just one. For example, let's create a list and map that to `key_1` in a dictionary. To access elements from the nested list, we will need to supply `key_1` to access the list and then a numerical index to access elements of the list:

```
>>> inner_list = ['a', 'b', 'c', 'd']
>>> print(inner_list[0])
a
>>> outer_dict = {'key_1': inner_list}
>>> print(outer_dict['key_1'])
['a', 'b', 'c', 'd']
>>> print(outer_dict['key_1'][3])
d
```

Now, let's switch gears, back to the task at hand, and leverage our new skills to search our dictionary to find vendor and product IDs. The `search_key()` function is defined on line 65 and takes the user-supplied VID and PID along with our parsed out `usb_dict` dictionary. We then start by querying `usb_dict` for the `vendor_key` value, using the `get()` method of a dictionary to attempt to get the requested key's value or return `None`, as specified on line 66, if the key is not found.

Please note that the data returned by the `get()` call, if successful, is the entire value for that key, or in this case a list, where element zero is the vendor name and element one is the dictionary of product details. We can then check, on line 67, to see whether the key was found; if it was unavailable, we print this to the user and exit on lines 68 and 69, as shown here:

```
065 def search_key(vendor_key, product_key, usb_dict):
066     vendor = usb_dict.get(vendor_key, None)
067     if vendor is None:
068         print('Vendor ID not found')
069         exit()
```

We can then repeat this logic for looking up the product information, though we first have to navigate to the product information. On line 71, we access element one of the vendor list, containing the product details dictionary, and perform the same `get()` method call to look up any name resolution for the PID. In the same manner, we check to see if the lookup failed and provide any available details to the user; in case it fails, we can at least give the vendor information:

```
071     product = vendor[1].get(product_key, None)
072     if product is None:
073         print('Vendor: {}\nProduct Id not found.'.format(
074             vendor[0]))
075         exit(0)
```

If everything resolves successfully, we can print the output to the user and the script will complete! Notice how, on line 77, in the format statement, we have to call the first element of the vendor variable since the value of the VID key lookup was a list, whereas the value of the PID key lookup is just the product's name. This is where things can get a little confusing, though feel free to reference the earlier sample data structure and add as many intermediate print statements to help with comprehension:

```
077     print('Vendor: {}\nProduct: {}'.format(vendor[0], product))
```

Running our first forensic script

The `usb_lookup.py` script requires two arguments—vendor and product IDs for the USB of interest. We can find this information by looking at a suspect `HKLM\SYSTEM\%CurrentControlSet%\Enum\USB` registry key. For example, supplying the vendor, `0951`, and product, `1643`, from the sub-key `VID_0951&PID_1643`, results in our script identifying the device as a Kingston DataTraveler G3:

```
(py3.7.1) C:\book\chapters\chapter_02>python usb_lookup.py 0951 1643
Vendor: Kingston Technology
Product: DataTraveler G3
```

Our data source is not an all-inclusive list, and if you supply a vendor or a product ID that does not exist in the data source, our script will print that the ID was not found. The full code for this and all of our scripts can be downloaded from `https://packtpub.com/books/content/support`.

Troubleshooting

At some point in your development career—probably by the time you write your first script—you will have encountered a Python error and received a **Traceback** message. A Traceback provides the context of the error and pinpoints the line that caused the issue. The issue itself is described as an exception, and usually provides a human-friendly message of the error.

Python has a number of built-in exceptions, the purpose of which is to help the developer in diagnosing errors in their code. A full listing of built-in exceptions can be found at `https://docs.python.org/3/library/exceptions.html`.

Let's look at a simple example of an exception, `AttributeError`, and what the Traceback looks like in this case:

```
>>> import math
>>> print(math.noattribute(5))
Traceback (most recent call last):
 File "<stdin>", line 1, in <module>
AttributeError: 'module' object has no attribute 'noattribute'
```

The Traceback indicates the file in which the error occurred, in this case, `stdin` or standard input, because this code was written in the interactive prompt. When working on larger projects or with a single script, the file will be the name of the script causing the error rather than `stdin`. The `in <module>` bit will be the name of the function that contains the faulty line of code, or `<module>` if the code is outside of a function.

Now, let's look at a slightly more complicated issue. To do this, let's use the data structure from our prior script. In the following code block, we are not accessing the VID data with the `get()` call, but instead hoping that it exists. Temporarily replace line 66 of the `usb_lookup.py` script with the following for this example:

```
066     vendor = usb_dict[vendor_key]
```

Now, if you run this updated code with a valid vendor key, you will get an expected result, though use a key such as `ffff` and see what occurs. Check if it looks like the following:

```
$ python usb_lookup.py ffff 1643
Traceback (most recent call last):
    File "usb_lookup.py", line 90, in <module>
        main(args.vid, args.pid)
    File "usb_lookup.py", line 62, in main
        search_key(vid, pid, usbs)
    File "usb_lookup.py", line 66, in search_key
        vendor = usb_dict[vendor_key]
KeyError: 'ffff'
```

The traceback here has three traces in the stack. The last trace at the bottom is where our error occurred. In this case, on line 66 of the `usb_lookup.py` file, the `search_key()` function generated a `KeyError` exception. Looking up what a `KeyError` exception is in the Python documentation would indicate that this is due to the key not existing in the dictionary. Most of the time, we will need to address the error at that specific error causing line. In our case, we employed the `get()` method of a dictionary to safely access key elements. Please revert the line back to its prior state at this time to prevent this error from occurring in the future!

Challenge

We recommend experimenting with the code to learn how it works or try to improve its functionality. For example, how can we further validate the VID and PID input to ensure they are valid? Can we perform this same check on the returned UID values on lines 55 and 59?

Another extension to our first script is to consider offline environments. How can we modify this code to allow someone to run in an air-gapped environment? What arguments can be used to change the behavior depending on the user's need for offline access?

Programs are constantly evolving and are never truly finished products. There are plenty of other improvements that can be made here and we invite you to create and share the modifications to this and all of your other forensic Python scripts.

Summary

This chapter continued from where we left off in previous chapter, and helped us build a solid Python foundation for later chapters. We covered advanced data types and object-oriented programming, developed our first scripts, and dived into traceback messages. At this point, you should start to become comfortable with Python, though repeat these two chapters and manually type out the code to help strengthen your comfort level as needed. We highly recommend to practice and experiment by either testing out ideas in the interactive prompt or modifying the scripts we developed. The code for this project can be downloaded from GitHub or Packt, as described in the *Preface*.

As we move away from theory and look into the core part of this book, we will start with simple scripts and work toward increasingly more complicated programs. This should allow a natural development of understanding programming and skills. In the next chapter, you will learn how to parse the `setupapi.dev.log` file on Windows systems to identify USB installation times.

3
Parsing Text Files

Text files, usually sourced from application or service logs, are common sources for artifacts in digital investigations. Log files can be quite large or contain data that makes human review difficult. A manual examination can devolve into a series of grep searches, which may or may not be fruitful; additionally, prebuilt tools may not have support for a specific log file format. For these instances, we will need to develop our own solution to properly parse and extract the relevant information. In this chapter, we will analyze the `setupapi.dev.log` file, which records device information on Windows machines. This log file is commonly examined, as it can extract the first connection time of USB devices on the system.

We will step through several iterations of the same code through this chapter. Though redundant, we encourage writing out each iteration for yourself. By rewriting the code, we will progress through the material together and find a more fitting solution, learn about bug handling, and implement efficiency measures. Please rewrite the code for yourself and test each iteration to see the changes in the output and code handling.

In this chapter, we will be covering the following topics:

- Identifying repetitive patterns in this log file for USB device entries
- Extracting and processing artifacts from text files
- Iteratively improving our script design and features
- Enhancing the presentation of data in a deduplicated and readable manner

The code for this chapter is developed and tested using Python 2.7.15 and Python 3.7.1.

Setup API

The `setupapi.dev.log` file is a Windows log file that tracks connection information for a variety of devices, including USB devices. Since USB device information generally plays an important role in many investigations, our script will help identify the earliest installation time of a USB device on a machine. This log is system-wide, not user-specific, and therefore provides only the installation time of a USB device's first connection to the system. In addition to logging this timestamp, the log contains the **vendor ID** (**VID**), **product ID** (**PID**), and the serial number of the device. With this information, we can paint a better picture of removable storage activity. On Windows XP, this file can be found at `C:\Windows\setupapi.log`; on Windows 7 through 10, this file can be found at `C:\Windows\inf\setupapi.dev.log`.

Introducing our script

In this section, we will build our `setupapi_parser.py` to parse the `setupapi.dev.log` file on Windows 7. Equipped with only modules from the standard library, we will open and read a `setupapi.log` file, identify and parse relevant USB information, and display it to the user in the console. As mentioned in the introduction, we will use an iterative build process to mimic a natural development cycle. Each iteration will build upon the previous while we explore new features and methods. We encourage the development of additional iterations, and there are challenges at the end of this chapter to compliment this.

Overview

Before developing any code, let's identify the requirements and features our script must possess to accomplish the desired task. We will need to execute the following steps:

1. Open the log file and read all lines
2. In each line, check for indicators of a USB device entry
3. Parse responsive lines for timestamp and device information
4. Output the result to the user

Now, let's examine the log file of interest to determine repetitive structures that we can use as footholds in our script to parse the relevant data. In the following sample USB entry, we can see the device information on line 1 following the text `Device Install (Hardware initiated)`. This device information contains the VID, PID, device revision, and the unique ID of the device. Each of these elements is separated by either a `&` or `_` character and may contain some additional inconsequential characters. The installation time is recorded on line 2, following the `Section start` text. For our purposes, we are only interested in these two lines. All other surrounding lines will be ignored, as they relate to operating system driver information:

```
001 >>>  [Setup online Device Install (Hardware initiated) -
pciven_15ad&dev_07a0&subsys_07a015ad&rev_013&18d45aa6&0&a9]
002 >>>  Section start 2010/11/10 10:21:12.593
003 ump: Creating Install Process: DrvInst.exe 10:21:12.593
004 ndv: Retrieving device info...
005 ndv: Setting device parameters...
006 ndv: Searching Driver Store and Device Path...
007 dvi: {Build Driver List} 10:21:12.640
```

Our first iteration – setupapi_parser_v1.py

The goal of our first iteration is to develop a functional prototype that we will improve upon in later iterations. We will continue to see the following code block in all our scripts, which provides basic documentation about the script and support for printing information (line 2) and opening files (line 3) in both version 2 and 3 of Python. The following is the licensing information and basic script descriptors that can be found in all of our scripts:

```
001 """First iteration of the setupapi.dev.log parser."""
002 from __future__ import print_function
003 from io import open
...
033 __authors__ = ["Chapin Bryce", "Preston Miller"]
034 __date__ = 20181027
035 __description__ = """This scripts reads a Windows 7 Setup API
036     log and prints USB Devices to the user"""
```

Our script involves three functions, which are outlined as follows. The `main()` function kicks off the script by calling the `parse_setupapi()` function. This function reads the `setupapi.dev.log` file and extracts the USB device and first installation date information. After processing, the `print_output()` function is called with the extracted information. The `print_output()` function takes the extracted information and prints it to the user in the console. These three functions work together to allow us to segment our code based on operations:

```
039 def main():
...
054 def parse_setupapi():
...
071 def print_output():
```

To run this script, we need to provide some code that calls the `main()` function. The following code block shows a Python feature that we will use in almost every one of our scripts throughout this book. This section of code will become more complex throughout this chapter, as we will be adding the ability to allow users to control input, output, and provide optional arguments.

Line 82 is simply an `if` statement that checks to see if this script is called from the command line. In more detail, the `__name__` attribute allows Python to tell us what function called the code. When `__name__` is equivalent to the `__main__` string, it indicates that it is the top-level script, and is therefore likely to be executed at the command line. This feature is especially important when designing code that may be called by another script. Someone else may import your functions into their code, and without this condition, it will likely result in our script immediately running when imported. We have the following code:

```
082 if __name__ == '__main__':
083     # Run the program
084     main()
```

As we can see in the following flowchart, the trunk function (our script as a whole) calls the `main()` function, which in turn calls `parse_setupapi()`, which finally calls the `print_output()` function:

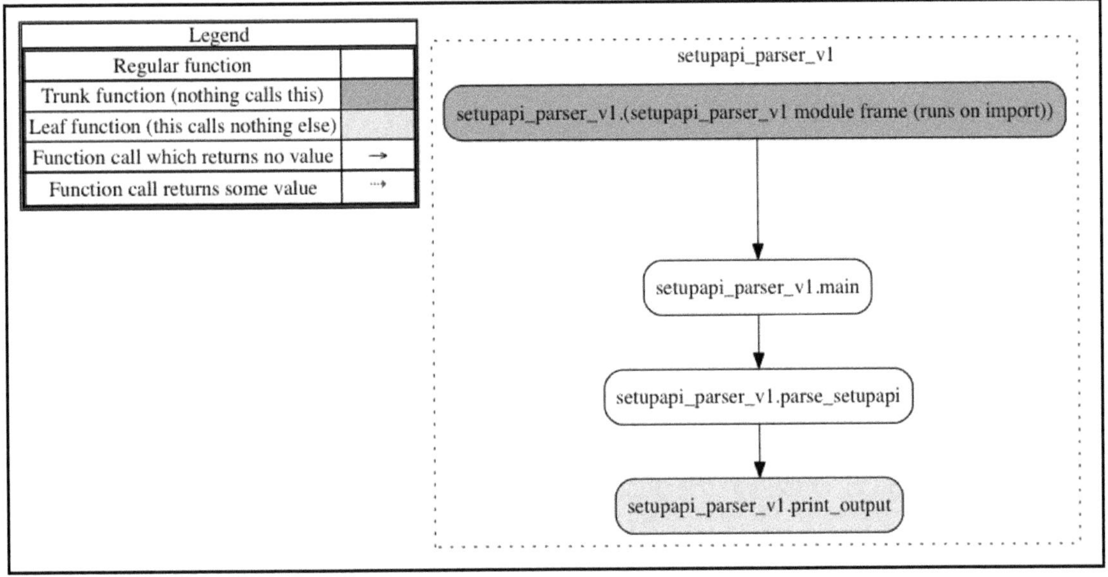

Designing the main() function

The `main()` function, defined on line 39, is fairly straightforward in this scenario. This function handles initial variable assignments and setup before calling `parse_setup()`. In the following code block, we create a docstring, surrounded with three double quotes where we document the purpose of the function, along with the data returned by it, as shown on lines 40 through 43. Pretty sparse, right? We'll enhance our documentation as we proceed as things might change drastically this early in development:

```
039 def main():
040     """
041     Primary controller for script.
042     :return: None
043     """
```

After the docstring, we hardcode the path to the `setupapi.dev.log` file on line 45. This means that our script can only function correctly if a log file with this name is located in the same directory as our script:

```
045     file_path = 'setupapi.dev.log'
```

On lines 48 through 50, we print our script information, including name and version, to the console, which notifies the user that the script is running. In addition, we print out 22 equal signs to provide a visual distinction between the setup information and any other output from the script:

```
047     # Print version information when the script is run
048     print('='*22)
049     print('SetupAPI Parser, v', __date__)
050     print('='*22)
```

Finally, on line 51, we call our next function to parse the input file. This function expects a `str` object that represents the path to the `setupapi.dev.log`. Though it may seem to defeat the purpose of a `main()` function, we will place the majority of the functionality in a separate function. This allows us to reuse code that's dedicated to the primary functionality in other scripts and for the `main()` function to act more as a primary controller. An example of this will be shown in the final iteration of this code. See the following line of code:

```
051     parse_setupapi(file_path)
```

Crafting the parse_setupapi() function

The `parse_setupapi()` function, defined on line 54, takes a string input that represents the full path to the Windows 7 `setupapi.dev.log` file, as detailed by the docstring on lines 55 through 59. On line 60, we open the file path provided by the `main()` function and read the data into a variable named `in_file`. This open statement didn't specify any parameters, so it uses default settings that open the file in read-only mode. This mode prevents us from accidentally writing to the file. In fact, trying to `write()` to a file that's been opened in read-only mode results in the following error and message:

```
IOError: File not open for reading
```

Although it does not allow writing to the file, working off a copy of the source evidence or the use of write-blocking technology should be used when handling digital evidence.

If there is any confusion regarding files and their modes, refer to `Chapter 1`, *Now for Something Completely Different*, for additional information. See the following code:

```
054 def parse_setupapi(setup_file):
055     """
056     Interpret the file
057     :param setup_file: path to the setupapi.dev.log
058     :return: None
059     """
060     in_file = open(setup_file)
```

On line 61, we read each line from the `in_file` variable into a new variable named `data` using the file object's `readlines()` method. This method returns a list where each element represents a single line in the file. Each element in the list is the string of text from the file delimited by the newline (`\n` or `\r\n`) character. At this newline character, the data is broken into a new element and fed as a new entry into the data list:

```
061     data = in_file.readlines()
```

With the content of the file stored in the variable data, we begin a `for` loop to walk through each individual line. This loop uses the `enumerate()` function, which wraps our iterator with a counter that keeps track of the number of iterations. This is desirable because we want to check for the pattern that identifies a USB device entry, then read the following line to get our date value. By keeping track of what element we are currently processing, we can easily pull out the next line we need to process with *data [n + 1]*, where *n* is the enumerated count of the current line being processed:

```
063     for i, line in enumerate(data):
```

Once inside the loop, on line 64, we evaluate whether the current line contains the string `device install (hardware initiated)`. To ensure that we don't miss valuable data, we will make the current line case insensitive by using the `.lower()` method to convert all characters in the string to lower case. If responsive, we execute lines 65 through 67. On line 65, we use the current iteration count variable, `i`, to access the responsive line within the data object:

```
064         if 'device install (hardware initiated)' in line.lower():
065             device_name = data[i].split('-')[1].strip()
```

After accessing the value, we call the `.split()` method on the string to split the values on the dash (-) character. After splitting, we access the second value in the split list and feed that string into the `strip()` function. The `.strip()` function, without any provided values, will strip whitespace characters on the left and right ends of the string. We process the responsive line so that it only contains USB identifying information.

The following is a log entry prior to processing with line 65:

```
>>> [Device Install (Hardware initiated) -
pciven_8086&dev_100f&subsys_075015ad&rev_014&b70f118&0&0888]
```

The following is the log entry after processing:

```
pciven_8086&dev_100f&subsys_075015ad&rev_014&b70f118&0&0888]
```

After converting the first line from the `setupapi.dev.log` USB entry, we then access the data variable on line 66 to obtain the date information from the following line. Since we know the date value sits on the line after the device information data, we can add one to the iteration count variable, `i`, to access that next line and get the line that contains the date. Similarly to device line parsing, we call the `.split()` function on the `start` string and extract the second element from the split that represents the date. Before saving the value, we need to call `.strip()` to remove whitespaces on both ends of the string:

```
066             date = data[i+1].split('start')[1].strip()
```

This process removes any other characters besides the date.

The following is a log entry prior to processing with line 66:

```
>>>  Section start 2010/11/10 10:21:14.656
```

The following is the log entry after processing:

```
2010/11/10 10:21:14.656
```

On line 67, we pass our extracted `device_name` and `date` values to the `print_output()` function. This function is called repeatedly for any responsive lines found in the loop. After the loop completes, the code on line 68 executes, which closes the `setupapi.dev.log` file that we initially opened, releasing the file from Python's use:

```
067             print_output(device_name, date)
068     in_file.close()
```

Developing the print_output() function

The `print_output()` function defined on line 71 allows us to control how the data is displayed to the user. This function requires two strings as input that represent the USB name and date, as defined by the docstring. On line 78 and 79, we print the USB data using the `.format()` method. As discussed in `Chapter 1`, *Now for Something Completely Different,* this function replaces the curly brackets (`{}`) with the data provided in the method call. A simple example like this doesn't show off the full power of the `.format()` method. However, this function can allow us to perform complex string formatting with ease. After printing the input, execution returns to the called function where the script continues the next iteration of the loop, as follows:

```
071 def print_output(usb_name, usb_date):
072     """
073     Print the information discovered
074     :param usb_name: String USB Name to print
075     :param usb_date: String USB Date to print
076     :return: None
077     """
078     print('Device: {}'.format(usb_name))
079     print('First Install: {}'.format(usb_date))
```

Running the script

We now have a script that takes a `setupapi.dev.log` file, as found on Windows 7, and outputs USB entries with their associated timestamps. The following screenshot shows how we can execute the script with a sample `setupapi.dev.log` file, which has been provided in the code bundle. Your output may vary depending on the `setupapi.dev.log` file you use the script on:

```
(py3.7.1) $ python setupapi_parser_v1.py
=======================
SetupAPI Parser, v 20181027
=======================
Device: root\rdp_kbd\0000]
First Install: 2016/03/10 14:58:21.526
Device: root\rdp_mou\0000]
First Install: 2016/03/10 14:58:21.526
Device: root\system\0000]
First Install: 2016/03/10 14:58:21.526
Device: root\umbus\0000]
First Install: 2016/03/10 14:58:21.558
Device: root\vdrvroot\0000]
First Install: 2016/03/10 14:58:22.884
Device: root\volmgr\0000]
```

Since `setupapi.dev.log` has numerous entries, we have pulled out two additional snippets from our command's output that focus on USB and USBSTOR devices:

```
First Install: 2016/03/10 14:59:49.589
Device: usb\vid_0e0f&pid_000b\6&103465e1&0&1]
First Install: 2016/03/10 14:59:49.604
Device: usb\vid_0e0f&pid_0002\6&b77da92&0&2]
First Install: 2016/03/10 14:59:49.994
Device: usb\vid_0e0f&pid_0003\6&b77da92&0&1]
First Install: 2016/03/10 14:59:50.306
Device: usb\vid_0e0f&pid_000b&mi_00\7&584f889&0&0000]
First Install: 2016/03/10 14:59:51.913
Device: USB\VID_0E0F&PID_0008\000650268328]
First Install: 2016/03/10 14:59:53.099
Device: USB\VID_0E0F&PID_0003&MI_00\7&2a7d3009&0&0000]
First Install: 2016/03/10 14:59:53.317
Device: USB\VID_0E0F&PID_0003&MI_01\7&2a7d3009&0&0001]
```

Our second snippet shows some details from the USBSTOR entries:

```
Device: BTH\MS_BTHPAN\8&20f38eb4&0&2]
First Install: 2016/03/10 14:59:56.468
Device: UMB\UMB\1&841921d&0&PrinterBusEnumerator]
First Install: 2016/03/10 15:05:23.422
Device: STORAGE\VolumeSnapshot\HarddiskVolumeSnapshot1]
First Install: 2016/03/10 20:29:16.962
Device: display\default_monitor\4&10c2e2d6&0&uid0]
First Install: 2016/03/10 20:30:08.761
Device: STORAGE\VolumeSnapshot\HarddiskVolumeSnapshot2]
First Install: 2016/03/10 20:49:56.453
Device: USB\VID_0BC2&PID_A003\NA538APY]
First Install: 2016/03/10 20:50:49.693
Device: USBSTOR\Disk&Ven_Seagate&Prod_Backup+_BK&Rev_0419\NA538APY&0]
First Install: 2016/03/10 20:50:53.316
Device: STORAGE\Volume\{c5232959
First Install: 2016/03/10 20:50:56.314
Device: STORAGE\Volume\{c5232959
First Install: 2016/03/10 20:50:56.314
Device: USB\VID_1F75&PID_0917\201207222733]
First Install: 2016/03/10 21:31:16.577
Device: USBSTOR\Disk&Ven_IS917&Prod_innostor&Rev_1.00\201207222733&0]
First Install: 2016/03/10 21:31:17.526
Device: STORAGE\Volume\_??_USBSTOR#Disk&Ven_IS917&Prod_innostor&Rev_1.00#201207222
733&0#{53f56307
First Install: 2016/03/10 21:31:18.312
Device: UMB\UMB\1&841921d&0&WpdBusEnumRoot]
First Install: 2016/03/10 21:31:19.903
Device: WpdBusEnumRoot\UMB\2&37c186b&0&STORAGE#VOLUME#_??_USBSTOR#DISK&VEN_IS917&P
ROD_INNOSTOR&REV_1.00#201207222733&0#]
First Install: 2016/03/10 21:31:20.325
```

Our current iteration seems to generate some false positives by extracting responsive lines that do not pertain solely to USB devices; let's see how we can address that.

Our second iteration – setupapi_parser_v2.py

With a functioning prototype, we now have some cleanup work to do. The first iteration was a proof of concept to illustrate how a `setupapi.dev.log` file can be parsed for forensic artifacts. With our second revision, we will clean up and restructure the code so that it will be easier to use in the future. In addition, we will integrate a more robust command-line interface, validate any user-supplied inputs, improve processing efficiency, and display any results in a better format.

On lines 2 through 6, we import the libraries that we will need for these improvements, alongside familiar cross-version support libraries. `argparse` is a library that we discussed at length in `Chapter 2`, *Python Fundamentals*, and is used to implement and structure arguments from the user. Next, we import `os`, a library we will use in this script to check the existence of input files before continuing. This will prevent us from trying to process a file that does not exist. The `os` module is used to access common operating system functionality in an operating system agnostic manner. That is to say, these functions, which may be handled differently on other operating systems, are treated the same and share the same module. We can use the `os` module to recursively walk through a directory, create new directories, and change the permissions of an object.

Finally, we import `sys`, which we will use to exit the script in case an error occurs to prevent faulty or improper output. After our imports, we have kept our licensing and documentation variables from before, modifying them to provide details about the second iteration:

```
001 """Second iteration of the setupapi.dev.log parser."""
002 from __future__ import print_function
003 import argparse
004 from io import open
005 import os
006 import sys
...
036 __authors__ = ["Chapin Bryce", "Preston Miller"]
037 __date__ = 20181027
038 __description__ = """This scripts reads a Windows 7 Setup API
039 log and prints USB Devices to the user"""
```

The functions defined in our previous script are still present here. However, these functions contain new code that allows for improved handling and flows logically in a different manner. Designing our code in a modularized manner allows us to repurpose functions in new or updated scripts, limiting the need for a major overhaul. This segmentation also allows for easier debugging when reviewing an error that's raised within a function:

```
def main()
...
def parse_setupapi()
...
def print_output()
```

The `if` statement serves the same purpose as the prior iteration. The additional code shown within this conditional allows the user to provide input to modify the script's behavior. In line 106, we create an `ArgumentParser` object with a description, default help formatting, and `epilog` containing author, version, and date information. This, in conjunction with the argument options, allows us to display information about the script that might be helpful to the user when running the `-h` switch. See the following code:

```
104 if __name__ == '__main__':
105     # Run this code if the script is run from the command line.
106     parser = argparse.ArgumentParser(
107         description=__description__,
108         epilog='Built by {}. Version {}'.format(
109             ", ".join(__authors__), __date__),
110         formatter_class=argparse.ArgumentDefaultsHelpFormatter
111     )
```

After defining the `ArgumentParser` object as `parser`, we add the `IN_FILE` parameter on line 113 to allow the user to specify which file to use for input. Already, this increases the usability of our script by adding flexibility in the input file path rather than hard coding the path. At line 115, we parse any provided arguments and store them in the `args` variable. Finally, we call the `main()` function on line 118, passing a string representing the file location of `setupapi.dev.log` to the function, as follows:

```
113     parser.add_argument('IN_FILE',
114         help='Windows 7 SetupAPI file')
115     args = parser.parse_args()
116 
117     # Run main program
118     main(args.IN_FILE)
```

Note the difference in our flowchart. Our script is no longer very linear. The `main()` function calls and accepts returned data from the `parse_setupapi()` method (indicated by the dashed arrow). The `print_output()` method is called to print the parsed data to the console:

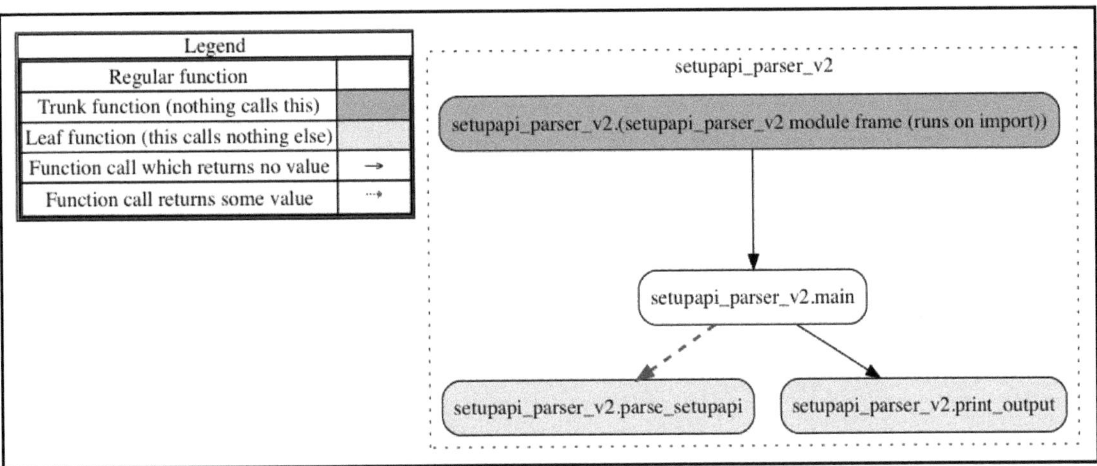

Improving the main() function

On line 42, we define the `main()` function that now accepts a new argument that we will call `in_file`. This argument, as defined by the docstring, is a string path to the `setupapi.dev.log` file to be analyzed:

```
042 def main(in_file):
043     """
044     Main function to handle operation
045     :param in_file: string path to Windows 7 setupapi.dev.log
046     :return: None
047     """
```

On line 48, we perform a validation of the input file to ensure that the file path and file exists using the `os.path.isfile()` function, which will return `true` if it is a file that's accessible by the script. As an aside, the `os.path.isdir()` function can be used to perform the same style of validation for directories. These functions work well with string inputs that represent either absolute or relative paths:

```
048     if os.path.isfile(in_file):
```

If the file path is valid, we print the version of the script. This time, we use the `.format()` method to create our desired string. Let's look at the formatters we've used on lines 49 and 51, starting with a colon to define our specified format. The caret (`^`) symbol indicates that we want to center the supplied object and have the padding to a minimum of 22 characters, using equal signs as padding. For example, the string `Hello World!` would be sandwiched between five equal signs on both sides. In the case of our script, we supply an empty string as the object to format because we only want 22 equal signs to create visual separation from the output.

Note that it is simpler to implement the `"=" * 22` logic from the prior iteration and that we have used the `format()` method to provide a demonstration of available features.

On line 50, the `.format()` method is used to print the script name and version strings, as follows:

```
049         print('{:=^22}'.format(''))
050         print('{} {}'.format('SetupAPI Parser, v', __date__))
051         print('{:=^22} \n'.format(''))
```

On line 52, we call the `parse_setupapi()` function and pass the `setupapi.dev.log` file, which we know is available. This function returns a list of USB entries, with one entry per discovered device. Each entry in `device_information` consists of two elements, that is, the device name, and the associated date value. On line 53, we iterate through this list using a `for` loop and feed each entry to the `print_output()` function on line 54:

```
052         device_information = parse_setupapi(in_file)
053         for device in device_information:
054             print_output(device[0], device[1])
```

On line 55, we handle the case where the provided file is not valid. This is a common way to handle errors that have been generated from invalid paths. Within this condition, we print on line 56 that the input is not a valid file.

If we wanted to use a built-in Python `Exception` class, we could raise an IOError and provide a message that the input file is not available at the specified path.

On line 57, we call `sys.exit()` to quit the program with an error of one. You may place any number here; however, since we defined this as one, we will know where the error was raised at exit:

```
055     else:
056         print('Input is not a file.')
057         sys.exit(1)
```

Tuning the parse_setupapi() function

The `parse_setupapi()` function accepts the path of the `setupapi.dev.log` file as its only input. Before opening the file, we must initialize the `device_list` variable on line 68 so that we can store extracted device records in a list:

```
060 def parse_setupapi(setup_log):
061     """
062     Read data from provided file for Device Install Events for
063         USB Devices
064     :param setup_log: str - Path to valid setup api log
065     :return: list of tuples - Tuples contain device name and date
066     in that order
067     """
068     device_list = list()
```

Starting on line 69, we open the input file in a novel manner; the `with` statement opens the file as `in_file` and allows us to manipulate data within the file without having to worry about closing the file afterward. Inside this `with` loop is a `for` loop that iterates across each line, which provides superior memory management. In the previous iteration, we used the `.readlines()` method to read the entire file into a list by line; though not very noticeable on smaller files, the `.readlines()` method on a larger file would cause performance issues on systems with limited resources:

```
069     with open(setup_log) as in_file:
070         for line in in_file:
```

Within the `for` loop, we leverage similar logic to determine whether the line contains our device installation indicators. If responsive, we extract the device information using the same manner as discussed previously.

By defining the `lower_line` variable on line 74, we can truncate the remaining code by preventing continuous calls to the `.lower()` method. Please note that lines 73 through 75 reflect one line of wrapped code:

On line 73, the backslash (\) character indicates to Python that it should ignore the newline character and continue reading on the next line. Then, at the end of line 74, we can return to anywhere without the need for the backslash, as our conditional is within parenthesis.

```
071             lower_line = line.lower()
072             # if 'Device Install (Hardware initiated)' in line:
073             if 'device install (hardware initiated)' in \
074                 lower_line and ('ven' in lower_line or
075                                 'vid' in lower_line):
```

As noted in the first iteration, a fair number of false positives were displayed in our output. That's because this log contains information related to many types of hardware devices, including those interfacing with PCI, and not just USB devices. To remove the noise, we will check to see what type of device it is.

We can split on the backslash character, as shown on lines 78 and 79, to access the first split element of the `device_name` variable and see if it contains the `usb` string. As mentioned in `Chapter 1`, *Now for Something Completely Different*, we need to escape a single backslash with another backslash so that Python knows to treat it as a literal backslash character. This will respond for devices labeled as USB and USBSTOR in the file. Some false positives will still exist, since mice, keyboards, and hubs will likely display as USB devices; however, we do not want to over-filter and miss relevant artifacts. If we discover that the entry does not contain the `usb` string, we execute the continue statement, telling Python to step through the next iteration of the `for` loop:

```
078                 if 'usb' not in device_name.split(
079                         '\\')[0].lower():
080                     continue
```

To retrieve the date, we need to use a different procedure to get the next line since we have not invoked the `enumerate()` function. To solve this challenge, we use the `next()` function on line 87 to step into the next line in the file. We then process this line in the same fashion as we discussed previously:

```
087                 date = next(in_file).split('start')[1].strip()
```

With the device's name and date processed, we append it to the `device_list` as a tuple, where the device's name is the first value and the date is the second. We need the double parenthesis, in this case, to ensure that our data is appended properly. The outer set is used by the `.append()` function. The inner parentheses allow us to build a tuple and append it as one value. If we did not have the inner parentheses, we would be passing the two elements as separate arguments to the `append()` function instead of a single tuple element. Once all of the lines have been processed in the `for` loop, the `with` loop will end and close the file. On line 90, the `device_list` is returned and the function exits.

```
088                 device_list.append((device_name, date))
089
090     return device_list
```

Modifying the print_output() function

This function is identical to the previous iteration, with the exception of the addition of the newline character `\n` on line 101. This helps separate entries in the console's output with an extra space. When iterating through the code, we will find that not all functions need updating to improve the user experience, accuracy, or efficiency of the code. Only by modifying an existing function will some sort of benefit be achieved:

```
093 def print_output(usb_name, usb_date):
094     """
095     Print the information discovered
096     :param usb_name: String USB Name to print
097     :param usb_date: String USB Date to print
098     :return: None
099     """
100     print('Device: {}'.format(usb_name))
101     print('First Install: {}\n'.format(usb_date))
```

Running the script

In this iteration, we address several issues from the proof of concept. These changes include the following:

- The improvement of resource management by iterating through a file rather than reading the entire file into a variable
- The addition of an argument to allow the user to provide the `setupapi.dev.log` file to parse
- The validation of the input file from the user

- The filtering of responsive hits to reduce noise in the output
- Improved formatting of our output for ease of review

The following screenshot shows a snippet of the output of our script upon execution:

```
(py3.7.1) $ python setupapi_parser_v2.py setupapi.dev.log
=======================
SetupAPI Parser, v 20181027
=======================

Device: usb\vid_0e0f&pid_000b\6&103465e1&0&1]
First Install: 2016/03/10 14:59:49.604

Device: usb\vid_0e0f&pid_0002\6&b77da92&0&2]
First Install: 2016/03/10 14:59:49.994

Device: usb\vid_0e0f&pid_0003\6&b77da92&0&1]
First Install: 2016/03/10 14:59:50.306

Device: usb\vid_0e0f&pid_000b&mi_00\7&584f889&0&0000]
First Install: 2016/03/10 14:59:51.913

Device: USB\VID_0E0F&PID_0008\000650268328]
First Install: 2016/03/10 14:59:53.099

Device: USB\VID_0E0F&PID_0003&MI_00\7&2a7d3009&0&0000]
First Install: 2016/03/10 14:59:53.317

Device: USB\VID_0E0F&PID_0003&MI_01\7&2a7d3009&0&0001]
First Install: 2016/03/10 14:59:53.317

Device: USB\VID_0BC2&PID_A003\NA538APY]
First Install: 2016/03/10 20:50:49.693

Device: USBSTOR\Disk&Ven_Seagate&Prod_Backup+_BK&Rev_0419\NA538APY&0]
First Install: 2016/03/10 20:50:53.316
```

Last but not least, we achieved considerable performance improvements over our previous design. The following screenshots display the impact on the machine's memory utilization. The first iteration is displayed on the left and the second is displayed on the right. The red lines highlight the start and finish time of our script. As we can see, we have reduced our resource utilization by iterating across the lines of the file with the `for` loop over the `readlines()` method. This is a small-scale example of resource management, but a larger input file would have a more dramatic impact on the system:

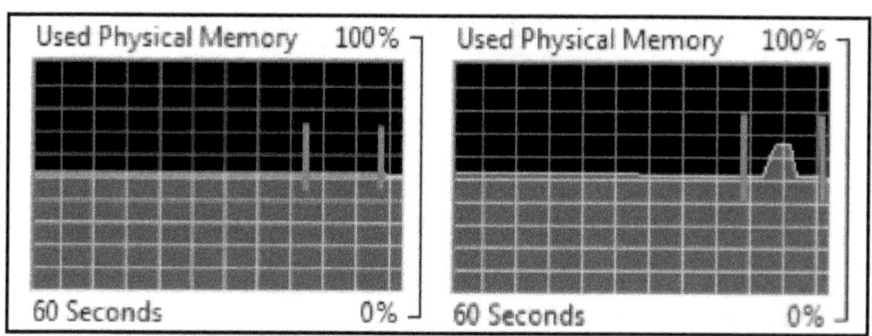

Our final iteration – setupapi_parser.py

In our final iteration, we will continue to improve the script by adding deduplication of processed entries and improving upon the output. Although the second iteration introduced the logic for filtering out non-USB devices, it does not deduplicate the responsive hits. We will deduplicate on the device name to ensure that there is only a single entry per device. In addition, we will integrate our `usb_lookup.py` script from `Chapter 2`, *Python Fundamentals*, to improve the utility of our script by displaying USB VIDs and PIDs for known devices.

We had to modify the code in the `usb_lookup.py` script to properly integrate it with the `setupapi` script. The differences between the two versions are subtle and are focused on reducing the number of function calls and improving the quality of the returned data. Throughout this iteration, we will discuss how we have implemented our custom USB VID/PID lookup library to resolve USB device names. On line 4, we import the `usb_lookup` script, as follows:

```
001 """Third iteration of the setupapi.dev.log parser."""
002 from __future__ import print_function
003 import argparse
004 from io import open
005 import os
006 import sys
007 import usb_lookup
...
037 __authors__ = ["Chapin Bryce", "Preston Miller"]
038 __date__ = 20181027
039 __description__ = """This scripts reads a Windows 7 Setup API
040     log and prints USB Devices to the user"""
```

As we can see in the following code block, we have added three new functions. Our prior functions have undergone minor modifications to accommodate new features. The majority of the modifications are in our new functions:

- The `parse_device_info()` function is responsible for splitting out the necessary information to look up the VID/PID values online and format the raw strings into a standard format for comparison
- The next function, `prep_usb_lookup()`, prepares and parses the database into a format that supports querying
- The `get_device_names()` function correlates matching device information with the database

With these new functions, we provide additional context for our investigators:

```
def main():
...
def parse_setupapi():
...
def parse_device_info():
...
def prep_usb_lookup():
...
def get_device_names():
...
def print_output():
```

We will add one argument to our parser before calling the `main()` function. The `--local` argument defined on lines 198 and 199 allow us to specify a local `usb.ids` file that we can use for parsing in an offline environment. The following code block shows our implementation of the arguments, spaced out over several lines to make it easier to read:

```
187 if __name__ == '__main__':
188     # Run this code if the script is run from the command line.
189     parser = argparse.ArgumentParser(
190         description=__description__,
191         epilog='Built by {}. Version {}'.format(
192             ", ".join(__authors__), __date__),
193         formatter_class=argparse.ArgumentDefaultsHelpFormatter
194     )
195
196     parser.add_argument('IN_FILE',
197         help='Windows 7 SetupAPI file')
198     parser.add_argument('--local',
199         help='Path to local usb.ids file')
200
201     args = parser.parse_args()
202
203     # Run main program
204     main(args.IN_FILE, args.local)
```

As with our prior iterations, we have generated a flow chart to map the logical course of our script. Please note that it uses the same legend as our other flow charts, though we omitted the legend due to the width of the graphic. Our `main()` function is executed and makes direct calls to five other functions. This layout builds upon the nonlinear design from the second iteration. In each iteration, we are continuing to add more control within the `main()` function. This function leans on others to perform tasks and return data rather than doing the work itself. This offers a form of high-level organization within our script and helps keep things simple by executing one function after another in a linear fashion:

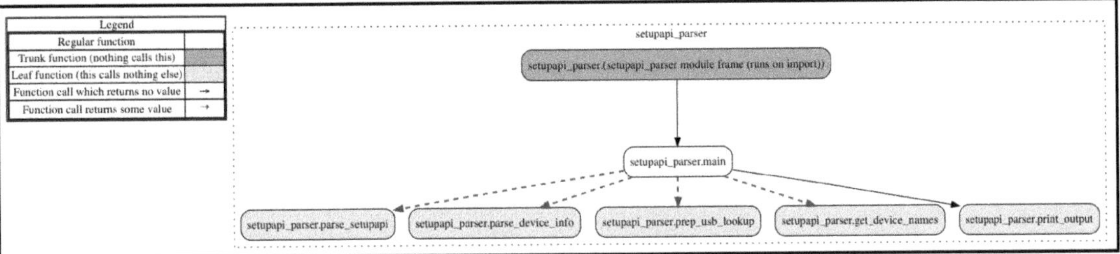

Extending the main() function

The `main()` function has remained mostly intact, only adding changes to look up the USB VID and PID information and present a superior output for the end user. One way we are facilitating this lookup is by providing a file path as the `local_usb_ids` parameter, which allows us to use an offline file for our VID/PID lookup database. To cut down on clutter in our output, we have elected to remove the script name and version printing. On line 51, a new function call to `prep_usb_info()` is made to initiate the setup of the VID/PID lookups. Our loop on line 52 has been reconfigured to hand each processed device entry to the `parse_device_info()` function on line 53. This new function is responsible for reading the raw string from the log file and attempts to split the VID and PID values for lookup:

```
042 def main(in_file, local_usb_ids=None):
043     """
044     Main function to handle operation
045     :param in_file: Str - Path to setupapi log to analyze
046     :return: None
047     """
048
049     if os.path.isfile(in_file):
050         device_information = parse_setupapi(in_file)
051         usb_ids = prep_usb_lookup(local_usb_ids)
052         for device in device_information:
053             parsed_info = parse_device_info(device)
```

The `if` statement on line 54 checks the value of the `parsed_info` variable to ensure that it was parsed correctly and can be compared against our known values. In the case that it is not prepared for this, the information is not queried or printed. See the following code:

```
054             if isinstance(parsed_info, dict):
055                 parsed_info = get_device_names(usb_ids,
056                     parsed_info)
```

Additional logic on line 57 checks to see whether the `parsed_info` value is not equivalent to `None`. A `None` value is assigned to `parsed_info` if the `parse_device_info()` function discovered that the device was not recorded as a USB, eliminating false positives:

```
057             if parsed_info is not None:
058                 print_output(parsed_info)
```

Finally, on line 59, we print to the console that we have completed parsing the log file. On lines 62 through 65, we address the situation where the `setupapi.dev.log` is not valid or accessible by our script and notify the user of the situation before exiting. The message that is printed before exiting the script is more detailed than in previous iterations. The more details we can provide to our users, especially regarding potential bugs, will improve their capability to determine the error and correct it on their own:

```
059         print('\n\n{} parsed and printed successfully.'.format(
060             in_file))
061
062     else:
063         print("Input: {} was not found. Please check your path "
064             "and permissions.".format(in_file))
065         sys.exit(1)
```

Adding to the parse_setup_api() function

This function has minor modifications that are focused on storing unique entries from the log file. We created a new variable named `unique_list` that is a `set` data type on line 76. Recall that a `set` must consist of hashable and unique elements, making it a perfect fit for this solution. Though it seems duplicative to have a list and set holding similar data, for simplicity of comparison and demonstration, we have created the second variable:

```
068 def parse_setupapi(setup_log):
069     """
070     Read data from provided file for Device Install Events for
071         USB Devices
072     :param setup_log: str - Path to valid setup api log
073     :return: tuple of str - Device name and date
```

```
074     """
075     device_list = list()
076     unique_list = set()
077     with open(setup_log) as in_file:
078         for line in in_file:
```

On line 79, we convert the line into lowercase to ensure that our comparisons are case-insensitive. At this point, we use the same logic to process the `device_name` and `date` values on lines 83 through 84. We have moved the code from the second iteration, which verified the device type, into our new `parse_device_info()` function:

```
079             lower_line = line.lower()
080             if 'device install (hardware initiated)' in \
081                     lower_line and ('vid' in lower_line or
082                                     'ven' in lower_line):
083                 device_name = line.split('-')[1].strip()
084                 date = next(in_file).split('start')[1].strip()
```

Before we store the `device_name` and `date` information in our `device_list`, we check to ensure that the `device_name` does not already exist in our `unique_list`. If it doesn't, we add the tuple on line 86, which contains the `device_name` and `date`. Afterward, we prevent that same device from being processed again by adding the entry to our `unique_list`. On line 89, we return our built list of tuples for the next stage of processing:

```
085                 if device_name not in unique_list:
086                     device_list.append((device_name, date))
087                     unique_list.add(device_name)
088 
089     return device_list
```

Creating the parse_device_info() function

This function interprets the raw string from the `setupapi.dev.log` and converts it into a dictionary with VID, PID, revision, unique ID, and date values. This is described in the docstring on lines 94 through 98. After the documentation, we initialize the variables we will use in this function on lines 101 through 104. This initialization provides default placeholder values, which will prevent future issues with the dictionary in scenarios where we cannot assign a value to these variables:

```
092 def parse_device_info(device_info):
093     """
094     Parses Vendor, Product, Revision and UID from a Setup API
095         entry
096     :param device_info: string of device information to parse
```

```
097        :return: dictionary of parsed information or original string
098            if error
099        """
100        # Initialize variables
101        vid = ''
102        pid = ''
103        rev = ''
104        uid = ''
```

After initialization, we split the `device_info` value, which is passed from the `parse_setup_api()` function into segments, using a single backslash as the delimiter. We need to escape this backslash with another to interpret it as a literal backslash character. This split on line 107 separates the device type segment from the string containing the VID and PID information. Following this split, we check to ensure that the device type entry reflects a USB device. If the device is not a USB, we return `None` to ensure that it is not processed further by this function and that we do not attempt to resolve VIDs or PIDs for this device. By adding this logic, we save ourselves from spending additional time and resources processing irrelevant entries:

```
106        # Split string into segments on \
107        segments = device_info[0].split('\\')
108
109        if 'usb' not in segments[0].lower():
110            return None
```

Next, we access the second element of the `segments` list, which contains the VID, PID, and revision data, delimited by an ampersand. Using `.split()`, we can access each of these values independently through the `for` loop on line 114. We convert the line to lower case to allow us to search in a case-insensitive fashion, through a series of conditionals, to determine what each item represents. On line 116, we check each item to see if it contains the keywords `ven` or `vid`. If the line does contain one of these indicators, we split only on the first underscore character (specified by the integer `1` as the second parameter). This allows us to extract the VID from the raw string. Note how we use `lower_item` for our comparisons and the `item` variable for storing values, preserving the original case of our data. This behavior is repeated for the `pid` variable, using the `dev`, `prod`, and `pid` indicators, and the `rev` variable, using the `rev` or `mi` indicators on lines 118 through 122, as follows:

```
114        for item in segments[1].split('&'):
115            lower_item = item.lower()
116            if 'ven' in lower_item or 'vid' in lower_item:
117                vid = item.split('_', 1)[-1]
118            elif 'dev' in lower_item or 'pid' in lower_item or \
119                    'prod' in lower_item:
```

```
120             pid = item.split('_', 1)[-1]
121         elif 'rev' in lower_item or 'mi' in lower_item:
122             rev = item.split('_', 1)[-1]
```

After parsing the VID, PID, and revision information, we attempt to extract the unique ID from the segments variable, which is normally the last element in the string. Because the entire line is wrapped in brackets, we strip the closing bracket from the rightmost entry in the segment on line 125. This removes the bracket, so it will not be included in our unique ID string:

```
124     if len(segments) >= 3:
125         uid = segments[2].strip(']')
```

On line 127, we use an `if` statement to determine whether the `vid` or `pid` received a value after initialization, and build a dictionary if we collected new information on lines 128 through 132. If these values were not filled out, we return the original string to allow the output of the entry without the additional formatting, as seen on line 134, to ensure that we are not missing any data due to a formatting error:

```
127     if vid != '' or pid != '':
128         return {'Vendor ID': vid.lower(),
129             'Product ID': pid.lower(),
130             'Revision': rev,
131             'UID': uid,
132             'First Installation Date': device_info[1]}
133     # Unable to parse data, returning whole string
134     return device_info
```

Forming the prep_usb_lookup() function

In this function, we call out to the `usb_lookup.py` script's `.get_usb_file()` function. Using the `local_usb_ids` parameter that's provided, we can confirm whether there is a known `usb.ids` file path that we should use for this lookup, or whether we should reach out to the online resource at `http://linux-usb.org/usb.ids` to read the known USB information into the `usb_file` variable on line 147. This database is an open source project that hosts the VID/PID lookup database, allowing users to reference and expand on the database:

```
137 def prep_usb_lookup(local_usb_ids=None):
138     """
139     Prepare the lookup of USB devices through accessing the most
140     recent copy of the database at http://linux-usb.org/usb.ids
141     or using the provided file and parsing it into a queriable
142     dictionary format.
```

```
143     """
144     if local_usb_ids:
145         usb_file = open(local_usb_ids, encoding='latin1')
146     else:
147         usb_file = usb_lookup.get_usb_file()
```

After downloading or using a local copy, we pass the file object to the `.parse_file()` function to process and then return the USB VID/PID data as a Python dictionary. Instead of creating a new variable for this functionality, we can just place the `return` keyword in front of the function call to immediately pass the value back, as shown on line 148:

```
148     return usb_lookup.parse_file(usb_file)
```

Constructing the get_device_names() function

This function's purpose is to pass the VID and PID information into the `usb_lookup` library and return resolved USB names. As defined by the docstring mentioned later, this function takes two dictionaries—the first contains the database of known devices from `prep_usb_lookup()`, and the second contains the extracted device entries from `parse_device_info()`. With this provided data, we will return a dictionary, updated with resolved vendor and product names:

```
151 def get_device_names(usb_dict, device_info):
152     """
153     Query `usb_lookup.py` for device information based on VID/PID.
154     :param usb_dict: Dictionary from usb_lookup.py of known
155         devices.
156     :param device_info: Dictionary containing 'Vendor ID' and
157         'Product ID' keys and values.
158     :return: original dictionary with 'Vendor Name' and
159         'Product Name' keys and values
160     """
```

This function calls the `usb_lookup.search_key()` function, passing the processed online USB dictionary and a two-element list containing the device's VID and PID as the first and second element, respectively. The `.search_key()` function returns either a responsive match or the `Unknown` string if no matches are discovered. This data is returned as a tuple and assigned to the `device_name` variable on line 161. We then split the two resolved values into new keys of our `device_info` dictionary on lines 165 and 166. Once we have expanded `device_info`, we can return it so that it can be printed to the console. See the following lines:

```
161     device_name = usb_lookup.search_key(
162         usb_dict, [device_info['Vendor ID'],
```

```
            device_info['Product ID']])

        device_info['Vendor Name'] = device_name[0]
        device_info['Product Name'] = device_name[1]

        return device_info
```

Enhancing the print_output() function

In this function, we have made some adjustments to improve the output to the console. With the addition of the separator defined on 178, we now have a line of 15 dashes visually breaking each entry from the output. As we can see, we have borrowed the same format string from the first iteration to add this break:

```
171 def print_output(usb_information):
172     """
173     Print formatted information about USB Device
174     :param usb_information: dictionary containing key/value
175         data about each device or tuple of device information
176     :return: None
177     """
178     print('{:-^15}'.format(''))
```

We have also modified the code to allow additional output for flexible fields. In this function, we need to handle two different data types, tuples and dictionaries, since some entries do not have a resolved vendor or product name. To handle this divide in formats, we must use the `isinstance()` function on line 180 to test the `usb_information` variable data type. If the value is a dictionary, we will print each of the keys and values to the console to display one key-value pair per line on line 182. This is possible through the combination of the `for` loop on line 181, which uses the `items()` method on a dictionary. This method returns a list of tuples, where the first tuple element is the key and the second is the value. Using this method, we can quickly extract the key-value pairs, as shown on lines 181 and 182:

```
180     if isinstance(usb_information, dict):
181         for key_name, value_name in usb_information.items():
182             print('{}: {}'.format(key_name, value_name))
```

If we need to print a tuple, we use two `print` statements, similar to the output from the prior iteration. Because this data is from a device that could not be parsed, it has a fixed format that is the same as our previous iteration. See the following lines:

```
    elif isinstance(usb_information, tuple):
        print('Device: {}'.format(usb_information[0]))
        print('Date: {}'.format(usb_information[1]))
```

Running the script

We have come a long way since our first script, as this version now does the following:

- Provides us with USB device information about the first installation time of a device on Windows 7
- Resolves additional device information using VID and PID data
- Prints output to the console in a format that is legible and informative

The following is an example execution of the script and illustration of the output:

```
(py3.7.1) $ python setupapi_parser.py setupapi.dev.log
---------------
Vendor ID: 0e0f
Product ID: 000b
Revision:
UID: 6&103465e1&0&1
First Installation Date: 2016/03/10 14:59:49.604
Vendor Name: VMware, Inc.
Product Name: unknown
---------------
Vendor ID: 0e0f
Product ID: 0002
Revision:
UID: 6&b77da92&0&2
First Installation Date: 2016/03/10 14:59:49.994
Vendor Name: VMware, Inc.
Product Name: Virtual USB Hub
```

The following screenshot has been included to highlight some of our storage devices further down the output:

```
Vendor ID: 0bc2
Product ID: a003
Revision:
UID: NA538APY
First Installation Date: 2016/03/10 20:50:49.693
Vendor Name: Seagate RSS LLC
Product Name: Backup Plus
---------------
Vendor ID: seagate
Product ID: backup+_bk
Revision: 0419
UID: NA538APY&0
First Installation Date: 2016/03/10 20:50:53.316
Vendor Name: unknown
Product Name: unknown
---------------
Vendor ID: 1f75
Product ID: 0917
Revision:
UID: 201207222733
First Installation Date: 2016/03/10 21:31:16.577
Vendor Name: Innostor Technology Corporation
Product Name: unknown
```

Challenge

For this chapter, we propose adding support for the Windows XP format of the `setupapi.log`. The user can supply a switch at the command line to indicate which type of log will be processed. For a more difficult task, our script could automatically identify the type of log file by fingerprinting unique structures found only in Windows XP versus the Windows 7 version.

Improving the deduplication process we used in this chapter would be a welcome addition. As we identified, some entries have UID values embedded in the device entry. This value is generally assigned by the manufacturer and could be used to deduplicate the entries. As you may note in the output, the UID can contain extra ampersand characters that may or may not be crucial to the UID structure and suggest their source. By applying some simple logic, possibly in a new function, we can improve deduplication based on UIDs.

Lastly, we can consider our output format. While it is useful to display things in a console-friendly format, we should consider adding support for a CSV or other report. This may be a good feature to revisit after working through the rest of the chapters of this book.

Summary

In this chapter, you learned how to parse a plain text file using Python. This process can be implemented for other log files, including those from firewalls, web servers, or other applications and services. Following these steps, we can identify repetitive data structures that lend themselves to scripts, process their data, and output results to the user. With our iterative build process, we implemented a test-then-code approach where we built a working prototype and then continually enhanced it into a viable and reliable forensic tool.

In addition to the text format we explored here, some files have a more concrete structure and are stored in a serialized format. Other files, such as HTML, XML, and JSON, file structure data in a manner that can be readily converted into a series of Python objects. The code for this project can be downloaded from GitHub or Packt, as described in the *Preface*.

In the next chapter, we will explore the methods in Python that we can use to parse, manipulate, and interact with these structured formats.

4
Working with Serialized Data Structures

In this chapter, we'll develop greater skills while working with nested lists and dictionaries by manipulating **JavaScript Object Notation** (**JSON**) structured data. Our artifact of interest is raw Bitcoin account data that contains, among other things, a list of all sent and received transactions. We'll access this dataset using a web **Application Programming Interface** (**API**) and parse it in a manner conducive to analysis.

APIs are created for software products and allow programmers to interface with the software in defined ways. Publicly accessible APIs aren't always available for the given software. When available, they expedite code development by offering methods to interact with the software, as the APIs will handle lower-level implementation details. Developers implement APIs to encourage others to build supporting programs and, additionally, control the manner in which other developers' code interacts with their software. By creating an API, developers are giving other programmers a controlled manner of interfacing with their program.

In this chapter, we'll use the web API from `https://www.blockchain.info` to query and receive Bitcoin account information for a given Bitcoin address. The JSON data that this API generates can be converted into Python objects using the JSON module from the standard library. Instructions and examples of their API can be found at `https://www.blockchain.info/api/blockchain_api`.

In this chapter, we'll cover the following:

- Discussing and manipulating serialized structures including **Extensible Markup Language** (**XML**) and JSON data
- Creating logs with Python
- Reporting results in a CSV output format

The code for this chapter was developed and tested using Python 2.7.15 and Python 3.7.1. The `bitcoin_address_lookup.v1.py` and `bitcoin_address_lookup.v2.py` scripts were developed to work with Python 3.7.1 and not Python 2.7.15.

Serialized data structures

Serialization is a process whereby data objects are preserved during storage on a computer system. Serializing data preserves the original type of the object. That's to say, we can serialize dictionaries, lists, integers, or strings into a file. Sometime later, when we deserialize this file, those objects will still maintain their original data type. Serialization is great because if, for example, we stored script objects to a text file, we wouldn't be able to feasibly reconstruct those objects into their appropriate data types as easily. As we know, reading a text file reads in data as a string.

XML and JSON are the two common examples of plain text-encoded serialization formats. You may already be accustomed to analyzing these files in forensic investigations. Analysts familiar with mobile device forensics will likely recognize application-specific XML files containing account or configuration details. Let's look at how we can leverage Python to parse XML and JSON files.

We can use the `xml` module to parse any markup language that includes XML and HTML data. The following `book.xml` file in the text contains the details about this book. If you've never seen XML data before, the first thing you may note is that it's similar in structure to HTML, another markup language, where contents are surrounded by opening and closing tags, as follows:

```
<?xml version="1.0" encoding="UTF-8"?>
<root>
  <authors>Preston Miller &amp; Chapin Bryce</authors>
  <chapters>
   <element>
     <chapterNumber>1</chapterNumber>
     <chapterTitle>Now for Something Completely Different</chapterTitle>
     <pageCount>30</pageCount>
   </element>
   <element>
     <chapterNumber>2</chapterNumber>
     <chapterTitle>Python Fundamentals</chapterTitle>
     <pageCount>25</pageCount>
   </element>
  </chapters>
  <numberOfChapters>13</numberOfChapters>
```

```
    <pageCount>500</pageCount>
    <publisher>Packt Publishing</publisher>
    <title>Learning Python for Forensics</title>
</root>
```

For analysts, XML and JSON files are easy to read because they're in plain text. However, a manual review becomes impractical when working with files containing thousands of lines. Fortunately, these files are highly structured, and even better, they're meant to be used by programs.

To explore XML, we need to use the `ElementTree` class from the `xml` module, which will parse the data and allow us to iterate through the children of the root node. In order to parse the data, we must specify the file being parsed. In this case, our `book.xml` file is located in the same working directory as the Python interactive prompt. If this weren't the case, we would need to specify the file path in addition to the filename. If you're using Python 2, please make sure to import `print_function` from `__future__` . We use the `getroot()` function to access the root-level node, as follows:

```
>>> import xml.etree.ElementTree as ET
>>> tree = ET.parse('book.xml')
>>> root = tree.getroot()
```

With the root element, let's use the `find()` function to search for the first instance of the `authors` tag in the XML file. Each element has different properties, such as `tag`, `attrib`, and `text`. The `tag` element is a string that describes the data, which in this case is `authors`. An attribute(s) or `attrib` are stored in a dictionary if present. Attributes are values assigned within a tag. For example, we could have created a `chapter` tag:

```
<chapter number=2, title="Python Fundamentals", count=20 />
```

The attributes for this object would be a dictionary with the keys number, title, and count and their respective values. To access the content between the tags (for example, `chapterNumber`), we would need to use the `text` attribute.

We can use the `findall()` function to find all occurrences of a specified child tag. In the following example, we're looking for every instance of `chapters/element` found in the dataset. Once found, we can use list indices to access specific tags within the `element` parent tag. In this case, we only want to access the chapter number and title in the first two positions of the element. Look at the following example:

```
>>> print(root.find('authors').text)
Preston Miller & Chapin Bryce
>>> for element in root.findall('chapters/element'):
... print('Chapter #{}'.format(element[0].text))
... print('Chapter Title: {}'.format(element[1].text))
```

```
...
Chapter #1
Chapter Title: Now for Something Completely Different
Chapter #2
Chapter Title: Python Fundamentals
```

There are a number of other methods we can use to process markup language files using the `xml` module. For the full documentation, please see `https://docs.python.org/3/library/xml.etree.elementtree.html`.

With XML covered, let's look at that same example stored as JSON data and, more importantly, how we use Python to interpret that data. Later, we're going to create a JSON file named `book.json`; note the use of keys, such as title, authors, publisher, and their associated values are separated by a colon. This is similar to how a dictionary is structured in Python. In addition, note the use of the square brackets for the `chapters` key and then how the embedded dictionary-like structures are separated by commas. In Python, this `chapters` structure is interpreted as a list containing dictionaries once it's loaded with the `json` module:

```
{
  "title": "Learning Python Forensics",
  "authors": "Preston Miller & Chapin Bryce",
  "publisher": "Packt Publishing",
  "pageCount": 500,
  "numberOfChapters": 13,
  "chapters":
  [
   {
    "chapterNumber": 1,
    "chapterTitle": "Now for Something Completely Different",
    "pageCount": 30
   },
   {
    "chapterNumber": 2,
    "chapterTitle": "Python Fundamentals",
    "pageCount": 25
   }
  ]
}
```

To parse this data structure using the `json` module, we use the `loads()` function. Unlike our XML example, we need to first open a file object before we can use `loads()` to convert the data. In the next code block, the `book.json` file, which is located in the same working directory as the interactive prompt, is opened and its contents are read into the `loads()` method. As an aside, we can use the `dump()` function to perform the reverse operation and convert Python objects into the JSON format for storage. As with the XML code block, if you're using Python 2, please import `print_function` from `__future__`:

```
>>> import json
>>> jsonfile = open('book.json', 'r')
>>> decoded_data = json.loads(jsonfile.read())
>>> print(type(decoded_data))
<class'dict'>
>>> print(decoded_data.keys())
dict_keys(['title', 'authors', 'publisher', 'pageCount',
'numberOfChapters', 'chapters'])
```

The module's `loads()` method reads the JSON file's string content and rebuilds the data into Python objects. As you can see in the preceding code, the overall structure is stored in a dictionary with key and value pairs. JSON is capable of storing the original data type of the objects. For example, `pageCount` is deserialized as an integer and `title` as a string object.

Not all the data is stored in the form of dictionaries. The `chapters` key is rebuilt as a list. We can use a `for` loop to iterate through `chapters` and print out any pertinent details:

```
>>> for chapter in decoded_data['chapters']:
... number = chapter['chapterNumber']
... title = chapter['chapterTitle']
... pages = chapter['pageCount']
... print('Chapter {}, {}, is {} pages.'.format(number, title, pages))
...
Chapter 1, Now For Something Completely Different, is 30 pages.
Chapter 2, Python Fundamentals, is 25 pages.
```

To be clear, the `chapters` key was stored as a list in the JSON file and contained nested dictionaries for each `chapter` element. When iterating through the list of dictionaries, we stored and then printed values associated with the dictionary keys to the user. We'll be using this exact technique on a larger scale to parse our Bitcoin JSON data. More details regarding the `json` module can be found at `https://docs.python.org/3/library/json.html`. Both the XML and JSON example files used in this section are available in the code bundle for this chapter. Other modules exist, such as `pickle` and `shelve`, which can be used for data serialization. However, they won't be covered in this book.

A simple Bitcoin web API

Bitcoin has caught the world by storm and is making headlines; it's the most successful and famous—or infamous, depending on whom you speak to—decentralized cryptocurrency. Bitcoin is regarded as an "anonymous" online cash substitute. SilkRoad, an illegal marketplace on the Tor network, which has been shut down, accepted Bitcoin as payment for illicit goods or services. Since gaining popularity, some websites and brick and mortar stores accept Bitcoins for payment. It has also gained vast public attention for climbing to unforeseen heights as its value rose well above everyone's expectations.

Bitcoin assigns individuals addresses to store their Bitcoins. These users can send or receive Bitcoins by specifying the address they would like to use. In Bitcoin, addresses are represented as 34 case-sensitive alphanumeric characters. Fortunately, all transactions are stored publicly on the blockchain. The blockchain keeps track of the time, input, output, and values for each transaction. In addition, each transaction is assigned a unique transaction hash.

Blockchain explorers are programs that allow an individual to search the blockchain. For example, we can search for a particular address or transaction of interest. One such blockchain explorer is at `https://www.blockchain.com/explorer` and is what we'll use to generate our dataset. Let's take a look at some of the data we'll need to parse.

Our script will ingest the JSON-structured transaction data, process it, and output this information to examiners in an analysis-ready state. After the user inputs the address of interest, we'll use the `blockchain.info` API to query the blockchain and pull down the relevant account data, including all associated transactions, as follows:

```
https://blockchain.info/address/%btc_address%?format=json
```

We'll query the preceding URL by replacing `%btc_address%` with the actual address of interest. For this exercise, we'll be investigating the `125riCXE2MtxHbNZkRtExPGAfbv7LsY3Wa` address. If you open a web browser and replace `%btc_address%` with the address of interest, we can see the raw JSON data that our script will be responsible for parsing:


```
{
 "hash160":"0be34924c8147535c5d5a077d6f398e2d3f20e2c",
 "address":"125riCXE2MtxHbNZkRtExPGAfbv7LsY3Wa",
 "n_tx":25,
 "total_received":80000000,
 "total_sent":80000000,
 "final_balance":0,
 "txs":
  [
```

```
        ...
      ]
  }
```

This is a more complicated version of our previous JSON example; however, the same rules apply. Starting with `hash160`, there's general account information, such as the address, number of transactions, balance, and total sent and received. Following that is the transaction array, denoted by the square brackets, that contains each transaction the address was involved in.

Looking at an individual transaction, a few keys stand out, such as the `addr` value from the input and output lists, time, and hash. When we iterate through the `txs` list, these keys will be used to reconstruct each transaction and display that information to the examiner. We have the following transaction:


```
"txs":[{
  "lock_time":0,
  "result":0,
  "ver":1,
  "size":225,
  "inputs":[
   {
     "sequence":4294967295,
     "prev_out":{
      "spent":true,
      "tx_index":103263818,
      "type":0,
      "addr":"125riCXE2MtxHbNZkRtExPGAfbv7LsY3Wa",
      "value":51498513,
      "n":1,
        "script":"76a9140be34924c8147535c5d5a077d6f398e2d3f20e2c88ac"
    },
"script":"4730440220673b8c6485b263fa15c75adc5de55c902cf80451c3c54f8e49df435
7ecd1a3ae022047aff8f9fb960f0f5b0313869b8042c7a81356e4cd23c9934ed1490110911c
e9012103e92a19202a543d7da710af28c956807c13f31832a18c1893954f905b339034fb"
  }],
  "time":1442766495,
  "tx_index":103276852,
  "vin_sz":1,
"hash":"f00febdc80e67c72d9c4d50ae2aa43eec2684725b566ec2a9fa9e8dbfc449827",
  "vout_sz":2,
  "relayed_by":"127.0.0.1",
  "out":[
   {
     "spent":false,
     "tx_index":103276852,
     "type":0,
```

```
    "addr":"12ytXWtNpxaEYW6ZvM564hVnsiFn4QnhAT",
    "value":100000,
    "n":0,
    "script":"76a91415ba6e75f51b0071e33152e5d34c2f6bca7998e888ac"
}
```


As with the previous chapter, we'll approach this task in a modular way by iteratively building our script. Besides working with serialized data structures, we're also going to introduce the concepts of creating logs and writing data to CSV files. Like `argparse`, the `logging` and `csv` modules will feature regularly in our forensic scripts.

Our first iteration – bitcoin_address_lookup.v1.py

The first iteration of our script will focus primarily on ingesting and processing the data appropriately. In this script, we'll print out transaction summaries for the account to the console. In later iterations, we'll add logging and outputting data to a CSV file. This script has been written and tested specifically for Python 3.7.1. The usage of the `urllib` library, a library we use to make HTTP requests, is structured differently in Python 2 and 3. In the final iteration of this script, we'll demonstrate the necessary code to make this script Python 2 and 3 compatible.

We'll use five modules in the initial version of the script. The `argparse`, `json`, `urllib`, and `sys` modules are all part of the standard library. The `unix_converter` module is the mostly unmodified script that we wrote in `Chapter 2`, *Python Fundamentals*, and is used here to convert Unix timestamps into the Bitcoin transaction data. The specific version of this module is available in the provided code for this chapter.
Both `argparse` and `urllib` have been used previously for user input and web requests, respectively. The `json` module is responsible for loading our transaction data into Python objects that we can manipulate:

```
"""First iteration of the Bitcoin JSON transaction parser."""
import argparse
import json
import urllib.request
import unix_converter as unix
import sys
...
__authors__ = ["Chapin Bryce", "Preston Miller"]
__date__ = 20181027
__description__ = """This scripts downloads address transactions
    using blockchain.info public APIs"""
```

Our script's logic is handled by five functions. The `main()` function, defined on line 42, serves as the coordinator between the other four functions. First, we pass the address supplied by the user to the `get_address()` function. This function is responsible for calling the `blockchain.info` API using `urllib` and returning the JSON data containing the transactions for that address.

Afterward, `print_transactions()` is called to traverse the nested dictionaries and lists and print out transaction details. In `print_transactions()`, function calls are made to `print_header()` and `get_inputs()`. The `print_header()` function is responsible for printing out non-transaction data, such as the number of transactions, current balance, and total sent and received values:

```
042 def main():
...
053 def get_address():
...
070 def print_transactions():
...
098 def print_header():
...
116 def get_inputs():
```

As seen before, we use `argparse` to create an `ArgumentParser` object and add the appropriate argument. Our only argument, `ADDR`, is a positional argument representing the Bitcoin address of interest. We call the `main()` function on line 145 and pass the `ADDR` argument:

```
128 if __name__ == '__main__':
129     # Run this code if the script is run from the command line.
130     parser = argparse.ArgumentParser(
131         description=__description__,
132         epilog='Built by {}. Version {}'.format(
133             ", ".join(__authors__), __date__),
134         formatter_class=argparse.ArgumentDefaultsHelpFormatter
135     )
136     parser.add_argument('ADDR', help='Bitcoin Address')
137     args = parser.parse_args()
138 
139     # Print Script Information
140     print('{:=^22}'.format(''))
141     print('{}'.format('Bitcoin Address Lookup'))
142     print('{:=^22} \n'.format(''))
143 
144     # Run main program
145     main(args.ADDR)
```

A flow diagram of our script can be seen as follows:

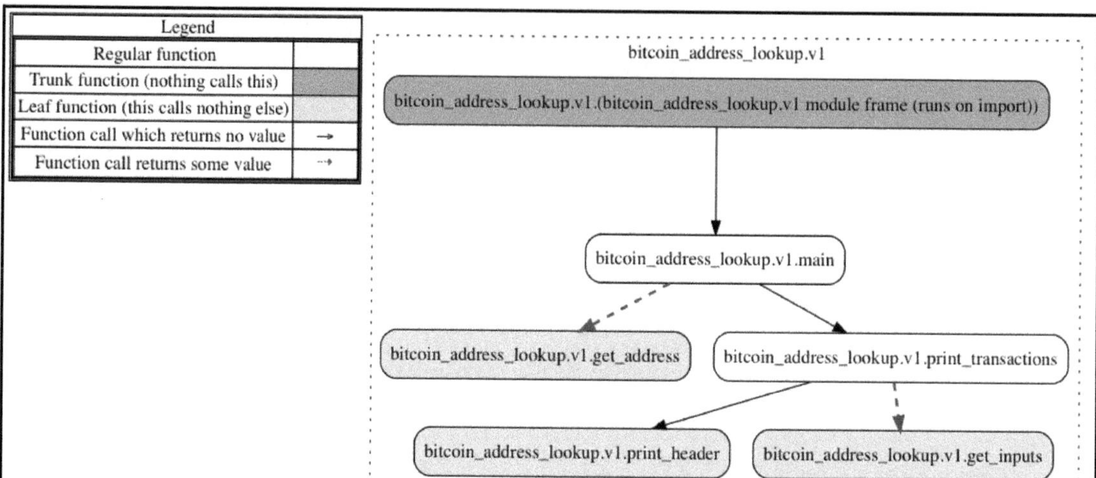

Exploring the main() function

The `main()` function is relatively simple. First, on line 48 we call the `get_address()` function and store the result in a variable named `raw_account`. This variable contains our JSON-formatted transaction data. In order to manipulate this data, we use the `json.loads()` function to deserialize the JSON data and store it in the account variable. At this point, our account variable is a series of dictionaries and lists that we can begin to traverse, which is exactly what we do in the `print_transactions()` function called on line 50:

```
042 def main(address):
043     """
044     The main function handles coordinating logic
045     :param address: The Bitcoin Address to lookup
046     :return: Nothing
047     """
048     raw_account = get_address(address)
049     account = json.loads(raw_account.read())
050     print_transactions(account)
```

Understanding the get_address() function

This is an integral, though a potentially error-prone, component of our script because it relies on the user correctly supplying data. The code itself is just a simple data request. However, when working with user supplied arguments, it isn't safe to assume that the user gave the script the correct data. Considering the length and somewhat random-looking sequence of a Bitcoin address, it's entirely possible that the user might supply an incorrect address. We'll catch any instance of `URLError` from the `urllib.error` module to handle a malformed input. `URLError` isn't part of the built-in exceptions we've talked about before and is a custom exception defined by the `urrlib` module:

```
053 def get_address(address):
054     """
055     The get_address function uses the blockchain.info Data API
056     to pull pull down account information and transactions for
057     address of interest
058     :param address: The Bitcoin Address to lookup
059     :return: The response of the url request
060     """
```

On line 62, we insert the user-supplied address into the `blockchain.info` API call using the string `format()` method. Then, we try to return the data requested using the `urllib.request.urlopen()` function. If the user supplies an invalid address or if the user doesn't have an internet connection, `URLError` will be caught. Once the error has been caught, we notify the user and exit the script, calling `sys.exit(1)` on line 67:

```
061     url = 'https://blockchain.info/address/{}?format=json'
062     formatted_url = url.format(address)
063     try:
064         return urllib.request.urlopen(formatted_url)
065     except urllib.error.URLError:
066         print('Received URL Error for {}'.format(formatted_url))
067         sys.exit(1)
```

Working with the print_transactions() function

This function handles the bulk of the processing logic in our code. This function traverses the transactions, or `txs`, list of embedded dictionaries from the loaded JSON data.

For each transaction, we'll print out its relative transaction number, the transaction hash, and the time of the transaction. Both the hash and time keys are easy to access as their values are stored in the outermost dictionary. The input and output details of the transaction are stored in an inner dictionary mapped to the input and output keys.

As is often the case, the time value is stored in Unix time. Luckily, in `Chapter 2`, *Python Fundamentals*, we wrote a script to handle such conversions, and once more we'll reuse this script by calling the `unix_converter()` method. The only change made to this function was removing the UTC label as these time values are stored in local time.

Because we imported `unix_converter` as `unix`, we must refer to the module as `unix`.

Let's take a quick look at the data structure we're dealing with. Imagine if we could pause the code during execution and inspect contents of variables, such as our account variable. At this point in this book, we'll just show you the contents of the `account` variable at this stage of execution. Later on in this book, we'll more formally discuss debugging in Python using the `pdb` module.

More information on the Python Debugger (`pdb`) is available in the documentation at `https://docs.python.org/3/library/pdb.html`.

In the following example, we can see the keys mapped to the first transaction in the `txs` list within the `account` dictionary. The `hash` and `time` keys are mapped to string and integer objects, respectively, which we can preserve as variables in our script:

```
>>> print(account['txs'][0].keys())
dict_keys(['ver', 'inputs', 'weight', 'block_height', 'relayed_by',
 'out', 'lock_time', 'result', 'size', 'time', 'tx_index', 'vin_sz',
 'hash', 'vout_sz'])
```

Next, we need to access the input and output details for the transaction. Let's take a look at the `out` dictionary. By looking at the keys, we can immediately identify the address, `addr`, and `value` sent as being valuable information. With an understanding of the layout and what data we want to present to the user, let's take a look at how we process each transaction in the `txs` list:

```
>>> print(account['txs'][0]['out'][0].keys())
dict_keys(['spent', 'tx_index', 'type', 'addr', 'value', 'n',
 'script'])
```

Before printing details of each transaction, we call and print basic account information parsed by the `print_header()` helper function to the console on line 77. On line 79, we begin to iterate through each transaction in the `txs` list. We've wrapped the list with the `enumerate()` function to update our counter, and the first variable in the `for` loop, `i`, to keep track of which transaction we're processing:

```
070 def print_transactions(account):
071     """
072     The print_transaction function is responsible for presenting
073     transaction details to end user.
074     :param account: The JSON decoded account and transaction data
075     :return:
076     """
077     print_header(account)
078     print('Transactions')
079     for i, tx in enumerate(account['txs']):
```

For each transaction, we print the relative transaction number, `hash`, and `time`. As we saw earlier, we can access `hash` or `time` by supplying the appropriate key. Remember that we do need to convert the Unix timestamp stored in the `time` key. We accomplish this by passing the value to the `unix_converter()` function:

```
080         print('Transaction #{}'.format(i))
081         print('Transaction Hash:', tx['hash'])
082         print('Transaction Date: {}'.format(
083             unix.unix_converter(tx['time'])))
```

On line 84, we begin to traverse the output list in the outside dictionary. This list is made up of multiple dictionaries with each representing an output for a given transaction. The keys we're interested in these dictionaries are the `addr` and `value` keys:

```
084         for outputs in tx['out']:
```

Be aware that the `value` value (not a typo) is stored as a whole number rather than a float and so a transaction of 0.025 BTC is stored as 2,500,000. We need to multiply this value by 10^{-8} to accurately reflect the value of the transaction. Let's call our helper function, `get_inputs()`, on line 85. This function will parse the input for the transaction separately and return the data in a list:

```
085             inputs = get_inputs(tx)
```

On line 86, we check to see whether there's more than one input address. That conditional will dictate what our print statement looks like. Essentially, if there's more than one input address, each address will be joined with an ampersand to clearly indicate the additional addresses.

The `print` statements on lines 87 and 91 use the string formatting method to appropriately display our processed data in the console. In these strings, we use the curly braces to denote three different variables. We use the `join()` function to convert a list into a string by joining on some delimiter. The second and third variables are the output `addr` and `value` keys, respectively:

```
086             if len(inputs) > 1:
087                 print('{} --> {} ({:.8f} BTC)'.format(
088                     ' & '.join(inputs), output['addr'],
089                     outputs['value'] * 10**-8))
090             else:
091                 print('{} --> {} ({:.8f} BTC)'.format(
092                     ''.join(inputs), outputs['addr'],
093                     outputs['value'] * 10**-8))
094
095         print('{:=^22}\n'.format(''))
```

Note how the designation for the value object is different from the rest. Because our value is a float, we can use string formatting to properly display the data to the correct precision. In the format descriptor, `{:.8f}`, the `8` represents the number of decimal places we want to allow. If there are more than eight decimal places, the value is rounded to the nearest number. `f` lets the `format()` method know that the input is expected to be of the float type. This function, while responsible for printing out the results to the user, uses two helper functions to perform its job.

The print_header() helper function

The `print_header()` helper function prints the account information to the console before transactions are printed. Specifically, the address, number of transactions, current balance, and total Bitcoins sent and received are displayed to the user. Take a look at the following code:

```
def print_header(account):
    """
    The print_header function prints overall header information
    containing basic address information.
    :param account: The JSON decoded account and transaction data
    :return: Nothing
    """
```

On lines 105 through 113, we print our values of interest using the string formatting method. During our program design, we chose to create this as a separate function in order to improve our code readability. Functionally, this code could have easily been, and originally was, in the `print_transactions()` function. It was separated to compartmentalize the different phases of execution. The purpose of the print statement on line 113 is to create a line of 22 left-aligned equal signs to visually separate the account information from the transactions in the console:

```
105     print('Address:', account['address'])
106     print('Current Balance: {:.8f} BTC'.format(
107         account['final_balance'] * 10**-8))
108     print('Total Sent: {:.8f} BTC'.format(
109         account['total_sent'] * 10**-8))
110     print('Total Received: {:.8f} BTC'.format(
111         account['total_received'] * 10**-8))
112     print('Number of Transactions:', account['n_tx'])
113     print('{:=^22}\n'.format(''))
```

The get_inputs() helper function

This helper function is responsible for obtaining the addresses responsible for sending the transaction. This information is found within multiple nested dictionaries. As there could be more than one input, we must iterate through one or more elements in the input list. As we find input addresses, we add them to an input list that's instantiated on line 123, as shown in the following code:

```
116 def get_inputs(tx):
117     """
118     The get_inputs function is a small helper function that returns
119     input addresses for a given transaction
120     :param tx: A single instance of a Bitcoin transaction
121     :return: inputs, a list of inputs
122     """
123     inputs = []
```

For each input, there's a dictionary key, `prev_out`, the value of which is another dictionary. The information we're looking for is mapped to the `addr` key within this inner dictionary. We append these addresses to our input list, which we return on line 126 after the `for` loop execution ends:

```
124     for input_addr in tx['inputs']:
125         inputs.append(input_addr['prev_out']['addr'])
126     return inputs
```

Running the script

Now, let's run our script and see the fruits of our labor. In the output mentioned later in the text, we can see that first the header information is printed to the user, followed by a number of transactions. The value objects are properly represented with the appropriate precision. For this particular example, there are four input values. Using the `' & '.join(inputs)` statement allows us to more clearly separate the different input values from each other:

```
(py3.7.1) C:\book\chapters\chapter_04>python bitcoin_address_lookup.v1.py 125riCXE2MtxHbNZkRtExPGAfbv7LsY3Wa
======================
Bitcoin Address Lookup
======================

Address: 125riCXE2MtxHbNZkRtExPGAfbv7LsY3Wa
Current Balance: 0.00000000 BTC
Total Sent: 0.80000000 BTC
Total Received: 0.80000000 BTC
Number of Transactions: 25
======================

Transactions
Transaction #0
Transaction Hash: 467a944dd0d7ed0bc41948675b48296094f04cbe035e048d6fa01c4eb5bb29c9
Transaction Date: 09/20/2015 11:56:24 PM
1J6bKdNo49s4c6fAjFFZgJLCgGphQrPvYM & 1FKGLnDiDa1b3dv8gimUJYAh8MzCo4Rook & 125riCXE2MtxHbNZkRtExPGAfbv7LsY3Wa & 1GxTRccWA3DztJasEtBG1wm
7pEcT7NogTE --> 1CbQp7zhUWbDeBSQTeeD6XnWNdH2GDYP1P (2.16686450 BTC)
1J6bKdNo49s4c6fAjFFZgJLCgGphQrPvYM & 1FKGLnDiDa1b3dv8gimUJYAh8MzCo4Rook & 125riCXE2MtxHbNZkRtExPGAfbv7LsY3Wa & 1GxTRccWA3DztJasEtBG1wm
7pEcT7NogTE --> 1GxTRccWA3DztJasEtBG1wm7pEcT7NogTE (0.25110936 BTC)
======================

Transaction #1
Transaction Hash: 399e3bc8b051def19a725888e2eb316c6247f8033fe4b875dd998f3ae42a6ff1
Transaction Date: 09/20/2015 10:17:58 PM
125riCXE2MtxHbNZkRtExPGAfbv7LsY3Wa --> 3HdbKdofxudExko4KPjAPgp4Jsy1Jy7fkq (0.00021762 BTC)
125riCXE2MtxHbNZkRtExPGAfbv7LsY3Wa --> 125riCXE2MtxHbNZkRtExPGAfbv7LsY3Wa (0.51281430 BTC)
======================
```

With our proof-of-concept complete, we can now iterate through and resolve some inherent issues in our current build. One problem is that we're not recording any data about the execution of our script. For example, an examiner's notes should contain the time, any errors or issues, and results of forensic processes. In the second iteration, we'll tackle this issue with the logging module. This module will store a log of our program's execution so the analyst has notes of when the program started, stopped, and any other relevant data regarding the process.

Our second iteration – bitcoin_address_lookup.v2.py

This iteration fixes one issue of our script by recording the details of execution. Really, we're using a log to create a chain of custody for the script. Our chain of custody will inform another party what our script did at various points in time and any errors encountered. Did we mention the traditional purpose of logging is for debugging? Nevertheless, our forensically commandeered log will be suitable in either scenario. This will serve as a brief tutorial on the basics of the logging module by using it in a real example. For more examples and references, please refer to the documentation at `https://docs.python.org/3/library/logging.html`.

We've added two modules to our imports: `os` and `logging`. If the user supplies the log file directory, we'll use the `os` module to append that directory and update the path of our log. In order to write a log, we'll use the `logging` module. Both of these modules are part of the standard library. See the following code:

```
"""Second iteration of the Bitcoin JSON transaction parser."""
import argparse
import json
import logging
import sys
import os
import urllib.request
import unix_converter as unix
...
__authors__ = ["Chapin Bryce", "Preston Miller"]
__date__ = 20181027
__description__ = """This scripts downloads address transactions
    using blockchain.info public APIs"""
```

Due to the additional code, our functions are defined later on in the script. However, their flow and purpose remain the same as before:

```
def main():
...
def get_address():
...
def print_transactions():
...
def print_header():
...
def get_inputs():
```

We've added a new optional argument, `-l`, on line 155. This optional argument can be used to specify the desired directory to write the log to. If it isn't supplied, the log is created in the current working directory:

```
146 if __name__ == '__main__':
147     # Run this code if the script is run from the command line.
148     parser = argparse.ArgumentParser(
149     description=__description__,
150     epilog='Built by {}. Version {}'.format(
151         ", ".join(__authors__), __date__),
152     formatter_class=argparse.ArgumentDefaultsHelpFormatter
153     )
154     parser.add_argument('ADDR', help='Bitcoin Address')
155     parser.add_argument('-l', help="""Specify log directory.
156         Defaults to current working directory.""")
157     args = parser.parse_args()
```

On line 159, we check whether the optional argument, `-l`, was supplied by the user. If it is, we use the `os.path.join()` function to append our desired log filename to the supplied directory and store it in a variable named `log_path`. If the optional argument isn't supplied, our `log_path` variable is just the filename of the log:

```
159     # Set up Log
160     if args.l:
161         if not os.path.exists(args.l):
162             os.makedirs(args.l)
163         log_path = os.path.join(args.l, 'btc_addr_lookup.log')
164     else:
165         log_path = 'btc_addr_lookup.log'
```

The logging object is created on line 165 using the `logging.basicConfig()` method. This method accepts a variety of keyword arguments. The `filename` keyword argument is the file path and the name of our log file that we stored in the `log_path` variable. The `level` keyword sets the level of the log. There are five different logging levels, in the default order of lowest to highest urgency:

- `DEBUG`
- `INFO`
- `WARN` (default level)
- `ERROR`
- `CRITICAL`

If the level isn't supplied, the log defaults to WARN. The level of the log ends up being very important. A log will only record an entry if the message is at the same level or higher than the log level. By setting the log to the DEBUG level, the lowest level, we can write messages of any level to the log:

```
logging.basicConfig(
    filename=log_path, level=logging.DEBUG,
    format='%(asctime)s | %(levelname)s | %(message)s',
    filemode='w')
```

Each level has a different significance and should be used appropriately. The DEBUG level should be used when logging technical details about program execution. The INFO level can be used to record the program start, stop, and success of various phases of execution. The remaining levels can be used when detecting potentially anomalous execution, when an error is generated, or at critical failures.

The format keyword specifies how we want to structure the log itself. Our log will have the following format:

```
time | level | message
```

For example, this format will create a log file with the local time when the entry is added, the appropriate level, and any message, all separated by pipes. To create an entry in the log, we can call the debug(), info(), warn(), error(), or critical() methods on our logging object and pass in the message as a string. For example, based on the following code, we would expect to see the following entry generated in our log:

```
logging.error("Blah Blah function has generated an error from the following
input: xyz123.")
```

The following is the log:

```
2015-11-06 19:51:47,446 | ERROR | Blah Blah function has generated an error
from the following input: xyz123.
```

Finally, the filemode='w' argument is used to overwrite previous entries in the log every time the script is executed. This means that only entries from the most recent execution will be stored in the log. If we wanted to append each execution cycle to the end of the log, we would omit this keyword argument. When omitted, the default file mode is a which, as you learned in Chapter 1, *Now for Something Completely Different*, allows us to append to the bottom of a pre-existing file.

We can begin writing information to the log after it has been configured. On lines 172 and 173, we record details of the user's system before program execution. We write this to the log at the `DEBUG` level due to the technically low-level nature of the content:

```
171     logging.info('Starting Bitcoin Lookup v. {}'.format(__date__))
172     logging.debug('System ' + sys.platform)
173     logging.debug('Version ' + sys.version.replace("\n", " "))
174
175     # Print Script Information
176     print('{:=^22}'.format(''))
177     print('{}'.format('Bitcoin Address Lookup'))
178     print('{:=^22} \n'.format(''))
179
180     # Run main program
181     main(args.ADDR)
```

This version of our script is largely the same and follows the same flow schematic as seen previously.

Modifying the main() function

The `main()` function, defined on line 44, is largely untouched. We've added two `INFO` level messages to the log regarding the script's execution on lines 50 and 52. The remainder of the method follows as seen in the first iteration:

```
044 def main(address):
045     """
046     The main function handles coordinating logic
047     :param address: The Bitcoin Address to lookup
048     :return: Nothing
049     """
050     logging.info('Initiated program for {} address'.format(
051         address))
052     logging.info(
053         'Obtaining JSON structured data from blockchain.info')
054     raw_account = get_address(address)
055     account = json.loads(raw_account.read())
056     print_transactions(account)
```

Improving the get_address() function

With the `get_address()` method, we've continued adding logging messages to our script. This time, when catching `URLError`, we stored the `Exception` object as `e` to extract additional information from it for debugging:

```
059 def get_address(address):
060     """
061     The get_address function uses the blockchain.info Data API
062     to pull pull down account information and transactions for
063     address of interest
064     :param address: The Bitcoin Address to lookup
065     :return: The response of the url request
066     """
```

For `URLError`, we'll want to log the `code`, `headers`, and `reason` attributes. These attributes contain information, such as the HTML error code—for example, `404` for a web page that isn't found—and a description of the reason for the error code. We'll store this data to preserve the context surrounding the error:

```
067     url = 'https://blockchain.info/address/{}?format=json'
068     formatted_url = url.format(address)
069     try:
070         return urllib.request.urlopen(formatted_url)
071     except urllib.error.URLError as e:
072         logging.error('URL Error for {}'.format(formatted_url))
073         if hasattr(e, 'code') and hasattr(e, 'headers'):
074             logging.debug('{}: {}'.format(e.code, e.reason))
075             logging.debug('{}'.format(e.headers))
076         print('Received URL Error for {}'.format(formatted_url))
077         logging.info('Program exiting...')
078         sys.exit(1)
```

Elaborating on the print_transactions() function

We define the `print_transaction()` function on line 81. We've made a few alterations to the function, starting on line 88 where we added an entry to log the current execution phase. Take a look at the following function:

```
081 def print_transactions(account):
082     """
083     The print_transaction function is responsible for presenting
084     transaction details to end user.
085     :param account: The JSON decoded account and transaction data
086     :return: Nothing
```

```
087     """
088     logging.info(
089         'Printing account and transaction data to console.')
090     print_header(account)
091     print('Transactions')
092     for i, tx in enumerate(account['txs']):
093         print('Transaction #{}'.format(i))
094         print('Transaction Hash:', tx['hash'])
095         print('Transaction Date: {}'.format(
096             unix.unix_converter(tx['time'])))
```

For the conditional statement starting on line 99, we add different cases using `if`, `elif`, and `else` statements to handle when the number of input values is greater than, equal to, or other than one. While rare, the first ever Bitcoin transaction, for example, had no input address. When an input address is absent, it's ideal to write a warning in the log that there are no detected inputs and print this information for the user, as follows:

```
097         for output in tx['out']:
098             inputs = get_inputs(tx)
099             if len(inputs) > 1:
100                 print('{} --> {} ({:.8f} BTC)'.format(
101                     ' & '.join(inputs), output['addr'],
102                     output['value'] * 10**-8))
103             elif len(inputs) == 1:
104                 print('{} --> {} ({:.8f} BTC)'.format(
105                     ''.join(inputs), output['addr'],
106                     output['value'] * 10**-8))
107             else:
108                 logging.warn(
109                     'Detected 0 inputs for transaction {}').format(
110                         tx['hash'])
111                 print('Detected 0 inputs for transaction.')
112
113         print('{:=^22}\n'.format(''))
```

Running the script

The remaining functions, `print_header()` and `get_inputs()`, weren't changed from the previous iteration. The entire code won't require modifications between iterations. By building a strong output module, we were able to avoid any adjustments to the reporting.

While results are still displayed in the console, we now have a written log of the program execution. Running the script with a specified `-l` switch will allow us to store the log in a specific directory. Otherwise, the current working directory is used. The following are the contents of the log after the script completed:

btc_addr_lookup.log

```
2018-12-01 11:14:09,308 | INFO | Starting Bitcoin Lookup v. 20181027
2018-12-01 11:14:09,308 | DEBUG | System win32
2018-12-01 11:14:09,308 | DEBUG | Version 3.7.1 (v3.7.1:260ec2c36a, Oct 20 2018, 14:57:15) [MSC v.1915 64 bit (AMD64)]
2018-12-01 11:14:09,316 | INFO | Initiated program for 125riCXE2MtxHbNZkRtExPGAfbv7LsY3Wa address
2018-12-01 11:14:09,316 | INFO | Obtaining JSON structured data from blockchain.info
2018-12-01 11:14:09,686 | INFO | Printing account and transaction data to console.
```

With logging accomplished, we've identified yet another area of enhancement for our code. For this particular address, we have a manageable number of transactions that get printed to the console. Imagine a case where there are hundreds of transactions for a single address. Navigating that output and being able to identify a specific transaction of interest isn't that straightforward.

Mastering our final iteration – bitcoin_address_lookup.py

In the final iteration, we'll write the output of our script to a CSV file rather than the console. This allows examiners to quickly filter and sort data in a manner conducive to analysis.

On line 4, we've imported the `csv` module that's a part of the standard library. Writing to a CSV file is fairly simple compared with other output formats, and most examiners are very comfortable with manipulating spreadsheets.

As mentioned previously in this chapter, in this final iteration of our script, we've added the necessary logic to detect whether Python 2 or Python 3 is being used to call the script. Depending on the version of Python, the appropriate `urllib` or `urllib2` functions are imported into this script. Note that we directly import the function, `urlopen()`, and `URLError`, which we plan to use so that we may call them directly in the script. This allows us to avoid using additional conditional statements later on to identify whether we should call `urllib` or `urllib2`:

```
001 """Final iteration of the Bitcoin JSON transaction parser."""
002 from __future__ import print_function
003 import argparse
004 import csv
005 import json
```

```
import logging
import sys
import os
if sys.version_info[0] == 2:
    from urllib2 import urlopen
    from urllib2 import URLError
elif sys.version_info[0] == 3:
    from urllib.request import urlopen
    from urllib.error import URLError
else:
    print("Unsupported Python version. Exiting..")
    sys.exit(1)
import unix_converter as unix
...
__authors__ = ["Chapin Bryce", "Preston Miller"]
__date__ = 20181027
__description__ = """This scripts downloads address transactions
    using blockchain.info public APIs"""
```

The main focus of this final iteration is the addition of the new function, `csv_writer()`. This function is responsible for writing the data returned by `parse_transactions()` to a CSV file. We'll need to modify the current version of `print_transactions()` to return the parsed data rather than printing it to the console. While this won't be an in-depth tutorial on the `csv` module, we'll discuss the basics of using this module in the current context. We'll use the `csv` module extensively and explore additional features throughout this book. Documentation for the `csv` module can be found at `http://docs.python.org/3/library/csv.html`.

Let's first open an interactive prompt to practice creating and writing to a CSV file. First, let's import the `csv` module that will allow us to create our CSV file. Next, we create a list named `headers`, which will store the column headers of our CSV file:

```
>>> import csv
>>> headers = ['Date', 'Name', 'Description']
```

Next, we'll open a file object using the built-in `open()` method with the appropriate file mode. In Python 2, a CSV file object should be opened in the `rb` or `wb` modes for reading and writing, respectively. In this case, we'll be writing to a CSV file so let's open the file in the `wb` mode. The `w` stands for write, and the `b` stands for binary mode.

In Python 3, a CSV file should be opened in the `w` mode with a newline character specified, as demonstrated here: `open('test.csv', 'w', newline='')`.

With our connection to the file object, `csvfile`, we now need to create a writer or reader (depending on our desired goal) and pass in the file object. There are two options—the `csv.writer()` or `csv.reader()` methods; both expect a file object as their input and accept various keyword arguments. The list object meshes well with the `csv` module, requiring little code to write the data to a CSV file. It isn't difficult to write a dictionary and other objects to a CSV file, but is out of scope here and will be covered in later chapters:

```
>>> with open('test.csv', 'wb') as csvfile:
...     writer = csv.writer(csvfile)
```

The `writer.writerow()` method will write one row using the supplied list. Each element in the list will be placed in sequential columns on the same row. If, for example, the `writerow()` function is called again with another list input, the data will now be written one row below the previous write operation:

```
...     writer.writerow(headers)
```

In practical situations, we've found that using nested lists is one of the simplest ways of iterating through and writing each row. In our final iteration, we'll store the transaction details in a list and append them within another list. We can then iterate through each transaction while writing the details to the CSV as we go along.

As with any file object, be sure to flush any data that's in a buffer to the file and then close the file. Forgetting these steps aren't the end of the world as Python will mostly handle this automatically, but they're highly recommended. After executing these last lines of code, a file called `test.csv` will be created in your working directory with the `Date`, `Name`, and `Description` headers as the first row. This same code will also work with the `csv` module in Python 3, with the exception of modifying the initial `open()` function as demonstrated previously:

```
...     csvfile.flush()
...     csvfile.close()
```

We've renamed the `print_transactions()` function to `parse_transactions()` to more accurately reflect its purpose. In addition, on line 159 we've added a `csv_writer()` function to write our transaction results to a CSV file. All other functions are similar to the previous iteration:

```
053 def main():
...
070 def get_address():
...
091 def parse_transactions():
...
123 def print_header():
```

```
...
142 def get_inputs():
...
159 def csv_writer():
```

Finally, we've added a new positional argument named `OUTPUT`. This argument represents the name and/or path for the CSV output. On line 230, we pass this output argument to the `main()` function:

```
195 if __name__ == '__main__':
196     # Run this code if the script is run from the command line.
197     parser = argparse.ArgumentParser(
198     description=__description__,
199     epilog='Built by {}. Version {}'.format(
200         ", ".join(__authors__), __date__),
201     formatter_class=argparse.ArgumentDefaultsHelpFormatter
202     )
203
204     parser.add_argument('ADDR', help='Bitcoin Address')
205     parser.add_argument('OUTPUT', help='Output CSV file')
206     parser.add_argument('-l', help="""Specify log directory.
207         Defaults to current working directory.""")
208
209     args = parser.parse_args()
210
211     # Set up Log
212     if args.l:
213         if not os.path.exists(args.l):
214             os.makedirs(args.l) # create log directory path
215         log_path = os.path.join(args.l, 'btc_addr_lookup.log')
216     else:
217         log_path = 'btc_addr_lookup.log'
218     logging.basicConfig(
219         filename=log_path, level=logging.DEBUG,
220         format='%(asctime)s | %(levelname)s | %(message)s',
221         filemode='w')
222
223     logging.info('Starting Bitcoid Lookup v. {}'.format(__date__))
224     logging.debug('System ' + sys.platform)
225     logging.debug('Version ' + sys.version.replace("\n", " "))
226
227     # Print Script Information
228     print('{:=^22}'.format(''))
229     print('{}'.format('Bitcoin Address Lookup'))
230     print('{:=^22} \n'.format(''))
231
232     # Run main program
233     main(args.ADDR, args.OUTPUT)
```

The following flow diagram exemplifies the differences between the first two iterations and our final version:

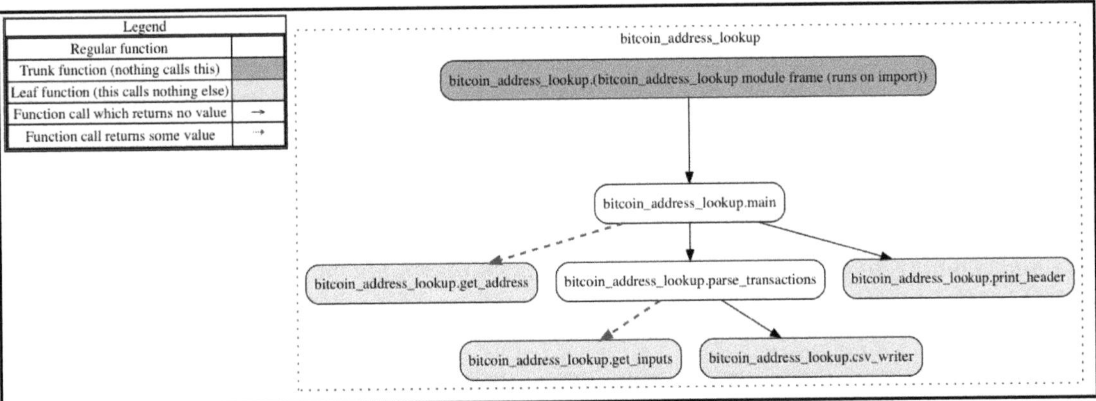

Enhancing the parse_transactions() function

This function, which was previously named `print_transactions()`, is used to process the transaction data so it can be ingested by our `csv_writer()`. Please note that the `print_header()` function call has now been moved into the `main()` function. We're also now passing an output argument to `parse_transactions()`:

```
091 def parse_transactions(account, output_dir):
092     """
093     The parse_transactions function appends transaction data into a
094     nested list structure so it can be successfully used by the
095     csv_writer function.
096     :param account: The JSON decoded account and transaction data
097     :param output_dir: The output directory to write the CSV
098     results
099     :return: Nothing
100     """
```

As we've seen previously, we must first iterate through the `transactions` list. As we traverse the data, we'll append it to a transaction list, which is created on line 104. This list represents a given transaction and its data. After we're finished appending transaction data, we append this list to the `transactions` list that serves as a container for all of the transactions:

```
101     msg = 'Parsing transactions...'
102     logging.info(msg)
```

```
103     print(msg)
104     transactions = []
105     for i, tx in enumerate(account['txs']):
106         transaction = []
```

In order to match an output address with its value, we create an `outputs` dictionary on line 107. On line 114, we create a key representing the address and value sent to it. Note that we use the newline character, `\n`, on lines 115 through 117 when combining multiple output addresses and their values so they're visually separate within one cell. We've also performed the same action in the `get_inputs()` function to handle multiple input values. This was a design choice we made because we've seen that there can be multiple output addresses. Rather than placing these in their own columns, we've opted to place them all in one column:

```
107         outputs = {}
108         inputs = get_inputs(tx)
109         transaction.append(i)
110         transaction.append(unix.unix_converter(tx['time']))
111         transaction.append(tx['hash'])
112         transaction.append(inputs)
113         for output in tx['out']:
114             outputs[output['addr']] = output['value'] * 10**-8
115         transaction.append('\n'.join(outputs.keys()))
116         transaction.append(
117             '\n'.join(str(v) for v in outputs.values()))
```

On line 118, we created a new value using the `sum()` built-in function, to sum the output values together. The `sum()` function is quite handy and accepts a list of `int` or `float` types as input and returns the sum:

```
118         transaction.append('{:.8f}'.format(sum(outputs.values())))
```

Now, we have all of our desired transaction details in the `transaction` list. We append the transaction to the `transactions` list on line 119. Once all transactions have been added to the `transactions` list, we call the `csv_writer()` method and pass in our `transactions` list and `output` directory:

```
119         transactions.append(transaction)
120     csv_writer(transactions, output_dir)
```

Once again, we've made no modifications to the `print_header()` or `get_address()` functions.

Developing the csv_writer() function

On line 159, we define our `csv_writer()` function. Before writing our transaction data to a CSV file, we log our current execution phase and create a `headers` variable. This `headers` list represents the columns in our spreadsheet and will be the first row written to the file, as follows:

```
159 def csv_writer(data, output_dir):
160     """
161     The csv_writer function writes transaction data into a CSV file
162     :param data: The parsed transaction data in nested list
163     :param output_dir: The output directory to write the CSV
164     results
165     :return: Nothing
166     """
167     logging.info('Writing output to {}'.format(output_dir))
168     print('Writing output.')
169     headers = ['Index', 'Date', 'Transaction Hash',
170         'Inputs', 'Outputs', 'Values', 'Total']
```

As with any user-supplied data, we must account for the possibility that the supplied data could be incorrect or generate an exception. For example, the user could specify a non-existent directory in the output path argument. On lines 173 and 175, we open the `csvfile` in the appropriate manner, depending on the version of Python being used, and write our CSV data under one `try` and `except` clause. If there's an issue with the user-supplied output, we'll receive an `IOError` exception.

We create our writer object on line 177 and write our `headers`, before iterating through our transactions list. Every transaction within the transactions list is written on its own row. Finally, on lines 181 and 182, we flush and close the CSV file:

```
171     try:
172         if sys.version_info[0] == 2:
173             csvfile = open(output_dir, 'wb')
174         else:
175             csvfile = open(output_dir, 'w', newline='')
176         with csvfile:
177             writer = csv.writer(csvfile)
178             writer.writerow(headers)
179             for transaction in data:
180                 writer.writerow(transaction)
181             csvfile.flush()
182             csvfile.close()
```

If `IOError` is generated, we write the error message and contextual information to the log before exiting with an error (any nonzero exit). If there are no errors generated, we log the completion of the script and exit without errors (also known as a zero exit), as seen on line 191 through 193:

```
183     except IOError as e:
184         logging.error("""Error writing output to {}.
185         \nGenerated message: {}.""".format(e.filename,
186         e.strerror))
187         print("""Error writing to CSV file.
188         Please check output argument {}""".format(e.filename))
189         logging.info('Program exiting.')
190         sys.exit(1)
191     logging.info('Program exiting.')
192     print('Program exiting.')
193     sys.exit(0)
```

Running the script

This iteration finally addresses the remaining issue we identified, which is a means of processing the data into an examination-ready state. Now if an address had hundreds or thousands of transactions, the examiner can analyze that data more efficiently than if it were displayed in a console.

This being said, as with most things, there's always room for improvement. For example, the way in which we've handled multiple input and output values means that it will have more than one address in a specific cell. This can be annoying when trying to filter for a specific address. The point here is that a script is never truly finished being developed and is always an ongoing process.

To run the script, we now must supply two arguments: the Bitcoin address and desired output. The following is an example of usage and output printed to the console when running our script:

```
(py3.7.1) C:\book\chapters\chapter_04>python bitcoin_address_lookup.py 125riCXE2MtxHbNZkRtExPGAfbv7LsY3Wa transactions.csv
=====================
Bitcoin Address Lookup
=====================

Address: 125riCXE2MtxHbNZkRtExPGAfbv7LsY3Wa
Current Balance: 0.00000000 BTC
Total Sent: 0.80000000 BTC
Total Received: 0.80000000 BTC
Number of Transactions: 25
=====================

Parsing transactions...
Writing output.
Program exiting.
```

The `transactions.csv` file will be written to the current working directory as specified. The following screenshot captures what this spreadsheet might look like:

Index	Date	Transaction Hash	Inputs	Outputs	Values	Total
0	9/20/2015 23:56	467a944dd0d7ed0bc41948675b4 8296094f04cbe035e048d6fa01c4e b5bb29c9	1J6bKdNo49s4c6fAjFFZgJLCgGphQrPvYM 1FKGLnDiDa1b3dv8gimUJYAh8MzCo4Rook 125riCXE2MtxHbNZkRtExPGAfbv7LsY3Wa 1GxTRccWA3DztJasEtBG1wm7pEcT7NogTE	1CbQp7zhUWbDeBSQTeeD6XnWNdH2GDYP1P 1GxTRccWA3DztJasEtBG1wm7pEcT7NogTE	2.1668645 0.25110936	2.4179739
1	9/20/2015 22:17	399e3bc8b051def19a725888e2eb 316c6247f8033fe4b875dd998f3ae 42a6ff1	125riCXE2MtxHbNZkRtExPGAfbv7LsY3Wa	3HdbKdofxudExko4KPjAPgp4Jsy1Jy7fkq 125riCXE2MtxHbNZkRtExPGAfbv7LsY3Wa	0.00021762 0.51281430000 00001	0.5130319
2	9/20/2015 20:11	4e569e655f322db5c7f9dcf7cd859 b95766f5fe958007a354db5ef9e06 018917	125riCXE2MtxHbNZkRtExPGAfbv7LsY3Wa	3GtGscT34cjR2Jay9UqcYMNwu7xA9GDYUX 125riCXE2MtxHbNZkRtExPGAfbv7LsY3Wa	0.00051253 0.51313192	0.5136445
3	9/20/2015 18:08	9032592a133bddd3270b449a3b6 a90698accb7836f03be6e3522435 2b1fab58e	125riCXE2MtxHbNZkRtExPGAfbv7LsY3Wa	18EdCZ7netnin52Mug6UjtZGSZUgdXUXu5 125riCXE2MtxHbNZkRtExPGAfbv7LsY3Wa	4.06800000000 00004e-05 0.51374445	0.5137851
4	9/20/2015 16:35	f00febdc80e67c72d9c4d50ae2aa4 3eec2684725b566ec2a9fa9e8dbfc 449827	125riCXE2MtxHbNZkRtExPGAfbv7LsY3Wa	12ytXWtNpxaEYW6ZvM564hVnsiFn4QnhAT 125riCXE2MtxHbNZkRtExPGAfbv7LsY3Wa	0.001 0.51388513	0.5148851
5	9/20/2015 15:17	e3d4ac28233722bf1094f90a86f4e ee2c19c8baa8a62dccc93c4b70197 016884	125riCXE2MtxHbNZkRtExPGAfbv7LsY3Wa	3FdYMAYiFn9Ns2vGBBmRrfRXSk2VWyXoJA 125riCXE2MtxHbNZkRtExPGAfbv7LsY3Wa	0.00019896 0.51498513	0.5151841

Challenge

For an additional challenge, modify the script so that each output and input address has its own cell. We recommend approaching this by determining the maximum number of input values or output addresses in a list of transactions. Knowing these values, you could build a conditional statement to modify the header so that it has the appropriate number of columns. In addition, you would need to write logic to skip those columns when you don't have multiple input or output values in order to preserve the correct spacing of data.

While specific to Bitcoin, examples in the wild may require similar logic when there exists a dynamic relationship between two or more data points. Tackling this challenge will help develop a logical and practical methodology that can be applied in future scenarios.

Summary

In this chapter, we gained greater familiarity with common serialized structures, Bitcoin, and CSV and with working with nested lists and dictionaries. Being able to manipulate lists and dictionaries is a vital skill, as data is often stored in mixed nested structures. Remember to always use the `type()` method to determine what type of data you're working with.

For this script, we (the authors) played around with the JSON data structure in the Python interactive prompt before writing the script. This allowed us to understand how to traverse the data structure correctly and the best manner to do so before writing any logic. The Python interactive prompt is an excellent sandbox to implement new features or to test new code. The code for this project can be downloaded from GitHub or Packt, as described in the *Preface*.

In the next chapter, we'll discuss a different method to store structured data. While learning how to integrate databases into our scripts, we'll create an active file listing script that stores all of its data in an SQLite3 format. Doing this will allow us to become more comfortable with storing and retrieving data from databases in Python using two different modules.

5
Databases in Python

In this chapter, we will leverage databases in our scripts so that we can accomplish meaningful tasks when working with large quantities of data. Using a simple example, we will demonstrate the capabilities and benefits of using a database backend in our Python scripts. We will store file metadata that has been recursively indexed from a given root directory into a database and then query it to generate reports. Although this may seem like a simple feat, the purpose of this chapter is to showcase the ways we can interact with a database in Python by creating an active file listing.

In this chapter, we will delve into the following topics:

- The basic design and implementation of SQLite3 databases
- Working with these databases in Python using built-in and third-party modules
- Understanding how to recursively iterate through directories in Python
- Understanding filesystem metadata and the methods for accessing it using Python
- Crafting CSV and HTML reports for easy review by our end user

The code for this chapter was developed and tested using Python 2.7.15 and Python 3.7.1. The `file_lister.py` script was developed to work with Python 3.7.1. The `file_lister_peewee.py` script was developed and tested using both Python 2.7.15 and Python 3.7.1.

An overview of databases

Databases provide an efficient means of storing large amounts of data in a structured manner. There are many types of databases, commonly broken into two categories: **SQL** or **NoSQL**. **SQL** (short for **Structured Query Language**) is designed to be a simple language that allows users to manipulate large datasets that are stored in a database. This includes common databases, such as MySQL, SQLite, and PostgreSQL. NoSQL databases are also useful and generally use JSON or XML to store data of varying structures, both of which were discussed as common serialized data types in the previous chapter.

Using SQLite3

SQLite3 is the latest version of SQLite and is one of the most common databases found in application development. This database, unlike others, is stored as a single file and does not require a server instance to be running or installed. For this reason, it is widely used due to its portability and is found in many applications for mobile devices, desktop applications, and web services. SQLite3 uses a slightly modified SQL syntax, though of the many SQL variations that exist, it is one of its simpler implementations. Naturally, there are some limitations to this lightweight database. These limitations include a restriction of one writer being connected to the database at a time, 140 TB of storage, and that it is not client-server based. Because our application will not execute multiple write statements simultaneously, uses less than 140 TB of storage, and does not require a client-server setup for distribution, we will be using SQLite for our example in this chapter.

Using SQL

Before developing our code, let's take a look at the basic SQL statements we will be using. This will help us understand how we can interact with databases even without Python. In SQL, commands are commonly written in uppercase, although they are case-insensitive. For this exercise, we will use uppercase to improve legibility. All SQL statements must end in a semicolon to execute, as it denotes the end of a statement.

If you would like to follow along, install a SQLite management tool, such as the command-line tool sqlite3. This tool can be downloaded from `https://www.sqlite.org/download.html`. The output shown in this section has been generated with the sqlite3 command-line tool, though the statements that have been given will generate the same database in most other sqlite3 graphical applications. When in doubt, use the official sqlite3 command-line tool.

To begin, we will create a table, a fundamental component of any database. If we compare a database to an Excel workbook, a table is tantamount to a worksheet. Tables contain named columns, as well as rows of data that are mapped to these columns. Just like how an Excel workbook may contain multiple worksheets, so too can a database contain multiple tables. To create a table, we will use the `CREATE TABLE` command, specifying the table name and then wrapping, in parentheses, the column names and their data types as a comma-separated list. Finally, we end the SQL statement with a semicolon:

```
>>> CREATE TABLE custodians (id INTEGER PRIMARY KEY, name TEXT);
```

As we can see in the `CREATE TABLE` statement, we specify the `id` and `name` columns in the `custodians` table. The `id` field is an integer and primary key. This designation of `INTEGER PRIMARY KEY` in SQLite3 will create an automatic index that sequentially increments for each added row, therefore creating an index of unique row identifiers. The `name` column has the data type of `TEXT`, which allows any character to be stored as a text string. SQLite supports five data types, two of which we've already introduced:

- `INTEGER`
- `TEXT`
- `REAL`
- `BLOB`
- `NULL`

The `REAL` data type allows floating point numbers (for example, decimals). The **BLOB** (short for **Binary Large OBject**) data type preserves any input data exactly as is, without casting it as a certain type. The `NULL` data type simply stores an empty value.

After creating the table, we can begin to add data to it. As we can see in the following code block, we can use the `INSERT INTO` command to insert data into the table. The syntax following this command specifies the table name, the columns to insert the data into, followed by the `VALUES` command specifying the values to be inserted. The columns and data must be wrapped in parentheses, as shown in the following code. Using the `null` statement as a value, the auto-incrementing feature of SQLite will step in and fill in this value with the next available unique integer. Remember that this auto-incrementing is only true because we designated it as `INTEGER PRIMARY KEY`. As a general rule, only one column in a table should have this designation:

```
>>> INSERT INTO custodians (id, name) VALUES (null, 'Chell');
>>> INSERT INTO custodians (id, name) VALUES (null, 'GLaDOS');
```

We've inserted two custodians, `Chell` and `GLaDOS`, and we let SQLite assign IDs to each of them. After the data has been inserted, we can select and view this information using the `SELECT` command. The basic syntax involves invoking the `SELECT` command, followed by the columns to select (or an asterisk `*` to designate all columns) and the `FROM` statement, indicating the table name following a trailing semicolon. As we can see in the following code, `SELECT` will print out a pipe (`|`) separated list of the values stored:

```
>>> SELECT * FROM custodians;
1|Chell
2|GLaDOS
```

In addition to showing only the desired columns from our table, we can also filter data on one or more conditions. The `WHERE` statement allows us to filter results and return only responsive items. For the purpose of the script in this chapter, we will stick to a simple `where` statement and only use the equals operator to return responsive values. When executed, the `SELECT-WHERE` statement returns only the custodian information where the `id` value is `1`. In addition, note that the order of the columns reflects the order in which they were specified:

```
>>> SELECT name,id FROM custodians WHERE id = 1;
Chell|1
```

There are more operations and statements available to interact with SQLite3 databases, although the preceding operations highlight all that we require for our scripts. We invite you to explore additional operations in the SQLite3 documentation, which can be found at `https://sqlite.org`.

Designing our script

The first iteration of our script focuses on performing the task at hand with a standard module, sqlite3, in a more manual fashion. This entails writing out each SQL statement and executing them as if you were working with the database itself. Although this is not a very Pythonic manner of handling a database, it demonstrates the methods that are used to interact with a database with Python. Our second iteration employs two third-party libraries: `peewee` and `jinja2`.

Peewee is an **object-relational mapper** (**ORM**), which is a term that's used to describe a software suite that uses objects to handle database operations. In short, this ORM allows the developer to call functions and define classes in Python that are interpreted as database commands. This layer of abstraction helps to standardize database calls and allows for multiple database backends to be easily interchanged. Peewee is a light ORM, as it is a single Python file that supports PostgreSQL, MySQL, and SQLite3 database connections. If we needed to switch our second script from SQLite3 to PostgreSQL, it would only require that we modify a few lines of code; our first script would require more attention to handle this same conversion. This being said, our first version does not require any dependencies beyond the standard Python installation for SQLite3 support, an attractive feature for tools that are designed to be portable and flexible while in the field.

Our `file_lister.py` script is a per-custodian metadata collection and reporting script. This is important in incident response or the discovery phase of an investigation, as it stores information about active files on a system or in a specified directory by custodian name. A custodian assignment system allows for multiple machines, directory paths, or network shares to be indexed and categorized by a single custodian name, regardless of whether the custodian is a user, machine, or device. To implement this system, we need to prompt the user for the custodian name, the path of the database to use, and the input or output information.

By allowing the examiner to add multiple custodians or paths into the same database, they can append to the files that have been found for a single custodian or add in as many custodians as they please. This is helpful in collections as the investigator can preserve as few or as many paths as they need, as we all know how unexpected devices show up once we are in the field. In addition, we can use the same script to create file listing reports, regardless of the number of collected files or custodians, as long as the custodian has at least one collected file.

In our design state, we don't only take into account our script but also the database and the relational model we will use. In our case, we are handling two separate items: custodians and files. These both make for good tables, as they are separate entries that share a common relation. In our scenario, a file has a custodian and a custodian may have one or more files; therefore, we will want to create a foreign key, relating files to a specific custodian. A foreign key is a reference to a primary key in another table. The primary key and the foreign key references are usually a unique value or an index that links the data together.

The following diagram represents the relational model for our database. We have two tables, custodians and files, and a one-to-many relationship between them. As defined earlier, this one-to-many relationship will allow us to assign many files to a single custodian. Using this relationship, we can ensure that our script will properly assign information in a structured and easy-to-manage manner:

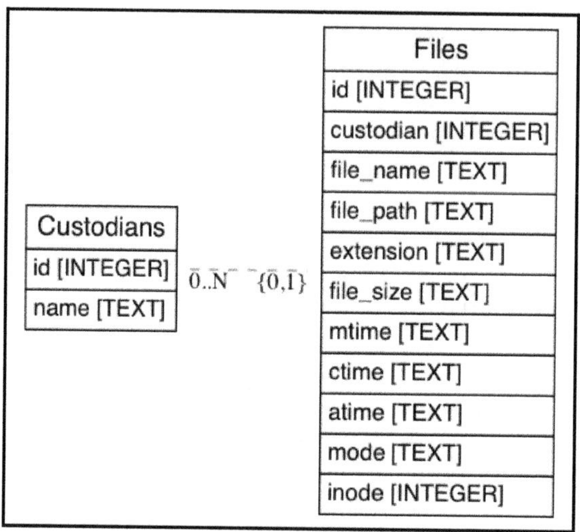

In this relational model, for example, we could have a custodian named JPriest who owns files located in a folder named `APB/`. Under this root folder, there are 40,000 files spread among 300 subdirectories, and we need to assign each of those 40,000 files to JPriest. Because custodian names may be long or complex, we want to assign JPriest an identifier, such as the integer 5, and write that to each row of the data being stored in the `Files` table. By doing this, we accomplish three things:

- We are saving space as we are storing only one character (`5`) instead of seven (JPriest) in each of the 40,000 rows
- We are maintaining a link between the JPriest user and their files
- If we ever needed to rename JPriest, we could change one row in our `Custodians` table and therefore update the custodian's name for all associated rows

Manually manipulating databases with Python – file_lister.py

As a note, this script will be designed to work only in Python 3 and was tested with Python 3.7.1. If you'd like the Python 2 version of the code after working through this section, please see `https://github.com/PacktPublishing/Learning-Python-for-Forensics` for the prior iteration.

In the first iteration of the script, we use several standard libraries to complete all of the functionality required for the full operation. Like we did in prior scripts, we are implementing `argparse`, `csv`, and `logging` for their usual purposes, which include argument handling, writing CSV reports, and logging program execution. For logging, we define our log handler, `logger`, on line 43. We have imported the `sqlite3` module to handle all database operations. Unlike our next iteration, we will only support SQLite databases through this script. The `os` module allows us to recursively step through files in a directory and any subdirectories. Finally, the `sys` module allows us to gather logging information about the system, and the `datetime` module is used to format timestamps as we encounter them on the system. This script does not require any third-party libraries. We have the following code:

```
001 """File metadata capture and reporting utility."""
002 import argparse
003 import csv
004 import datetime
005 import logging
006 import os
007 import sqlite3
008 import sys
...
038 __authors__ = ["Chapin Bryce", "Preston Miller"]
039 __date__ = 20181027
040 __description__ = '''This script uses a database to ingest and
041     report meta data information about active entries in
042      directories.'''
043 logger = logging.getLogger(__name__)
```

Following our import statements, we have our `main()` function, which takes the following user inputs: custodian name, target input directory or output file, and a path to the database to use. The `main()` function handles some high-level operations, such as adding and managing custodians, error handling, and logging. It first initializes the database and tables, and then checks whether the custodian is in the database. If it is not, that custodian is added to the database. The function allows us to handle the two possible run options: to recursively ingest the base directory, capturing all subobjects and their metadata, and to read the captured information from the database into a report using our writer functions.

The `init_db()` function, which is called by `main()`, creates the database and default tables if they do not exist. The `get_or_add_custodian()` function, in a similar manner, checks to see whether a custodian exists. If it does, it returns the ID of the custodian, otherwise it creates the custodian table. To ensure that the custodian is in the database, the `get_or_add_custodian()` function is run again after a new entry is added.

After the database has been created and the custodian table exists, the code checks whether the source is an input directory. If so, it calls `ingest_directory()` to iterate through the specified directory and scan all subdirectories to collect file-related metadata. Captured metadata is stored in the `Files` table of the database with a foreign key to the `Custodians` table to tie each custodian to their file(s). During the collection of metadata, we call the `format_timestamp()` function to cast our collected timestamps into a standard string format.

If the source is an output file, the `write_output()` function is called, passing the open database cursor, output file path, and custodian name as arguments. The script then determines whether the custodian has any responsive results in the `Files` table and passes them to the `write_html()` or `write_csv()` function, based on the output file path's extension. If the extension is `.html`, then the `write_html()` function is called to create an HTML table using Bootstrap CSS, which displays all of the responsive results for the custodian. Otherwise, if the extension is `.csv`, then the `write_csv()` function is called to write the data to a comma-delimited file. If neither of the extensions is supplied in the output file path, then a report is not generated and an error is raised that the file type could not be interpreted:

```
def main(custodian, target, db):
...
def init_db(db_path):
...
def get_or_add_custodian(conn, custodian):
...
def get_custodian(conn, custodian):
...
def ingest_directory(conn, target, custodian_id):
```

```
...
207 def format_timestamp(timestamp):
...
219 def write_output(conn, target, custodian):
...
254 def write_csv(conn, target, custodian_id):
...
280 def write_html(conn, target, custodian_id, custodian_name):
```

Now, let's look at the required arguments and the setup for this script. On lines 321 through 339, we build out the `argparse` command-line interface with the required positional arguments `CUSTODIAN` and `DB_PATH`, and the optional arguments `--input`, `--output`, and `-l`:

```
320 if __name__ == '__main__':
321     parser = argparse.ArgumentParser(
322     description=__description__,
323     epilog='Built by {}. Version {}'.format(
324         ", ".join(__authors__), __date__),
325     formatter_class=argparse.ArgumentDefaultsHelpFormatter
326     )
327     parser.add_argument(
328         'CUSTODIAN', help='Name of custodian collection is of.')
329     parser.add_argument(
330         'DB_PATH', help='File path and name of database to '
331                         'create or append metadata to.')
332     parser.add_argument(
333         '--input', help='Base directory to scan.')
334     parser.add_argument(
335         '--output', help='Output file to write to. use `.csv` '
336                          'extension for CSV and `.html` for HTML')
337     parser.add_argument(
338         '-l', help='File path and name of log file.')
339     args = parser.parse_args()
```

On lines 341 through 347, we check that either the `--input` or `--output` argument was supplied by the user. We create a variable, `arg_source`, which is a tuple containing the mode of operation and the corresponding path specified by the argument. If neither of the mode arguments were supplied, an `ArgumentError` is raised and prompts the user for an input or output. This ensures that the user provides the required arguments when there are one or more options:

```
341     if args.input:
342         arg_source = ('input', args.input)
343     elif args.output:
344         arg_source = ('output', args.output)
345     else:
```

```
346         raise argparse.ArgumentError(
347             'Please specify input or output')
```

On lines 349 through 368, we can see the log configuration that we used in previous chapters and check for the `-l` argument, making a path to the log if necessary. We also log the script version and the operating system information on lines 366 through 368:

```
349     if args.l:
350         if not os.path.exists(args.l):
351             os.makedirs(args.l) # create log directory path
352         log_path = os.path.join(args.l, 'file_lister.log')
353     else:
354         log_path = 'file_lister.log'
355
356     logger.setLevel(logging.DEBUG)
357     msg_fmt = logging.Formatter("%(asctime)-15s %(funcName)-20s"
358         "%(levelname)-8s %(message)s")
359     strhndl = logging.StreamHandler(sys.stdout)
360     strhndl.setFormatter(fmt=msg_fmt)
361     fhndl = logging.FileHandler(log_path, mode='a')
362     fhndl.setFormatter(fmt=msg_fmt)
363     logger.addHandler(strhndl)
364     logger.addHandler(fhndl)
365
366     logger.info('Starting File Lister v.' + str(__date__))
367     logger.debug('System ' + sys.platform)
368     logger.debug('Version ' + sys.version)
```

With the logging squared away, we can create a dictionary, which defines the arguments passed into the `main()` function using kwargs. Kwargs, or keyword arguments, provide a means of passing arguments as dictionary key-value pairs, where the keys match the parameter name and are assigned a corresponding value. To pass a dictionary to a function or class as kwargs instead of a value, we must specify two asterisks preceding the dictionary name, as seen on line 373. If we did not use kwargs, we would have needed to pass the `args.custodian`, `arg_source`, and `args.db_path` arguments as individual positional arguments. There is more advanced functionality with kwargs, and examples of this can be found at `https://docs.python.org/3.7/faq/programming.html`. We have the following code:

```
370     args_dict = {'custodian': args.CUSTODIAN,
371                  'target': arg_source, 'db': args.DB_PATH}
372
373     main(**args_dict)
```

Refer to the following flowchart to understand how each function is linked together:

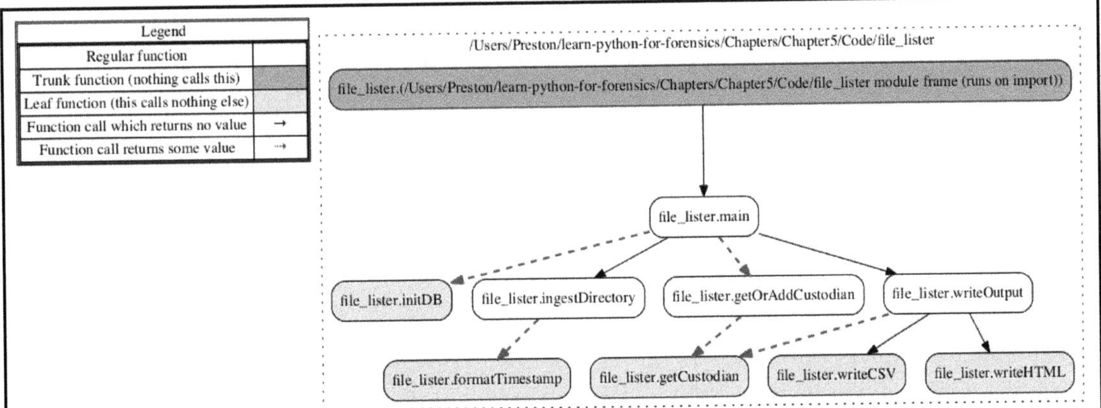

Building the main() function

The `main()` function is broken up into two phases: database initialization and input/output (I/O) processing. Database initialization, inclusive of the docstring, occurs on lines 46 through 57, where we define and document the inputs for the function. Note that the input variables match the keys of the `args_dict` that is passed as a keyword argument to the function. If `args_dict` did not have those exact keys defined, we would receive a `TypeError` when calling the function. See the following code:

```
046 def main(custodian, target, db):
047     """
048     The main function creates the database or table, logs
049         execution status, and handles errors
050     :param custodian: The name of the custodian
051     :param target: tuple containing the mode 'input' or 'output'
052         as the first elemnet and a file path as the second
053     :param db: The filepath for the database
054     :return: None
055     """
```

On line 57, we call the `init_db()` function, passing the path to the database and assigning the returned database connection to the `conn` variable. The database connection object is handled by the `sqlite3` Python library. We use this object to communicate with the database by translating all calls from Python into SQL. With the connection object, we can call the cursor object. A cursor is an object that is used to send and receive data through the connection; we will define it in the functions where we want to interact with the database, since we want to keep cursors limited in scope, whereas we can share the database connection between functions:

```
056     logger.info('Initiating SQLite database: ' + db)
057     conn = init_db(db)
```

After additional logging, we call `get_or_add_custodian()`, passing the connection object and custodian name to the function. By passing the open connection, we allow the function to interact with the database and define its own cursor. If the `custodian_id` is found, we move forward and skip the `while` loop on line 61; otherwise, we rerun the `get_or_add_custodian()` function until we have added the custodian and retrieved a custodian ID:

```
058     logger.info('Initialization Successful')
059     logger.info('Retrieving or adding custodian: ' + custodian)
060     custodian_id = get_or_add_custodian(conn, custodian)
061     while not custodian_id:
062         custodian_id = get_or_add_custodian(conn, custodian)
063     logger.info('Custodian Retrieved')
```

Once we have a custodian ID to work with, we need to determine whether the source is specified as input or output. If on line 64 the source is an `input`, then we run the `ingest_directory()` function, which iterates through the provided root directory and gathers associated metadata about any subfiles. Once complete, we commit (save) our changes to the database and log its completion:

```
064     if target[0] == 'input':
065         logger.info('Ingesting base input directory: {}'.format(
066             target[1]))
067         ingest_directory(conn, target[1], custodian_id)
068         conn.commit()
069         logger.info('Ingest Complete')
```

If the source is an `output`, the `write_output()` function is called to handle writing the output in the specified format. If the source type cannot be determined, we raise an `argparse.ArgumentError` error, stating that the arguments cannot be interpreted. After running the desired mode, we end the function by closing our database connections and log completion of the script, as follows:

```
    elif target[0] == 'output':
        logger.info('Preparing to write output: ' + target[1])
        write_output(conn, target[1], custodian)
    else:
        raise argparse.ArgumentError(
            'Could not interpret run time arguments')

    conn.close()
    logger.info('Script Completed')
```

Initializing the database with the init_db() function

The `init_db()` function is called on line 87 of the `main()` function to perform the basic tasks of creating the database and the initial structure within it. First, we need to check whether the database already exists, and if it does, connect to it and return the connection object. Regardless of whether a file exists or not, we can use the `sqlite3` library's `connect()` method to open or create a file as a database. This connection is used to allow communication between Python objects and the database. We also specifically use a cursor object, assigned as `cur` on line 94, to keep track of the position we are at among executed statements. This cursor is required to interact with our database:

```
081 def init_db(db_path):
082     """
083     The init_db function opens or creates the database
084     :param db_path: The filepath for the database
085     :return: conn, the sqlite3 database connection
086     """
087     if os.path.exists(db_path):
088         logger.info('Found Existing Database')
089         conn = sqlite3.connect(db_path)
090     else:
091         logger.info('Existing database not found. '
092                     'Initializing new database')
093         conn = sqlite3.connect(db_path)
094         cur = conn.cursor()
```

If the database does not exist, then we must create a new database, connect to it, and initialize the tables. As mentioned in the SQL section of this chapter, we must create these tables by using the `CREATE TABLE` statement, followed by the column names and their data types. In the `Custodians` table, we need to create an auto-incrementing `id` column to provide an identifier for the `name` column, which will hold the custodian's names.

To do this, we must first build our query in the `sql` variable on line 96. After assignment, we pass this variable to the `cur.execute()` method, which executes our SQL statement through the cursor object. At this point, the cursor talks to the connection object from before, which then communicates with the database. Take a look at the following code:

```
096         sql = """CREATE TABLE Custodians (
097                 cust_id INTEGER PRIMARY KEY, name TEXT);"""
098         cur.execute(sql)
```

On line 99, we create another SQL query using `PRAGMA`, which allows us to modify the database's configuration. By default, in SQLite3, foreign keys are disabled, preventing us from referencing data from one table in another. Using the `PRAGMA` statement, we can enable this feature for our database by setting `foreign_keys` to `1`:

```
099         cur.execute('PRAGMA foreign_keys = 1;')
```

We repeat the table creation process for the `Files` table, adding many more fields to account for the file metadata. On lines 100 through 105, we write out the list of field names and their associated data types. We are able to wrap this string across multiple lines by using triple quotes and have Python interpret it as a single string value. As we've already seen, we need columns to store an ID (in a similar fashion to the `Custodians` table), the filename, file path, extension, size, modified time, created time, accessed time, mode, and inode number.

The `mode` attribute specifies the permissions of the file and is based on the UNIX permissions standard, whereas the `inode` attribute is the unique number that identifies filesystem objects in UNIX-based systems. Both of these elements are further described in the *Understanding the ingest_directory() function* section, where they are extracted from the files. After creating the two tables and defining their structures, we execute the final SQL statement on line 106 and return the connection object:

```
100         sql = """CREATE TABLE Files(id INTEGER PRIMARY KEY,
101             custodian INTEGER NOT NULL, file_name TEXT,
102             file_path TEXT, extension TEXT, file_size INTEGER,
103             mtime TEXT, ctime TEXT, atime TEXT, mode TEXT,
104             inode INTEGER, FOREIGN KEY (custodian)
105             REFERENCES Custodians(cust_id));"""
106         cur.execute(sql)
```

```
        conn.commit()
    return conn
```

Checking for custodians with the get_or_add_custodian() function

At this point, the database is initialized and ready for further interaction. The `get_or_add_custodian()` function is called to check for the existence of the custodian and to pass along the ID if it is found. If the custodian does not exist, the function will add the custodian to the `Custodians` table. On line 120, we call the `get_custodian()` function to check and see whether the custodian exists. On line 122, we use a conditional to check whether `id` is not empty, and if so, assign the ID of the custodian to the `cust_id` variable. The SQLite library returns tuples for backward compatibility, the first element of which will be our ID of interest:

```
111 def get_or_add_custodian(conn, custodian):
112     """
113     The get_or_add_custodian function checks the database for a
114         custodian and returns the ID if present;
115         Or otherwise creates the custodian
116     :param conn: The sqlite3 database connection object
117     :param custodian: The name of the custodian
118     :return: The custodian ID or None
119     """
120     cust_id = get_custodian(conn, custodian)
121     cur = conn.cursor()
122     if cust_id:
123         cust_id = cust_id[0]
```

If the custodian is not found, we insert it into the table for future use. In lines 125-126, we craft a SQL statement to insert the custodian into the `Custodians` table. Note the `null` string in the `VALUES` section; this is interpreted by SQLite as a `NoneType` object. SQLite converts `NoneType` objects in our primary key field to an auto-incrementing integer. Following the `null` value is our custodian string. SQLite requires that string values be wrapped in quotes, similar to Python.

We must use double quotes to wrap our query that contains single quotes. This prevents any issues with a string breaking due to an error with the quotes. If you see a syntax error in this section of the code, be sure to check the quotes used on lines 125-126.

Finally, we execute this statement and return the empty `cust_id` variable so that the `main()` function will have to check for the custodian in the database again and rerun this function. The next pass should detect our inserted value and allow the `main()` function to proceed. We have the following code:

```
    else:
        sql = """INSERT INTO Custodians (cust_id, name) VALUES
            (null, '{}') ;""".format(custodian)
        cur.execute(sql)
        conn.commit()
    return cust_id
```

Although we could call the `get_custodian()` function here (or grab the ID after the insert) for validation purposes, we have the `main()` function check for the custodian again. Feel free to implement one of these alternative solutions and see in what ways it impacts the performance and stability of the code.

Retrieving custodians with the get_custodian() function

The `get_custodian()` function is called to retrieve the custodian ID from the SQLite database. Using a simple `SELECT` statement, we select the `id` column from the `Custodian` table, where we match the name provided by the user to the `name` column. We use the string `format()` method to insert the custodian name into the SQL statement. Note that we still have to wrap the inserted string in single quotes, as follows:

```
def get_custodian(conn, custodian):
"""
The get_custodian function checks the database for a
    custodian and returns the ID if present
:param conn: The sqlite3 database connection object
:param custodian: The name of the custodian
:return: The custodian ID
"""
cur = conn.cursor()
sql = "SELECT cust_id FROM Custodians "\
    "WHERE name='{}';".format(custodian)
```

After executing this statement, we use the `fetchone()` method on line 144 to return a single result from the statement. This is the first time our script requests data out of the database. To acquire data, we use any of the `fetchone()`, `fetchmany()`, or `fetchall()` functions to gather data from the executed statement. These three methods are only available to the cursor object. The `fetchone()` method is the better option here as we anticipate a single custodian to be returned by this statement. This custodian ID is captured and returned in the `data` variable:

```
143     cur.execute(sql)
144     data = cur.fetchone()
145     return data
```

Understanding the ingest_directory() function

The `ingest_directory()` function handles the input mode for our script and recursively captures the metadata of files from a user-supplied root directory. On line 158, we set up our database cursor before a `count` variable, which will keep count of the number of files stored in the `Files` table:

```
148     def ingest_directory(conn, target, custodian_id):
149     """
150     The ingest_directory function reads file metadata and stores
151         it in the database
152     :param conn: The sqlite3 database connection object
153     :param target: The path for the root directory to
154         recursively walk
155     :param custodian_id: The custodian ID
156     :return: None
157     """
158     cur = conn.cursor()
159     count = 0
```

The most important part of this function is the `for` loop on line 160. This loop uses the `os.walk()` method to break apart a provided directory path into an iterative array that we can step through. There are three components of the `os.walk()` method. They are generally named `root`, `folders`, and `files`. The `root` value is a string that represents the path of the base directory we are currently walking during the specific loop iteration. As we traverse through subfolders, they will be appended to the root value. The `folders` and `files` variables provide lists of folder and filenames within the current root, respectively. Although these variables may be renamed as you see fit, this is a good naming convention to prevent overwriting Python statements, such as `file` or `dir`, which are already used in Python. In this instance, though, we do not need the `folders` list from `os.walk()`, so we will name it as a single underscore (_):

```
160     for root, _, files in os.walk(target):
```

This is a common practice for assigning a value to a variable that is unused in the code. For this reason, only use a single underscore to represent unused data. Where possible, try to redesign your code to not return unwanted values.

Within the loop, we begin iterating over the `files` list to access information about each file. On line 162, we create a file-specific dictionary, `meta_data`, to store the collected information, as follows:

```
161         for file_name in files:
162             meta_data = dict()
```

On line 163, we use a try-except clause to catch any exceptions. We know we said not to do that, but hear us out first. This catch-all is in place so that any error within a discovered file does not cause the script to crash and stop. Instead, the filename and error will be written to the log before skipping that file and continuing execution. This can help an examiner quickly locate and troubleshoot specific files. This is important as some errors may occur on Windows systems due to filesystem flags and naming conventions that cause errors in Python. Different errors will then occur on macOS and Linux/UNIX systems, making it hard to predict all of the instances where the script will crash. This is an excellent example of why logging is important, as we can review errors that have been generated by our script.

Within the try-except clause, we store the different properties of the file's metadata to keys. To begin, we record the filename and full path on lines 163 and 164. Note how the dictionary keys share the name with the columns they belong to in the `Files` table. This format will make our lives easier later in the script. The file path is stored using the `os.path.join()` method, which combines separate paths into a single one using the operating system's specific path separator.

On line 167, we gather the file extension by using the `os.path.splitext()` method to split the extension after the last `.` in the filename. Since this function on line 167 creates a list, we select the last element to ensure that we store the extension. In some situations, the file may not have an extension (for example, a `.DS_Store` file), in which case the last value in the returned list is an empty string. Be aware that this script does not check file signatures to confirm that the file type matches the extension; the process of checking file signatures can be automated:

```
163             try:
164                 meta_data['file_name'] = file_name
165                 meta_data['file_path'] = os.path.join(root,
166                                                       file_name)
167                 meta_data['extension'] = os.path.splitext(
168                     file_name)[-1]
```

Exploring the os.stat() method

On line 170, we use `os.stat()` to collect our metadata for the file. This method reaches out to the system's `stat` library to gather information about the supplied file. By default, this method returns an object with all of the available data gathered about each file. Because this information varies between platforms, we have selected only the most cross-platform properties for our script, as defined in the `os` library documentation; more information can be found at `https://docs.python.org/3/library/os.html#os.stat_result`. This list includes creation time, modified time, accessed time, file mode, file size, inode number, and mode. SQLite will accept the data types in string format, though we will store them in the script with the correct data types in case we need to modify them or use special characteristics of the specific types.

The file mode is best displayed as an octal integer, so we must use the Python `oct()` function to convert it into a readable state, as shown on line 171:

```
170                 file_stats = os.stat(meta_data['file_path'])
171                 meta_data['mode'] = str(oct(file_stats.st_mode))
```

The file mode is a three-digit integer representing the read, write, and execute permissions of a file object. The permissions are defined in the following table and use the numbers 0-7 to determine the permissions that are assigned. Each digit represents permissions for the file's owner, the group the file is assigned to, and all other users. The number 777, for example, allows full permissions to anyone, and 600 means that only the owner can read and write to the file. Beyond each individual digit, octal representation allows us to assign additional permissions for a file by adding digits. For example, the value 763 grants the owner full permissions (700), read and write permissions to the group (040 + 020), and write and execute permissions to everyone else (002 + 001). You will probably never see 763 as a permission set, though it makes for a fun example here:

Permission	Description
700	Full file owner permissions
400	An owner has read permission
200	An owner has write permission
100	An owner has execute permission
070	Full group permissions
040	A group has read permission
020	A group has write permission
010	A group has execute permission
007	Full permissions for others (not in the group or the owner)
004	Others have read permission
002	Others have write permission
001	Others have execute permission

The following table shows additional file type information, which is provided by Python's `os.stat()` method. The three-hashes in the table indicate where the file permissions we just discussed are located within the number. The first two rows of the following table are self-explanatory, and symbolic links represent references to other locations in a filesystem. For example, in the following table, the value 100777 represents a regular file, with full permissions for the owner, groups, and anyone else. Although it may take time to get accustomed to this, this system is very useful for identifying the permissions of files and who has access to them:

File type	Description
040###	Directory
100###	Regular file

120###	Symbolic link

The `inode` value, a unique identifier of filesystem objects, is the next value we will capture on line 172. Although this is a feature that's only found in Linux/UNIX/macOS-based systems, Python converts the record number for NTFS into the same object for uniformity. On line 173, we assign the file size, which is represented by the number of allocated bytes as an integer. On lines 174 through 179, we assign the accessed, modified, and created timestamps to the dictionary, in that order. Each timestamp is converted from a float into a string using our `format_timestamps()` function. We have now collected the necessary data to complete a row in our `Files` table:

```
172                 meta_data['inode'] = int(file_stats.st_ino)
173                 meta_data['file_size'] = int(file_stats.st_size)
174                 meta_data['atime'] = format_timestamp(
175                     file_stats.st_atime)
176                 meta_data['mtime'] = format_timestamp(
177                     file_stats.st_mtime)
178                 meta_data['ctime'] = format_timestamp(
179                     file_stats.st_ctime)
```

The exception mentioned earlier in this section is defined on line 180 and logs any errors that are encountered while collecting metadata:

```
180             except Exception as e:
181                 logger.error(
182                     'Error processing file: {} {}'.format(
183                         meta_data.get('file_path', None),
184                         e.__str__()))
```

Lastly, outside of our try-except clause, we add the `custodian_id` to our `meta_data` dictionary so that we can store it alongside our record. We can now construct our SQL statement for inserting the new file metadata record. As we saw previously, we will construct an insert statement on line 186 and add placeholders for the column and value names. Using the `.format()` method, we will insert our `meta_data` key and value data. On line 187, we join the `meta_data` keys into a string where each key is separated by double quotes and a comma. On line 188, we join a comma-separated list of commas, inserting one question mark per value as a placeholder for our `execute()` call. An example of the generated string in the `sql` variable is shown here:

```
INSERT INTO Files
    ("custodian","ctime","mtime","extension","inode",
     "file_size","file_name","mode","atime","file_path")
VALUES
    (?, ?, ?, ?, ?, ?, ?, ?, ?, ?)
```

This allows us to then provide a list of our values, as seen within the try block on lines 189-190, to the SQLite3 Python library to craft the correct insert statement for the database. We need to convert our dictionary values into a tuple for support with SQLite3, as shown in the call on line 190:

```
185                 meta_data['custodian'] = custodian_id
186                 sql = 'INSERT INTO Files ("{}") VALUES ({})'.format(
187                     '","'.join(meta_data.keys()),
188                     ', '.join('?' for x in meta_data.values()))
189                 try:
190                     cur.execute(sql, tuple(meta_data.values()))
```

Now, we can close our except clause and provide error handling and logging for SQLite3 library errors on lines 191 through 197. After our error handling, we increment our file processing count by 1 and move to the next file, which can be found in either of our two for loops:

```
191                 except (sqlite3.OperationalError,
192                         sqlite3.IntegrityError) as e:
193                     logger.error(
194                         "Could not insert statement {}"
195                         " with values: {}".format(
196                             sql, meta_data.values()))
197                     logger.error("Error message: {}".format(e))
198                 count += 1
```

Once our innermost for loop completes, we use the `commit()` method to save the new records in our database. We also run the `commit()` method again once our outer for loop finishes, before logging that the directory ingestion is complete and providing the user with a count of files handled:

```
199         conn.commit()
200     conn.commit()
201     logger.info('Stored meta data for {} files.'.format(count))
```

Developing the format_timestamp() helper function

This comparatively small function interprets integer timestamps as human-readable strings. Because the Python `os.stat()` module returns the time as a count of seconds since the epoch, 1/1/1970, we need to use the `datetime` library to perform this transformation. Using the `datetime.datetime.fromtimestamp()` function, we can parse the float to a `datetime` object, which we name `ts_datetime` on line 211. With the date as a `datetime` object, we can now use the `strftime()` method to format the date using our desired format, `YYYY-MM-DD HH:MM:SS`, on line 212. With the string ready to be inserted into the database, we return the value to the calling function:

```
204 def format_timestamp(timestamp):
205     """
206     The format_timestamp function formats an integer to a string
207     timestamp
208     :param timestamp: An integer timestamp
209     :return: ts_format, a formatted (YYYY-MM-DD HH:MM:SS) string
210     """
211     ts_datetime = datetime.datetime.fromtimestamp(timestamp)
212     ts_format = ts_datetime.strftime('%Y-%m-%d %H:%M:%S')
213     return ts_format
```

Short utility functions like this are useful to incorporate into larger scripts. One advantage is that if we wanted to update our date format, we only have to change it in one location, versus finding every use of `strftime()`. This smaller function also increases the readability of our code. The `ingest_directory()` function is already pretty sizable, and adding this logic three times over could become confusing to the next person to review the code. These functions are useful in string formatting or common conversions, though as you are designing your own script, consider what utility functions you can create to make your life easier.

Configuring the write_output() function

If the output destination is specified by the user, the `write_output()` function is called. Once invoked, we select the custodian ID from the database using the `get_custodian()` function, which is called on line 225. If found, we need to build a new query to determine the number of files associated with the custodian using the `COUNT()` SQL function. If the custodian is not found, an error is logged to alert the user that the custodian was unresponsive, as we can see on lines 234 through 237:

```
216 def write_output(conn, target, custodian):
217     """
218     The write_output function handles writing either the CSV or
219     HTML reports
220     :param conn: The sqlite3 database connection object
221     :param target: The output filepath
222     :param custodian: Name of the custodian
223     :return: None
224     """
225     custodian_id = get_custodian(conn, custodian)
226     cur = conn.cursor()
227     if custodian_id:
228         custodian_id = custodian_id[0]
229         sql = "SELECT COUNT(id) FROM Files "\
230               "where custodian = {}".format(
231                   custodian_id)
232         cur.execute(sql)
233         count = cur.fetchone()
234     else:
235         logger.error(
236             'Could not find custodian in database. Please check '
237             'the input of the custodian name and database path')
```

If the custodian is found and the number of stored files is greater than zero, we check what type of report to generate. The conditional statements starting on line 239 check the size of `count` and the extension of the source. If `count` is not greater than zero or does not contain a value, then an error is logged on line 240. Otherwise, we check for the CSV file extension on line 241 and the HTML file extension on line 243, calling the respective function if we find a match. If the source does not end in either of those file extensions, then an error is logged, stating that the file type could not be determined. Finally, if the code reaches the else statement on line 247, we log the fact that an unknown error occurred. We can see all of this in the following code:

```
239     if not count or not count[0] > 0:
240         logger.error('Files not found for custodian')
241     elif target.endswith('.csv'):
242         write_csv(conn, target, custodian_id)
```

```
243     elif target.endswith('.html'):
244         write_html(conn, target, custodian_id, custodian)
245     elif not (target.endswith('.html')or target.endswith('.csv')):
246         logger.error('Could not determine file type')
247     else:
248         logger.error('Unknown Error Occurred')
```

Designing the write_csv() function

If the file extension is CSV, we can start iterating through the entries stored in the Files table. The SQL statement on line 261 uses the `WHERE` statement to identify only files related to the specific custodian. The `cur.description` value that's returned is a tuple of tuples, with eight elements in each of the nested tuples, representing our column names. The first value in each tuple is the column name, whereas the remaining seven are empty strings that are left in place for backward compatibility purposes. Using list comprehension on line 265, we iterate through these tuples and build the list of column names by selecting only the first element from each item in the returned tuples. This one-line statement allows us to condense a simple for loop into a single statement that generates the desired list:

```
251 def write_csv(conn, target, custodian_id):
252     """
253     The write_csv function generates a CSV report from the
254     Files table
255     :param conn: The Sqlite3 database connection object
256     :param target: The output filepath
257     :param custodian_id: The custodian ID
258     :return: None
259     """
260     cur = conn.cursor()
261     sql = "SELECT * FROM Files where custodian = {}".format(
262         custodian_id)
263     cur.execute(sql)
264 
265     cols = [description[0] for description in cur.description]
```

A list comprehension is a succinct method for generating a list with a single-line for loop. These are generally used to filter the content of a list or provide some form of transformation. On line 265, we are using it to perform a structural transformation, extracting only the first item from each element of the `cur.description` list and storing it as columns. This is because the Python SQLite bindings return the column names as a nested tuple where the first element of each subtuple is the column's name.

With the column names prepared, we log that the CSV report is being written and open the output file in `wb` mode on line 267. We then initialize a writer by calling the `csv.writer()` method on line 268 and passing the file object. After this file is opened, we write the column rows by calling on the `csv_writer` object to `writerow()`, which writes a single row.

At this point, we will loop through the results by iterating over the cursor, where it will return a row for each iteration of the loop until exiting when no more rows are responsive to the original query. For each row that's returned, we need to call the `writerow()` method again, as shown on line 272. We then flush the new data to the file on line 273 to ensure that the data is written to disk. Finally, we log that the report is complete and stored at the user-specified location. We have the following code:

```
266     logger.info('Writing CSV report')
267     with open(target, 'w', newline="") as csv_file:
268         csv_writer = csv.writer(csv_file)
269         csv_writer.writerow(cols)
270 
271         for entry in cur:
272             csv_writer.writerow(entry)
273         csv_file.flush()
274     logger.info('CSV report completed: ' + target)
```

Composing the write_html() function

If the user specifies an HTML report, the `write_html()` function is called to read data from the database, generate the HTML tags for our data, and, using Bootstrap styling, create a table with our file metadata. Because this is HTML, we can customize it to create a professional-looking report that can be converted into a PDF or viewed by anyone with a web browser. If additional HTML elements prove to be useful in your version of the report, they can easily be added to the following strings and customized with logos, highlighting by extension, responsive tables, graphs, and much more, which is possible if you use various web styles and scripts.

Since this book is focused on the design of Python scripts, we won't be diving into detail about HTML, CSS, or other web design languages. Where we use these features, we will describe the basics of why they are used and how to implement them, though we recommend using related resources (such as `http://www.w3schools.com`) to learn more about those topics if they are of interest to you.

This function begins similarly to write_csv(): we select the files that belong to the custodian in a SQL statement on line 287. Once executed, we again gather our cols using list comprehension on line 291. With our column names, we define the table_header HTML string using the join() function on our list and separating each value with <th></th> tags on line 292. For all except the first and last element, this will enclose each element in a <th>{{ element }}</th> tag. Now, we need to close the first and last element tags to ensure that they form the proper table header. For the beginning of the string, we append the <tr><th> tags to define the table row <tr> for the entire row, and the table header <th> for the first entry. Likewise, we close the table header and table row tags at the end of the string on line 293, as follows:

```
277 def write_html(conn, target, custodian_id, custodian_name):
278     """
279     The write_html function generates an HTML report from the
280         Files table
281     :param conn: The sqlite3 database connection object
282     :param target: The output filepath
283     :param custodian_id: The custodian ID
284     :return: None
285     """
286     cur = conn.cursor()
287     sql = "SELECT * FROM Files where custodian = {}".format(
288         custodian_id)
289     cur.execute(sql)
290
291     cols = [description[0] for description in cur.description]
292     table_header = '</th><th>'.join(cols)
293     table_header = '<tr><th>' + table_header + '</th></tr>'
294
295     logger.info('Writing HTML report')
```

On line 297, we open our HTML file in w mode as the html_file variable. With the file open, we begin to build our HTML code, starting with the <html><body> tags that are used to initialize HTML documents on line 298. Next, we connect to the custom style sheet that's hosted online to provide the Bootstrap styles for our table. We do this by using the <link> tag, with the type and the source of the style sheet, which is located at https://www.bootstrapcdn.com/.

Now, let's define the header of our HTML report so that we can ensure it contains the custodian ID and name. We will do this by using the <h1></h1> or heading 1 tags. For our table, we use the table tags on line 302 and the Bootstrap styles (table, table-hover, and table-striped) we would like to implement.

For additional information on Bootstrap, visit `http://getbootstrap.com`. While this script uses Bootstrap CSS version 3.3.5, explore the more recent updates to Bootstrap and see if you can implement the newer features in your code.

With this header information in the HTML string, we can write it to the file, first writing the HTML header and style sheet information on line 304, followed by the column names for our table on line 305, as follows:

```
297     with open(target, 'w') as html_file:
298         html_string = """<html><body>\n
299             <link rel="stylesheet"
300
href="https://maxcdn.bootstrapcdn.com/bootstrap/3.3.5/css/bootstrap.min.css
">
301             <h1>File Listing for Custodian ID: {}, {}</h1>\n
302             <table class='table table-hover table-striped'>\n
303             """.format(custodian_id, custodian_name)
304             html_file.write(html_string)
305             html_file.write(table_header)
```

Now, let's iterate over the records in the database and write them to the table as individual rows. We begin by joining each element in the table data tags (`<td></td>`) that specify the table cell content. We use list comprehension before joining the data on line 308 and converting it to the string value that the `join()` method requires:

```
307         for entry in cur:
308             row_data = "</td><td>".join(
309                 [str(x) for x in entry])
```

On line 310, we add a new line character (`\n`) followed by a `<tr>` table row tag and the initial `<td>` tag to open the table data for the first element. The newline character reduces the loading time in some HTML viewers, as it breaks the data into multiple lines. We also have to close the last table data tag and the entire table row, as seen at the end of line 310. The row data is written to the file on line 311. Finally, within the loop for the table rows, we `.flush()` the content to the file. With the table data built, we can close the table, body, and the HTML tags on line 313. Once outside of the `for` loop, we log the report's status and location on line 315:

```
310             html_string = "\n<tr><td>" + row_data + "</td></tr>"
311             html_file.write(html_string)
312             html_file.flush()
313         html_string = "\n</table>\n</body></html>"
314         html_file.write(html_string)
315     logger.info('HTML Report completed: ' + target)
```

Running the script

In this iteration, we have highlighted the process that's required for reading all of the file metadata of a directory recursively, storing it into a database, extracting it out of the database, and generating reports from the data. This iteration uses basic libraries to handle the necessary SQL and HTML operations in a fairly manual fashion. The next iteration focuses on using Python objects to perform this same functionality. Both iterations are final versions of the scripts and are fully functional. The separate iterations demonstrate different methods to accomplish the same task.

To run our script, we need to first supply it with the name of the custodian, the location of the database to create or read from, and the desired mode. In the first example, we specify the input mode and pass the root directory to index. In the second example, we create a CSV report with the output mode and supply an appropriate file path:

```
(py3.7.1) C:\book\chapters\chapter_05>python file_lister.py chapters ch7_listing.sqlite --input ..\chapter_07
2018-12-01 15:00:01,033 <module>          INFO     Starting File Lister v.20181027
2018-12-01 15:00:01,033 <module>          DEBUG    System win32
2018-12-01 15:00:01,038 <module>          DEBUG    Version 3.7.1 (v3.7.1:260ec2c36a, Oct 20 2018, 14:57:15) [MSC v.1915 64 bit (AMD64)]
2018-12-01 15:00:01,040 main              INFO     Initiating SQLite database: ch7_listing.sqlite
2018-12-01 15:00:01,042 init_db           INFO     Existing database not found. Initializing new database
2018-12-01 15:00:01,103 main              INFO     Initialization Successful
2018-12-01 15:00:01,103 main              INFO     Retrieving or adding custodian: chapters
2018-12-01 15:00:01,129 main              INFO     Custodian Retrieved
2018-12-01 15:00:01,129 main              INFO     Ingesting base input directory: ..\chapter_07
2018-12-01 15:00:01,234 ingest_directory  INFO     Stored meta data for 21 files.
2018-12-01 15:00:01,234 main              INFO     Ingest Complete
2018-12-01 15:00:01,239 main              INFO     Script Completed

(py3.7.1) C:\book\chapters\chapter_05>python file_lister.py chapters ch7_listing.sqlite --output  chapters.csv
2018-12-01 15:01:17,180 <module>          INFO     Starting File Lister v.20181027
2018-12-01 15:01:17,180 <module>          DEBUG    System win32
2018-12-01 15:01:17,183 <module>          DEBUG    Version 3.7.1 (v3.7.1:260ec2c36a, Oct 20 2018, 14:57:15) [MSC v.1915 64 bit (AMD64)]
2018-12-01 15:01:17,185 main              INFO     Initiating SQLite database: ch7_listing.sqlite
2018-12-01 15:01:17,186 init_db           INFO     Found Existing Database
2018-12-01 15:01:17,188 main              INFO     Initialization Successful
2018-12-01 15:01:17,188 main              INFO     Retrieving or adding custodian: chapters
2018-12-01 15:01:17,190 main              INFO     Custodian Retrieved
2018-12-01 15:01:17,195 main              INFO     Preparing to write output: chapters.csv
2018-12-01 15:01:17,196 write_csv         INFO     Writing CSV report
2018-12-01 15:01:17,199 write_csv         INFO     CSV report completed: chapters.csv
2018-12-01 15:01:17,200 main              INFO     Script Completed
```

The output of the preceding script can be viewed in the following screenshot. Here, we have simply created a generic CSV report containing the captured metadata of the indexed files for this chapter's custodian:

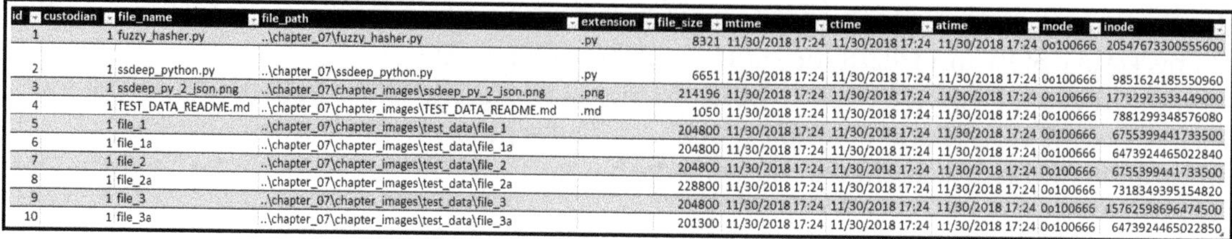

id	custodian	file_name	file_path	extension	file_size	mtime	ctime	atime	mode	inode
1	1	fuzzy_hasher.py	..\chapter_07\fuzzy_hasher.py	.py	8321	11/30/2018 17:24	11/30/2018 17:24	11/30/2018 17:24	0o100666	20547673300555600
2	1	ssdeep_python.py	..\chapter_07\ssdeep_python.py	.py	6651	11/30/2018 17:24	11/30/2018 17:24	11/30/2018 17:24	0o100666	9851624185550960
3	1	ssdeep_py_2_json.png	..\chapter_07\chapter_images\ssdeep_py_2_json.png	.png	214196	11/30/2018 17:24	11/30/2018 17:24	11/30/2018 17:24	0o100666	17732923533449000
4	1	TEST_DATA_README.md	..\chapter_07\chapter_images\TEST_DATA_README.md	.md	1050	11/30/2018 17:24	11/30/2018 17:24	11/30/2018 17:24	0o100666	7881299348576080
5	1	file_1	..\chapter_07\chapter_images\test_data\file_1		204800	11/30/2018 17:24	11/30/2018 17:24	11/30/2018 17:24	0o100666	6755399441733500
6	1	file_1a	..\chapter_07\chapter_images\test_data\file_1a		204800	11/30/2018 17:24	11/30/2018 17:24	11/30/2018 17:24	0o100666	6473924465022840
7	1	file_2	..\chapter_07\chapter_images\test_data\file_2		204800	11/30/2018 17:24	11/30/2018 17:24	11/30/2018 17:24	0o100666	6755399441733500
8	1	file_2a	..\chapter_07\chapter_images\test_data\file_2a		228800	11/30/2018 17:24	11/30/2018 17:24	11/30/2018 17:24	0o100666	7318349395154820
9	1	file_3	..\chapter_07\chapter_images\test_data\file_3		204800	11/30/2018 17:24	11/30/2018 17:24	11/30/2018 17:24	0o100666	15762598696474500
10	1	file_3a	..\chapter_07\chapter_images\test_data\file_3a		201300	11/30/2018 17:24	11/30/2018 17:24	11/30/2018 17:24	0o100666	6473924465022850

Automating databases further – file_lister_peewee.py

In this iteration, we will use third-party Python modules to automate our SQL and HTML setup further. This will introduce extra overhead; however, our script will be simpler to implement and more streamlined, which will allow us to easily develop further functionality. Developing with an eye toward the future helps prevent us from rewriting the entire script for every minor feature request.

We have imported the majority of the standard libraries required in the prior version and added the third-party `unicodecsv` module (version 0.14.1). This module wraps around the built-in `csv` module and automatically provides Unicode support for the CSV output. To keep things familiar, we can even name it `csv` by using the `import...as...` statement on line 8. As mentioned previously in this chapter, `peewee` (version 2.8.0) and `jinja2` (version 2.8) are the two libraries that can handle our SQLite and HTML operations. As these last three imports are third-party libraries, they will need to be installed on the user's machine for our code to run properly and can be done so with `pip`:

```
001 """File metadata capture and reporting utility."""
002 import argparse
003 import datetime
004 from io import open
005 import logging
006 import os
007 import sys
008 import unicodecsv as csv
009 import peewee
010 import jinja2
```

Following the import statements and license, we define our common script metadata and logging handler. On line 46, we add the `database_proxy` object, which is used to create the Peewee base model for the `Custodian` and `Files` class tables. We also add the `get_template()` function, which builds a template HTML table using `jinja2`. The other functions largely resemble their counterparts in the previous iteration, with minor adjustments here and there. However, we have removed the `get_custodian()` function as Peewee has that functionality builtin:

```
040 __authors__ = ["Chapin Bryce", "Preston Miller"]
041 __date__ = 20181027
042 __description__ = '''This script uses a database to ingest and
043     report meta data information about active entries in
044     directories.'''
045 logger = logging.getLogger(__name__)
046 database_proxy = peewee.Proxy()
047
048 class BaseModel(peewee.Model):
...
052 class Custodians(BaseModel):
...
055 class Files(BaseModel):
...
069 def get_template():
...
106 def main(custodian, target, db):
...
138 def init_db(db):
...
150 def get_or_add_custodian(custodian):
...
167 def ingest_directory(source, custodian_model):
...
216 def format_timestamp(ts):
...
226 def write_output(source, custodian_model):
...
253 def write_csv(source, custodian_model):
...
282 def write_html(source, custodian_model):
```

The code block under the `if __name__ == '__main__'` conditional that defines command-line arguments and sets up logging is identical to the prior iteration. We will not repeat these implementation details here as we can simply copy and paste the section from the previous iteration, saving a few trees. While that section has remained unchanged, the overall flow of our script has seen minor modifications, as shown in the following flow diagram:

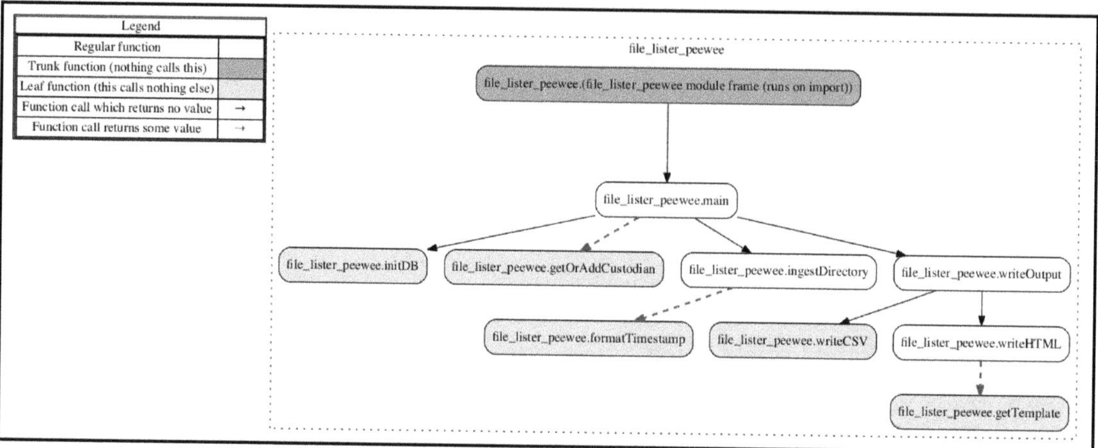

Peewee setup

Peewee, the object relational manager library that was described at the beginning of this chapter, is excellent at database management in Python. It uses Python classes to define settings for the database, including table configurations, the location of the database, and how to handle different Python data types. On line 46, we must first create an anonymous database connection using the Peewee `Proxy()` class, which allows us to redirect the information into the previously specified format. This variable must be declared before any Peewee operations, as per its documentation (`http://docs.peewee-orm.com/en/3.6.0/`).

Following the initialization of the proxy, we define our first Python class used in this book, thus creating a `BaseModel` class that defines the database to use. As part of the Peewee specification, we must link the `database_proxy` to the `database` variable within the `Meta` class of our `BaseModel` object.

While this required configuration may not make the most sense at the moment, continue through the rest of this chapter and revisit this section after completing and running the script, as the purpose of these modules will become clearer. Additionally, the aforementioned documentation does an excellent job at demonstrating the features and the usage of Peewee.

We must include the base model, as defined on lines 48 through 50, as the minimum setup for Peewee to create the database:

```
046 database_proxy = peewee.Proxy()
047
048 class BaseModel(peewee.Model):
049     class Meta:
050         database = database_proxy
```

Next, we create the `Custodians` table that's defined on line 60. This table inherits the `BaseModel` properties and therefore has the `BaseModel` class within its parentheses. This is usually used to define arguments that are needed for a function, but with classes, it can also allow us to assign a parent class to inherit data from. In this script, the `BaseModel` class is the child of `peewee.Model` and the parent to the `Custodians` and (soon to be discussed) `Files` tables. Keep in mind that Peewee describes tables as class models and that the library will be creating a table named `Custodians` for us; more on this in a bit.

After initialization, we add a text field, `name`, to the `Custodians` table on line 61. The `unique=True` keyword creates an auto-incrementing index column in addition to our `name` column. This table configuration will be used later to create the table, and then insert data into it and retrieve information out of it:

```
052 class Custodians(BaseModel):
053     name = peewee.TextField(unique=True)
```

The `Files` table has many more fields and several new data types. As we already know, SQLite only manages the text, integers, none, and BLOB data types, and so a few of these types may look out of place. Using the `DateTimeField` as an example, Peewee can take any Python `date` or `datetime` object. Peewee will automatically store it as a text value in the database and can even preserve its original time zone. When the data is called out of the table, Peewee attempts to convert this value back into a `datetime` object or into a formatted string. Although the date is still stored as a text value in the database, Peewee transforms the data in transit to provide better support and functionality in Python. Although we could replicate this functionality manually, like we did in our prior script, this is one of the many useful features that are bundled into Peewee.

On lines 56 through 66, we create typed columns, which reflect primary and foreign keys, text, timestamps, and integers. The `PrimaryKeyField` specifies unique and primary key attributes and is assigned to the `id` column. The `ForeignKeyField` has the `Custodians` class as the argument, as Peewee uses this to relate it back to the index in the `Custodians` class we defined. Following the two special key fields are a series of fields that we described earlier in this chapter:

```
055 class Files(BaseModel):
056     id = peewee.PrimaryKeyField(unique=True, primary_key=True)
057     custodian = peewee.ForeignKeyField(Custodians)
058     file_name = peewee.TextField()
059     file_path = peewee.TextField()
060     extension = peewee.TextField()
061     file_size = peewee.IntegerField()
062     atime = peewee.DateTimeField()
063     mtime = peewee.DateTimeField()
064     ctime = peewee.DateTimeField()
065     mode = peewee.TextField()
066     inode = peewee.IntegerField()
```

This completes the entire setup for the database we created previously using a SQL query in the first script. Although it is lengthier in comparison, it does prevent us from having to write our own SQL queries and, when working with larger databases, it is even more essential. For example, a larger script with many modules would greatly benefit from using Peewee to define and handle database connections. Not only would it provide uniformity across the modules, it also allows cross-compatibility with different database backends. Later in this chapter, we will showcase how to change the database type between PostgreSQL, MySQL, and SQLite. Although the Peewee setup is verbose, it adds many features and saves us from having to develop our own functions to handle database transactions.

Jinja2 setup

Now, let's discuss the configuration of the other new module. Jinja2 allows us to create powerful text templates using a Pythonic syntax for text expansion and logic evaluation. Templates also allow us to develop a reusable block of text versus needing to build our table rows and columns line by line within our Python script's `for` loops. Although the prior script takes a simplistic approach by forming an HTML file from strings, this template is more robust, dynamic, and most importantly, more sustainable.

This function defines one variable, `html_string`, which holds our Jinja2 template. This string captures all of the HTML tags and data to be processed by Jinja2. Although we place this information in a single variable, we could also place the text in a file to avoid the extra line count in our code. On lines 76 and 77, we can see identical information to the previous iteration's `write_html()` function:

```
069 def get_template():
070     """
071     The get_template function returns a basic template for our
072     HTML report
073     :return: Jinja2 Template
074     """
075     html_string = """
076         <html>\n<head>\n<link rel="stylesheet"
077         href="https://maxcdn.bootstrapcdn.com/bootstrap/3.3.5/
css/bootstrap.min.css">
```

On lines 78 through 80, we open the <body> and <h1> header tags, followed by a string containing two instances of a Python object wrapped in spaced double curly braces (`{{ ... }}`). Jinja2 looks for a provided dictionary key or object name that matches the name of the string inside of the spaced braces. In the case of lines 79 and 80, the `custodian` variable is an object with `id` and `name` attributes. Using the same syntax as in Python, we can call the object's attribute and insert them into the HTML when the template is executed:

```
078         </head>\n<body>\n<h1>
079         File Listing for Custodian {{ custodian.id }},
080         {{ custodian.name }}</h1>\n
```

The <table> tag, on line 81, specifies the Bootstrap CSS classes we use to style our table. On line 82, we open the table row <tr> tag, followed by a newline `\n` character and a new template operator. The curly braces surrounding percentage symbols (`{% ... %}`) indicate to Jinja2 that the template contains an operation, such as a loop, that it needs to evaluate. In our case, on line 83 we start a for loop, similar in syntax to Python's for loop, though missing the closing colon. Skipping ahead to line 85, we use the same syntax to surround the `endfor` statement, notifying Jinja2 that the loop is complete. We must do this because the HTML is not tab or space sensitive and cannot automatically determine the boundary of a loop like Python's indented code.

It is a good practice to include spaces between the Jinja2 template syntax and the value we would like Jinja2 to insert into the configured placeholders. For example, `{{ Document_Title }}` reads a lot easier than `{{Document_Title}}`.

On line 84, we then wrap the newly defined header variable in the table header <th> tags. After the loop completes, we close the table row <tr> tag on line 86. Through this loop, we have generated a table row, <tr>, containing a list of the table headers, <th>, as follows:

```
081         <table class="table table-hover table-striped">\n
082         <tr>\n
083         {% for header in table_headers %}
084             <th>{{ header }}</th>
085         {% endfor %}
086         </tr>\n
```

Next, we open a new loop to iterate over each reported column, creating a new table row <tr> and wrapping each element in a table data <td> tag. Because each column of the database is an attribute of the Peewee-returned row object, we can specify the column name using the following format: entry.column_name. Through this simple for loop, we build a table in an easy-to-read and extensible format:

```
087         {% for entry in file_listing %}
088             <tr>
089                 <td>{{ entry.id }}</td>
090                 <td>{{ entry.custodian.name }}</td>
091                 <td>{{ entry.file_name }}</td></td>
092                 <td>{{ entry.file_path }}</td>
093                 <td>{{ entry.extension }}</td>
094                 <td>{{ entry.file_size }}</td>
095                 <td>{{ entry.atime }}</td>
096                 <td>{{ entry.mtime }}</td>
097                 <td>{{ entry.ctime }}</td>
098                 <td>{{ entry.mode }}</td>
099                 <td>{{ entry.inode }}</td>
100             </tr>\n
101         {% endfor %}
```

After the {% endfor %} statement, we can complete this HTML template by closing the open HTML tags and closing the multiline string with three double quotes. With the html_string built, we call the Jinja2 templating engine to interpret the built string. To do so, we call and return the output of the jinja2.Template() function on line 103. This allows us to use this template whenever we need to generate an HTML report. We could have also supplied Jinja2 with an HTML file using the same markup as the template to load. This is especially helpful when building more complex or multi-page HTML content:

```
102         </table>\n</body>\n</html>"""
103     return jinja2.Template(html_string)
```

Updating the main() function

This function is almost identical to the `main()` function we saw in the previous iteration, albeit with a few exceptions. To begin, on line 117 we do not need to catch a returned value from `init_db()` as `peewee` handles that for us after initialization. We have also removed the `while` loop when calling `get_or_add_custodian`, as the logic of the function has been supplemented by Peewee, rendering the sanity check unnecessary. We assign the returned custodian table to a variable named `custodian_model` since Peewee refers to each table as a model.

In our case, the `Custodians` and `Files` classes are models in Peewee that represent the `Custodians` and `Files` tables in SQLite. In Peewee terms, a set of data returned from one model is referred to as a model instance.

The data returned on line 120 is identical in nature to what was returned by the `SELECT` statements in the previous instance of the script, though it is a model instance that's handled by Peewee:

```
106 def main(custodian, target, db):
107     """
108     The main function creates the database or table, logs
109         execution status, and handles errors
110     :param custodian: The name of the custodian
111     :param target: tuple containing the mode 'input' or 'output'
112         as the first element and its arguments as the second
113     :param db: The file path for the database
114     :return: None
115     """
116     logger.info('Initializing Database')
117     init_db(db)
118     logger.info('Initialization Successful')
119     logger.info('Retrieving or adding custodian: ' + custodian)
120     custodian_model = get_or_add_custodian(custodian)
```

The third modification involves modifying how we handle the different modes for our script. Now, we only need to provide the `target` and the `custodian_model` variables since we can access the database via the `peewee` model classes that we have already built. This behavior will be illustrated within each function to demonstrate how to insert and access data in the tables. The remainder of the function remains the same from our prior iteration:

```
121     if target[0] == 'input':
122         logger.info('Ingesting base input directory: {}'.format(
123             target[1]))
```

```
        ingest_directory(target[1], custodian_model)
        logger.info('Ingesting Complete')
    elif target[0] == 'output':
        logger.info(
            'Preparing to write output for custodian: {}'.format(
                custodian))
        write_output(target[1], custodian_model)
        logger.info('Output Complete')
    else:
        logger.error('Could not interpret run time arguments')

    logger.info('Script Complete')
```

Adjusting the init_db() function

The `init_db()` function is where we define the database type (for example, PostgreSQL, MySQL, or SQLite). Although we are using SQLite in this example, we could use another database type to call a separate `peewee` function on line 144, such as `PostgresqlDatabase()` or `MySQLDatabase()`. On line 144, we must pass the path to the file we want Peewee to write the database to. If we prefer to only have the database temporarily, we could pass the special string `:memory:` to have Peewee host the SQLite database in memory. There are two downsides to the memory option: one is that the database is not persistent after the script exits, and the second is the database's contents must fit in memory, which may not be possible on older machines or with large databases. With our use case, we must write the database to disk as we may wish to rerun the script against the same database to create additional preservations or reports:

```
138 def init_db(db):
139     """
140 The init_db function opens or creates the database
141     :param db_path: The file path for the database
142     :return: conn, the sqlite3 database connection
143     """
144     database = peewee.SqliteDatabase(db)
```

After creating our database object, we have to initialize the `database_proxy` we created on line 46 and update it to reference the newly created SQLite database. This proxy connection tells Peewee how to route the data from the models into our SQLite instance.

We had to create this proxy earlier to allow us to specify the model data before we initiate the database connection. The use of this proxy also allowed us to ask the user where they'd like to store the database, and through a proxy, we can create a placeholder that we can later assign to the SQLite (or other) database handler.

More information about proxy usage is available in the Peewee documentation at `http://docs.peewee-orm.com/en/3.6.0/peewee/database.html?highlight=proxy#dynamically-defining-a-database`.

Once connected to the proxy, we can create the necessary tables, thus calling the `create_tables()` method on our Peewee database object. As you can see, we had to create a list of the models first so that when we called `create_tables()`, we could reference the tables (and their schemas) to create.

The `safe=True` argument is required here as we want to ignore the table if it exists in the database so that we do not overwrite or lose data. If we were to expand the functionality of the tool or needed another table, we would need to remember to add it to the list on line 146 so that the table would be created. As mentioned in the `main()` function, we do not need to return any connection or cursor object here, as the data flows through the `peewee` model classes we defined earlier:

```
145 database_proxy.initialize(database)
146 table_list = [Custodians, Files] # Update with any new tables
147 database.create_tables(table_list, safe=True)
```

Modifying the get_or_add_custodian() function

This function is much simpler than the prior iteration. All we must do is call the `get_or_create()` method on our `Custodians` model and pass the field identifier, `name`, and the value it should respond to, `custodian`. With this call, we will have an instance from the model and a Boolean value of whether the row was created or not. Using this `created` Boolean value, we can add a logging statement to alert the user that a custodian was either added to the database or that an existing custodian was retrieved. On line 164, we return the model instance to the calling function, as follows:

```
150 def get_or_add_custodian(custodian):
151     """
152     The get_or_add_custodian function gets the custodian by name
153         or adds it to the table
154     :param custodian: The name of the custodian
155     :return: custodian_model, custodian peewee model instance
```

```
    """
    custodian_model, created = Custodians.get_or_create(
        name=custodian)
    if created:
        logger.info('Custodian added')
    else:
        logger.info('Custodian retrieved')

    return custodian_model
```

Improving the ingest_directory() function

While one of the more complex functions in this script, it is almost identical to the prior iteration, as the method to gather this information has not varied. The new additions here include the initialization on line 177 of a list we will use to collect the dictionaries of file metadata and the assignment of the passed `custodian_model` instance instead of an integer value for the custodian. We also generate the `ddate` value, set to a default timestamp, to insert into `peewee` in the case that the script is unable to retrieve a date value and needs to store a partial record. The default timestamp values will be set to the minimum value for Python's `datetime` library to ensure that date encoding and decoding are still functional.

On line 207, we append the `meta_data` dictionary to the `file_data` list. What's missing, however, is the code to build a complex SQL insert statement and a list of column names and their values. Instead, we iterate over the `file_data` list and write the data in a more efficient manner, as described in a moment; for now, we have the following code:

```
167 def ingest_directory(source, custodian_model):
168     """
169     The ingest_directory function reads file metadata and stores
170         it in the database
171     :param source: The path for the root directory to
172         recursively walk
173     :param custodian_model: Peewee model instance for the
174         custodian
175     :return: None
176     """
177     file_data = []
178     for root, _, files in os.walk(source):
179         for file_name in files:
180             ddate = datetime.datetime.min
181             meta_data = {
182                 'file_name': None, 'file_path': None,
183                 'extension': None, 'mode': -1, 'inode': -1,
```

```
            'file_size': -1, 'atime': ddate, 'mtime': ddate,
            'ctime': ddate, 'custodian': custodian_model.id}
        try:
            meta_data['file_name'] = os.path.join(file_name)
            meta_data['file_path'] = os.path.join(root,
                file_name)
            meta_data['extension'] = os.path.splitext(
                file_name)[-1]

            file_stats = os.stat(meta_data['file_path'])
            meta_data['mode'] = str(oct(file_stats.st_mode))
            meta_data['inode'] = str(file_stats.st_ino)
            meta_data['file_size'] = str(file_stats.st_size)
            meta_data['atime'] = format_timestamp(
                file_stats.st_atime)
            meta_data['mtime'] = format_timestamp(
                file_stats.st_mtime)
            meta_data['ctime'] = format_timestamp(
                file_stats.st_ctime)
        except Exception as e:
            logger.error(
                'Error processing file: {} {}'.format(
                    meta_data['file_path'], e.__str__()))
        file_data.append(meta_data)
```

On line 209, we start to insert file metadata into the database. Because we may have several thousands of lines of data in our list, we need to batch the inserts to the database to prevent any resource exhaustion issues. The loop on 209 uses the `range` function, starting at `0` and continuing through the length of the `file_data` list in increments of `50`. This means that `x` will be an increment of `50` until we reach the last element, where it will catch all remaining items.

By doing this, on line 210, we can insert data into `Files` using the `.insert_many()` method. Within the insert, we access entries from `x` through `x+50` to insert `50` elements of the list at a time. This method is a change of philosophy from the previous iteration where we inserted each line as it was gathered. Here, we are inserting, batches of rows at the same time using a simplified statement to perform the `INSERT` actions. Finally, on line 211, we need to execute each task that we have performed to commit the entries to the database. At the end of the function, we log the count of the files that have been inserted, as follows:

```
209     for x in range(0, len(file_data), 50):
210         task = Files.insert_many(file_data[x:x+50])
211         task.execute()
212     logger.info('Stored meta data for {} files.'.format(
213         len(file_data)))
```

Feel free to adjust the unit of 50 rows to execute as an insert. Tweaking this number on your system may produce improved performance, although this sweet spot tends to vary depending on the available resources.

You may also want to look into inserting records once our `file_data` list gets to a certain length to help with memory management. For example, if the `file_data` list exceeds 500 records, pause the collection, insert the whole list (that is, 50 records at a time), clear the list, and then resume the metadata collection. On larger collections, you should notice a significant reduction in memory usage.

A closer look at the format_timestamp() function

This function serves the same purpose as the prior iteration, but returns a `datetime` object instead, since Peewee uses this object to write the data to the cell for `datetime` values. As we saw in the previous iteration, by using the `fromtimestamp()` method, we can convert the integer date value into a `datetime` object with ease. We can return the `datetime` object as is because Peewee handles the rest of the string formatting and conversion for us. This is shown in the following code:

```
216 def format_timestamp(ts):
217     """
218     The format_timestamp function converts an integer into a
219     datetime object
220     :param ts: An integer timestamp
221     :return: A datetime object
222     """
223     return datetime.datetime.fromtimestamp(ts)
```

Converting the write_output() function

In this function, we can see how to query a `peewee` model instance. On line 235, we need to select a count of files where the custodian is equal to the custodian's `id`. We first call `select()` on the model to signify we wish to select data, followed by the `where()` method to specify the column name, `Files.custodian`, and the value, `custodian_model.id`, to evaluate. This is followed by the `count()` method to provide an integer of the number of responsive results. Note that the `count` variable is an integer, not a tuple, like it was in the previous iteration:

```
226 def write_output(source, custodian_model):
227     """
```

```
228     The write_output function handles writing either the CSV or
229         HTML reports
230     :param source: The output filepath
231     :param custodian_model: Peewee model instance for the
232         custodian
233     :return: None
234     """
235     count = Files.select().where(
236         Files.custodian == custodian_model.id).count()
237
238     logger.info("{} files found for custodian.".format(count))
```

On line 240, we follow the same logic from the prior iteration to check and see whether some lines were responsive, followed by statements to validate the output extension to engage the correct writer or provide the user's accurate error information. Note that, this time, we pass along the custodian model instance versus an `id` or name on lines 243 and 247, as Peewee performs operations best on existing model instances:

```
240     if not count:
241         logger.error('Files not found for custodian')
242     elif source.endswith('.csv'):
243         write_csv(source, custodian_model)
244     elif source.endswith('.html'):
245         write_html(source, custodian_model)
246     elif not (source.endswith('.html') or \
247         source.endswith('.csv')):
248         logger.error('Could not determine file type')
249     else:
250         logger.error('Unknown Error Occurred')
```

Simplifying the write_csv() function

The `write_csv()` function uses a new method from the `peewee` library, allowing us to retrieve data from the database as dictionaries. Using the familiar `Files.select().where()` statement, we append the `dicts()` method to convert the result into Python dictionaries. This dictionary format is an excellent input for our reports, as the built-in CSV module has a class named `DictWriter`. As its name suggests, this class allows us to pass a dictionary of information to be written as a row of data in a CSV file. Now that we have our query staged, we can log to the user that we are starting to write the CSV report:

```
253 def write_csv(source, custodian_model):
254     """
255     The write_csv function generates a CSV report from the Files
256         table
```

```
    :param source: The output filepath
    :param custodian_model: Peewee model instance for the
        custodian
    :return: None
    """
    query = Files.select().where(
        Files.custodian == custodian_model.id).dicts()
    logger.info('Writing CSV report')
```

Next, we define our column names for our CSV writer and open the user-specified output file using the `with...as...` statement. To initialize the `csv.DictWriter` class, we pass the open file object and column headers that correspond to the table's column names (and therefore the dictionary key names). After initialization, we call the `writeheader()` method and write the table's header at the top of the spreadsheet. Finally, to write the row content, we open a `for` loop on our query object to iterate over the rows and write them to the file with the `.writerow()` method. Using the `enumerate` method, we can provide the user with a status update every 10,000 rows to let them know that our code is hard at work for larger file reports. After writing those status updates (and rows, of course), we add some additional log messages for the user and exit the function. Although we are calling the `csv` library, remember that it is actually our `unicodecsv` import. This means that we will encounter less encoding errors while generating our output versus using the standard `csv` library:

```
    cols = [u'id', u'custodian', u'file_name', u'file_path',
        u'extension', u'file_size', u'ctime', u'mtime',
        u'atime', u'mode', u'inode']

    with open(source, 'wb') as csv_file:
        csv_writer = csv.DictWriter(csv_file, cols)
        csv_writer.writeheader()
        for counter, row in enumerate(query):
            csv_writer.writerow(row)
            if counter % 10000 == 0:
                logger.debug('{:,} lines written'.format(counter))
        logger.debug('{:,} lines written'.format(counter))

    logger.info('CSV Report completed: ' + source)
```

Condensing the write_html() function

We will need the `get_template()` function we designed earlier to generate our HTML report. On line 291, we call this pre-built Jinja2 template object and store it in the `template` variable. When referencing the template, we need to provide a dictionary with three keys: `table_headers`, `file_listing`, and `custodian`. These three keys are required as they are what we chose as placeholders in our template. On line 292, we build out the table headers as a list of strings, formatted in the order we wish to display them:

```
282 def write_html(source, custodian_model):
283     """
284     The write_html function generates an HTML report from the
285         Files table
286     :param source: The output file path
287     :param custodian_model: Peewee model instance for the
288         custodian
289     :return: None
290     """
291     template = get_template()
292     table_headers = [
293         'Id', 'Custodian', 'File Name', 'File Path',
294         'File Extension', 'File Size', 'Created Time',
295         'Modified Time', 'Accessed Time', 'Mode', 'Inode']
```

Afterwards, we create our `file_data` list for the `file_listing` key on line 296 by using a similar `select` statement that's found in the CSV function. This list allows us to access the attributes individually within the template, as specified earlier. We could have placed this logic within the template file as well, but we thought it best to place malleable logic in a function versus a template. Take a look at lines 296 and 297:

```
296     file_data = Files.select().where(
297         Files.custodian == custodian_model.id)
```

With all three of these elements gathered, we create a dictionary with the keys to match the data in our template on line 299. After a log statement, we open the source using a `with...as...` statement. To write the template data, we call the `render()` method on our `template` object, passing our already built dictionary as a `kwarg` on line 307. The `render()` method evaluates the statements and logic found in the template and places the provided data in the correct location to form an HTML report. This method also returns the raw HTML as a string, so we have encapsulated it in a `write()` call to immediately write the data to the file. Once written, we log the path to the source, as well as its successful completion:

```
299     template_dict = {
300         'custodian': custodian_model,
```

```
            'table_headers': table_headers,
            'file_listing': file_data}

    logger.info('Writing HTML report')

    with open(source, 'w') as html_file:
        html_file.write(template.render(**template_dict))

    logger.info('HTML Report completed: ' + source)
```

Running our new and improved script

This iteration highlights the use of additional Python third-party libraries to handle many of the operations we previously performed in a more manual manner. In this instance, we used Peewee and Jinja2 to further automate database management and HTML reporting. These two libraries are popular methods for handling this type of data and are either bundled into or have ports for other Python suites, such as Flask and Django.

In addition, this iteration closely resembles the first to demonstrate the differences in the two methods in a clearer manner. One of the goals of this book is to introduce as many methods for performing a task in Python as possible. The purpose of this chapter is not to create a better iteration, but to showcase different methods to accomplish the same tasks and add new skills to our toolbox. This is the last chapter where we will be creating multiple iterations of a script; the chapters going forward are focused on more expansive singular scripts as we begin to expand on our forensic coding capabilities.

Note that the way in which we execute our script has not changed. We still need to specify a custodian, a path to a database, and the type of mode. You may notice that this script is considerably slower than our previous script. Sometimes, when using automated solutions, our code can suffer due to additional overhead or the inefficient implementation of the module. Here, we've lost some efficiency by moving away from a more bare-bones and manual process. However, this script is more maintainable and does not require the developer to have in-depth knowledge of SQL.

For this iteration, we opted to generate our Bootstrap-based HTML report. What this report lacks in analytical capacity, it gains in portability and simplicity. This is a professional looking page, thanks to Bootstrap, and can be searched for specific files of interest or printed out for those that prefer the paper-and-pen approach:

File Listing for Custodian 1, lpff

Id	Custodian	File Name	File Path	File Extension	File Size	Created Time	Modified Time	Accessed Time	Mode	Inode
1	lpff	.DS_Store	./.DS_Store		8196	2018-12-04 18:32:06.271613	2019-01-06 09:49:11.716346	2019-01-06 09:49:11.716346	0o100644	8596377387
2	lpff	cover.png	./cover.png	.cover	25433	2018-12-11 08:14:07.775540	2018-12-11 08:14:07.775540	2018-12-11 08:14:07.775540	0o100755	8596372884
3	lpff	README.md	./README.md	.md	817	2018-12-11 08:14:07.777037	2016-06-07 13:12:53	2018-05-05 16:16:08.056954	0o100755	8596372883
4	lpff	metadata_parser.py	./chapter_08/metadata_parser.py	.py	5339	2018-12-11 08:21:03.883265	2018-12-03 07:49:23.772684	2018-12-03 07:49:23.772684	0o100755	8611348725
5	lpff	img_42.jpg	./chapter_08/img_42.jpg	.jpg	426508	2018-12-11 08:21:03.797925	2018-12-01 10:42:18.516989	2018-12-01 10:42:18.516989	0o100755	8611319406
6	lpff	kml_writer.py	./chapter_08/writers/kml_writer.py	.py	2882	2018-12-11 08:21:04.445378	2018-12-03 07:49:23.777603	2018-12-03 07:49:23.777603	0o100755	8611348734
7	lpff	__init__.py	./chapter_08/writers/__init__.py	.py	1348	2018-12-11 08:21:03.956158	2018-12-03 07:49:23.776738	2018-12-03 07:49:23.776738	0o100755	8611348732
8	lpff	csv_writer.py	./chapter_08/writers/csv_writer.py	.py	2615	2018-12-11 08:21:04.213078	2018-12-03 07:49:23.777187	2018-12-03 07:49:23.777187	0o100755	8611348733
9	lpff	office_parser.py	./chapter_08/plugins/office_parser.py	.py	6343	2019-01-06 07:48:05.564649	2019-01-06 07:47:50.172905	2019-01-06 07:47:50.172905	0o100755	8612176123
10	lpff	__init__.py	./chapter_08/plugins/__init__.py	.py	1370	2018-12-11 08:21:03.886521	2018-12-03 07:49:23.773134	2018-12-03 07:49:23.773134	0o100755	8611348726

Challenge

As always, we challenge you to add new features to this script and extend it using the knowledge and available resources that you have. For this chapter, we first challenge you to hash the indexed files using MD5 or SHA1 and store that information in the database. You can use the built-in `hashlib` library to handle hashing operations; more on this and other hashing techniques in `Chapter 7`, *Fuzzy Hashing*.

In addition, consider adding user-specified filters for particular file extensions for the collection. These features can be implemented without major renovation to the code, though you may find it easiest and more beneficial to your understanding to start from scratch and build the script with one or more of these new features in mind.

One more extension that we can add to our code is parsing the file's modes into separate columns for ease of querying in our database and reports. While the number we store is compact and the format is generally understood, splitting out the value into separate columns can help non-technical reviewers understand these file's properties and allow easier queries against the database in case we want to identify all files with a specified permission set. We could either perform this operation in our collection module or keep our current database schema and interpret the modes while generating our reports.

Summary

This chapter focused on the use of databases in script development. We explored how to use and manipulate a SQLite database in Python to store and retrieve information about file listings. We discussed when and how a database is a correct solution to store this information, as it has a fixed data structure and could be a large dataset.

In addition, we discussed multiple methods of interacting with databases, a manual process to show how databases work at a lower level, and a more Pythonic example where a third-party module handles these low-level interactions for us. We also explored a new type of report, using HTML to create a different output that can be viewed without additional software, and manipulating it to add new styles and functionality as we see fit. Overall, this section builds on the underlying goal of demonstrating different ways we can use Python and supporting libraries to solve forensic challenges. The code for this project can be downloaded from GitHub or Packt, as described in the *Preface*.

In the next chapter, we will learn how to parse binary data and registry hives using third-party libraries. Learning how to parse binary data will become a fundamental skill for the forensic developer and will be performed by many of the libraries that are featured throughout the remainder of this book.

6
Extracting Artifacts from Binary Files

Parsing binary data is an indispensable skill. Inevitably, we are tasked with analyzing artifacts that are unfamiliar or undocumented. This issue is compounded when the file of interest is a binary file. Rather than analyzing a text-like file, we often need to use our favorite hex editor to begin reverse engineering the file's internal binary structure. Reverse engineering the underlying logic of binary files is out of scope for this chapter. Instead, we will work with a binary object whose structure is already well-known. This will allow us to highlight how to use Python to parse these binary structures automatically once the internal structure is understood. In this chapter, we will examine the `UserAssist` registry key from the `NTUSER.DAT` registry hive.

This chapter illustrates how to extract Python objects from binary data and generate an automatic Excel report. We will use three modules to accomplish this task: `struct`, `yarp`, and `xlsxwriter`. Although the `struct` module is included in the standard installation of Python, both `yarp` and `xlsxwriter` must be installed separately. We will cover how to install these modules in their respective sections.

The `struct` library is used to parse the binary object into Python objects. Once we have parsed the data from the binary object, we can write our findings into a report. In past chapters, we have reported results in the CSV or HTML files. In this chapter, we will create an Excel report containing tables and summary charts of the data.

In this chapter, we will cover the following topics:

- Understanding the `UserAssist` artifact and its binary structure
- An introduction to ROT-13 encoding and decoding
- Installing and manipulating registry files with the `yarp` module
- Using `struct` to extract Python objects from binary data
- Creating worksheets, tables, and charts using `xlsxwriter`

The code for this chapter was developed and tested using Python 2.7.15 and Python 3.7.1

UserAssist

The `UserAssist` artifact identifies **graphical user interface** (**GUI**) application execution on Windows machines. This artifact stores differing amounts of information depending on the version of Windows OS. To identify the data specific to certain applications, we have to decode the registry key name as it is stored as the ROT13-encoded path and name of the application. As an example, the `UserAssist` value data for Windows XP and Vista is 16 bytes in length, and it stores the following:

- The last execution time in UTC (in FILETIME format)
- Execution count
- Session ID

The last execution time information is stored as a Windows FILETIME object. This is another common representation of time that differs from the UNIX timestamps we've seen in previous chapters. We will show how this timestamp can be interpreted within Python and displayed as human-readable, later in this chapter. The execution count represents the number of times the application has been launched.

Windows 7 and higher store even more data than their predecessors. Windows 7 `UserAssist` values are 72 bytes in length and, in addition to the three previously mentioned artifacts, store the following:

- Focus count
- Focus time

The focus count is the number of times the application was clicked on to bring it back into focus. For example, when you have two applications opened, only one is in focus at a given time. The other application is inactive until it is clicked on again. The focus time is the total amount of time a given application was in focus, and it is expressed in milliseconds.

This registry artifact does not store the execution of command-line-based programs or GUI applications that are Windows startup programs.

The `UserAssist` registry key is located within the `NTUSER.DAT` registry hive found in the root folder of every user's home directory. Within this hive, the `UserAssist` key is found at `SOFTWARE\Microsoft\Windows\CurrentVersion\Explorer\UserAssist`. Subkeys of the `UserAssist` key consist of known GUIDs and their respective count subkey. Within the count subkey of each GUID, there may be numerous values related to program execution. This structure is demonstrated here:

```
SOFTWARE\Microsoft\Windows\CurrentVersion\Explorer\UserAssist
.{GUID_1}
..Count
.{GUID_2}
..Count
```

The values within the count subkey store the application execution information we are interested in parsing. Each value's name under the count subkey represents the ROT-13-encoded path and name of the executable. This makes it difficult to identify executables at first glance. Let's fix that.

Understanding the ROT-13 substitution cipher – rot13.py

ROT-13 is a simple substitution cipher that transforms text and substitutes each character with another, thirteen characters after it. For example, the letter `a` would be substituted with the letter `n` and vice versa. Elements such as numbers, special characters, and a character's case are unaffected by the cipher. While Python does offer a built-in way of decoding ROT-13, we are going to pretend that it doesn't exist and manually decode ROT-13 data. We will use the built-in ROT-13 decoding method in our script.

Before we pretend that this functionality doesn't exist, let's quickly use it to illustrate how we could encode and decode ROT-13 data with Python 2:

```
>>> original_data = 'Why, ROT-13?'
>>> encoded_data = original_data.encode('rot-13')
>>> print encoded_data
Jul, EBG-13?
>>> print encoded_data.decode('rot-13')
Why, ROT-13?
```

Decoding or encoding with ROT-13 in Python 3 requires a slightly different approach with the native `codecs` library:

```
>>> import codecs
>>> enc = codecs.getencoder('rot-13')
```

```
>>> enc('Why, ROT-13?')
('Jul, EBG-13?', 12)
>>> enc('Why, ROT-13?')[0]
'Jul, EBG-13?'
```

Now, let's look at how you might approach this if it weren't already built-in. While you should never reinvent the wheel, we want to take this opportunity to practice list operations and introduce a tool to audit code. The code from the `rot13.py` script in the code bundle for this chapter is demonstrated next.

The `rot_code()` function defined at line 32 accepts a ROT-13-encoded or ROT-13-decoded string. On line 39, we have `rot_chars`, a list of characters in the alphabet. As we iterate through each character in the supplied input, we will use this list to substitute the character with its counterpart 13 elements away. As we execute this substitution, we will store them in the substitutions list instantiated in line 43:

```
032 def rot_code(data):
033     """
034      The rot_code function encodes/decodes data using string
035      indexing
036      :param data: A string
037      :return: The rot-13 encoded/decoded string
038      """
039      rot_chars = ['a', 'b', 'c', 'd', 'e', 'f', 'g', 'h', 'i',
040      'j', 'k', 'l', 'm', 'n', 'o', 'p', 'q', 'r', 's', 't',
041      'u', 'v', 'w', 'x', 'y', 'z']
042
043      substitutions = []
```

On line 46, we begin to walk through each character, `c`, in the data string. On line 49, we use a conditional statement to determine if the character is uppercase or lowercase. We do this to preserve the case of the character as we process it:

```
045      # Walk through each individual character
046      for c in data:
047
048          # Walk through each individual character
049          if c.isupper():
```

On line 54, we attempt to identify the index of the character in our list. If the character is a non-alphabetical character, we will receive a `ValueError` exception. Non-alphabetical characters, such as numbers or special characters, are appended to the substitutions list unmodified as these types of values are not encoded by ROT-13:

```
051              try:
052                  # Find the position of the character in
```

```
053                 # rot_chars list
054                 index = rot_chars.index(c.lower())
055             except ValueError:
056                 substitutions.append(c)
057                 continue
```

Once we have found the index of the character, we can calculate the corresponding index 13 characters away by subtracting 13. For values less than 13, this will be a negative number. Fortunately, list indexing supports negative numbers and works splendidly here. Before appending the corresponding character to our substitutions list, we use the string `upper()` function to return the character to its original case:

```
059             # Calculate the relative index that is 13
060             # characters away from the index
061             substitutions.append(
062             (rot_chars[(index-13)]).upper())
```

The `else` statement of the conditional block handles lowercase characters. The following code block is substantially the same functionality as what we just covered. The difference is that we never use lowercase or uppercase because the character is already in the proper case to be processed:

```
064         else:
065
066             try:
067                 # Find the position of the character in
068                 # rot_chars list
069                 index = rot_chars.index(c)
070             except ValueError:
071                 substitutions.append(c)
072                 continue
073
074             substitutions.append(rot_chars[((index-13))])
```

Finally, on line 76, we collapse the substitutions list to a string using the `join()` method. We join on an empty string so that each element of the list is appended without any separating characters. If this script is invoked from the command line, it will print out the processed string, `Jul, EBG-13?`, which we know corresponds to `ROT-13?`. We have the following code:

```
076     return ''.join(substitutions)
077
078 if __name__ == '__main__':
079     print(rot_code('Jul, EBG-13?'))
```

The following screenshot illustrates how we can import our `rot13` module and call the `rot_code()` method to either decode or encode a string:

```
(py2.7.15) C:\book\chapters\chapter_06>python
Python 2.7.15 (v2.7.15:ca079a3ea3, Apr 30 2018, 16:30:26) [MSC v.1500 64 bit (A
MD64)] on win32
Type "help", "copyright", "credits" or "license" for more information.
>>> import rot13
>>> data = 'Why, ROT-13?!'.encode('rot13')
>>> print data
Jul, EBG-13?!
>>> print rot13.rot_code(data)
Why, ROT-13?!
>>> print rot13.rot_code('Why, ROT-13?!')
Jul, EBG-13?!
>>>
```

Make sure that the Python interactive prompt is opened in the same directory as the `rot13.py` script. Otherwise, an `ImportError` will be generated.

Evaluating code with timeit

Let's now audit our module and see if it is superior to the built-in method (spoiler: it's not!) We mentioned that you should never reinvent the wheel unless absolutely required. There's a good reason: most built-in or third-party solutions have been optimized for performance and security. How does our `rot_code()` function stack up against the built-in function? We can use the `timeit` module to calculate the time a function or line of code takes to execute.

Let's compare the difference between the two methods of decoding ROT-13 values. Supplying the Python interpreter with `-m` executes a named module if its parent directory is found in the `sys.path` list. The `timeit` module can be called directly from the command line using the `-m` switch.

We can see what directories are in scope by importing the `sys` module and printing `sys.path`. To extend the items available through `sys.path`, we can append new items to it using list attributes, such as append or extend.

The `timeit` module supports a variety of switches, and can be used to run individual lines of code or entire scripts. The `-v` switch prints more verbose output, and is increasingly more verbose when supplied with additional `v` switches. The `-n` switch is the number of times to execute the code or script (for example, the number of executions per measuring period). We can use the `-r` switch to specify how many times to repeat a measurement (defaults to `3`). Increasing this will allow us to calculate a more accurate average execution speed. Finally, the `-s` switch is a statement to be run once on the first round of execution, in this case, to allow us to import the script we made. For further documentation, please visit `http://docs.python.org/3/library/timeit.html` or run `python -m timeit -h`.

The output generated on our computer when timing both methods is captured in the following screenshot. Performance may vary depending on the machine. For our first test, we measured the time it took to run three one million cycles of our script. On the first cycle, we imported our module, `rot13`, before calling it. On the second test, we similarly measured three one-million cycles of the built-in Python 2 `decode()` functions:

```
(py2.7.15) C:\book\chapters\chapter_06>python -m timeit -vv -n 1000 -s
    "import rot13" "rot13.rot_code('Why, ROT-13?!')"
raw times: 0.01793 0.01775 0.01775
1000 loops, best of 3: 17.75 usec per loop

(py2.7.15) C:\book\chapters\chapter_06>python -m timeit -vv -n 1000
    "'Why, ROT-13?!'.decode('rot-13')"
raw times: 0.001702 0.001185 0.001168
1000 loops, best of 3: 1.168 usec per loop
```

It turns out that there is good reason to not reinvent the wheel. Our custom `rot_code()` function is significantly slower than the built-in method when run a thousand times. Odds are we will not call this function a thousand times; for the `UserAssist` key, this function will likely be called only hundreds of times. However, if we were working with more data or had a particularly slow script, we could begin timing individual functions or lines of code to identify poorly optimized code.

As an aside, you can also use the `time.time()` function before and after a function call and calculate the elapsed time by subtracting the two times. This alternative approach is slightly simpler to implement but not as robust.

You have now learned about the `UserAssist` artifact, ROT-13 encoding, and a mechanism to audit our code. Let's shift focus and examine other modules that will be used in this chapter. One of those modules, `yarp`, will be used to access and interact with the `UserAssist` key and values.

Working with the yarp library

The **yarp** (short for **Yet Another Registry Parser**) library can be used to obtain keys and values from registry hives. Python provides a built-in registry module named `_winreg`; however, this module only works on Windows machines. The `_winreg` module interacts with the registry on the system running the module. It does not support opening external registry hives.

The `yarp` library allows us to interact with supplied registry hives and can be run on non-Windows machines. The `yarp` library can be downloaded from `https://github.com/msuhanov/yarp`. On the project's GitHub page, click on the releases section to see a list of all stable versions and download the desired version. For this chapter, we use version 1.0.25. Once the archived file is downloaded and extracted, we can run the included `setup.py` file to install the module. In a Command Prompt, execute the following code in the module's top-level directory:

```
python setup.py install
```

This should install the `yarp` library successfully on your machine. We can confirm by opening the Python interactive prompt and typing `import yarp`. We will receive an error if the module was not installed successfully. With `yarp` installed, let's begin learning how we can leverage this module for our needs.

First, we need to import the `Registry` class from the `yarp` module. Then, we use the `RegistryHive` function and pass it the registry object we want to query. In this example, we have copied the `NTUSER.DAT` registry file to our current working directory, which allows us to supply just the filename and not the path. Next, we use the `find_key` method to navigate to our key of interest. In this case, we are interested in the `RecentDocs` registry key. This key contains recent active files separated by extension:

```
>>> from yarp import Registry
>>> reg_file = open('NTUSER.DAT', 'rb')
>>> reg = Registry.RegistryHive(reg_file)
>>> recent_docs =
reg.find_key('SOFTWARE\Microsoft\Windows\CurrentVersion\Explorer\RecentDocs
')
```

If we print the recent_docs variable, we can see that it contains 151 values with 75 subkeys, which may contain additional values and subkeys. In addition, we can use the last_written_timestamp() method to see the last written time of the registry key:

```
>>> print(recent_docs)
RegistryKey, name: RecentDocs, subkeys: 75, values: 151

>>> print(recent_docs.last_written_timestamp()) # Last Written Time
datetime.datetime(2018, 11, 20, 3, 14, 40, 286516)
```

We can iterate over the values in the recent_docs key using the subkeys() function in a for loop. For each value, we can access the name(), value(), and values_count() methods, among others. When accessing a value (as opposed to a subkey), we can also access the value's raw data by using the raw_data() function. For our purposes, we use the raw_data() function when we want to work with the underlying binary data. We have the following code:

```
>>> for i, value in enumerate(recent_docs.subkeys()):
...     print('{}) {}: {}'.format(i, value.name(), value.values_count()))
...
0) .001: 2
1) .1: 2
2) .7z: 2
3) .AAE: 2
...
```

Another useful feature of the yarp module is a provided means of querying for a certain subkey or value. This is provided by the subkey(), value(), or find_key() functions. A None value is generated when a subkey is not present when using the subkey() function:

```
>>> if recent_docs.subkey('.docx'):
...     print('Found docx subkey.')
...
Found docx subkey.
>>> if recent_docs.subkey('.1234abcd') is None:
...     print('Did not find 1234abcd subkey.')
...
None
```

The find_key() function takes a path and can find a subkey recursively through multiple levels. The subkey() and value() functions search only child elements. We can use these functions to confirm that a key or value exists before trying to navigate to them. yarp has a number of other relevant features not covered here, including recovering deleted registry keys and values, carving registry keys and values, and supporting transaction log files.

With the `yarp` module, finding keys and their values is straightforward. However, when the values are not strings and are instead binary data, we have to rely on another module to make sense of the mess. For all binary needs, the `struct` module is an excellent candidate.

Introducing the struct module

The `struct` module is part of the standard Python library and is incredibly useful. The `struct` library is used to convert C structures to or from binary data. Full documentation for this module can be found at `http://docs.python.org/3/library/struct.html`.

For forensic purposes, the most important function in the struct module is the `unpack()` method. This method takes a format string representing the objects to be extracted from the binary data. It is important that the size dictated by the format string correlates to the size of the binary data supplied to the function.

The format string informs the `unpack()` function of what kind of data is in the binary object and how it should be interpreted. If we do not correctly identify the types of data or try to unpack more or less than what is provided, the `struct` module will throw an exception. The following is a table of the most common characters we use to build our format strings. The standard size column indicates the expected size of the binary object in bytes:

Character	**Python object**	**Standard size (bytes)**
`h`	Integer	2
`i`	Integer	4
`q`	Integer	8
`s`	String	1
`x`	N/A	N/A

There are additional characters that can be used in format strings. For example, other characters can interpret binary data as floats, Booleans, and other various C structures. The `x` character is simply a padding character that can be used to ignore bytes we're not interested in.

Additionally, an optional starting character can be used to define byte order, size, and alignment. The default is native byte order, size, and alignment. As we cannot predict the environment the script might be running on, it is often not advisable to use any native option. Instead, we can specify little or big endian byte order with standard sizes using the `<" and ">` symbols, respectively. Let's practice with a few examples.

First, open an interactive prompt and import `struct`. Next, we assign 0x01000000 to a variable. In Python 3, hex notation is specified by an escape character and an `x` before every two hexadecimal characters. The length of our hex data is four bytes, and to interpret this as an integer, we use the `i` character. Interpreting the hex as a little endian integer returns a value of `1`:

```
>>> import struct
>>> raw_data = b'\x01\x00\x00\x00' # Integer (1)
>>> print(struct.unpack('<i', raw_data)) # Little-Endian
(1,)
```

The `<i` and `>i` represents the string format. We are telling the `unpack()` method to interpret `raw_data` as a four-byte integer in little or big endian byte ordering. The struct module returns the unpacked data as a tuple. By default, Python will print a single element tuple in parenthesis with a trailing comma, as seen in the following output:

```
>>> print(struct.unpack('>i', raw_data)) # Big-Endian
(16777216,)
>>> print(type(struct.unpack('>i', raw_data)))
<class 'tuple'>
```

Let's look at another example. We can interpret `rawer_data` as three 4-byte integers by using three `i` characters. Alternatively, we can prepend a number to the format character to parse multiple values in a row. In both cases, when interpreted as a little endian, we receive the integers `1`, `5`, and `4`. If we aren't interested in the middle integer, we can skip it with the `4x` character:

```
>>> rawer_data = b'\x01\x00\x00\x00\x05\x00\x00\x00\x04\x00\x00\x00'
>>> print(struct.unpack('<iii', rawer_data))
(1, 5, 4)
>>> print(struct.unpack('<3i', rawer_data))
(1, 5, 4)
>>> print(struct.unpack('<i4xi', rawer_data)) # "skip" 4 bytes
(1, 4)
```

We raised the possibility of errors with struct earlier in this section. Now, let's purposely create errors with struct to understand what they mean. We receive an error for the following two examples because we tried to `unpack()` more or fewer values than were actually present in the `rawer_data` variable used previously. This can cause some initial frustration when trying to unpack a large amount of binary data. Always be sure to check the math, the byte order, and whether the size is standard or native:

```
>>> print(struct.unpack('<4i', rawer_data))
struct.error: unpack requires a buffer of 16 bytes
>>> print(struct.unpack('<2i', rawer_data))
struct.error: unpack requires a buffer of 8 bytes
```

Let's take it one step further and parse a `UserAssist` value using the struct module. We will parse a Windows XP value, which represents the easiest scenario as it is only 16 bytes in length. The byte offsets of a Windows XP UserAssist value are recorded in the following table:

Byte offset	Value	Object
0-3	Session ID	Integer
4-7	Count	Integer
8-15	FILETIME	Integer

The following hex dump is saved into the file `Neguhe Qrag.bin`. The file is packaged with the code bundle that can be downloaded from `https://packtpub.com/books/content/support`:

```
0000: 0300 0000 4800 0000  |....H...
0010: 01D1 07C4 FA03 EA00  |........
```

When unpacking data from a file object, we need to open it in the `rb` mode rather than the default `r` mode to ensure that we can read the data as bytes. Once we have the raw data, we can parse it using our specific character format. We know that the first 8 bytes are two 4-byte integers (`2i`), and then one 8-byte integer (`q`) representing the FILETIME of the `UserAssist` value. We can use indexing on the returned tuple to print out each extracted integer:

```
>>> rawest_data = open('Neguhe Qrag.bin', 'rb').read()
>>> parsed_data = struct.unpack('<2iq', rawest_data)
>>> print('Session ID: {}, Count: {}, FILETIME: {}'.format(parsed_data[0],
parsed_data[1], parsed_data[2]))
...
Session ID: 3, Count: 72, FILETIME: 6586952011847425
```

Once we have parsed the `UserAssist` values in our script, we will present the results in a report-ready format. In the past, we have used CSV and HTML for output reports. Frequently, reports are often reviewed in spreadsheet format using software such as Microsoft Excel. To provide reports that fully leverage this software, we will learn how to create XSLX-formatted spreadsheets as an output of our script.

Creating spreadsheets with the xlsxwriter module

`xlsxwriter` (version 1.1.2) is a useful third-party module that can write data to Excel spreadsheets. There are a plethora of Excel-supported modules for Python, but we chose this module because it was highly robust and well-documented. As the name suggests, this module can only be used to write Excel spreadsheets. The `xlsxwriter` module supports cell and conditional formatting, charts, tables, filters, and macros, among others. This module can be installed with `pip`:

```
pip install xlsxwriter==1.1.2
```

Adding data to a spreadsheet

Let's quickly create a script named `simplexlsx.v1.py` for this example. On lines 2 and 3, we import the `xlsxwriter` and `datetime` modules. The data we are going to be plotting, including the column names, is stored as nested lists in the `school_data` variable. Each list is a row of information we will want to store in the Excel spreadsheet, with the first element containing the column names:

```
002 import xlsxwriter
003 from datetime import datetime
...
033 school_data = [['Department', 'Students', 'Cumulative GPA',
034                 'Final Date'],
035                ['Computer Science', 235, 3.44,
036                datetime(2015, 7, 23, 18, 0, 0)],
037                ['Chemistry', 201, 3.26,
038                datetime(2015, 7, 25, 9, 30, 0)],
039                ['Forensics', 99, 3.8,
040                datetime(2015, 7, 23, 9, 30, 0)],
041                ['Astronomy', 115, 3.21,
042                datetime(2015, 7, 19, 15, 30, 0)]]
```

The `write_xlsx()` function, defined on line 45, is responsible for writing our data to a spreadsheet. First, we must create our Excel spreadsheet using the `Workbook()` function and supplying the desired name of the file as an input. On line 53, we create a worksheet using the `add_worksheet()` function. This function can take the desired title of the worksheet or use the default name `Sheet N`, where `N` represents a number:

```
045 def write_xlsx(data):
046     """
047     The write_xlsx function creates an XLSX spreadsheet from a
048     list of lists
049     :param data: A list of lists to be written in the spreadsheet
050     :return: Nothing
051     """
052     workbook = xlsxwriter.Workbook('MyWorkbook.xlsx')
053     main_sheet = workbo
ok.add_worksheet('MySheet')
```

The `date_format` variable stores a custom number format we will use to display our `datetime` objects in the desired human-readable format. On line 58, we begin to enumerate through our data to write. The conditional on line 59 is used to handle the first item, the column names, in the data list. We use the `write()` function and supply a numerical row and column. Alternatively, for instance, rather than using numerical values to represent the column and row to write the data to, we could have also used Excel notation such as `A1` to signify the data should be written to the first column and row:

```
055     date_format = workbook.add_format(
056     {'num_format': 'mm/dd/yy hh:mm:ss AM/PM'})
057 
058     for i, entry in enumerate(data):
059         if i == 0:
060             main_sheet.write(i, 0, entry[0])
061             main_sheet.write(i, 1, entry[1])
062             main_sheet.write(i, 2, entry[2])
063             main_sheet.write(i, 3, entry[3])
```

The `write()` method will try to write the appropriate data type for an object when it can detect that data's type. However, we can use different write methods to specify the correct format. These specialized writers preserve the data type in Excel, so we can use the appropriate data type-specific Excel functions for the object. Since we know the data types within the entry list, we can manually specify when to use the general `write()` function versus the `write_number()` function:

```
064         else:
065             main_sheet.write(i, 0, entry[0])
066             main_sheet.write_number(i, 1, entry[1])
067             main_sheet.write_number(i, 2, entry[2])
```

For the fourth entry in the list, the `datetime` object, we supply the `write_datetime()` function with our `date_format` defined on line 55. After our data is written to the workbook, we use the `close()` function to close and save our spreadsheet. On line 73, we call the `write_xlsx()` function, passing it the `school_data` list we built earlier, as follows:

```
068             main_sheet.write_datetime(i, 3, entry[3], date_format)
069 
070     workbook.close()
071 
072 
073 write_xlsx(school_data)
```

A table of `write` functions and the objects they preserve is presented as follows:

Function	**Supported objects**
`write_string`	`str`
`write_number`	`int`, `float`, `long`
`write_datetime`	`datetime` objects
`write_boolean`	`bool`
`write_url`	`str`

When the script is invoked at the command line, a spreadsheet named `MyWorkbook.xlsx` is created. When we convert this to a table, we can sort by any of our values and use Excel functions and features we are all familiar with. Had we failed to preserve the data types, values such as our dates might be displayed differently than intended:

	A	B	C	D
1	Department	Students	Cumulative GPA	Final Date
2	Computer Science	235	3.44	07/23/15 06:00:00 PM
3	Chemistry	201	3.26	07/25/15 09:30:00 AM
4	Physics	99	3.8	07/23/15 09:30:00 AM
5	Astronomy	115	3.21	07/19/15 03:30:00 PM

Building a table

Being able to write data to an Excel file and preserve the object type is already a step up over CSV, but we can do better. Often, the first thing an examiner will do with an Excel spreadsheet is convert the data into a table and begin the frenzy of sorting and filtering the data set. However, we can convert our data range to a table using `xlsxwriter`. In fact, writing a table with `xlsxwriter` is arguably easier than writing each row individually. The code discussed in this section is represented in the `simplexlsx.v2.py` file.

For this iteration, we have removed the initial list in the `school_data` variable that contained the column names. Our new `write_xlsx()` function writes the header separately, which we will see later:

```
034 school_data = [['Computer Science', 235, 3.44,
035                  datetime(2015, 7, 23, 18, 0, 0)],
036                  ['Chemistry', 201, 3.26,
037                  datetime(2015, 7, 25, 9, 30, 0)],
038                  ['Forensics', 99, 3.8,
039                  datetime(2015, 7, 23, 9, 30, 0)],
040                  ['Astronomy', 115, 3.21,
041                  datetime(2015, 7, 19, 15, 30, 0)]]
```

Lines 44 through 55 are identical to the previous iteration of the function. Writing our table to the spreadsheet is accomplished on line 58. See the following code:

```
044 def write_xlsx(data):
045     """
046     The write_xlsx function creates an XLSX spreadsheet from a
047     list of lists
```

```
048     :param data: A list of lists to be written in the spreadsheet
049     :return: Nothing
050     """
051     workbook = xlsxwriter.Workbook('MyWorkbook.xlsx')
052     main_sheet = workbook.add_worksheet('MySheet')
053
054     date_format = workbook.add_format(
055     {'num_format': 'mm/dd/yy hh:mm:ss AM/PM'})
```

The `add_table()` function takes multiple arguments. First, we pass a string representing the top-left and bottom-right cells of the table in Excel notation. We use the length variable, defined on line 56, to calculate the necessary length of our table. The second argument is a little more confusing; this is a dictionary with two keys, data and columns. The `data` key has the value of our data variable, which is perhaps poorly named in this case. The `columns` key defines each column header and, optionally, its format, as seen on line 62:

```
056     length = str(len(data) + 1)
057
058     main_sheet.add_table(('A1:D' + length),
059     {'data': data,
060     'columns': [{'header': 'Department'}, {'header': 'Students'},
061                 {'header': 'Cumulative GPA'},
062                 {'header': 'Final Date', 'format': date_format}]})
063
064     workbook.close()
```

In fewer lines than the previous example, we've managed to create a more useful output built as a table. Now, our spreadsheet has our specified data already converted into a table and ready to be sorted.

There are more possible keys and values that can be supplied during the construction of a table. Please consult the documentation (`http://xlsxwriter.readthedocs.org`) for more details on advanced usage.

This process is simple when we are working with nested lists representing each row of a worksheet. Data structures not in this format require a combination of both methods demonstrated in our previous iterations to achieve the same effect. For example, we can define a table to span across a certain number of rows and columns and then use the `write()` function for those cells. However, to prevent unnecessary headaches, we recommend keeping data in nested lists where possible.

Creating charts with Python

Finally, let's create a chart with `xlsxwriter`. The module supports a variety of different chart types, including line, scatter, bar, column, pie, and area. We use charts to summarize data in meaningful ways. This is particularly useful when working with large datasets, allowing examiners to gain some preliminary understanding of the data before getting into the weeds.

Let's modify the previous iteration yet again to display a chart. We will save this modified file as `simplexlsx.v3.py`. On line 65, we are going to create a variable named `department_grades`. This variable will be our chart object created by the `add_chart()` method. For this method, we pass in a dictionary specifying keys and values. In this case, we specify the type of the chart to be a column chart:

```
065     department_grades = workbook.add_chart({'type':'column'})
```

On line 66, we use the `set_title()` function and again pass in a dictionary of parameters. We set the name key equal to our desired title. At this point, we need to tell the chart what data to plot. We do this with the `add_series()` function. Each category key maps to the Excel notation specifying the horizontal axis data. The vertical axis is represented by the `values` key. With the data to plot specified, we use the `insert_chart()` function to plot the data in the spreadsheet. We give this function a string representing the cell that will act as an anchor to plot the top-left corner of the chart to:

```
066     department_grades.set_title(
067     {'name':'Department and Grade distribution'})
068     department_grades.add_series(
069     {'categories':'=MySheet!$A$2:$A$5',
070     'values':'=MySheet!$C$2:$C$5'})
071     main_sheet.insert_chart('A8', department_grades)
072     workbook.close()
```

Running this version of the script will convert our data into a table and generate a column chart, comparing departments by their cumulative grades. We can clearly see that, unsurprisingly, the Physics department has the highest GPA earners in the school's program. This information is easy enough to eyeball for such a small dataset. However, when working with data orders of greater magnitude, creating summarizing graphics can be particularly useful to understand the big picture:

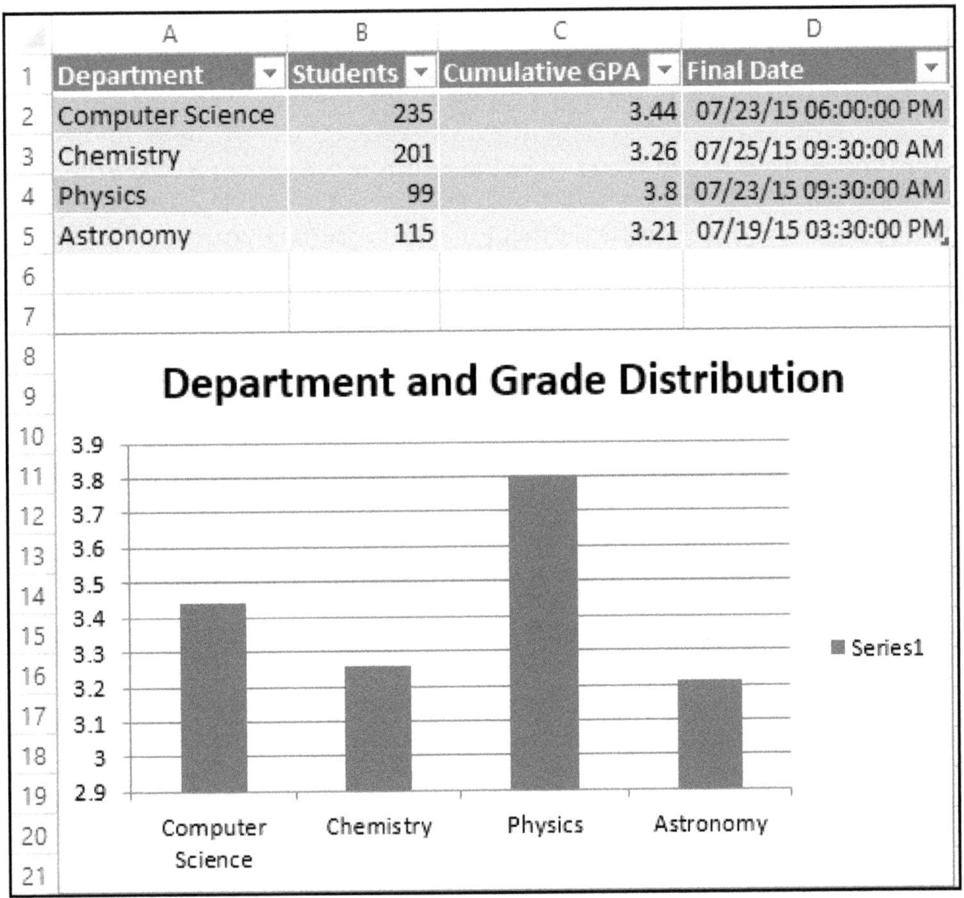

Be aware that there is a great deal of additional functionality in the `xlsxwriter` module that we will not use in our script. This is an extremely powerful module, and we recommend it for any operation that requires writing Excel spreadsheets.

The UserAssist framework

Our `UserAssist` framework is made up of three scripts, `userassist_parser.py`, `csv_writer.py`, and `xlsx_writer.py`. The `userassist_parser.py` script handles the bulk of the processing logic and then passes the results to the CSV or XLSX writer. The directory structure of our framework is shown as follows. Our writers are contained within a directory named `Writers`. Remember that for a directory to be searchable by Python, it needs to include the `__init__.py` file. This file may be empty, contain functions and classes, or contain code to be executed upon import:

```
|-- userassist_parser.py
|-- Writers
    |-- __init__.py
    |-- csv_writer.py
    |-- xlsx_writer.py
```

Developing our UserAssist logic processor – userassist_parser.py

The `userassist_parser.py` script is responsible for handling user input, creating a log file, and parsing `UserAssist` data from the `NTUSER.DAT` file. On lines 2 through 9, we import familiar and new modules to facilitate our tasks. The `yarp` and `struct` modules will grant us access to and then extract objects from the `UserAssist` binary data, respectively. We import our `xlsx_writer` and `csv_writer` modules, which are in the `Writers` directory. Other used modules have been introduced in previous chapters:

```
001 """UserAssist parser leveraging the YARP library."""
002 from __future__ import print_function
003 import argparse
004 import struct
005 import sys
006 import logging
007 import os
008 from Writers import xlsx_writer, csv_writer
009 from yarp import Registry
```

The KEYS variable defined as an empty list on line 45 will store parsed UserAssist values. The main() function, defined on line 48, will handle all coordinating logic. It calls functions to parse the UserAssist key and then to write the results. The create_dictionary() function uses the Registry module to find and store UserAssist value names and raw data in a dictionary for each GUID.

On line 134, we define the parse_values() function, which processes the binary data of each UserAssist value using struct. During this method, we determine if we are working with Windows XP- or Windows 7-based UserAssist data based on length. The get_name() function is a small function that separates the executable name from the full path:

```
045 KEYS = []
...
048 def main():
...
085 def create_dictionary():
...
134 def parse_values():
...
176 def get_name():
```

On lines 202 through 212, we create our argument parser object, which takes two positional arguments and one optional argument. Our REGISTRY input is the NTUSER.DAT file of interest. The OUTPUT argument is the path and filename of the desired output file. The optional -l switch is the path of the log file. If this is not supplied, the log file is created in the current working directory:

```
202 if __name__ == '__main__':
203     parser = argparse.ArgumentParser(description=__description__,
204                                      epilog='Developed by ' +
205                                      __author__ + ' on ' +
206                                      __date__)
207     parser.add_argument('REGISTRY', help='NTUSER Registry Hive.')
208     parser.add_argument('OUTPUT',
209     help='Output file (.csv or .xlsx)')
210     parser.add_argument('-l', help='File path of log file.')
211 
212     args = parser.parse_args()
```

If the user supplies a log path, we check on line 215 if the path exists. If it does not exist, we use the `os.makedirs()` function to create the log directory. In either case, we instantiate the `log_path` variable with the supplied directory and the log file. On line 220, we create our log and write startup details in the same manner as previous chapters, before calling `main()` on line 227:

```
214     if args.l:
215         if not os.path.exists(args.l):
216             os.makedirs(args.l)
217         log_path = os.path.join(args.l, 'userassist_parser.log')
218     else:
219         log_path = 'userassist_parser.log'
220     logging.basicConfig(filename=log_path, level=logging.DEBUG,
221                         format=('%(asctime)s | %(levelname)s | '
222                         '%(message)s'), filemode='a')
223 
224     logging.info('Starting UserAssist_Parser')
225     logging.debug('System ' + sys.platform)
226     logging.debug('Version ' + sys.version)
227     main(args.REGISTRY, args.OUTPUT)
```

The following flow chart depicts the interconnected functions within our `UserAssist` framework. Here, we can see how the `main()` function calls and receives data from the `create_dictionary()` and `parse_values()` functions. The `parse_values()` function separately calls the `get_name()` function:

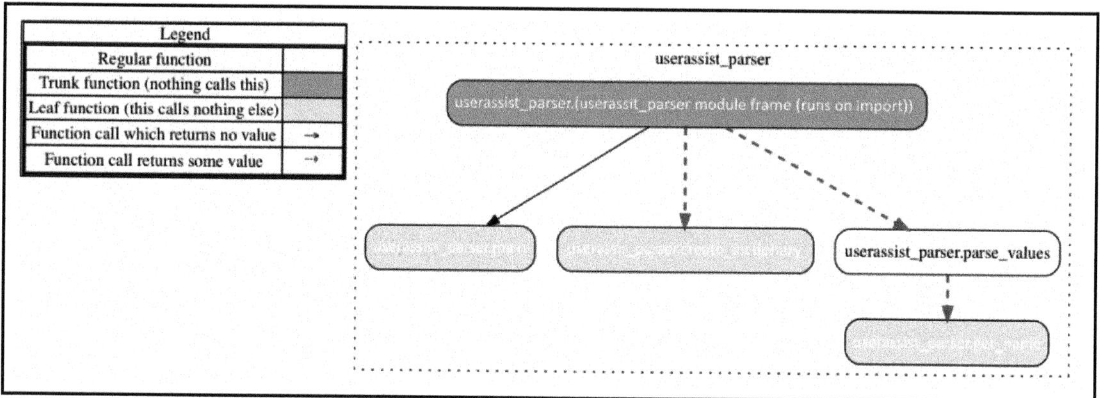

Evaluating the main() function

The `main()` function sends the registry file to be processed before calling the appropriate methods to write the `out_file`. On line 61, we call the `create_dictionary()` function to create a list of dictionaries containing `UserAssist` data mapped to the executable's name:

```
048 def main(registry, out_file):
049     """
050     The main function handles main logic of script.
051     :param registry: Registry Hive to process
052     :param out_file: The output path and file
053     :return: Nothing.
054     """
055     if os.path.basename(registry).lower() != 'ntuser.dat':
056         print(('[-] {} filename is incorrect (Should be '
057                'ntuser.dat)').format(registry))
058         logging.error('Incorrect file detected based on name')
059         sys.exit(1)
060     # Create dictionary of ROT-13 decoded UA key and its value
061     apps = create_dictionary(registry)
```

Next, this dictionary is fed into the `parse_values()` method that appends parsed data to the `KEYS` list we created on line 45. This function returns an integer representing the type of `UserAssist` data parsed. This function returns a value of `0` for Windows XP `UserAssist` values and `1` for Windows 7. We log this information for troubleshooting purposes:

```
062     ua_type = parse_values(apps)
063
064     if ua_type == 0:
065         logging.info('Detected XP-based Userassist values.')
066
067     else:
068         logging.info(('Detected Win7-based Userassist values. '
069                       'Contains Focus values.'))
```

Once data is processed, it can be sent to our writers. We use the `endswith()` method to identify what the extension is of the user-supplied output. If the output ends with `.xlsx` or `.csv`, we send the data to our `excel_writer()` or `csv_writer()` functions, respectively, as follows:

```
071     # Use .endswith string function to determine output type
072     if out_file.lower().endswith('.xlsx'):
073         xlsx_writer.excel_writer(KEYS, out_file)
074     elif out_file.lower().endswith('.csv'):
075         csv_writer.csv_writer(KEYS, out_file)
```

If the user does not include an extension in their output, we write a warning to the log and write the data to a CSV file in the current working directory. We chose a CSV output because it represents the simplest and most portable option of our supported output formats. In addition, if the user wanted to examine their data in a spreadsheet application, they could easily import and convert the CSV document to an XLSX format:

```
076     else:
077     print(('[-] CSV or XLSX extension not detected in '
078            'output. Writing CSV to current directory.'))
079     logging.warning(('.csv or .xlsx output not detected. '
080                      'Writing CSV file to current '
081                      'directory.'))
082     csv_writer.csv_writer(KEYS, 'Userassist_parser.csv')
```

Both writers accept the same arguments: `KEYS` and `out_file`. The `KEYS` list, which was defined on line 45, is a container of `UserAssist` dictionaries. We packaged our data as a list of dictionaries in order to use the dictionary keys to dictate which headers were present. The `out_file` is the path and name of the desired output.

Defining the create_dictionary() function

The `create_dictionary()` function prepares the `UserAssist` data for processing. This function pulls all values within each `UserAssist` GUID key. It creates a dictionary where the keys are the ROT-13 decoded executable name, and the values are the respective binary data. This binary data is extracted now, so we can process it in a later function:

```
085 def create_dictionary(registry):
086     """
087     The create_dictionary function creates a list of dictionaries
088     where keys are the ROT-13 decoded app names and values are
089     the raw hex data of said app.
090     :param registry: Registry Hive to process
091     :return: apps_list, A list containing dictionaries for
092     each app
093     """
```

On line 97, we try to open the registry file provided by the user. If there is an error accessing the input file, we catch the error, log it, and exit gracefully with an error code of `2`:

```
094     try:
095         # Open the registry file to be parsed
096         registry_file = open(registry, "rb")
097         reg = Registry.RegistryHive(registry_file)
098     except (IOError, UnicodeDecodeError) as e:
```

```
099         msg = 'Invalid NTUSER.DAT path or Registry ID.'
100         print('[-]', msg)
101         logging.error(msg)
102         sys.exit(2)
```

If we can open the registry file, we then try to navigate to the `UserAssist` key. We use a conditional to catch the scenario where the `UserAssist` key is not found in the supplied registry file. Note that, for this error, we use the integer, `3`, to differentiate from our previous exit scenario:

```
104     # Navigate to the UserAssist key
105     ua_key = reg.find_key(
106     ('SOFTWARE\\Microsoft\\Windows\\CurrentVersion\\Explorer'
107     '\\UserAssist'))
108     if ua_key is None:
109         msg = 'UserAssist Key not found in Registry file.'
110         print('[-]', msg)
111         logging.error(msg)
112         sys.exit(3)
```

On line 113, we create a list named `apps_list`, which will store `UserAssist` dictionaries. If we were able to find the `UserAssist` key, we loop through each `ua_subkey`, a GUID, and check their count subkey. This is an important step; as Windows has evolved, more GUIDs have been added to the `UserAssist` key. Rather than hardcoding these values, which could miss new GUIDs added in future versions of Windows, we opted for a more dynamic process that will discover and handle new GUIDs across many versions of Windows:

```
113     apps_list = []
114     # Loop through each subkey in the UserAssist key
115     for ua_subkey in ua_key.subkeys():
116         # For each subkey in the UserAssist key, detect a subkey
117         # called Count that has more than 0 values to parse.
```

This process involves checking each GUIDs that has a subkey named `Count`, which stores the actual `UserAssist` application values. On line 118, we determine if the GUID has a subkey named `Count` with one or more values. This ensures that we find all the `UserAssist` values present on the system:

```
118         if(ua_subkey.subkey('Count') and
119         ua_subkey.subkey('Count').values_count() > 0):
```

We create an apps dictionary on line 120 and begin to loop through each value under the `Count` subkey. For each value, we add the ROT-13-decoded name as the key, and associate it with its `raw_data` as the value. Once all the values in the GUID have been added to the dictionary, it is appended to `apps_list` and the cycle repeats. Once all of the GUIDs have been processed, our list is returned to the `main()` function:

```
120             apps = {}
121             for v in ua_subkey.subkey('Count').values():
122                 if sys.version_info[0] == 2:
123                     apps[v.name().encode('utf-8').decode(
124                     'rot-13')] = v.data_raw()
125                 elif sys.version_info[0] == 3:
126                     import codecs
127                     enc = codecs.getencoder('rot-13')
128                     apps[enc(str(v.name()))[0]] = v.data_raw()
129
130                 apps_list.append(apps)
131     return apps_list
```

Extracting data with the parse_values() function

The `parse_values()` function takes the list of GUID dictionaries as its input and uses struct to parse the binary data. As we've discussed, there are two types of `UserAssist` keys we will support: Windows XP and Windows 7. The following two tables break down the relevant data structures we will parse. Windows XP-based keys are 16 bytes in length and contain a Session ID, Count, and FILETIME timestamp:

Byte offset	**Value**	**Object**
0-3	Session ID	Integer
4-7	Count	Integer
8-15	FILETIME	Integer

Windows 7 artifacts are 72 bytes in length containing a session ID, count, focus count/time, and FILETIME timestamp:

Byte offset	**Value**	**Object**
0-3	Session ID	Integer
4-7	Count	Integer
8-11	Focus count	Integer

12-15	Focus time	Integer
16-59	???	N/A
60-67	FILETIME	Integer
68-71	???	N/A

On lines 143 through 146, we set up our function by instantiating the `ua_type` variable and logging execution status. This `ua_type` variable will be used to document which type of `UserAssist` value we're working with. On lines 148 and 149, we loop through each value in each dictionary to identify its type and parse it:

```
134 def parse_values(data):
135     """
136     The parse_values function uses struct to unpack the raw value
137     data from the UA key
138     :param data: A list containing dictionaries of UA
139     application data
140     :return: ua_type, based on the size of the raw data from
141     the dictionary values.
142     """
143     ua_type = -1
144     msg = 'Parsing UserAssist values.'
145     print('[+]', msg)
146     logging.info(msg)
147 
148     for dictionary in data:
149         for v in dictionary.keys():
```

On lines 151 and 159, we use the `len()` function to identify the type of `UserAssist` key. For Windows XP-based data, we need to extract two 4-byte integers followed by an 8-byte integer. We also want to interpret this data in little endian using standard sizes. We accomplish this on line 152 with `<2iq` as the struct format string. The second argument we pass to the unpack method is the raw binary data for the particular key from the GUID dictionary:

```
150             # WinXP based UA keys are 16 bytes
151             if len(dictionary[v]) == 16:
152                 raw = struct.unpack('<2iq', dictionary[v])
153                 ua_type = 0
154                 KEYS.append({'Name': get_name(v), 'Path': v,
155                 'Session ID': raw[0], 'Count': raw[1],
156                 'Last Used Date (UTC)': raw[2],
157                 'Focus Time (ms)': '', 'Focus Count': ''})
```

The Windows 7-based data is slightly more complicated. There are bytes in the middle and end of the binary data that we are not interested in parsing and yet, because of the nature of struct, we must account for them in our format. The format string we use for this task is `<4i44xq4x`, which accounts for the four 4-byte integers, the 44 bytes of intervening space, the 8-byte integer, and the remaining 4 bytes we will ignore:

```
158             # Win7 based UA keys are 72 bytes
159             elif len(dictionary[v]) == 72:
160                 raw = struct.unpack('<4i44xq4x', dictionary[v])
161                 ua_type = 1
162                 KEYS.append({'Name': get_name(v), 'Path': v,
163                 'Session ID': raw[0], 'Count': raw[1],
164                 'Last Used Date (UTC)': raw[4],
165                 'Focus Time (ms)': raw[3],'Focus Count': raw[2]})
```

As we parse `UserAssist` records, we append them to the `KEYS` list for storage. When we append the parsed values, we wrap them in curly braces to create our inner dictionary object. We also call the `get_name()` function on the `UserAssist` value name to separate the executable from its path. Note that regardless of the type of `UserAssist` key, we still create the same keys in our dictionary. This will ensure that all our dictionaries have the same structure and will help streamline our CSV and XLSX output functions.

If a `UserAssist` value is not 16 or 72 bytes (which can happen), then that value is skipped and the user is notified of the name and size that was passed over. From our experience, these values were not forensically relevant, and so we decided to pass on them. On line 173, the `UserAssist` type is returned to the `main()` function:

```
166             else:
167                 # If the key is not WinXP or Win7 based -- ignore.
168                 msg = 'Ignoring {} value that is {} bytes'.format(
169                 str(v), str(len(dictionary[v])))
170                 print('[-]', msg)
171                 logging.info(msg)
172                 continue
173     return ua_type
```

Processing strings with the get_name() function

The `get_name()` function uses string operations to separate the executable from the path name. From testing, we found that a colon, backslash, or both characters were present in the path. Because this pattern exists, we can try to split this information using these characters to extract the name:

```
176 def get_name(full_name):
177     """
178     the get_name function splits the name of the application
179     returning the executable name and ignoring the
180     path details.
181     :param full_name: the path and executable name
182     :return: the executable name
183     """
```

On line 185, we check to see if both colon and backslashes are in the `full_name` variable. If this is true, we use the `rindex()` function to get the index of the rightmost occurrence of the substring for both elements. On line 187, we check to see if the right-most index for the colon is found later in the string than the backslash. The element with the greatest index is used as the delimiter for the `split()` function. To get the last substring in the list (our executable name), we use the `-1` index:

```
184     # Determine if '\\' and ':' are within the full_name
185     if ':' in full_name and '\\' in full_name:
186         # Find if ':' comes before '\\'
187         if full_name.rindex(':') > full_name.rindex('\\'):
188             # Split on ':' and return the last element
189             # (the executable)
190             return full_name.split(':')[-1]
191         else:
192             # Otherwise split on '\\'
193             return full_name.split('\\')[-1]
```

On lines 196 and 198, we handle the alternative scenarios and split on either the colon or backslash, and return the last element in the list of substrings:

```
194     # When just ':' or '\\' is in the full_name, split on
195     # that item and return the last element (the executable)
196     elif ':' in full_name:
197         return full_name.split(':')[-1]
198     else:
199         return full_name.split('\\')[-1]
```

This completes the logic in our `userassist_parser.py` script. Now, let's turn our attention to our two writer functions responsible for writing our parsed data in a useful format.

Writing Excel spreadsheets – xlsx_writer.py

The `xlsx_writer.py` script contains the logic for creating an excel document containing our processed `UserAssist` values. In addition to this, this script also creates an additional worksheet that contains summarizing charts of our data. The `xlsxwriter` is imported on line 1 and is the third-party module we use to create the Excel document. The `itemgetter` function, imported on line 3, will be used and explained in the sorting functions later in this section. We have seen the `datetime` and `logging` modules from previous chapters:

```
001 from __future__ import print_function
002 import xlsxwriter
003 from operator import itemgetter
004 from datetime import datetime, timedelta
005 import logging
```

There are six functions in the `xlsx_writer.py` script. The coordinating logic is handled by the `excel_writer()` function defined on line 36. This function creates our Excel workbook object and then hands it off to the `dashboard_writer()` and `userassist_writer()` functions to create the dashboard and `UserAssist` worksheets, respectively.

The remaining three functions, `file_time()`, `sort_by_count()`, and `sort_by_date()`, are helper functions used by the dashboard and `UserAssist` writers. The `file_time()` function is responsible for converting FILETIME objects that we parsed from the raw `UserAssist` data into `datetime` objects. The sorting functions are used to sort the data by either count or date. We use these sorting functions to answer some basic questions about our data. What are the most-used applications? What are the least-used applications? What were the last 10 applications used on the machine (according to `UserAssist`)?

```
036 excel_writer():
...
071 dashboard_writer():
...
156 userassist_writer():
...
201 file_time():
...
214 sort_by_count():
...
227 sort_by_date():
```

Controlling output with the excel_writer() function

The `excel_writer()` function is the glue for this script. The headers list on line 47 is a list containing our desired column names. These column names also conveniently correlate to the keys in our `UserAssist` dictionaries we will be writing. On line 49, we create the `Workbook` object we will write to. On the next line, we create our `title_format`, which controls the color, font, size, and other style options for our spreadsheet header. We have the following code:

```
036 def excel_writer(data, out_file):
037     """
038     The excel_writer function handles the main logic of writing
039     the excel output
040     :param data: the list of lists containing parsed UA data
041     :param out_file: the desired output directory and filename
042     for the excel file
043     :return: Nothing
044     """
045     print('[+] Writing XLSX output.')
046     logging.info('Writing XLSX to ' + out_file + '.')
047     headers = ['Name', 'Path', 'Session ID', 'Count',
048     'Last Used Date (UTC)', 'Focus Time (ms)', 'Focus Count']
049     wb = xlsxwriter.Workbook(out_file)
050     title_format = wb.add_format({'bold': True,
051     'font_color': 'white', 'bg_color': 'black', 'font_size': 30,
052     'font_name': 'Calibri', 'align': 'center'})
```

The `title_format` is similar to the `date_format` we created when we previously discussed the `xlsxwriter` module. This format is a dictionary containing keywords and values. Specifically, we'll use this format when creating a title and subtitle rows so it sticks out from other data in our spreadsheet.

On lines 54 through 59, we convert our dictionaries back into lists. This might seem to you as though we made the wrong data type choice to store our data, and perhaps you have a point. However, storing our data in lists will immensely simplify writing out XSLX output. Once we see how the CSV writer handles the data, it will become clearer why we originally use dictionaries. In addition, the use of dictionaries allows us to easily understand the stored data without need for review of the code or documentation:

```
054     # A temporary list that will store dictionary values
055     tmp_list = []
056     for dictionary in data:
057         # Adds dictionary values to a list ordered by the headers
058         # Adds an empty string is the key does not exist
059         tmp_list.append([dictionary.get(x, '') for x in headers])
```

We use list comprehension to append data from our dictionary in the proper order. Let's break it down. On line 59, we iterate through each `UserAssist` dictionary. As we know, dictionaries do not store data by index and instead store by key mapping. However, we want our data to be written in a certain order as dictated by our headers list. The `x` in the headers loop allows us to iterate over that list. For each `x`, we use the `get()` method to return the value for `x` if found in the dictionary or an empty string.

On line 61 and 62, we call the two worksheet writers for the dashboard and `UserAssist` data. After the last of those functions exit, we `close()` the workbook object. It is incredibly important to close the workbook. Failing to do so will throw an exception that might prevent us from transferring our Excel document from memory to disk. Take a look at the following code:

```
061     dashboard_writer(wb, tmp_list, title_format)
062     userassist_writer(wb, tmp_list, headers, title_format)
063
064     wb.close()
065     msg =('Completed writing XLSX file. '
066           'Program exiting successfully.')
067     print('[*]', msg)
068     logging.info(msg)
```

Summarizing data with the dashboard_writer() function

The aim of the `dashboard_writer()` function is to provide the analyst or reviewer with some graphics that summarize our `UserAssist` data. We chose to present the top 10, bottom 10, and most recent 10 executables to the user. This function is our longest and requires the most logic.

On line 81, we add our dashboard worksheet object to the workbook. Next, we merge the first row from the `A` to `Q` columns and write our company name, `XYZ Corp`, using our title format created in the `excelWriter()` function. Similarly, we create a subtitle row to identify this worksheet as our dashboard on line 83, as follows:

```
071 def dashboard_writer(workbook, data, ua_format):
072     """
073     the dashboard_writer function creates the 'Dashboard'
074     worksheet, table, and graphs
075     :param workbook: the excel workbook object
076     :param data: the list of lists containing parsed UA data
077     :param ua_format: the format object for the title and
078     subtitle row
079     :return: Nothing
080     """
```

```
081     dashboard = workbook.add_worksheet('Dashboard')
082     dashboard.merge_range('A1:Q1', 'XYZ Corp', ua_format)
083     dashboard.merge_range('A2:Q2', 'Dashboard', ua_format)
```

On line 87, we create and add a `date_format` to the workbook in order to properly format our dates. On lines 92 and 93, we make function calls to the two sorting functions. We use list slicing to carve the sorted data to create our sublists: `topten`, `leastten`, and `lastten`. For the `topten` executables used by count, we grab the last 10 elements in the sorted list. For the `leastten`, we simply perform the inverse. For the `lastten`, we grab the first 10 results in the sorted dates list, as follows:

```
085     # The format to use to convert datetime object into a human
086     # readable value
087     date_format = workbook.add_format({
088     'num_format': 'mm/dd/yy h:mm:ss'})
089
090     # Sort our original input by count and date to assist with
091     # creating charts.
092     sorted_count = sort_by_count(data)
093     sorted_date = sort_by_date(data)
094
095     # Use list slicing to obtain the most and least frequently
096     # used UA apps and the most recently used UA apps
097     topten = sorted_count[-10:]
098     leastten = sorted_count[:10]
099     lastten = sorted_date[:10]
```

On line 103, we iterate over the elements in the `lastten` list. We must convert each timestamp into a `datetime` object. The `datetime` object is stored in the first index of the `UserAssist` list we created and is converted by the `file_time()` function:

```
101     # For the most recently used UA apps, convert the FILETIME
102     # value to datetime format
103     for element in lastten:
104         element[1] = file_time(element[1])
```

On lines 108 through 116, we create our three tables for our top, bottom, and most recent data points. Note how these tables start on row 100. We chose to place them far away from the top of the spreadsheet so the user sees the tables we will add instead of the raw data. As we saw when describing tables in the `xlsxwriter` section, the second argument of the `add_table()` function is a dictionary containing keywords for header names and formats. There are other keywords that could be provided for additional functionality. For example, we use the `format` keyword to ensure that our `datetime` objects are displayed as desired using our `date_format` variable. We have the following code:

```
106     # Create a table for each of the three categories, specifying
107     # the data, column headers, and formats for specific columns
108     dashboard.add_table('A100:B110',
109     {'data': topten, 'columns': [{'header': 'App'},
110     {'header': 'Count'}]})
111     dashboard.add_table('D100:E110',
112     {'data': leastten, 'columns': [{'header': 'App'},
113     {'header': 'Count'}]})
114     dashboard.add_table('G100:H110',
115     {'data': lastten, 'columns': [{'header': 'App'},
116     {'header': 'Date (UTC)', 'format': date_format}]})
```

On lines 118 to 153, we create our charts for the three tables. After instantiating `top_chart` as a pie chart, we set the title and the scale in the *X* and *Y* direction. During testing, we realized that the figure would be too small to adequately display all of the information, and so we used a larger scale:

```
118     # Create the most used UA apps chart
119     top_chart = workbook.add_chart({'type': 'pie'})
120     top_chart.set_title({'name': 'Top Ten Apps'})
121     # Set the relative size to fit the labels and pie chart within
122     # chart area
123     top_chart.set_size({'x_scale': 1, 'y_scale': 2})
```

On line 127, we add the series for our pie chart; identifying the categories and values is straightforward. All we need to do is define the rows and columns we want to plot. The `data_labels` key is an additional option that can be used to specify the value's format of the plotted data. In this case, we chose the `'percentage'` option as seen on line 130, as follows:

```
125     # Add the data as a series by specifying the categories and
126     # values
127     top_chart.add_series(
128     {'categories': '=Dashboard!$A$101:$A$110',
129     'values': '=Dashboard!$B$101:$B$110',
130     'data_labels': {'percentage': True}})
```

```
131     # Add the chart to the 'Dashboard' worksheet
132     dashboard.insert_chart('A4', top_chart)
```

With this setup, our pie chart will be split based on usage count, the legend will contain the name of the executable, and the percentage will show the relative execution in comparison to the other nine executables. After creating the chart, we call `insert_chart()` to add it to the dashboard worksheet. The `least_chart` is created in the same manner, as follows:

```
134     # Create the least used UA apps chart
135     least_chart = workbook.add_chart({'type': 'pie'})
136     least_chart.set_title({'name': 'Least Used Apps'})
137     least_chart.set_size({'x_scale': 1, 'y_scale': 2})
138
139     least_chart.add_series(
140     {'categories': '=Dashboard!$D$101:$D$110',
141     'values': '=Dashboard!$E$101:$E$110',
142     'data_labels': {'percentage': True}})
143     dashboard.insert_chart('J4', least_chart)
```

Finally, we create and add the `last_chart` to our spreadsheet. In an effort to save trees, this is handled in the same fashion as we previously discussed. This time, however, our chart is a column chart and we've modified the scale to be appropriate for the type of chart:

```
145     # Create the most recently used UA apps chart
146     last_chart = workbook.add_chart({'type': 'column'})
147     last_chart.set_title({'name': 'Last Used Apps'})
148     last_chart.set_size({'x_scale': 1.5, 'y_scale': 1})
149
150     last_chart.add_series(
151     {'categories': '=Dashboard!$G$101:$G$110',
152     'values': '=Dashboard!$H$101:$H$110'})
153     dashboard.insert_chart('D35', last_chart)
```

Writing artifacts in the userassist_writer() function

The `userassist_writer()` function is similar to the previous dashboard function. The difference is that this function creates a single table containing our raw data without any of the additional accouterments. On lines 167 through 169, we create the `UserAssist` worksheet object and add our title and subtitle to the spreadsheet. On line 173, we once again create a `date_format` to properly display dates, as follows:

```
156 def userassist_writer(workbook, data, headers, ua_format):
157     """
158     The userassist_writer function creates the 'UserAssist'
159     worksheet and table
```

```
160     :param workbook: the excel workbook object
161     :param data: the list of lists containing parsed UA data
162     :param headers: a list of column names for the spreadsheet
163     :param ua_format: the format object for the title and subtitle
164     row
165     :return: Nothing
166     """
167     userassist = workbook.add_worksheet('UserAssist')
168     userassist.merge_range('A1:H1', 'XYZ Corp', ua_format)
169     userassist.merge_range('A2:H2', 'Case ####', ua_format)
170
171     # The format to use to convert datetime object into a
172     # human readable value
173     date_format = workbook.add_format(
174     {'num_format': 'mm/dd/yy h:mm:ss'})
```

On line 178, we loop through the outer list and convert the FILETIME object into a `datetime` object using our prebuilt function. We also add an integer to the beginning of the list so that examiners can quickly determine how many `UserAssist` records are there by looking at the index:

```
176     # Convert the FILETIME object to datetime and insert the 'ID'
177     # value as the first element in the list
178     for i, element in enumerate(data):
179         element[4] = file_time(element[4])
180         element.insert(0, i + 1)
```

On line 188, we begin creating our `UserAssist` table. We use the length variable, created in line 184, to determine the appropriate number distance to the bottom-right corner of the table. Note that the length is the length of the list plus three. We added three to this length because we need to account for our title and subtitle rows, taking up the first two columns, and the difference between how Python and Excel count. We have the following code:

```
182     # Calculate how big the table should be. Add 3 to account for
183     # the title and header rows.
184     length = len(data) + 3
185
186     # Create the table; depending on the type (WinXP v. Win7) add
187     # additional headers
188     userassist.add_table(('A3:H' + str(length)),
189                          {'data': data,
190                          'columns': [{'header': 'ID'},
191                          {'header': 'Name'},
192                          {'header': 'Path'},
193                          {'header': 'Session ID'},
194                          {'header': 'Count'},
195                          {'header': 'Last Run Time (UTC)',
```

```
                        'format': date_format},
                        {'header': 'Focus Time (MS)'},
                        {'header': 'Focus Count'}]})
```

Defining the file_time() function

This is a very small helper function. The FILETIME object we parsed with the struct library is an 8-byte integer representing the count of 100-nanosecond units since 01/01/1601. This date is used by most Microsoft operating systems and applications as a common reference point in time.

Therefore, to get the date it represents, we need to add the FILETIME value to the `datetime` object representing 01/01/1601 with the `timedelta()` function. The `timedelta` function calculates the number of days and hours an integer represents. We can then add the output from the `timedelta()` function directly to the `datetime` object to arrive at the correct date. In order to arrive at the correct magnitude, we need to divide the FILETIME value by `10`, as follows:

```
def file_time(ft):
    """
    The file_time function converts the FILETIME objects into
    datetime objects
    :param ft: the FILETIME object
    :return: the datetime object
    """
    if ft is not None and ft != 0:
        return datetime(1601, 1, 1) + timedelta(microseconds=ft / 10)
    else:
        return 0
```

Processing integers with the sort_by_count() function

The `sort_by_count()` function sorts the inner lists based on their execution count value. This is a somewhat complicated one-liner, so let's take it apart step by step. To begin, let's focus on the `sorted(data, key=itemgetter(3))` step first. Python includes a built-in `sorted()` method to sort data by a key, normally an integer. We can supply the `sorted()` function with a key to tell it what to sort by and return a new sorted list.

As with any new piece of code, let's look at a simple example in the interactive prompt:

```
>>> from operator import itemgetter
>>> test = [['a', 2], ['b', 5], ['c', -2], ['d', 213], ['e', 40], ['f', 1]]
>>> print(sorted(test, key=itemgetter(1)))
[['c', -2], ['f', 1], ['a', 2], ['b', 5], ['e', 40], ['d', 213]]
>>> print(sorted(test, key=itemgetter(1), reverse=True))
[['d', 213], ['e', 40], ['b', 5], ['a', 2], ['f', 1], ['c', -2]]
>>> print(sorted(test, key=itemgetter(0)))
[['a', 2], ['b', 5], ['c', -2], ['d', 213], ['e', 40], ['f', 1]]
```

In the preceding example, we've created an outer list that contains inner lists with two elements: a character and a number. Next, we sort this list and use the number in the first index of the inner lists as the key. By default, `sorted()` will sort in ascending order. To sort in descending order, you need to supply the `reverse=True` argument. If we wanted to sort by letter, we would provide the `itemgetter()` with the value of `0` to specify to sort on elements found at that location.

Now, all that is left is to understand what `x[0:5:3]` means. Why are we even doing this in the first place? We are using list slicing to only grab the first and third element, that is, the name and count of the executable, to use for our table.

Remember that slicing notation supports three optional components: *List[x:y:z]*, were, *x* = start index, *y* = end index, *z* = step.

In this example, we start at index 0 and stop at index 5, taking steps of 3. If we do this, we will only get the elements at the zero and third position of the list before reaching the end.

Now, the statement `x[0:5:3]` for x in `sorted(data, key=itemgetter(3))` will loop through the newly sorted list and only retain the zero and third-positioned elements in each list. We then wrap this entire statement in a pair of square brackets in order to preserve our outer and inner list structure that `xlsxwriter` prefers.

The list object also has a `sort()` method that is syntactically similar to the `sorted()` function. However, the `sort()` function is more memory-friendly as it does not create a new list, but rather sorts the current list in place. Because memory consumption is not a big concern for a dataset, that might contain a few hundred entries at most and, as we did not want to modify the original list, we chose to use the `sorted()` function. We have the following code:

```
def sort_by_count(data):
    """
```

```
    The sort_by_count function sorts the lists by their count
    element
    :param data: the list of lists containing parsed UA data
    :return: the sorted count list of lists
    """
    # Return only the zero and third indexed item (the name and
    # count values) in the list after it has been sorted by the
    # count
    return [x[0:5:3] for x in sorted(data, key=itemgetter(3))]
```

Processing datetime objects with the sort_by_date() function

The `sort_by_date()` function is very similar to the `sort_by_count()` function except that it uses different indices. Since a `datetime` object is really just a number, we can easily sort by that as well. Supplying `reverse=True` allows us to sort in descending order.

Once again, we're first creating a new sorted list using the datetime in position 4 as the key. We are then only retaining the zero- and fourth-positioned elements in each list and wrapping all of that inside another list to preserve our nested list structure:

```
def sort_by_date(data):
    """
    The sort_by_date function sorts the lists by their datetime
    object
    :param data: the list of lists containing parsed UA data
    :return: the sorted date list of lists
    """
    # Supply the reverse option to sort by descending order
    return [x[0:6:4] for x in sorted(data, key=itemgetter(4),
    reverse=True)]
```

Writing generic spreadsheets – csv_writer.py

The `csv_writer.py` script is fairly straightforward compared with the previous two scripts we've written. This script is responsible for the CSV output of our `UserAssist` data. The `csv_writer.py` script has two functions: `csv_writer()` and the helper function, `file_time()`. We explained the `file_time()` function in the `xlsx_writer` section, and it will not be repeated here as it has the same implementation.

Understanding the csv_writer() function

The `csv_writer()` function, defined on line 38, is slightly different from the way we have been creating CSV output in previous chapters. We normally start by creating our headers list, creating a writer object, and writing the headers list and each sublist in our data variable. This time, instead of using `writer()`, we will use the `DictWriter()` method to handle writing our `UserAssist` dictionaries for us:

```
001 from __future__ import print_function
002 import sys
003 if sys.version_info[0] == 2:
004     import unicodecsv as csv
005 elif sys.version_info[0] == 3:
006     import csv
007 from datetime import datetime, timedelta
008 import logging
...
038 def csv_writer(data, out_file):
039     """
040     The csv_writer function writes the parsed UA data to a csv
041     file
042     :param data: the list of lists containing parsed UA data
043     :param out_file: the desired output directory and filename
044     for the csv file
045     :return: Nothing
046     """
047     print('[+] Writing CSV output.')
048     logging.info('Writing CSV to ' + out_file + '.')
```

On line 49, we do still create our headers list as normal. However, this list plays a more important role. This list contains the name of each key that will appear in our `UserAssist` dictionaries and in the order we want to display them. The `DictWriter()` method will allow us to then order our dictionaries by this list to ensure that our data is presented in the appropriate sequence. Depending on whether Python 2 or 3 is running the code, we open the `csvfile` using the appropriate method. Look at the following code:

```
049     headers = ['ID', 'Name', 'Path', 'Session ID', 'Count',
050     'Last Used Date (UTC)', 'Focus Time (ms)', 'Focus Count']
051
052     if sys.version_info[0] == 2:
053         csvfile = open(out_file, "wb")
054     elif sys.version_info[0] == 3:
055         csvfile = open(out_file, "w", newline='',
056         encoding='utf-8')
```

We start by creating our `csvfile` object and our writer. The `DictWriter()` method takes a file object as its required argument and optional keyword arguments. The `fieldnames` argument will ensure that the dictionary keys are written in the appropriate order. The `extrasaction` keyword is set to ignore scenarios where a dictionary contains a keyword that is not in the `fieldnames` list. If this option was not set, we would receive an exception if there was an extra unaccounted-for key in the dictionary. In our scenario, we should never encounter this issue as we have hardcoded the keys. However, if for some reason there are extra keys, we would rather the `DictWriter()` ignore them than crash, as follows:

```
058     with csvfile:
059         writer = csv.DictWriter(csvfile, fieldnames=headers,
060         extrasaction='ignore')
```

With the `DictWriter()` object, we can call the `writeheader()` method to automatically write the supplied field names:

```
061         # Writes the header from list supplied to fieldnames
062         # keyword argument
063         writer.writeheader()
```

Note that we do some additional processing on each dictionary before writing it. First, we add the ID key to the current loop count. Next, on line 71, we call the `fileTime()` method to convert the FILETIME object into a `datetime` format. Finally, on line 73, we write our dictionary to the CSV output file:

```
065         for i, dictionary in enumerate(data):
066             # Insert the 'ID' value to each dictionary in the
067             # list. Add 1 to start ID at 1 instead of 0.
068             dictionary['ID'] = i + 1
069             # Convert the FILETIME object in the fourth index to
070             # human readable value
071             dictionary['Last Used Date (UTC)'] = file_time(
072             dictionary['Last Used Date (UTC)'])
073             writer.writerow(dictionary)
```

After all the dictionaries have been written, we `flush()` and `close()` the handle on the `csvfile` object. And with that, we log the successful completion of our CSV script. All that's left at this point is to actually run our new framework:

```
075         csvfile.flush()
076         csvfile.close()
077         msg = 'Completed writing CSV file. Program exiting
successfully.'
078         print('[*]', msg)
079         logging.info(msg)
```

Running the UserAssist framework

Our script is capable of parsing both Windows XP- and Windows 7-based `UserAssist` keys. However, let's focus our attention on the differences between the CSV and XLSX output options. Using the `xlsxwriter` module and seeing the output should make the advantages of writing directly to an excel file over CSV clear. While you do lose the portability of the CSV document, you gain a lot more functionality. The following is the screenshot of running the `userassist.py` script against a Vista `NTUSER.DAT` and creating an XLSX output:

```
(py3.7.1) $ python userassist_parser.py --help
usage: userassist_parser.py [-h] [-l L] REGISTRY OUTPUT

This scripts parses the UserAssist Key from NTUSER.DAT.

positional arguments:
  REGISTRY     NTUSER Registry Hive.
  OUTPUT       Output file (.csv or .xlsx)

optional arguments:
  -h, --help  show this help message and exit
  -l L        File path of log file.

Developed by Preston Miller & Chapin Bryce on 20181119
(py3.7.1) $ python userassist_parser.py NTUSER.DAT ntuser.xlsx
[+] Parsing UserAssist values.
[-] Ignoring UEME_CTLSESSION value that is 8 bytes
[-] Ignoring UEME_CTLSESSION value that is 8 bytes
[-] Ignoring UEME_CTLSESSION value that is 8 bytes
[-] Ignoring UEME_CTLSESSION value that is 8 bytes
[-] Ignoring UEME_CTLSESSION value that is 8 bytes
[-] Ignoring UEME_CTLSESSION value that is 8 bytes
[-] Ignoring UEME_CTLSESSION value that is 8 bytes
[-] Ignoring UEME_CTLSESSION value that is 8 bytes
[+] Writing XLSX output.
[*] Completed writing XLSX file. Program exiting successfully.
```

The CSV output is not capable of preserving Python objects or crafting report-ready spreadsheets. The upside of a CSV report, besides the portability, is that writing the module itself is very simple. We were able to write the main logic in just a few lines of code compared with over 100 lines for the Excel document, which clearly took more time to develop.

Being able to write a customized Excel report is great, but comes at a time cost. It might not always be a feasible addition for the forensic developer as time constraints often play a large role in the development cycle and dictate what you can and cannot do. However, if time permits, this can save the hassle of performing this process manually by the examiner and allow more time for analysis.

Challenge

We talked extensively about the additions that Windows 7 brought to the `UserAssist` artifact. However, there are even more changes that we did not account for in our current implementation of the `UserAssist` framework. With Windows 7, some common folder names were replaced with GUIDs. The following is a table of some examples of folders and their respective GUIDs:

Folder	**GUID**
`UserProfiles`	`{0762D272-C50A-4BB0-A382-697DCD729B80}`
`Desktop`	`{B4BFCC3A-DB2C-424C-B029-7FE99A87C641}`
`Documents`	`{FDD39AD0-238F-46AF-ADB4-6C85480369C7}`
`Downloads`	`{374DE290-123F-4565-9164-39C4925E467B}`

An improvement to our script might involve finding these and other common folder GUIDs, and replacing them with the true path. A list of some of these common GUIDs can be found on Microsoft's MSDN website at `http://msdn.microsoft.com/en-us/library/bb882665.aspx`.

Alternatively, the graph we chose to chart the last 10 executables may not be the best way of presenting dates graphically. It might be worthwhile to create a more timeline-focused graph to better represent that data. Try using some of the other built-in graphs and their features to become more familiar with the graphing features of `xlsxwriter`.

Summary

This was a module-centric chapter, where we added three new modules to our toolkit. In addition, we gained an understanding of the `UserAssist` artifact and how to parse it. While these concepts are important, our brief detour with `timeit` may prove most valuable going forward.

As developers, there will be times where the execution of our scripts is lacking or, on large datasets, takes an absurd amount of time. In these situations, modules such as `timeit` can help audit and evaluate code to identify more efficient solutions for a given situation. The code for this project can be downloaded from GitHub or Packt, as described in the *Preface*.

In the next chapter, we will introduce how to hash files in Python. Specifically, we will focus on hashing blocks of data to identify identical and similar files. This is referred to as "fuzzy hashing." This technique is useful when evaluating objects that share a similar root, such as malware. We could take a known sample of malware we suspect was used on a system, fuzzy hash it, and search for matches on the system. Instead of finding an identical match, we receive a 90% match on an obscure file, which upon further inspection turns out to be a new variant of the malware that might otherwise have gone unnoticed. We will cover multiple methods to implement this functionality and the logic behind the process.

7 Fuzzy Hashing

Hashing is one of the most common processes run in DFIR. This process allows us to summarize file content and assign a representative and repeatable signature that represents the file's content. We generally employ file and content hashes using algorithms such as MD5, SHA1, and SHA256. These hash algorithms are valuable as we can use them for integrity validation since a change to even one byte of a file's content will completely alter the resulting hash value. These hashes are also commonly used to form whitelists to exclude known or irrelevant content, or alert lists that quickly identify known interesting files. In some cases, though, we need to identify near matches—something that our MD5, SHA1, and SHA256 algorithms can't handle on their own.

One of the most common utilities that assists with similarity analysis is ssdeep, developed by Jessie Kornblum. This tool is an implementation of the spamsum algorithm, developed by Dr. Andrew Tridgell, which generates a base64 signature representing file content. These signatures can be used, independently of the file's content, to help to determine the confidence that two files are similar. This allows for a less computationally intense comparison of these two files and presents a relatively short signature that can be shared or stored easily.

In this chapter, we'll do the following:

- Hash data using MD5, SHA1, and SHA256 algorithms with Python
- Discuss how to hash streams of data, files, and directories of files
- Explore how the spamsum algorithm works and implement a version in Python
- Leverage the compiled ssdeep library via Python bindings for increased performance and features

The code for this chapter was developed and tested using Python 2.7.15 and Python 3.7.1.

Background on hashing

Hashing data is a common technique in the forensics community to `fingerprint` a file. Normally, we create a hash of an entire file; however, in the script we'll build later in this chapter, we'll hash segments of a file to evaluate the similarity between two files. Before diving into the complexities of fuzzy hashing, let's walk through how Python can generate cryptographic hashes such as MD5 and SHA1 values.

Hashing files in Python

As previously discussed, there are multiple algorithms commonly used by the DFIR community and tools. Before generating a file hash, we must decide which algorithm we would like to use. This can be a tough question, as there are multiple factors to consider. The **Message Digest Algorithm 5** (**MD5**) produces a 128-bit hash and is one of the most commonly used cryptographic hash algorithms across forensic tools. The algorithm is relatively lightweight and the resulting hash is short in length, when compared with other algorithms. Since cryptographic hashes have a fixed length output, selecting an algorithm with a shorter length can help in reducing the impact on system resources.

However, the main issue with MD5 is the probability of hash collisions. A hash collision is where two different input values result in the same hash, an issue that is a product of having a fixed length hash value. This is an issue in forensics, as we rely on the hash algorithm to be a unique fingerprint to represent the integrity of data. If the algorithm has known collisions, the hash may no longer be unique and can't guarantee integrity. For this reason, MD5 isn't recommended for use as the primary hash algorithm in most forensic situations.

In addition to MD5, there are several other common cryptographic hash algorithms including the **Secure Hash Algorithm** (**SHA**) family. The SHA family consists of SHA-1 (160-bit), SHA-256 (256-bit), and SHA-512 (512-bit) to name a few of the more prominent algorithms used in forensics. The SHA-1 algorithm frequently accompanies the MD5 hash in most forensic tools. Recently a research group discovered collisions in the SHA-1 algorithm and shared their findings on their site, `https://shattered.io/`. Like MD5, SHA-1 is now losing popularity in the field.

Leveraging one of these hash algorithms is fairly straightforward in Python. In the following code block, we'll demonstrate the examples of hashing with the MD5, SHA-1, and SHA-256 algorithms in the interpreter.

To facilitate this, we'll need to import the standard library, `hashlib`, and provide data to generate a hash of. After importing `hashlib`, we create a hashing object using the `md5()` method. Once defined as `m`, we can use the `.update()` function to add data to the algorithm and the `hexdigest()` method to generate the hexadecimal hash we're accustomed to seeing from other tools. This process can be handled by a single line as demonstrated here:

```
>>> import hashlib
>>> m = hashlib.md5()
>>> m.update('This will be hashed!')
>>> m.hexdigest()
'0fc0cfd05cc543be3a2f7e7ed2fe51ea'
>>> hashlib.md5('This will be hashed!').hexdigest()
'0fc0cfd05cc543be3a2f7e7ed2fe51ea'
>>> hashlib.sha1('This will be hashed!').hexdigest()
'5166bd094f3f27762b81a7562d299d887dbd76e3'
>>> hashlib.sha256('This will be hashed!').hexdigest()
'03bb6968581a6d6beb9d1d863b418bfdb9374a6ee23d077ef37df006142fd595'
```

In the preceding example, we hashed a string object. But what about files? After all, that's what we're truly interested in doing.

To hash a file, we need to pass the contents of the file to the hash object. As seen in the code block, we begin by opening and writing to a file to generate some sample data that we can hash. After the setup, we close and then reopen the file for reading and use the `read()` method to read the full content of the file into the `buffer` variable. At this point, we provide the `buffer` value as the data to hash and generate our unique hash value. See the following code:

```
>>> output_file = open('output_file.txt', 'w')
>>> output_file.write('TmV2ZXIgR29ubmEgR212ZSBZb3UgVXA=')
>>> output_file.close()
>>> input_file = open('output_file.txt', 'r')
>>> buffer = input_file.read()
>>> hashlib.sha1(buffer).hexdigest()
'aa30b352231e2384888e9c78df1af47a9073c8dc'
>>> hashlib.md5(buffer).hexdigest()
'1b49a6fb562870e916ae0c040ea52811'
>>> hashlib.sha256(buffer).hexdigest()
'89446e08f985a9c201fa969163429de3dbc206bd7c7bb93e490631c308c653d7'
```

The hashing method shown here is good for small files or streams of data. We need to adjust our approach some if we want to be able to more flexibly handle files.

Hashing large files – hashing_example.py

Our first script in this chapter is short and to the point; it'll allow us to hash a provided file's content with a specified cryptographic algorithm. This code will likely be more useful as a feature within a larger script, such as our file listing utility; we'll demonstrate a standalone example to walk through how to handle hashing files in a memory-efficient manner.

To begin, we only need two imports, `argparse` and `hashlib`. Using these two built-in libraries, we'll be able to generate hashes, as shown in the prior example. On line 33, we list out the supported hash algorithms. This list should only contain algorithms available as a module within `hashlib`, as we'll call (for example) `md5` from the list as `hashlib.md5()`. The second constant defined, on line 34, is `BUFFER_SIZE`, which is used to control how much of a file to read at a time. This value should be smaller, 1 MB in this instance, to preserve the amount of memory required per read, although we also want a number large enough to limit the number of reads we have to perform on the file. You may find this number is adjusted based on the system you choose to run it on. For this reason, you may consider specifying this as an argument instead of a constant:

```
001 """Sample script to hash large files effiently."""
002 import argparse
003 import hashlib
...
033 HASH_LIBS = ['md5', 'sha1', 'sha256', 'sha512']
034 BUFFER_SIZE = 1024**3
```

Next, we define our arguments. This is very brief as we're only accepting a filename and an optional algorithm specification:

```
036 parser = argparse.ArgumentParser()
037 parser.add_argument("FILE", help="File to hash")
038 parser.add_argument("-a", "--algorithm",
039     help="Hash algorithm to use", choices=HASH_LIBS,
040     default="sha512")
041 args = parser.parse_args()
```

Once we know the specified arguments, we'll translate the selected algorithm from an argument into a function we can call. To do this, we use the `getattr()` method as shown on line 43. This built-in function allows us to retrieve functions and properties from an object (such as a method from a library, as shown in the following code). We end the line with `()` as we want to call the specified algorithm's initialization method and create an instance of the object as `alg` that we can use to generate the hash. This one-liner is the equivalent of calling `alg = hashlib.md5()` (for example), but performed in an argument-friendly fashion:

```
043 alg = getattr(hashlib, args.algorithm)()
```

On line 45, we open the file for reading, which we start on line 47 by reading the first buffer length into our `buffer_data` variable. We then enter a `while` loop where we update our hash algorithm object on line 49 before getting the next buffer of data on line 50. Luckily for us, Python will read all of the data from `input_file`, even if `BUFFER_SIZE` is greater than what remains in the file. Additionally, Python will exit the loop once we reach the end of the file and close it for us when exiting the `with` context. Lastly, on line 52, we print the `.hexdigest()` of the hash we calculated:

```
045 with open(args.FILE, 'rb') as input_file:
046
047     buffer_data = input_file.read(BUFFER_SIZE)
048     while buffer_data:
049         alg.update(buffer_data)
050         buffer_data = input_file.read(BUFFER_SIZE)
051
052 print(alg.hexdigest())
```

Creating fuzzy hashes

Now that we've mastered how to generate cryptographic hashes, let's work on generating fuzzy hashes. We'll discuss a few techniques we could employ for similarity analysis, and walk through a basic example of how ssdeep and spamsum employ rolling hashing to help generate more resilient signatures.

It may go without saying that our most accurate approach to similarity analysis is to compare the byte content of two files, side by side, and look for differences. While we may be able to accomplish this using command-line tools or a difference analysis tool (such as kdiff3), this only really works at a small scale. Once we move from comparing two small files to comparing many small files, or a few medium-sized files, we need a more efficient approach. This is where signature generation comes into play.

To generate a signature, we must have a few things figured out:

- What alphabet we want to use for our signature
- How we want to segment the file into summarizable blocks
- The technique for converting our block summary into a character from our alphabet

While the alphabet is an optional component, it allows us humans to better review and understand the data. We can always store it as integers and save a tiny bit of computational resources. Base64 is a common choice for the alphabet and is used by both spamsum and ssdeep.

For the aforementioned second and third items, let's discuss a few techniques for slicing up our file and generating our hash value. For this example (and to keep things simple), let's use the following character sequence as our file content:

```
abcdefghijklmnopqrstuvwxyz01
```

Our first approach is to slice the file into equal sized blocks. The first row in the following example is our file content, and the second is the numeric ASCII value for each character in our first row. For this example, we've decided to split our file into 4-byte blocks with the vertical bars and color-coded numeric ASCII values:

Fixed block Original	content	a	b	c	d	e	f	g	h	i	j	k	l	m	n	o	p	q	r	s	t	u	v	w	x	y	z	0	1
	ascii val	97	98	99	100	101	102	103	104	105	106	107	108	109	110	111	112	113	114	115	116	117	118	119	120	121	122	48	49
	ascii sum	394				410				426				442				458				474				340			
Kaq6KaU	b64 char	K				a				q				6				K				a				U			

We then summarize each of these 4-byte blocks by summing the ASCII value of the four characters, as shown in the third row of the table. We then convert this summarization of our file content into our base64 representation by taking 394 modulo 64 (*394 % 64*) which is 10, or **K** in the base64 alphabet. This base64 value, as you may have guessed, is on the fourth row.

The letter **K** becomes our summarization of the first block, **a** for the second, and it continues until we have our complete file signature of **Kaq6KaU**.

In the next diagram, there's a slightly modified version of our original file. As seen below, someone replaced **jklmn** with **hello**. We can now run our hashing algorithm against this file to get a sense of how much has changed between the two versions:

Fixed block	content	a	b	c	d	e	f	g	h	i	h	e	l	l	o	o	p	q	r	s	t	u	v	w	x	y	z	0	1
replacement	ascii sum	394				410				418				442				458				474				340			
Kai6KaU	b64 char	K				a				i				6				K				a				U			

Using the same technique, we calculate the new hash value of **Kai6KaU**. If we wanted to compare the similarity of our two files, we should be able to use our signatures to facilitate our comparison, right? So in this case, we have one letter difference between our signatures, meaning our two file streams are largely similar!

As you may have spotted, there's an issue here: we've found a hash collision when using our algorithm. In the prior example, the fourth block of each file is different; the first is **mnop** and the second is **loop**. Since we're summing our file content to determine our signature value, we're bound to get an unhealthy amount of collisions. These collisions may cause us to think files are more similar when they aren't, and unfortunately are a product of summarizing file content without the use of a cryptographic hash algorithm. For this reason, we have to find a better balance between summarizing file content and encountering hash collisions.

Our next example demonstrates what happens when insertion occurs. As you can see in the following diagram, the letter **h** was inserted after **mn**, adding one byte to the file and causing the entire content to shift right by one. In this instance, our last block will just contain the number 1, though some implementations may handle this differently:

Fixed block	content	a	b	c	d	e	f	g	h	i	j	k	l	m	n	h	o	p	q	r	s	t	u	v	w	x	y	z	0	1	N/A	N/A	N/A
insertion	ascii sum	394				410				426				434				454				470				411				49			
KaqyGWbx	b64 char	K				a				q				y				G				W				b				x			

Using our same formula, we calculate a hash of **KaqyGUbx**. This hash is largely different than **Kaq6KaU**. In fact, once we reach the block containing the change, the hash is completely different even though we have similar content in the latter half of the file.

This is one of the main reasons that using a fixed block size isn't the best approach for similarity analysis. Any shift in content moves data across the boundaries and will cause us to calculate completely different hashes for similar content. To address that, we need to be able to set these boundaries in another way.

Context Triggered Piecewise Hashing (CTPH)

As you probably guessed, this is where CTPH comes into play. Essentially, we're aiming to calculate reset points with this technique. Reset points, in this case, are boundaries similar to the 4-byte boundaries we used in the prior example, as we use these reset points to determine the amount of a file we want to summarize. The notable exception is that we pick the boundaries based on file content (our context triggering) versus fixed windows. What this means is we use a rolling hash, as employed by ssdeep and spamsum, to calculate values throughout the file; when this specific value is found, a boundary line is drawn and the content since the prior boundary is summarized (the piecewise hash). In the following example, we're using a simplified calculation to determine whether we've reached a reset point.

While both spamsum and ssdeep calculate the reset point number for each file, for our example, we'll use *7* to keep things simple. This means whenever our rolling hash has a value of *7*, we'll summarize the content between this boundary and the previous. As an additional note, this technique is meant for files with more than 28 bytes, so our hashes here will be really short and, therefore, less useful outside of our illustrative purposes.

Before jumping into the example, let's talk through what a rolling hash is. Once again, we'll use the same example file content we used previously. We then use what's known as a rolling hash to calculate our value for each byte of the file. A rolling hash works by calculating a hash value for all of the characters within a certain window of the file. In our case, we'll have a window size of three. The window movement in our file would look like this across the first four iterations:

- `['a', '', ''] = [97, 0, 0]`
- `['a', 'b', ''] = [97, 98, 0]`
- `['a', 'b', 'c'] = [97, 98, 99]`
- `['b', 'c', 'd'] = [98, 99, 100]`

As you can see, this rolling window would continue through the file, adding a new byte each iteration and removing the oldest byte, in FIFO style. To generate a hash of this window, we would then perform a series of further calculation against the values in the window.

For this example, as you likely guessed, we'll sum the ASCII values to keep things simple. This sum is shown in the first row of the following example. To keep the numbers smaller though, we'll then take our summed ASCII values (*S*) modulo 8 (*S % 8*) and use this integer to look for our boundaries in the file content. This number is found in the second row of the following screenshot. If *S % 8 == 7*, we've reached a reset point and can create a summarization of the prior block.

The ssdeep and spamsum algorithms handle this rolling window calculation differently, though the product of the calculation is used in the same manner. We have simplified the calculation to make this process easier to discuss.

Since our reset point is 7, as previously selected, we'll define a chunk of a file any time our rolling hash calculation returns a seven. This is represented in the following screenshot with horizontal lines showing the blocks we've set within the file.

For each block, we'll calculate our signature in the same way as before: summing up the ASCII integer values of the content within the entire block (as shown in the fourth row) and applying modulo 64 to get the character for the signature (as seen in the last row). Please remember that the only relationship between rows 2 and 4 in this example is that row 2 tells us when to set the reset point and calculate the number shown in row 4. These two hashes are algorithmically independent of one another by design. Row 4 is still the summation of the ASCII values for $a + b + c + d + e + f$ and not the summation of our rolling hash output:

	sum of window	97	195	294	297	300	303	306	309	312	315	318	321	324	327	330	333	336	339	342	345	348	351	354	357	360	363	291	219
Context based	rolling hash	1	3	6	1	4	7	2	5	0	3	6	1	4	7	2	5	0	3	6	1	4	7	2	5	0	3	3	3
Original	content	a	b	c	d	e	f	g	h	i	j	k	l	m	n	o	p	q	r	s	t	u	v	w	x	y	z	0	1
	ascii sum	597						852								916								579					
VUUD	b64 char	V						U								U								D					

This produces the signature **VUUD**. While much shorter, we now have context triggered hashes. As previously described, we've accomplished this by using the rolling hash to define our boundaries (the context triggering), and the summation of our block (piecewise hashing) to identify common chunks of the file that we can compare to files with similar reset point sizes (or other files with a reset point of 7).

For our final example, let's revisit what happens when we perform the same insertion of the letter **h**. Using our rolling hash to calculate our context-based blocks (as shown in the first row), we can calculate the summarization of blocks using the same algorithm and generate the signature **VUH1D**:

Context based	rolling hash	1	3	6	1	4	7	2	5	0	3	6	1	4	7	3	5	7	0	3	6	1	4	7	2	5	0	3	3	3
Insertion	content	a	b	c	d	e	f	g	h	i	j	k	l	m	n	h	o	p	q	r	s	t	u	v	w	x	y	z	0	1
	ascii sum	597						852								327			693						579					
VUH1D	b64 char	V						U								H			1						D					

As you can see, this technique is more resilient to insertions and allows us to more accurately compare differences in files than using the fixed blocks. In this case, our signatures are showing that the two files are more different than they are, though this technique is more accurate than our fixed block calculation as it understands that the tail of our file is the same between our two versions.

Obviously, this technique requires files larger than 28 bytes in order to produce accurate results, though hopefully this simplification can help depict how these fuzzy hashes are formed. With this understanding, let's start working on our script.

Implementing fuzzy_hasher.py

This script was tested with both Python versions 2.7.15 and 3.7.1 and doesn't leverage any third-party libraries.

While we'll get to the internals of the fuzzy hashing algorithm, let's start our script as we have the others. We begin with our imports, all standard libraries that we've used before as shown in the following. We also define a set of constants on lines 36 through 47. Lines 37 and 38 define our signature alphabet, in this case all of the base64 characters. The next set of constants are used in the spamsum algorithm to generate the hash. `CONTEXT_WINDOW` defines the amount of the file we'll read for our rolling hash. `FNV_PRIME` is used to calculate the hash while `HASH_INIT` sets a starting value for our hash. We then have `SIGNATURE_LEN`, which defines how long our fuzzy hash signature should be. Lastly, the `OUTPUT_OPTS` list is used with our argument parsing to show supported output formats—more on that later:

```
001 """Spamsum hash generator."""
002 import argparse
003 import logging
004 import json
005 import os
006 import sys
007
008 """ The original spamsum algorithm carries the following license:
009 Copyright (C) 2002 Andrew Tridgell <tridge@samba.org>
010
011 This program is free software; you can redistribute it and/or
012 modify it under the terms of the GNU General Public License
013 as published by the Free Software Foundation; either version 2
014 of the License, or (at your option) any later version.
015
016 This program is distributed in the hope that it will be useful,
017 but WITHOUT ANY WARRANTY; without even the implied warranty of
018 MERCHANTABILITY or FITNESS FOR A PARTICULAR PURPOSE. See the
019 GNU General Public License for more details.
020
021 You should have received a copy of the GNU General Public License
022 along with this program; if not, write to the Free Software
023 Foundation, Inc.,
024 51 Franklin Street, Fifth Floor, Boston, MA 02110-1301, USA.
```

```

CHANGELOG:
Implemented in Python as shown below by Chapin Bryce &
Preston Miller
"""

__authors__ = ["Chapin Bryce", "Preston Miller"]
__date__ = 20181027
__description__ = '''Generate file signatures using
    the spamsum algorithm.'''

# Base64 Alphabet
ALPHABET = 'ABCDEFGHIJKLMNOPQRSTUVWXYZ'
ALPHABET += 'abcdefghijklmnopqrstuvwxyz0123456789+/'

# Constants for use with signature calculation
CONTEXT_WINDOW = 7
FNV_PRIME = 0x01000193
HASH_INIT = 0x28021967
SIGNATURE_LEN = 64

# Argument handling constants
OUTPUT_OPTS = ['txt', 'json', 'csv']
logger = logging.getLogger(__file__)
```

This script has three functions: `main()`, `fuzz_file()`, and `output()`. The `main()` function acts as our primary controller, handling the processing of directories versus single files and calling the `output()` function to display the result of the hashing. The `fuzz_file()` function accepts a file path and generates a spamsum hash value. The `output()` function then takes the hash and filename and displays the values in the specified format:

```
def main(file_path, output_type):
...
def fuzz_file(file_path):
...
def output(sigval, filename, output_type='txt'):
```

The structure of our script is fairly straightforward, as emphasized by the following diagram. As illustrated by the dashed line, the `fuzz_file()` function is the only function that returns a value. This is true as our `output()` function displays content on the console instead of returning it to `main()`:

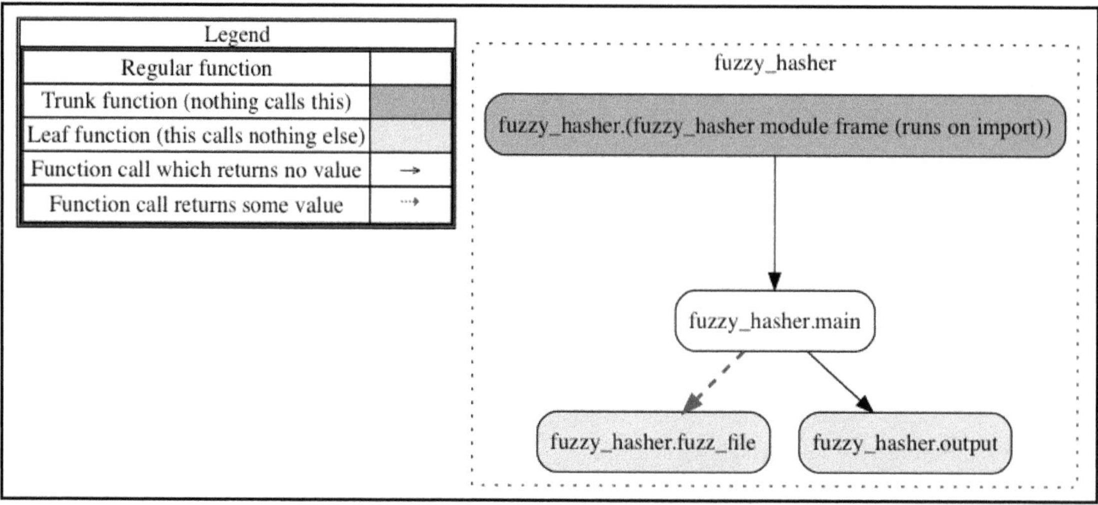

Finally, our script ends with argument handling and log initiation. For command-line arguments, we're accepting a path to a file or folder to process and the format of our output. Our output will be written to the console, with current options for text, CSV, and JSON output types. Our logging parameter is standard and looks very similar to our other implementations, with the notable difference that we're writing the log messages to `sys.stderr` instead so that the user can still interact with the output generated by `sys.stdout`:

```
if __name__ == '__main__':
    parser = argparse.ArgumentParser(
        description=__description__,
        epilog='Built by {}. Version {}'.format(
            ", ".join(__authors__), __date__),
        formatter_class=argparse.ArgumentDefaultsHelpFormatter
    )
    parser.add_argument('PATH',
        help='Path to file or folder to generate hashes for. '
             'Will run recursively.')
    parser.add_argument('-o', '--output-type',
        help='Format of output.', choices=OUTPUT_OPTS,
        default="txt")
    parser.add_argument('-l', help='specify log file path',
```

```
        default="./")

    args = parser.parse_args()

    if args.l:
        if not os.path.exists(args.l):
            os.makedirs(args.l) # create log directory path
            log_path = os.path.join(args.l, 'fuzzy_hasher.log')
    else:
        log_path = 'fuzzy_hasher.log'

    logger.setLevel(logging.DEBUG)
    msg_fmt = logging.Formatter("%(asctime)-15s %(funcName)-20s"
        "%(levelname)-8s %(message)s")
    strhndl = logging.StreamHandler(sys.stderr) # Set to stderr
    strhndl.setFormatter(fmt=msg_fmt)
    fhndl = logging.FileHandler(log_path, mode='a')
    fhndl.setFormatter(fmt=msg_fmt)
    logger.addHandler(strhndl)
    logger.addHandler(fhndl)

    logger.info('Starting Fuzzy Hasher v. {}'.format(__date__))
    logger.debug('System ' + sys.platform)
    logger.debug('Version ' + sys.version.replace("\n", " "))

    logger.info('Script Starting')
    main(args.PATH, args.output_type)
    logger.info('Script Completed')
```

With this framework, let's explore how our `main()` function is implemented.

Starting with the main() function

Our main function accepts two parameters: the file path and output type. We first check the output type to ensure it's in the `OUTPUT_OPTS` list, just in case the function was called from other code that did not validate. If it is an unknown output format, we'll raise an error and exit the script:

```
def main(file_path, output_type):
    """
    The main function handles the main operations of the script
    :param file_path: path to generate signatures for
    :param output_type: type of output to provide
    :return: None
    """

```

```
059     # Check output formats
060     if output_type not in OUTPUT_OPTS:
061         logger.error(
062             "Unsupported output format '{}' selected. Please "
063             "use one of {}".format(
064                 output_type, ", ".join(OUTPUT_OPTS)))
065         sys.exit(2)
```

We then start working with the file path, getting its absolute file path on line 67, and checking whether it's a directory on line 69. If so, we begin to iterate over the directory and subdirectories to find and process all files within. The code on lines 71 through 73 should look familiar from `Chapter 5`, *Databases in Python*. On line 74, we call the `fuzz_file()` function to generate our hash value, `sigval`. This `sigval` value is then provided, along with the filename and output format, to our `output()` function:

```
067     # Check provided file path
068     file_path = os.path.abspath(file_path)
069     if os.path.isdir(file_path):
070         # Process files in folders
071         for root, _, files in os.walk(file_path):
072             for f in files:
073                 file_entry = os.path.join(root, f)
074                 sigval = fuzz_file(file_entry)
075                 output(sigval, file_entry, output_type)
```

The remainder of our `main()` function handles single file processing and error handling for invalid paths. If, as seen on lines 76 through 79, the path is a file, we'll process it the same as we did before, generating the hash with `fuzz_file()` and passing the values to our `output()` function. Lastly, on lines 80 through 84, we handle errors with accessing the specified file or folder path:

```
076     elif os.path.isfile(file_path):
077         # Process a single file
078         sigval = fuzz_file(file_path)
079         output(sigval, file_path, output_type)
080     else:
081         # Handle an error
082         logger.error("Error - path {} not found".format(
083             file_path))
084         sys.exit(1)
```

Creating our fuzzy hashes

Before we dive into the code for our `fuzz_file()` function, let's talk briefly about the moving parts here:

- A rolling hash
- A calculated reset point that is derived from the file's size
- Two traditional hashes, in this case leveraging the FNV algorithm

The rolling hash is similar to our earlier example in that it's used to identify the boundaries that we'll summarize using our traditional hashes. In the case of ssdeep and spamsum, the reset point that the rolling hash is compared to (set to `7` in our prior example) is calculated based on the file's size. We'll show the exact function for determining this value in a bit, though we wanted to highlight that this means only files with the same block size can be compared. While there is more to talk about conceptually, let's start working through the code and applying these concepts.

We now move to the fun function: `fuzz_file()`. This function accepts a file path and uses the constants found at the beginning of the file to handle the calculation of the signature:

```
def fuzz_file(file_path):
    """
    The fuzz_file function creates a fuzzy hash of a file
    :param file_path (str): file to read.
    :return (str): spamsum hash
    """
```

Generating our rolling hash

The following code block is our rolling hash function. Now, it may seem odd to have a function within a function, though this design has a few advantages. First, it's useful for organization. This rolling hash code block is only used by our `fuzz_file()` function and, by nesting it inside this function, we can inform the next person who reads our code that this is the case. Secondly, by placing this function within `fuzz_file()`, we can assure anyone who imports our code as a module doesn't misuse the rolling hash function. And while there are multiple other efficiencies and management reasons for selecting this design, we wanted to incorporate this feature into this script to introduce you to the concept. As you see in our other scripts, this isn't always used for specialized functions but is a tool that you can employ in your scripts to refine their design.

This nested function takes two arguments, shortened to `nb` for `new_byte` and `rh` for our rolling hash tracking dictionary. In our prior example, to calculate the rolling hash, we added the ASCII values of the entire window together. In this function, we'll perform a series of calculations to help us generate a rolling hash of a larger 7-byte window:

```
    def update_rolling_hash(nb, rh):
        """
        Update the rolling hash value with the new byte
        :param nb (int): new_byte as read from file
        :param rh (dict): rolling hash tracking dictionary
        :return: computed hash value to compare to reset_point
        """
```

The `rh` rolling hash tracking dictionary is used to keep an eye on the moving parts within this rolling hash. There are three numbers that are stored as `r1`, `r2`, and `r3`. These numbers face additional calculations, as shown in the following code block, and the sum of the three are returned as the integer representing the rolling hash for that frame of the file.

The other two elements tracked by the dictionary are `rn` and `rw`. The `rn` key holds the offset the rolling hash is at within the file and is used to determine what character in the window is replaced by the `nb`, `new_byte`, value. This window, as you may have guessed, is stored in `rw`. Unlike our prior example where each character in the window was shifted left for each calculation of the rolling hash, this implementation just replaces the oldest character in the array. This improves efficiency as it results in one operation instead of eight:

```
        # Calculate R2
        rh['r2'] -= rh['r1']
        rh['r2'] += (CONTEXT_WINDOW * nb)

        # Calculate R1
        rh['r1'] += nb
        rh['r1'] -= rh['rw'][rh['rn'] % CONTEXT_WINDOW]

        # Update RW and RN
        rh['rw'][rh['rn'] % CONTEXT_WINDOW] = nb
        rh['rn'] += 1

        # Calculate R3
        rh['r3'] = (rh['r3'] << 5) & 0xFFFFFFFF
        rh['r3'] = rh['r3'] ^ nb

        # Return the sum of R1 + R2 + R3
        return rh['r1'] + rh['r2'] + rh['r3']
```

This logic is computationally the same as that used by ssdeep and spamsum. To start, we compute the `r2` value by subtracting `r1` and adding the product of `CONTEXT_WINDOW` and `new_byte`. We then update the `r1` value by adding `new_byte` and subtracting the oldest byte within the window. This means that `r1` stores the sum of the entire window, similarly to our entire rolling hash algorithm in the earlier example.

On line 111, we start updating our window, replacing the oldest byte with our `new_byte` character. After this, we increment the `rn` value so that it accurately tracks the offset within the file.

Finally, we calculate our `r3` value, which uses some operations we haven't introduced at this point. The << operator is a bitwise operator that shifts our value to the left, in this case by five places. This is effectively the same as us multiplying our value by 2**5. The second new bitwise operator on line 115 is `&`,which in Python is a bitwise `AND` statement. This operator evaluates each bit for the values on either side of the operation, position by position, and if they're both equal to `1`, they're enabled in that position of the output; otherwise, they're disabled. As a note, two `0` values in the same position do not result in `1` when using a bitwise `AND` statement. The third new bitwise operator is on line 116 and is `^`, or the exclusive `OR` operator, also called an XOR operation. This works mostly as the opposite of our bitwise `AND` statement, where if the bits between the two values, position by position, are different, `1` is returned for that position and if they're the same, `0` is returned.

More information on bitwise operations in Python is available at `https://wiki.python.org/moin/BitwiseOperators`.

With our bitwise operations out of the way, we return the sum of `r1`, `r2`, and `r3` for further use in our fuzzy hash calculation.

Preparing signature generation

Moving back into our `fuzz_file()` function, we evaluate the provided file to see whether it has any content, and if so, open the file. We store this file size for later use:

```
122     fsize = os.stat(file_path).st_size
123     if fsize == 0:
124         logger.warning("File is 0-bytes. Skipping...")
125         return ""
126     open_file = open(file_path, 'rb')
```

We now start with our first factor in the hashing algorithm, the **reset point**. This value is noted as the first value in a signature, as it's used to determine what hashes can be compared. To calculate this number, we start with `3`, as selected in the spamsum algorithm as a minimum reset point. We then double the reset point, as shown on line 130, until it's larger than the `filesize / 64`:

```
129     reset_point = 3
130     while reset_point * 64 < fsize:
131         reset_point *= 2
```

Once we have our initial reset point, we read our file into memory as `bytearray` since we want to read each character as a byte that we can interpret. We then set up our `while` loop, which we'll use to adjust the `reset_point` size if we need to—more on that later on:

```
134     complete_file = bytearray(open_file.read())
135     done = False
136     while not done:
```

Once within our `while` loop, we'll initiate our hashing objects. The first object is `rolling_hash`, a dictionary with five keys. The `r1`, `r2`, and `r3` keys are used to compute the hash; the `rn` key tracks the position of the cursor in the file; the `rw` key holds a list the size of the `CONTEXT_WINDOW` constant. This is the dictionary that's referenced heavily in our `update_rolling_hash()` function. It may be helpful to re-read that section now that you've seen what the `rolling_hash` dictionary looks like.

Following this dictionary, we have `trad_hash1` and `trad_hash2` initialized with the `HASH_INIT` constant. Lastly, we initialize the two signatures, `sig1` and `sig2`. The variable `trad_hash1` is used to populate the `sig1` value, and similarly, `trad_hash2` is used to populate the `sig2` value. We'll show how we calculate these traditional hashes and update our signatures shortly:

```
138         rolling_hash = {
139             'r1': 0,
140             'r2': 0,
141             'r3': 0,
142             'rn': 0,
143             'rw': [0 for _ in range(CONTEXT_WINDOW)]
144         }
145         trad_hash1 = HASH_INIT
146         trad_hash2 = HASH_INIT
147         sig1 = ""
148         sig2 = ""
```

Once we've initialized our hash values, we can start iterating through the file as seen on line 151. On line 153, we calculate the rolling hash using the latest byte from the file and the `rolling_hash` dictionary. Remember that dictionaries can be passed into a function and updated, and can retain their updated values outside of the function without needing to be returned. This allows a simpler interface with our rolling hash function. This function simply returns the calculated rolling hash, which is in the form of an integer as previously discussed. This rolling hash allows us to hash a moving (or rolling) window of data through a byte stream and is used to identify when in our file we should add a character to our signature:

```
151         for new_byte in complete_file:
152             # Calculate our rolling hash
153             rh = update_rolling_hash(new_byte, rolling_hash)
```

After calculating the rolling hash value, we need to update our traditional hashes. These hashes use the **Fowler–Noll–Vo** (**FNV**) hash, where we multiply the former value of the hash against the fixed prime, defined as one of our constants, before being XOR'd (^ as previously discussed) against the new byte of data. Unlike the rolling hash, these hash values continue to increment with each new byte and grow in size until we reach one of our boundaries:

```
156             trad_hash1 = (trad_hash1 * FNV_PRIME) ^ new_byte
157             trad_hash2 = (trad_hash2 * FNV_PRIME) ^ new_byte
```

These boundaries are evaluated by two conditionals, one for each of our hash/signature pairs. Lines 161 through 164 are functionally equivalent to lines 165 through 168, with the exception of which traditional hash and signature is in use. For simplicity, we'll walk through the first.

On lines 161 and 162 (due to line wrapping), we have our first conditional statement, which evaluates whether the product of our rolling hash modulo `reset_point`, is equal to `reset_point - 1`. We also ensure that our overall signature length is less than the maximum signature length minus 1. If these conditions are met, we've reached a boundary and will convert our traditional hash into a character of our signature, as shown on line 163. After adding a character to our signature, we then reset our traditional hash back to the initial value, meaning the next block of data will have a hash value starting from the same point as the prior block.

As mentioned, this is repeated for the second signature, with the notable exception that the second signature is modifying `reset_point` (by multiplying it by two) and the maximum signature length (by dividing it by two). This second reset point was added to address the desire for the spamsum signature to be short—64 characters by default. This means that the primary signature may be cut off and the tail of the file may represent one character of the signature. To combat this, spamsum added the second signature to generate a value that represents more, if not all, of the file. This second signature effectively has a `reset_point` twice as large as the first signature:

```
            # Check if our rolling hash reaches a reset point
            # If so, update sig and reset trad_hash
            if (rh % reset_point == reset_point - 1
                    and len(sig1) < SIGNATURE_LEN - 1):
                sig1 += ALPHABET[trad_hash1 % 64]
                trad_hash1 = HASH_INIT
            if (rh % (reset_point * 2) == (reset_point * 2) - 1
                    and len(sig2) < (SIGNATURE_LEN / 2) - 1):
                sig2 += ALPHABET[trad_hash2 % 64]
                trad_hash2 = HASH_INIT
```

This is the end of our for loop; this logic will repeat until we've reached the end of the file, though the signatures will only grow to 63 and 31 characters in length, respectively. After our `for` loop exists, we evaluate whether we should start the `while` loop (beginning on line 136) over again. We would want to do this if our first signature was less than 32 characters and our `reset_point` wasn't the default value of `3`. If we have too short a signature, we halve our `reset_point` value and re-run our entire calculation again. This means that we need every efficiency possible within this `while` loop, as we could be re-processing content over and over:

```
        # If sig1 is too short, change block size and recalculate
        if len(sig1) < SIGNATURE_LEN / 2 and reset_point > 3:
            reset_point = reset_point // 2
            logger.debug("Shortening block size to {}".format(
                reset_point))
        else:
            done = True
```

If our signature length is greater than 32 characters, we exit our `while` loop and generate the last character for our signature. If the product of our rolling hash isn't equal to zero, we add the last character to each signature, as shown on lines 180 and 181:

```
178     # Add any values from the tail to our hash
179     if rh != 0:
180         sig1 += ALPHABET[trad_hash1 % 64]
181         sig2 += ALPHABET[trad_hash2 % 64]
```

```

    # Close the file and return our new signature
    open_file.close()
    return "{}:{}:{}".format(reset_point, sig1, sig2)
```

At this point, we can close the file and return our full spamsum/ssdeep signature. This signature has three, hopefully recognizable, parts:

- Our `reset_point` value
- The primary signature
- The secondary signature

Providing the output

Our last function, luckily, is a whole lot simpler than the previous one. This function provides output of the signature and filename in one of the supported formats. In the past, we've written separate functions to handle separate formats, though in this case we've opted to place them all in the same function. This design decision is because we want to provide results in near-real time, especially if the user is processing a number of files. Since our logs are redirected to `STDERR`, we can use the `print()` function to provide results on `STDOUT`. This allows flexibility to our users, who can pipe the output into another program (such as grep) and perform additional processing on the results:

```
def output(sigval, filename, output_type='txt'):
    """Write the output of the script in the specified format
    :param sigval (str): Calculated hash
    :param filename (str): name of the file processed
    :param output_type (str): Formatter to use for output
    """
    if output_type == 'txt':
        print("{} {}".format(sigval, filename))
    elif output_type == 'json':
        print(json.dumps({"sig": sigval, "file": filename}))
    elif output_type == 'csv':
        print("{},\"{}\"".format(sigval, filename))
    else:
        raise NotImplementedError(
            "Unsupported output type: {}".format(output_type))
```

Running fuzzy_hasher.py

The following screenshot shows us how we can generate our fuzzy hashing on a set of files within a directory and perform post-processing on the output. In this case, we're hiding the log messages by sending `STDERR` to `/dev/null`. Then, we pipe our output into `jq`, a utility that formats and queries JSON data, to present our output in a nicely formatted manner:

```
(py3.7.1) $ python fuzzy_hasher.py test_data/ -o json 2>/dev/null | jq '.'
{
  "sig": "6144:c4AYyuHeJ6r+/c+KbACreaDFBWb630KP14uEpRI2:/pj+/Gdas18vd",
  "file": "/book/ch7/test_data/file_1"
}
{
  "sig": "6144:CM25l7OAZxLp9SQr2GlFOYXwYvThLa0Au6W6zcfZ:B25l7OAvSQr20FOxuEzch",
  "file": "/book/ch7/test_data/file_3"
}
{
  "sig": "3072:txY051DcDOz1ZgHSDWYI9TNiqg3fEZvTXbG9wXnvaa9yCqTEmo/y/kOkaCu0/M:PY
UpDdI9TlX1LG4nvaaUTayMnMIM",
  "file": "/book/ch7/test_data/file_4"
}
{
  "sig": "6144:oQfHmO1mMsDPU/PAyLqq59Toq3sjEF33kH2:FuQdsDPZq3sjaH1",
  "file": "/book/ch7/test_data/file_5"
}
{
  "sig": "3072:xI3BjBl25lQ8fBgLpLu8ASJm5S5vBTDBfdAF6WpstZ/Xg3LXzIVGbJf2/Izc2w:mn
myLdv1yovOF6TUvf229w",
  "file": "/book/ch7/test_data/file_2"
}
```

There are a few things you may have identified in this output. The first we'll highlight is that the files aren't in alphabetical order. This is because our `os.walk` function doesn't preserve alphabetical order by default when it iterates through a path. The second thing is, even though all of these files are identical in size, they vary in block size. What this means is that some of these files (containing random content) didn't have enough blocks and therefore the signatures were too short. This means we needed to halve the block size and try again, so when we move to the comparison component, we can compare files with enough similar blocks. On the other hand, the second signature in the files with the 3,072 blocks (`file_2` and `file_4`) can be compared in part to the first signature of the other files with block sizes of 6,144.

We've provided these test files for your use and comparison to confirm our implementation matches yours and the output of the next script.

Using ssdeep in Python – ssdeep_python.py

This script was tested with both Python 2.7.15 and 3.7.1, and requires the ssdeep version 3.3 third-party library.

As you may have noticed, the prior implementation is almost prohibitively slow. In situations like this, it's best to leverage a language, such as C, that can perform this operation much faster. Luckily for us, spamsum was originally written in C, then further expanded by the ssdeep project, also in C. One of the expansions the ssdeep project provides us with is Python bindings. These bindings allow us to still have our familiar Python function calls while offloading the heavy calculations to our compiled C code. Our next script covers the implementation of the ssdeep library in a Python module to produce the same signatures and handle comparison operations.

In this second example of fuzzy hashing, we're going to implement a similar script using the ssdeep Python library. This allows us to leverage the ssdeep tool and the spamsum algorithm, which has been widely used and accepted in the fields of digital forensics and information security. This code will be the preferred method for fuzzy hashing in most scenarios as it's more efficient with resources and produces more accurate results. This tool has seen wide support in the community, and many ssdeep signatures are available online. For example, the VirusShare and VirusTotal websites host hashes from ssdeep on their sites. This public information can be used to check for known malicious files that match or are similar to executable files on a host machine, without the need to download the malicious files.

One weakness of ssdeep is that it doesn't provide information beyond the matching percentage and can't compare files with significantly different block sizes. This can be an issue as ssdeep automatically generates the block size based on the size of the input file. The process allows ssdeep to run more efficiently and accommodates scaling much better than our script; however, it doesn't provide a manual solution to specify a block size. We could take our prior script and hardcode our block size, though that introduces other (previously discussed) issues.

This script starts the same as the other, with the addition of the new import of the ssdeep library. To install this library, run `pip install ssdeep==3.3`, or if that fails, you can run `BUILD_LIB=1 pip install ssdeep==3.3` as per the documentation at `https://pypi.python.org/pypi/ssdeep`. This library wasn't built by the developer of ssdeep, but another member of the community who created the bindings Python needs to communicate with the C-based library. Once installed, it can be imported as seen on line 7:

```
001 """Example script that uses the ssdeep python bindings."""
002 import argparse
003 import logging
```

```
004 import os
005 import sys
006
007 import ssdeep
```

This iteration has a similar structure to our previous one, though we hand off all of our calculations to the `ssdeep` library. Though we may be missing our hashing and comparison functions, we're still using our main and output functions in a very similar manner:

```
047 def main():
...
104 def output():
```

Our program flow has also remained similar to our prior iteration, though it's missing the internal hashing function we developed in our prior iteration. As seen in the flow diagram, we still make calls to the `output()` function in the `main()` function:

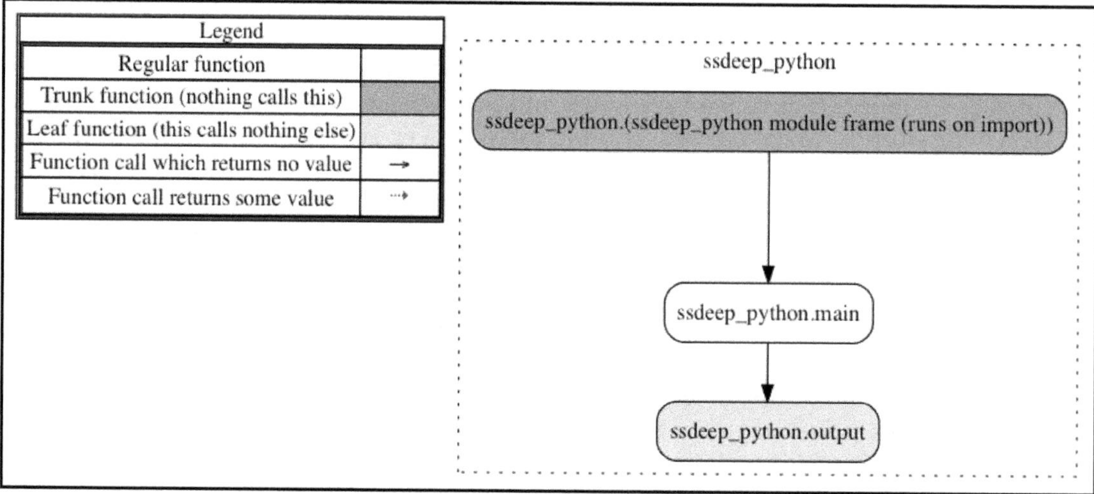

Our argument parsing and logging configurations are nearly identical to the prior script. The major difference is that we've introduced one new file path argument and renamed our argument that accepted files or folders. On line 134, we once more create the `argparse` object to handle our two positional arguments and two optional output format and logging flags. The remainder of this code block is consistent with the prior script, with the exception of renaming our log files:

```
134 if __name__ == '__main__':
135     parser = argparse.ArgumentParser(
136         description=__description__,
137         epilog='Built by {}. Version {}'.format(
```

```
            ", ".join(__authors__), __date__),
        formatter_class=argparse.ArgumentDefaultsHelpFormatter
    )
    parser.add_argument('KNOWN',
        help='Path to known file to use to compare')
    parser.add_argument('COMPARISON',
        help='Path to file or directory to compare to known. '
        'Will recurse through all sub directories')
```

Revisiting the main() function

This `main()` function is very similar to the prior script, though it has a few additional lines of code as we've added some functionality. This script starts the same with checking that the output type is a valid format, as shown on lines 56 through 62. We then add another conditional on line 63 that allows us to print the CSV header row since this output is more complicated than the last iteration:

```
047 def main(known_file, comparison, output_type):
048     """
049     The main function handles the main operations of the script
050     :param known_file: path to known file
051     :param comparison: path to look for similar files
052     :param output_type: type of output to provide
053     :return: None
054     """
055 
056     # Check output formats
057     if output_type not in OUTPUT_OPTS:
058         logger.error(
059             "Unsupported output format '{}' selected. Please "
060             "use one of {}".format(
061                 output_type, ", ".join(OUTPUT_OPTS)))
062         sys.exit(2)
063     elif output_type == 'csv':
064         # Special handling for CSV headers
065         print('"similarity","known_file","known_hash",'
066               '"comp_file","comp_hash"')
```

Now that we've handled the output format validation, let's pivot to our files for comparison. To start, we'll get the absolute path for both our known file and comparison path for consistency to our prior script. Then, on line 73, we check to ensure our known file exists. If it does, we then calculate the ssdeep hash on line 78. This calculation is completely handled by ssdeep; all we need to do is provide a valid file path to the `hash_from_file()` method. This method returns a string value containing our ssdeep hash, the same product as our `fuzz_file()` function in our prior script. The big difference here is speed improvements through the use of efficient C code running in the `ssdeep` module:

```
068     # Check provided file paths
069     known_file = os.path.abspath(known_file)
070     comparison = os.path.abspath(comparison)
071
072     # Generate ssdeep signature for known file
073     if not os.path.exists(known_file):
074         logger.error("Error - path {} not found".format(
075             comparison))
076         sys.exit(1)
077
078     known_hash = ssdeep.hash_from_file(known_file)
```

Now that we have our known hash value, we can evaluate our comparison path. In case this path is a directory, as shown on line 81, we'll walk through the folder and it's subfolders looking for files to process. On line 86, we generate a hash of this comparison file as we had for the known file. The next line introduces the `compare()` method, allowing us to provide two hashes for evaluation. This compare method returns an integer between (and including) 0 and 100, representing the confidence that these two files have similar content. We then take all of our parts, including the filenames, hashes, and resulting similarity, and provide them to our output function along with our formatting specification. This logic continues until we've recursively processed all of our files:

```
080     # Generate and test ssdeep signature for comparison file(s)
081     if os.path.isdir(comparison):
082         # Process files in folders
083         for root, _, files in os.walk(comparison):
084             for f in files:
085                 file_entry = os.path.join(root, f)
086                 comp_hash = ssdeep.hash_from_file(file_entry)
087                 comp_val = ssdeep.compare(known_hash, comp_hash)
088                 output(known_file, known_hash,
089                        file_entry, comp_hash,
090                        comp_val, output_type)
```

Our next conditional handles the same operations, but for a single file. As you can see, it uses the same `hash_from_file()` and `compare()` functions as in the directory operation. Once all of our values are assigned, we pass them in the same manner to our `output()` function. Our final conditional handles the case where an error on input is found, notifying the user and exiting:

```
092     elif os.path.isfile(comparison):
093         # Process a single file
094         comp_hash = ssdeep.hash_from_file(comparison)
095         comp_val = ssdeep.compare(known_hash, comp_hash)
096         output(known_file, known_hash, file_entry, comp_hash,
097                comp_val, output_type)
098     else:
099         logger.error("Error - path {} not found".format(
100             comparison))
101         sys.exit(1)
```

Redesigning our output() function

Our last function is `output()`; this function takes our many values and presents them cleanly to the user. Just like our prior script, we'll support TXT, CSV, and JSON output formats. To show a different design for this type of function, we'll use our format specific conditionals to build out a template. This template will then be used to print our contents in a formatted manner. This technique is useful if we plan on changing our output function (in this case `print()`) to another output function down the road:

```
104 def output(known_file, known_hash, comp_file, comp_hash, comp_val,
105            output_type='txt'):
106     """Write the output of the script in the specified format
107     :param sigval (str): Calculated hash
108     :param filename (str): name of the file processed
109     :param output_type (str): Formatter to use for output
110     """
```

To begin, we need to convert our one integer value, `comp_val`, into a string for compatibility with our templates. With this complete on line 112, we'll build our template for the text format. The text format gives us the freedom to display the data in a way that we find useful for visual review. The following is one option, though feel free to make modifications.

On lines 113 and 114, we're able to build our template with named placeholders by using the curly braces surrounding our placeholder identifier. Skipping ahead to lines 127 to 132, you can see that when we call `msg.format()`, we provide our values as arguments using the same names as our placeholders. This tells the `format()` method which placeholder to fill with which value. The main advantage of naming our placeholders is that we can arrange the values however we want when we call the `format()` method, and even have the elements in different positions between our template formats:

```
111     comp_val = str(comp_val)
112     if output_type == 'txt':
113         msg = "{similarity} - {known_file} {known_hash} | "
114         msg += "{comp_file} {comp_hash}"
```

Next is our JSON formatting. The `json.dumps()` method is the preferred way to output dictionaries as JSON content, though in this case we'll explore how you can accomplish a similar goal. Using our same templating method, we build out a dictionary where the keys are fixed strings and the values are the placeholders. Since the templating syntax uses a single curly brace to indicate a placeholder, we must escape the single curly brace with a second curly brace. This means our entire JSON object it wrapped in an extra curly brace—don't fear, only one of the two curly braces will display on print:

```
115     elif output_type == 'json':
116         msg = '{{"similarity": {similarity}, "known_file": '
117         msg += '"{known_file}", "known_hash": "{known_hash}", '
118         msg += '"comparison_file": "{comp_file}", '
119         msg += '"comparison_hash": "{comp_hash}"}}'
```

Lastly, we have our CSV output, which uses the named placeholder templating again. As you may have noticed, we wrapped each value in double quotes to ensure that any commas within the values don't cause formatting issues down the line:

```
120     elif output_type == 'csv':
121         msg = '"{similarity}","{known_file}","{known_hash}"'
122         msg += '"{comp_file}","{comp_hash}"'
```

The only reason we have our `msg` variable on multiple lines here is for word wrapping. There's nothing else stopping you from having one long string as a format template. Lastly, we have our `else` conditional, which will catch any unsupported output type:

```
123     else:
124         raise NotImplementedError(
125             "Unsupported output type: {}".format(output_type))
```

After our conditional, we print out the template with the applied values in place of the placeholders. If we wanted to support a new or alternate format, we could add a new conditional above and create the desired template without needing to re-implement this `print()` function:

```
    print(msg.format(
        similarity=comp_val,
        known_file=known_file,
        known_hash=known_hash,
        comp_file=comp_file,
        comp_hash=comp_hash))
```

Running ssdeep_python.py

We can now run our script, providing, for example, `test_data/file_3` as our known file and the whole `test_data/` folder as our comparison set. Using the JSON output again, we can see the result of our templating in the two following screenshots:

```
(py3.7.1) $ python ssdeep_python.py test_data/file_3 test_data/ -o json \
>                   2> /dev/null | jq '.'
{
  "similarity": 0,
  "known_file": "/book/ch7/test_data/file_3",
  "known_hash": "6144:CM2517OAZxLp9SQr2GlFOYXwYvThLa0Au6W6zcfZ:B2517OAvSQr20FOxuEz
ch",
  "comparison_file": "/book/ch7/test_data/file_2a",
  "comparison_hash": "3072:xI3BjBl2rrEWtrMlQ8fBgLpLu8ASJm5S5vBTDBfdAF6WpstZ/Xg3LXz
IVGbJf2/5:mnG4yLdvlyovOF6TUvf229w"
}
{
  "similarity": 0,
  "known_file": "/book/ch7/test_data/file_3",
  "known_hash": "6144:CM2517OAZxLp9SQr2GlFOYXwYvThLa0Au6W6zcfZ:B2517OAvSQr20FOxuEz
ch",
  "comparison_file": "/book/ch7/test_data/file_1a",
  "comparison_hash": "6144:c4AYyleJ6rjL/c+KbACreaDFBWb630KP14uEpRI2:/pyf/Gdas18vd"
}
{
  "similarity": 0,
  "known_file": "/book/ch7/test_data/file_3",
  "known_hash": "6144:CM2517OAZxLp9SQr2GlFOYXwYvThLa0Au6W6zcfZ:B2517OAvSQr20FOxuEz
ch",
  "comparison_file": "/book/ch7/test_data/file_1",
  "comparison_hash": "6144:c4AYyuHeJ6r+/c+KbACreaDFBWb630KP14uEpRI2:/pj+/Gdas18vd"
}
```

The following is our continued output:

```
{
   "similarity": 96,
   "known_file": "/book/ch7/test_data/file_3",
   "known_hash": "6144:CM25l7OAZxLp9SQr2G1FOYXwYvThLa0Au6W6zcfZ:B25l7OAvSQr20FOxuEz
ch",
   "comparison_file": "/book/ch7/test_data/file_3a",
   "comparison_hash": "6144:v5l7OAZxLp9SQr2G1FOYXwYvThLa0Au6W6zcfZ:v5l7OAvSQr20FOxu
Ezch"
}
{
   "similarity": 100,
   "known_file": "/book/ch7/test_data/file_3",
   "known_hash": "6144:CM25l7OAZxLp9SQr2G1FOYXwYvThLa0Au6W6zcfZ:B25l7OAvSQr20FOxuEz
ch",
   "comparison_file": "/book/ch7/test_data/file_3",
   "comparison_hash": "6144:CM25l7OAZxLp9SQr2G1FOYXwYvThLa0Au6W6zcfZ:B25l7OAvSQr20F
OxuEzch"
}
{
   "similarity": 0,
   "known_file": "/book/ch7/test_data/file_3",
   "known_hash": "6144:CM25l7OAZxLp9SQr2G1FOYXwYvThLa0Au6W6zcfZ:B25l7OAvSQr20FOxuEz
ch",
   "comparison_file": "/book/ch7/test_data/file_2",
   "comparison_hash": "3072:xI3BjBl25lQ8fBgLpLu8ASJm5S5vBTDBfdAF6WpstZ/Xg3LXzIVGbJf
2/Izc2w:mnmyLdvlyovOF6TUvf229w"
}
```

You'll also notice that this script, using the `ssdeep` library, produces the same signatures as our prior implementation! One thing to notice is the speed difference between these two scripts. Using the tool time, we ran our two scripts against the same folder of these six files. As seen in the following screenshot, there's a significant performance boost in using our `ssdeep` imported module:

```
(py3.7.1) $ time python fuzzy_hasher.py test_data/ > /dev/null 2>&1

real    1m2.316s
user    0m59.688s
sys     0m0.659s
(py3.7.1) $ time python ssdeep_python.py test_data/file_3 test_data/ \
>                       > /dev/null 2>&1

real    0m0.209s
user    0m0.163s
sys     0m0.029s
```

Additional challenges

You've created a script that implements the spamsum algorithm to generate ssdeep compatible hashes! With this, there are a few additional challenges to pursue.

First, we're providing six sample files, found in the previously mentioned `test_data/` directory. These files are available to confirm you're getting the same hashes as those printed and to allow you to perform some additional testing. The `file_1`, `file_2`, and `file_3` files are our originals, whereas the instances with an appended `a` are a modified version of the original. The accompanying `README.md` file contains a description of the alterations we performed, though in short, we have the following:

- `file_1` with a relocation of some file content to a later portion of the file
- `file_2` with an insertion in the early portion of the file
- `file_3` with a removal of the start of the file

We encourage you to perform additional testing to learn about how ssdeep responds to different types of alterations. Feel free to further alter the original files and share your findings with the community!

Another challenge is to study the ssdeep or spamsum code and learn how it handles the comparison component with the goal of adding it into the first script.

We can also explore developing code to expose the content of, for example, word documents and generate ssdeep hashes of the document's content instead of the binary file. This can be applied to other file types and doesn't have to be limited to text content. For example, if we discover that an executable is packed, we may also want to generate a fuzzy hash of the unpacked byte content.

Lastly, there are other similarity analysis utilities out there. To name one, the `sdhash` utility takes a different approach to identifying similarities between two files. We recommend you spend some time with this utility, running it against your and our provided test data to see how it performs with different types of modifications and alterations. More information on `sdhash` is available on the website: `http://roussev.net/sdhash/sdhash.html`.

References

- Kornblum, J. (2006). *Identifying Almost Identical Files Using Context Triggered Piecewise Hashing*, Digital Investigation, 91-97. Retrieved October 31, 2015, from `http://dfrws.org/2006/proceedings/12-Kornblum.pdf`
- Stevens, M. Karpmanm P. Peyrin, T. (2015), *RESEARCHERS URGE: INDUSTRY STANDARD SHA-1 SHOULD BE RETRACTED SOONER*, retrieved October 31, 2015, from `https://ee788fc4-a-62cb3a1a-s-sites.googlegroups.com/site/itstheshappening/shappening_PR.pdf`

Summary

Hashing is a critical component of the DFIR workflow. While most use cases of hashing are focused on integrity checking, the use of similarity analysis allows us to learn more about near matches and file relations. This process can provide insight for malware detection, identification of restricted documents in unauthorized locations, and discovery of closely related items based on content only. Through the use of third-party libraries, we're able to lean on the power behind the C languages with the flexibility of the Python interpreter and build powerful tools that are user and developer friendly. The code for this project can be downloaded from GitHub or Packt, as described in the *Preface*.

A fuzzy hash is a form of metadata, or data about data. Metadata also includes embedded attributes such as document editing time, image geolocation information, and source application. In the next chapter, you'll learn how to extract embedded metadata from various files including images, audio files, and office documents.

8
The Media Age

Metadata, or data describing data, is a powerful artifact an examiner can leverage to answer investigative questions. Broadly speaking, metadata can be found through examination of filesystems and embedded elements. File permissions, MAC timestamps, and file size are recorded at the filesystem level. However, for specific file types, such as JPEGs, additional metadata is embedded within the file itself.

Embedded metadata is more specific to the object in question. This embedded metadata can provide additional sources of timestamps, the author of a particular document, or even GPS coordinates for a photo. Entire software applications, such as Phil Harvey's ExifTool, exist to extract embedded metadata from files and collate it with filesystem metadata.

This chapter will cover the following topics:

- Using first- and third-party libraries to extract metadata from files
- Understanding **Exchangeable Image File Format** (**EXIF**), ID3, and Microsoft Office embedded metadata
- Learning to build frameworks to facilitate rapid development and integration of scripts

The code for this chapter was developed and tested using Python 2.7.15 and Python 3.7.1.

Creating frameworks in Python

Frameworks are incredibly useful for large-scale projects in Python. We previously called the `UserAssist` script a framework in `Chapter 6`, *Extracting Artifacts from Binary Files;* however, it doesn't really fit that model. The frameworks we build will have an abstract top layer, which will act as the controller of the program. This controller will be responsible for executing plugins and writers.

A plugin is code contained in a separate script that adds a specific feature to the framework. Once developed, a plugin should be easily integrated into an existing framework in a few lines of code. A plugin should also execute standalone functionality and not require modification of the controller to operate. For example, we'll write one plugin to specifically process EXIF metadata and another to process Office metadata. An advantage of the framework model is that it allows us to group many plugins together in an organized manner and execute them all for a shared objective, such as extracting various types of embedded metadata from files.

Building out frameworks requires some forethought and planning. It's vital to plan out and test the types of data structures you want to use for your framework. Some data structures are better suited for different tasks. Consider the types of input and output your framework will handle and let that guide your decision to the appropriate data type. Having to rewrite your framework after discovering a more optimal data structure can be a frustrating and time-consuming task.

Without this step, a framework can rapidly get out of hand and become an absolute bogged down mess. Imagine scenario where each plugin requires its own unique arguments, and worse, returns different types of data that require special handling. For example, one plugin might return a list of dictionaries and another plugin may return a dictionary of dictionaries. Most of your code would be written to convert these data types into a common form for your writers. For your sanity, we recommend creating standardized input and output that each plugin adheres to. This will have the benefit of making your framework much easier to understand and more stable from unnecessary conversion errors.

Writers take processed data from the plugins and write them to output files. An example of a writer we're familiar with is a CSV writer. In previous chapters, our CSV writers take processed data input and write it to a file. In larger projects, such as this, we might have writers for various types of output. For example, in this chapter, we'll develop a Google Earth KML writer to plot GPS data we extract from embedded EXIF metadata.

Introduction to EXIF metadata

EXIF metadata is a standard that's used for image and audio file tags that are created by devices and applications. Most commonly, this kind of embedded metadata is associated with JPEG files. However, EXIF metadata is also present in TIFF, WAV, and other files. In JPEG files, EXIF metadata can contain technical camera settings used to take the photo such as the shutter speed, F-stop, and ISO values. These may not be inherently useful to an examiner, but tags containing the make, model, and GPS location of the photo can be used for attributing an individual to a crime. Each of these elements are associated with a tag. For example, the make metadata is EXIF tag 271 or `0x010F`. A list of tags can be found at `http://www.exiv2.org/tags.html`.

EXIF metadata is stored at the beginning of JPEG images and, if present, is located at byte offset 24. The EXIF header begins with the hex `0x45786966`, which is Exif in ASCII. The following is a hex dump of the first 52 bytes of a JPEG image:

```
lpf@ubuntu: ~/Desktop
lpf@ubuntu:~$ cd Desktop/
lpf@ubuntu:~/Desktop$ xxd -l 52 img_42.jpg
0000000: ffd8 ffe0 0010 4a46 4946 0001 0101 0048  ......JFIF.....H
0000010: 0048 0000 ffe1 9cd6 4578 6966 0000 4d4d  .H......Exif..MM
0000020: 002a 0000 0008 000b 010f 0002 0000 0006  .*..............
0000030: 0000 089e                                ....
lpf@ubuntu:~/Desktop$
```

Note the EXIF header starting at offset 24. The hex `0x4D4D` following it represents Motorola or big-endian byte alignment. The `0x010F` tag ID at byte offset 40 is the EXIF `Make` metadata tag. Each tag is made up of four components:

Byte offset	Name	Description
0-1	ID	The tag ID representing a specific EXIF metadata element
2-3	Type	Type of data (integer,+ string, and so on)
4-7	Length	The length of the data
8-11	Offset	The offset from the byte alignment value

In the preceding table, the `Make` tag has a data type of 2, equating to an ASCII string, is 6 bytes long, and is located 2,206 bytes from the byte alignment value of `0x4D4D`. The second screenshot shows a 52 byte slice of data `2206` bytes from the beginning of the file. Here, we can see Nokia, the make of the phone that was used to take the photograph, as a 6 byte long ASCII string:

```
lpf@ubuntu: ~/Desktop
lpf@ubuntu:~/Desktop$ xxd -s 2206 -l 52 img_42.jpg
000089e: 0000 0000 0000 0000 0000 0000 0000 0000  ................
00008ae: 0000 0000 0000 0000 0000 0000 0000 4e6f  ..............No
00008be: 6b69 6100 4c75 6d69 6120 3633 3500 0000  kia.Lumia 635...
00008ce: 0048 0000                                .H..
lpf@ubuntu:~/Desktop$
```

If we were so inclined, we could use `struct` and parse through the header and grab the pertinent EXIF metadata. Fortunately, the third-party **Python Imaging Library**, PIL, module already supports EXIF metadata and makes this task much simpler.

Introducing the Pillow module

Pillow (version 5.3.0) is an actively maintained fork of the Python Imaging Library and is an extensive module that can archive, display, and process image files. A full description of this module can be read at `http://www.pillow.readthedocs.io`. This library can be installed using `pip` as follows:

```
pip install pillow==5.3.0
```

PIL provides a function named `_getexif()`, which returns a dictionary of tags and their values. Tags are stored in their decimal format rather than hexadecimal. Interpreting `0x010F` in big-endian corresponds to the decimal value 271 for the `Make` tag. Rather than doing this the hard way with `struct`, we can simply query whether a tag exists and, if it does, then process the value:

```
>>> from PIL import Image
>>> image = Image.open('img_42.jpg')
>>> exif = image._getexif()
>>> if 271 in exif.keys():
...     print('Make:', exif[271])
...
Make: Nokia
```

Introduction to ID3 metadata

The ID3 metadata container is often associated with MP3 files. There are two versions of the embedded structure: ID3v1 and ID3v2. The ID3v1 version is the final 128 bytes of the file and has a different structure from the updated format. The newer version, which we'll focus on, is located at the beginning of the file and is variable in length.

An ID3 tag has a simpler structure compared with EXIF tags. The first 16 bytes are evenly split between the tag ID and the length of the metadata. Following that is the metadata itself. The following screenshot contains the first 144 bytes of an MP3 file:

```
lpf@ubuntu: ~/Desktop
lpf@ubuntu:~/Desktop$ xxd -l 144 music.mp3
0000000: 4944 3303 0000 0000 1f76 5453 5300 0000  ID3......vTSS...
0000010: 0014 0000 004c 6f67 6963 2045 7870 7265  .....Logic Expre
0000020: 7373 2039 2e30 2e31 5450 3100 0000 000b  ss 9.0.1TP1.....
0000030: 0000 0054 6865 2041 7274 6973 7454 5032  ...The ArtistTP2
0000040: 0000 0000 1100 0000 5468 6520 416c 6275  ........The Albu
0000050: 6d20 4172 7469 7374 5443 4d00 0000 000e  m ArtistTCM.....
0000060: 0000 0054 6865 2043 6f6d 706f 7365 7200  ...The Composer.
0000070: 5441 4c00 0000 000a 0000 0054 6865 2041  TAL........The A
0000080: 6c62 756d 5454 3100 0000 000d 0000 0054  lbumTT1........T
lpf@ubuntu:~/Desktop$
```

The file signature of MP3 files is the ASCII ID3. Shortly after the signature, we can see different tags, such as TP1, TP2, and TCM. These are metadata tags for the artist, band, and composer, respectively. The next 8 bytes following TP1 is the length represented by the hex `0x0B` or 11. Following the 2 byte buffer is the data for the artist formerly known as `The Artist`. `The Artist` is 10 bytes long with an additional single null byte (0x00) prepended to the data for a total of 11 bytes. We'll use a module named Mutagen to load the file and read any ID3 tags that are present.

Some MP3 files may not have embedded ID3 metadata. In this case, the tags we can see in the previous screenshot may not be present.

Introducing the Mutagen module

Mutagen (version 1.41.1) is capable of reading and writing different audio metadata formats. Mutagen supports a wide variety of embedded audio formats, such as ASF, FLAC, M4A, and MP3 (ID3). The full documentation for this module can be found at `http://www.mutagen.readthedocs.io`. We can install this module with `pip` as follows:

```
pip install mutagen==1.41.1
```

Using Mutagen is straightforward. We need to create an ID3 object by opening our MP3 file and then, as with PIL, look for specific tags in a dictionary, as follows:

```
>>> from mutagen import id3
>>> id = id3.ID3('music.mp3')
>>> if 'TP1' in id.keys():
...     print('Artist:', id['TP1'])
...
Artist: The Artist
```

Introduction to Office metadata

With the launch of Office 2007, Microsoft introduced a new proprietary format for their office products, such as `.docx`, `.pptx`, and `.xlsx` files. These documents are actually a zipped directory consisting of XML and binary files. These documents have a great deal of embedded metadata stored in the XML files within the document. The two XML files we'll look at are `core.xml` and `app.xml`, which store different types of metadata.

The `core.xml` file stores metadata related to the document such as author, the revision number, and who last modified the document. The `app.xml` file stores metadata that's more specific to the contents of the file. For example, Word documents store page, paragraph, line, word, and character counts, whereas a PowerPoint presentation stores information related to slides, hidden slides, and note count, among others.

To view this data, use an archive utility of your choice and unzip an existing 2007 or higher version Office document. You may need to add a `.zip` extension to the end of your file to get the option to unzip the archive with your tool of choice. The following is a screenshot of the contents of an unzipped Word document:

Name	Date Modified	Size	Kind
_rels	Nov 5, 2015, 11:41 PM	--	Folder
[Content_Types].xml	Jan 1, 1980, 12:00 AM	2 KB	XML Document
customXml	Today, 10:38 AM	--	Folder
_rels	Nov 5, 2015, 11:41 PM	--	Folder
item1.xml.rels	Jan 1, 1980, 12:00 AM	296 bytes	Document
item1.xml	Jan 1, 1980, 12:00 AM	254 bytes	XML Document
itemProps1.xml	Jan 1, 1980, 12:00 AM	341 bytes	XML Document
docProps	Nov 5, 2015, 11:41 PM	--	Folder
app.xml	Jan 1, 1980, 12:00 AM	1 KB	XML Document
core.xml	Jan 1, 1980, 12:00 AM	903 bytes	XML Document
word	Today, 10:38 AM	--	Folder
_rels	Nov 5, 2015, 11:41 PM	--	Folder
document.xml.rels	Jan 1, 1980, 12:00 AM	2 KB	Document
footnotes.xml.rels	Jan 1, 1980, 12:00 AM	343 bytes	Document
document.xml	Jan 1, 1980, 12:00 AM	540 KB	XML Document
endnotes.xml	Jan 1, 1980, 12:00 AM	2 KB	XML Document
fontTable.xml	Jan 1, 1980, 12:00 AM	3 KB	XML Document
footer1.xml	Jan 1, 1980, 12:00 AM	2 KB	XML Document
footnotes.xml	Jan 1, 1980, 12:00 AM	8 KB	XML Document
media	Nov 5, 2015, 11:41 PM	--	Folder
image1.png	Jan 1, 1980, 12:00 AM	30 KB	PNG image
image2.png	Jan 1, 1980, 12:00 AM	22 KB	PNG image
numbering.xml	Jan 1, 1980, 12:00 AM	18 KB	XML Document
settings.xml	Jan 1, 1980, 12:00 AM	9 KB	XML Document
styles.xml	Jan 1, 1980, 12:00 AM	33 KB	XML Document
theme	Nov 5, 2015, 11:41 PM	--	Folder
theme1.xml	Jan 1, 1980, 12:00 AM	7 KB	XML Document
webSettings.xml	Jan 1, 1980, 12:00 AM	511 bytes	XML Document

In the `docProps` folder, we can see our two XML files, which contain the metadata related to our specific word document. The word directory contains the actual word document itself in `document.xml` and any inserted media stored in the media subdirectory. Now, let's take a look at the `core.xml` file:

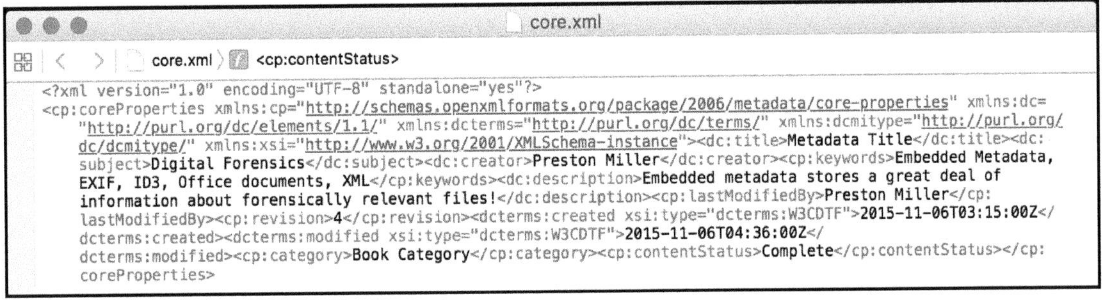

```
core.xml
core.xml > <cp:contentStatus>
<?xml version="1.0" encoding="UTF-8" standalone="yes"?>
<cp:coreProperties xmlns:cp="http://schemas.openxmlformats.org/package/2006/metadata/core-properties" xmlns:dc=
    "http://purl.org/dc/elements/1.1/" xmlns:dcterms="http://purl.org/dc/terms/" xmlns:dcmitype="http://purl.org/
    dc/dcmitype/" xmlns:xsi="http://www.w3.org/2001/XMLSchema-instance"><dc:title>Metadata Title</dc:title><dc:
    subject>Digital Forensics</dc:subject><dc:creator>Preston Miller</dc:creator><cp:keywords>Embedded Metadata,
    EXIF, ID3, Office documents, XML</cp:keywords><dc:description>Embedded metadata stores a great deal of
    information about forensically relevant files!</dc:description><cp:lastModifiedBy>Preston Miller</cp:
    lastModifiedBy><cp:revision>4</cp:revision><dcterms:created xsi:type="dcterms:W3CDTF">2015-11-06T03:15:00Z</
    dcterms:created><dcterms:modified xsi:type="dcterms:W3CDTF">2015-11-06T04:36:00Z</
    dcterms:modified><cp:category>Book Category</cp:category><cp:contentStatus>Complete</cp:contentStatus></cp:
    coreProperties>
```

In `Chapter 4`, *Working with Serialized Data Structures*, we discussed serialized data and mentioned that XML was a popular format for data serialization. XML works on the concept of directives, namespaces, and tags and is similar to another popular markup language, HTML. Most XML files begin with header directives detailing the version, encoding, and any instructions to parsers.

The `core.xml` file also contains five namespaces that are declared only once at the beginning of the file and are then referred to by their assigned namespace variable thereafter. The primary purpose of namespaces is to avoid name conflict resolutions and are created using the `xmlns` attribute.

After the namespaces, we have a variety of tags, similar to HTML, such as the title, subject, and creator. We can use an XML parser, such as `lxml`, to iterate through these tags and process them.

Introducing the lxml module

The `lxml` (version 4.2.5) third-party module has Python bindings to the C `libxml2` and `libxslt` libraries. This module is a very popular XML parser for its speed and can be used to parse HTML files. We'll use this module to walk through each `child` tag and print out those of interest. Full documentation for this library can be found at `http://www.lxml.de`. Once again, installing a library is made simple using `pip`:

```
pip install lxml==4.2.5
```

Let's take a look at how to iterate through the `core.xml` file in the interactive prompt. The `etree` or element tree API provides a simple mechanism of iterating through children in the XML file. First, we need to parse an XML file into an element tree. Next, we get the root-level element in the tree. With the root, we can walk through each child using the `root.iter()` function and print out the tag and text values. Note that the tag contains the fully expanded namespace. In just a few lines of code, we can now parse basic XML files with ease using `lxml`:

```
>>> import lxml.etree.ElementTree as ET
>>> core = ET.parse('core.xml')
>>> root = core.getroot()
>>> for child in root.iter():
...     print(child.tag, ':', child.text)
...
{http://purl.org/dc/elements/1.1/}title : Metadata Title
{http://purl.org/dc/elements/1.1/}subject : Digital Forensics
{http://purl.org/dc/elements/1.1/}creator : Preston Miller & Chapin Bryce
...
```

The Metadata_Parser framework overview

Now that we understand the concept of frameworks and what kind of data we're dealing with, we can examine the specifics of our framework implementation. Rather than a flow diagram, we use a high-level diagram to show how the scripts interact with each other:

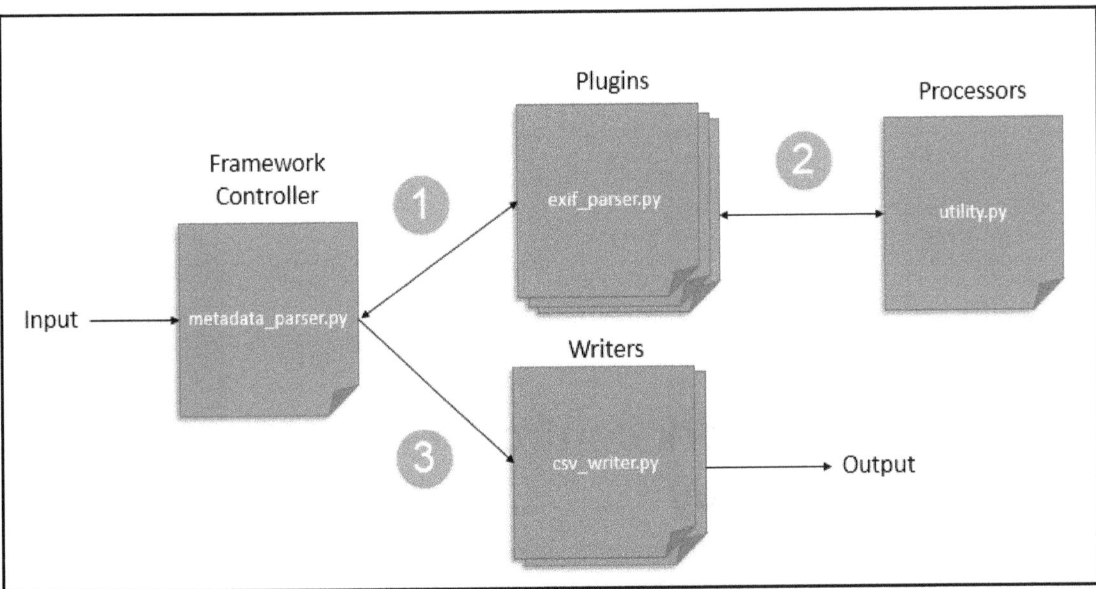

This framework is going to be controlled by the `metadata_parser.py` script. This script will be responsible for launching our three plugin scripts and then shuttling the returned data to the appropriate writer plugins. During processing, the plugins make calls to processors to help validate data or perform other processing functions. We have two writer plugins, one for CSV output and another to plot geotagged data using Google Earth's KML format.

Each plugin will take an individual file as its input and store the parsed metadata tags in a dictionary. This dictionary is then returned to `metadata_parser.py` and is appended to a list. Once all of our input files are processed, we send these lists of dictionaries to writers. We use the `DictWriter` from the `csv` module to write our dictionary output to a CSV file.

Similar to Chapter 6, *Extracting Artifacts from Binary Files,* we'll have multiple Python directories to organize our code in a logical manner. To use these packages, we need to make the directory searchable with an `__init__.py` script and then import the directory in the code:

```
|-- metadata_parser.py
|-- plugins
    |-- __init__.py
    |-- exif_parser.py
    |-- id3_parser.py
    |-- office_parser.py
|-- processors
    |-- __init__.py
    |-- utility.py
|-- writers
    |-- __init__.py
    |-- csv_writer.py
    |-- kml_writer.py
```

Our main framework controller – metadata_parser.py

The `metadata_parser.py` script contains a single function, `main()`, on line 45 that handles coordinating logic between our plugins and writers. At the top of the script, we call our imports we will use for this chapter. On lines 8 and 9, we specifically import our plugins and writers directories that we've created as follows:

```
001 """EXIF, ID3, and Office Metadata parser."""
002 from __future__ import print_function
003 import argparse
004 import os
005 import sys
006 import logging
007
008 import plugins
009 import writers
...
045 def main(input_dir, output_dir):
```

On line 133, we set up the arguments for our program. This script takes two positional arguments, an input and output directory, and an optional log argument to change the directory and name of the log file. Lines 142 through 154 focus on setting up the log, as in previous chapters. The lines are as follows:

```
131 if __name__ == '__main__':
132
133     parser = argparse.ArgumentParser(description=__description__,
134                                      epilog='Developed by ' +
135                                      __author__ + ' on ' +
136                                      __date__)
137     parser.add_argument('INPUT_DIR', help='Input Directory')
138     parser.add_argument('OUTPUT_DIR', help='Output Directory')
139     parser.add_argument('-l', help='File path of log file.')
140     args = parser.parse_args()
141
142     if args.l:
143         if not os.path.exists(args.l):
144             os.makedirs(args.l)
145         log_path = os.path.join(args.l, 'metadata_parser.log')
146     else:
147         log_path = 'metadata_parser.log'
148     logging.basicConfig(filename=log_path, level=logging.DEBUG,
149                         format=('%(asctime)s | %(levelname)s | '
150                         '%(message)s'), filemode='a')
151
152     logging.info('Starting Metadata_Parser')
153     logging.debug('System ' + sys.platform)
154     logging.debug('Version ' + sys.version)
```

On line 156, we create our output directory if the supplied output directory doesn't exist. This output directory is created with the `makedirs()` function. This function accepts a string representing the file path to a directory and creates the directory and any intermediate directories that don't exist in the file path. On line 159, we check whether the supplied input is a directory and whether it exists. If so, on line 161, the `main()` function is called, and the input and output directory arguments are passed. If the input doesn't exist or isn't a directory, we log and print the error and exit with status code 1. We have the following code:

```
156     if not os.path.exists(args.OUTPUT_DIR):
157         os.makedirs(args.OUTPUT_DIR)
158
159     if(os.path.exists(args.INPUT_DIR) and
160     os.path.isdir(args.INPUT_DIR)):
161         main(args.INPUT_DIR, args.OUTPUT_DIR)
162     else:
```

```
        msg =('Supplied input directory doesn't exist or is'
        'not a directory')
        print('[-]', msg)
        logging.error(msg)
        sys.exit(1)
```

Controlling our framework with the main() function

On lines 57 through 59, we create our lists that will store the returned dictionaries from our plugin calls. But before we can call our plugins, we need to generate a file listing from the user's input directory argument. We do this on line 65 with the `os.walk()` function, which we used in previous chapters. A new argument, `topdown`, is passed to our directory walking loop. This allows us to control the flow of the iteration and step through the directory from the top level down to the furthest level. This is the default behavior, though it can be specified to ensure the anticipated behavior. For each file, we need to `join()` it with the root to generate the full path to the file:

```
045 def main(input_dir, output_dir):
046     """
047     The main function generates a file listing, sends files to be
048     processed, and output written.
049     :param input_dir: The input directory to scan for suported
050         embedded metadata containing files
051     :param output_dir: The output directory to write metadata
052         reports to
053     :return: Nothing.
054     """
055     # Create lists to store each supported embedded metadata
056     # before writing to output
057     exif_metadata = []
058     office_metadata = []
059     id3_metadata = []
060
061     # Walk through list of files
062     msg = 'Generating file listing and running plugins.'
063     print('[+]', msg)
064     logging.info(msg)
065     for root, subdir, files in os.walk(input_dir, topdown=True):
066         for file_name in files:
067             current_file = os.path.join(root, file_name)
068             ext = os.path.splitext(current_file)[1].lower()
```

Finally, on line 68, we separate the extension from the full path using the `os.path.splitext()` function. The `splitext()` function takes a string representing a file path and returns a list with the path as the first element and the extension as the second element. We could have also used the `split()` function, splitting on the period and accessing the last element of the newly formed list:

```
>>> '/path/to/metadata_image.jpg'.split('.')[-1]
jpg
```

After we have `current_file`, we look at its extension on lines 71, 83, and 96 to determine whether any of our existing plugins are appropriate. If our file is a JPEG image, then the conditional on line 71 will evaluate to `True`. On line 73, we call our `exif_parser()` function, which is found in the `exif_parser.py` script within the plugins subdirectory. Because we're only matching on extension, this function call is wrapped around `try` and `except` to handle situations where we raise an error in the `exif_parser()` function due to mismatching file signatures:

```
070             # PLUGINS
071             if ext == '.jpeg' or ext == '.jpg':
072                 try:
073                     ex_metadata, exif_headers =
plugins.exif_parser.exif_parser(
074                     current_file)
075                     exif_metadata.append(ex_metadata)
076                 except TypeError:
077                     print(('[-] File signature mismatch. '
078                         'Continuing to next file.'))
079                     logging.error((('JPG & TIFF File Signature '
080                     'check failed for ' + current_file)))
081                     continue
```

If the function doesn't raise an error, it'll return the EXIF metadata for that particular file and the headers for the CSV writer. On line 75, we append the EXIF metadata results to our `exif_metadata` list and continue processing the other input files:

```
083             elif ext == '.docx' or ext == '.pptx' or ext == '.xlsx':
084                 try:
085                     of_metadata, office_headers =
plugins.office_parser.office_parser(
086                     current_file)
087                     office_metadata.append(of_metadata)
088                 except TypeError:
089                     print(('[-] File signature mismatch. '
090                         'Continuing to next file.'))
091                     logging.error((('DOCX, XLSX, & PPTX File '
092                     'Signature check failed for ' + current_file))
```

```
093                     )
094                     continue
095
096             elif ext == '.mp3':
097                 try:
098                     id_metadata, id3_headers =
plugins.id3_parser.id3_parser(
099                     current_file)
100                     id3_metadata.append(id_metadata)
101                     except TypeError:
102                         print(('[-] File signature mismatch. '
103                             'Continuing to next file.'))
104                         logging.error((('MP3 File Signature check '
105                             'failed for ' + current_file)))
106                         continue
```

Note the similar structure employed for the other two plugins. All plugins take only one input, `current_file`, and return two output values, the metadata dictionary and CSV headers. Only eight lines of code are required to properly call and then store the results of each plugin. A few more lines of code are required to write the stored data to an output file.

Once we've iterated through all of the files, we can begin writing any necessary output. On lines 113, 119, and 123, we check to see whether any of the metadata lists contain dictionaries. If they do, we call the `csv_writer()` function in the `csv_writer.py` script under the writers subdirectory. For EXIF metadata, we also call the `kml_writer()` function on line 114 to plot GPS coordinates:

```
108     # WRITERS
109     msg = 'Writing output to ' + output_dir
110     print('[+]', msg)
111     logging.info(msg)
112
113     if len(exif_metadata) > 0:
114         writers.kml_writer.kml_writer(exif_metadata,
115             output_dir, 'exif_metadata.kml')
116         writers.csv_writer.csv_writer(exif_metadata, exif_headers,
117             output_dir, 'exif_metadata.csv')
118
119     if len(office_metadata) > 0:
120         writers.csv_writer.csv_writer(office_metadata,
121             office_headers, output_dir, 'office_metadata.csv')
122
123     if len(id3_metadata) > 0:
124         writers.csv_writer.csv_writer(id3_metadata, id3_headers,
125             output_dir, 'id3_metadata.csv')
126
127     msg = 'Program completed successfully -- exiting..'
```

```
    print('[*]', msg)
    logging.info(msg)
```

This completes the controller logic for our framework. The main processing occurs in each individual plugin file. Now, let's look at our first plugin.

Parsing EXIF metadata – exif_parser.py

The `exif_parser` plugin is the first we'll develop and is relatively simple due to our reliance on the PIL module. There are three functions within this script: `exif_parser()`, `get_tags()`, and `dms_to_decimal()`. The `exif_parser()` function, on line 39, is the entry point into this plugin and takes a string representing a filename as its only input. This function primarily serves as coordinating logic for the plugin.

The `get_tags()` function on line 62 is responsible for parsing the EXIF tags from our input file. Finally, the `dms_to_decimal()` function on line 172 is a small helper function, which is responsible for converting GPS coordinates into decimal format. Take a look at the following code:

```
001 from datetime import datetime
002 import os
003 from time import gmtime, strftime
004
005 from PIL import Image
006
007 import processors
...
039 def exif_parser():
...
062 def get_tags():
...
172 def dms_to_decimal():
```

Understanding the exif_parser() function

This function serves three purposes: it validates the input file, extracts the tags, and returns the processed data to `metadata_parser.py`. To validate an input value, we'll evaluate its file signature against known signatures. Rather than relying on the extension of a file, which can be incorrect, we check the signature to avoid any additional sources of error.

Checking a file's signature, sometimes referred to as its magic number, typically consists of examining the first couple of bytes of a file and comparing that with known signatures for that file type. Gary Kessler has a great list of file signatures documented on his website, `https://www.garykessler.net/library/file_sigs.html`:

```
039 def exif_parser(filename):
040     """
041     The exif_parser function confirms the file type and sends it
042     to be processed.
043     :param filename: name of the file potentially containing EXIF
044     metadata.
045     :return: A dictionary from get_tags, containing the embedded
046     EXIF metadata.
047     """
```

On line 50, we create a list of known file signatures for JPEG images. On line 52, we call the `check_header()` function in the `utility.py` script in the processors subdirectory. This function will evaluate to `True` if the header of the file matches one of the supplied known signatures:

```
049     # JPEG signatures
050     signatures = ['ffd8ffdb','ffd8ffe0', 'ffd8ffe1', 'ffd8ffe2',
051         'ffd8ffe3', 'ffd8ffe8']
052     if processors.utility.check_header(
053             filename,signatures, 4) == True:
054         return get_tags(filename)
055     else:
056         print(('File signature doesn't match known '
057             'JPEG signatures.'))
058         raise TypeError(('File signature doesn't match '
059             'JPEG object.'))
```

If we do have a legitimate JPEG file, we call and return the results of the `get_tags()` function on line 54. Alternatively, if `check_header()` returns `False`, then we have a mismatch and we raise a `TypeError` exception to our parent script, `metadata_parser.py`, to handle the situation appropriately.

Developing the get_tags() function

The `get_tags()` function, with the help of the PIL module, parses EXIF metadata tags from our JPEG image. On line 72, we create a list of headers for our CSV output. This list contains all of the possible keys that might be created in our EXIF dictionary in the order we want them to be displayed in a CSV file. As all JPEG images may not have the same or any embedded EXIF tags, we'll run into the scenario where some dictionaries have more tags than others. By supplying the writer with the list of ordered keys, we'll ensure that the fields are written in the appropriate order and columns:

```
062 def get_tags(filename):
063     """
064     The get_tags function extracts the EXIF metadata from the data
065     object.
066     :param filename: the path and name to the data object.
067     :return: tags and headers, tags is a dictionary containing
068     EXIF metadata and headers are the order of keys for the
069     CSV output.
070     """
071     # Set up CSV headers
072     headers = ['Path', 'Name', 'Size', 'Filesystem CTime',
073     'Filesystem MTime', 'Original Date', 'Digitized Date', 'Make',
074     'Model', 'Software', 'Latitude', 'Latitude Reference',
075     'Longitude', 'Longitude Reference', 'Exif Version', 'Height',
076     'Width', 'Flash', 'Scene Type']
```

On line 77, we open the JPEG file using the `Image.open()` function. Once again, we perform one final validation step using the `verify()` function. This function checks for any file corruption and raises errors if encountered. Otherwise, on line 84, we call the `_getexif()` function, which returns a dictionary of EXIF metadata:

```
077     image = Image.open(filename)
078
079     # Detects if the file is corrupt without decoding the data
080     image.verify()
081
082     # Descriptions and values of EXIF tags
083     # http://www.exiv2.org/tags.html
084     exif = image._getexif()
```

On line 86, we create our dictionary, `tags`, which will store metadata about our file object. On lines 87 through 94, we populate the dictionary with some filesystem metadata, such as the full path, name, size, and create and modify timestamps. The `os.path.basename()` function takes the full pathname and returns the filename. For example, `os.path.basename('Users/LPF/Desktop/myfile.txt')` would simply return `myfile.txt`.

Using the `getsize()` function will return the file size in bytes. The larger the number, the less useful it is for humans. We're more accustomed to seeing sizes with common prefixes, such as MB, GB, and TB. The `convert_size()` processor function does just this to make the data more useful for the human analyst.

On lines 91 and 93, we convert the integer returned by `os.path.getctime()`, representing the creation time expressed in seconds since the epoch. The epoch, `01/01/1970 00:00:00`, can be confirmed by calling `time.gmtime(0)`. We use the `gmtime()` function to convert these seconds into a time-structured object (similar to `datetime`). We use the `strftime` to format the time object into our desired date string:

```
086         tags = {}
087         tags['Path'] = filename
088         tags['Name'] = os.path.basename(filename)
089         tags['Size'] = processors.utility.convert_size(
090             os.path.getsize(filename))
091         tags['Filesystem CTime'] = strftime('%m/%d/%Y %H:%M:%S',
092             gmtime(os.path.getctime(filename)))
093         tags['Filesystem MTime'] = strftime('%m/%d/%Y %H:%M:%S',
094             gmtime(os.path.getmtime(filename)))
```

On line 95, we check whether there are any keys in the `exif` dictionary. If there are, we iterate through each key and check its value. The values we're querying for are from the EXIF tags described at `http://www.exiv2.org/tags.html`. There are many potential EXIF tags, but we're going to query for only some of the more forensically relevant ones.

If the particular tag does exist in the `exif` dictionary, then we transfer the value to our tags dictionary. Some tags require some additional processing, such as timestamp, scene, flash, and GPS tags. The timestamp tags are displayed in a format that's inconsistent with how we're representing other timestamps. For example, the time from tag 36867 on line 99 is separated by colons and in a different order:

```
2015:11:11 10:32:15
```

In line 100, we use the `strptime` function to convert our existing time string into a `datetime` object. In the very next line, we use the `strftime` function to convert it into our desired date string format:

```
095     if exif:
096         for tag in exif.keys():
097             if tag == 36864:
098                 tags['Exif Version'] = exif[tag]
099             elif tag == 36867:
100                 dt = datetime.strptime(exif[tag],
101                 '%Y:%m:%d %H:%M:%S')
102                 tags['Original Date'] = dt.strftime(
103                 '%m/%d/%Y %H:%M:%S')
104             elif tag == 36868:
105                 dt = datetime.strptime(exif[tag],
106                 '%Y:%m:%d %H:%M:%S')
107                 tags['Digitized Date'] = dt.strftime(
108                 '%m/%d/%Y %H:%M:%S')
```

The scene (`41990`) and flash (`37385`) tags have an integer value rather than a string. As we mentioned previously, the online documentation (`http://www.exiv2.org/tags.html`) explains what these integers represent. In these two scenarios, we create a dictionary containing the potential integers as keys and their descriptions as values. We check whether the tag's value is a key in our dictionary. If it's present, we store the description in the tags dictionary rather than the integer. Again, this is for the purpose of making analysis easier on the examiner. Seeing a string explanation of the scene or flash tag is more valuable than a number representing that explanation:

```
109             elif tag == 41990:
110                 # Scene tags
111                 #
http://www.awaresystems.be/imaging/tiff/tifftags/privateifd/exif/scenecaptu
retype.html
112                 scenes = {0: 'Standard', 1: 'Landscape',
113                 2: 'Portrait', 3: 'Night Scene'}
114                 if exif[tag] in scenes:
115                     tags['Scene Type'] = scenes[exif[tag]]
116                 else:
117                     pass
118             elif tag == 37385:
119                 # Flash tags
120                 #
http://www.awaresystems.be/imaging/tiff/tifftags/privateifd/exif/flash.html
121                 flash = {0: 'Flash did not fire',
122                 1: 'Flash fired',
123                 5: 'Strobe return light not detected',
```

```
124                    7: 'Strobe return light detected',
125                    9: 'Flash fired, compulsory flash mode',
126                    13: 'Flash fired, compulsory flash mode, return light
not detected',
127                    15: 'Flash fired, compulsory flash mode, return light
detected',
128                    16: 'Flash did not fire, compulsory flash mode',
129                    24: 'Flash did not fire, auto mode',
130                    25: 'Flash fired, auto mode',
131                    29: 'Flash fired, auto mode, return light not
detected',
132                    31: 'Flash fired, auto mode, return light detected',
133                    32: 'No flash function',
134                    65: 'Flash fired, red-eye reduction mode',
135                    69: 'Flash fired, red-eye reduction mode, return light
not detected',
136                    71: 'Flash fired, red-eye reduction mode, return light
detected',
137                    73: 'Flash fired, compulsory flash mode, red-eye
reduction mode',
138                    77: 'Flash fired, compulsory flash mode, red-eye
reduction mode, return light not detected',
139                    79: 'Flash fired, compulsory flash mode, red-eye
reduction mode, return light detected',
140                    89: 'Flash fired, auto mode, red-eye reduction mode',
141                    93: 'Flash fired, auto mode, return light not detected,
red-eye reduction mode',
142                    95: 'Flash fired, auto mode, return light detected,
red-eye reduction mode'}
143                if exif[tag] in flash:
144                    tags['Flash'] = flash[exif[tag]]
145            elif tag == 271:
146                tags['Make'] = exif[tag]
147            elif tag == 272:
148                tags['Model'] = exif[tag]
149            elif tag == 305:
150                tags['Software'] = exif[tag]
151            elif tag == 40962:
152                tags['Width'] = exif[tag]
153            elif tag == 40963:
154                tags['Height'] = exif[tag]
```

Finally, on line 155, we look for the GPS tags that are stored as a nested dictionary under the key 34853. If the latitude and longitude tags exist, we pass them to the `dms_to_decimal()` function to convert them into a more suitable manner for the KML writer:

```
155            elif tag == 34853:
```

```
                for gps in exif[tag]:
                    if gps == 1:
                        tags['Latitude Reference'] = exif[tag][gps]
                    elif gps == 2:
                        tags['Latitude'] = dms_to_decimal(
                        exif[tag][gps])
                    elif gps == 3:
                        tags['Longitude Reference'] = exif[tag][gps]
                    elif gps == 4:
                        tags['Longitude'] = dms_to_decimal(
                        exif[tag][gps])
                    else:
                        pass
    return tags, headers
```

Adding the dms_to_decimal() function

The `dms_to_decimal()` function converts GPS coordinates from degree minute second format into decimal. A simple formula exists to convert between the two formats. The GPS data we extract from our EXIF metadata contains three tuples within another tuple. Each interior tuple represents the numerator and denominator of the degree, minute, or second. First, we need to separate the individual degree, min, and second numerators from their denominators in the nested tuples. The following diagram highlights how we can convert our extracted GPS data into decimal format:

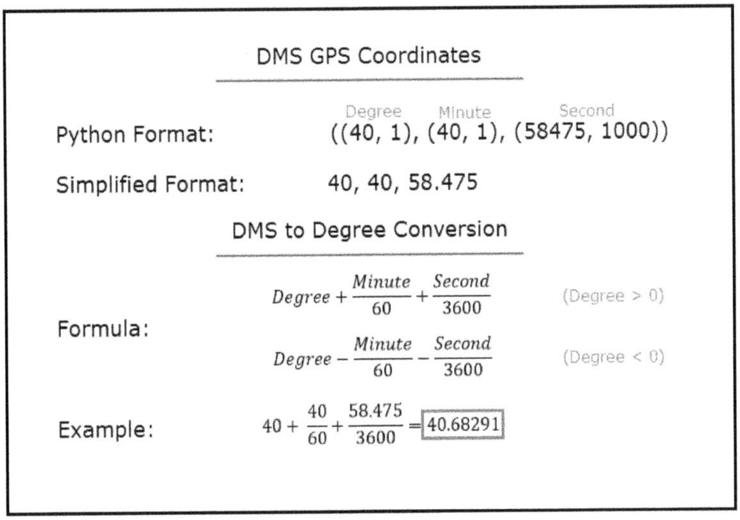

DMS GPS Coordinates

Python Format: ((40, 1), (40, 1), (58475, 1000)) (Degree, Minute, Second)

Simplified Format: 40, 40, 58.475

DMS to Degree Conversion

Formula:

$$Degree + \frac{Minute}{60} + \frac{Second}{3600} \quad \text{(Degree > 0)}$$

$$Degree - \frac{Minute}{60} - \frac{Second}{3600} \quad \text{(Degree < 0)}$$

Example:

$$40 + \frac{40}{60} + \frac{58.475}{3600} = \boxed{40.68291}$$

On line 178, we use list comprehension to create a list containing the first element of every element in the tuple. We then unpack this list into the three elements: `deg`, `min`, and `sec`. The formula we use is dependent on whether the degree value is positive or negative.

If `deg` is positive, then we add the minutes and seconds. We divide seconds by 360,0000 rather than 3,600 because originally we did not divide the seconds' value by its denominator. If `deg` is negative, we instead subtract the minutes and seconds as follows:

```
172 def dms_to_decimal(dms):
173     """
174     Converts GPS Degree Minute Seconds format to Decimal format.
175     :param dms: The GPS data in Degree Minute Seconds format.
176     :return: The decimal formatted GPS coordinate.
177     """
178     deg, min, sec = [x[0] for x in dms]
179     if deg > 0:
180         return "{0:.5f}".format(deg + (min / 60.) + (
181             sec / 3600000.))
182     else:
183         return "{0:.5f}".format(deg - (min / 60.) - (
184             sec / 3600000.))
```

Parsing ID3 metdata – id3_parser.py

`id3_parser` is similar to `exif_parser` we've previously discussed. The `id3_parser()` function defined on line 37 checks the file signature and then calls the `get_tags()` function. The `get_tags()` function relies on the `mutagen` module to parse MP3 and ID3 tags:

```
001 import os
002 from time import gmtime, strftime
003
004 from mutagen import mp3, id3
005
006 import processors
..
037 def id3_parser():
...
059 def get_tags():
```

Understanding the id3_parser() function

This function is identical to the `exif_parser()` function, with the exception of the signature that's used to check file headers. The MP3 format has only one file signature, `0x494433`, unlike the JPEG format. When we call the `check_header()` function, we supply the file, known signature, and the number of bytes to read from the header. If the signatures match, we call and return the results of the `get_tags()` function, as follows:

```
def id3_parser(filename):
    """
    The id3_parser function confirms the file type and sends it to
    be processed.
    :param filename: name of the file potentially containing exif
    metadata.
    :return: A dictionary from get_tags, containing the embedded
    EXIF metadata.
    """
```

Although it might be boring to see the same type of logic in each plugin, this greatly simplifies the logic of our framework. In scenarios with larger frameworks, creating things in the same uniform manner helps those maintaining the code sane. Copying and pasting a pre-existing plugin and working from there is often a good way to ensure that things are developed in the same manner. See the following code:

```
    # MP3 signatures
    signatures = ['494433']
    if processors.utility.check_header(
    filename, signatures, 3) == True:
        return get_tags(filename)
    else:
        print(('File signature doesn't match known '
        'MP3 signatures.'))
        raise TypeError(('File signature doesn't match '
        'MP3 object.'))
```

Revisiting the get_tags() function

The `get_tags()` function follows the same logic we used for our EXIF plugin. Like any good programmer, we copied that script and made a few modifications to fit ID3 metadata. In the `get_tags()` function, we first need to create our CSV headers on line 69. These headers represent the possible keys our dictionary might possess and the order we want to see them in our CSV output:

```
059 def get_tags(filename):
060     """
061     The get_tags function extracts the ID3 metadata from the data
062     object.
063     :param filename: the path and name to the data object.
064     :return: tags and headers, tags is a dictionary containing ID3
065     metadata and headers are the order of keys for the CSV output.
066     """
067
068     # Set up CSV headers
069     header = ['Path', 'Name', 'Size', 'Filesystem CTime',
070     'Filesystem MTime', 'Title', 'Subtitle', 'Artist', 'Album',
071     'Album/Artist', 'Length (Sec)', 'Year', 'Category',
072     'Track Number', 'Comments', 'Publisher', 'Bitrate',
073     'Sample Rate', 'Encoding', 'Channels', 'Audio Layer']
```

On line 74, we create our tags dictionary and populate it with some filesystem metadata in the same manner as the EXIF plugin, as follows:

```
074     tags = {}
075     tags['Path'] = filename
076     tags['Name'] = os.path.basename(filename)
077     tags['Size'] = processors.utility.convert_size(
078         os.path.getsize(filename))
079     tags['Filesystem CTime'] = strftime('%m/%d/%Y %H:%M:%S',
080         gmtime(os.path.getctime(filename)))
081     tags['Filesystem MTime'] = strftime('%m/%d/%Y %H:%M:%S',
082         gmtime(os.path.getmtime(filename)))
```

Mutagen has two classes that we can use to extract metadata from MP3 files. The first class, `MP3`, has some standard metadata stored in MP3 files, such as the bitrate, channels, and length in seconds. Mutagen has built-in functions to access this information. First, we need to create an MP3 object, which is accomplished on line 85, using the `mp3.MP3()` function. Next, we can use the `info.bitrate()` function, for example, to return the bitrate of the MP3 file. We store these values in our tags dictionary in lines 88 through 92, as follows:

```
084     # MP3 Specific metadata
085     audio = mp3.MP3(filename)
```

```
    if 'TENC' in audio.keys():
        tags['Encoding'] = audio['TENC'][0]
        tags['Bitrate'] = audio.info.bitrate
        tags['Channels'] = audio.info.channels
        tags['Audio Layer'] = audio.info.layer
        tags['Length (Sec)'] = audio.info.length
        tags['Sample Rate'] = audio.info.sample_rate
```

The second class, `ID3`, extracts ID3 tags from an MP3 file. We need to first create an ID3 object using the `id3.ID3()` function. This will return a dictionary of ID3 tags as keys. Sound familiar? This is what we were presented with in the previous plugin. The only difference is that the value in the dictionaries are stored in a slightly different format:

```
{'TPE1': TPE1(encoding=0, text=[u'The Artist']),...}
```

To access the value, `The Artist`, we need to treat the value as a list and specify the element in the zeroth index.

In a similar manner, we look for each of our tags of interest and store the first element in the value in the tags dictionary. At the end of this process, we return the tags and header objects back to `id3_parser()`, which in turn returns it to the `metadata_parser.py` script:

```
    # ID3 embedded metadata tags
    id = id3.ID3(filename)
    if 'TPE1' in id.keys():
        tags['Artist'] = id['TPE1'][0]
    if 'TRCK' in id.keys():
        tags['Track Number'] = id['TRCK'][0]
    if 'TIT3' in id.keys():
        tags['Subtitle'] = id['TIT3'][0]
    if 'COMM::eng' in id.keys():
        tags['Comments'] = id['COMM::eng'][0]
    if 'TDRC' in id.keys():
        tags['Year'] = id['TDRC'][0]
    if 'TALB' in id.keys():
        tags['Album'] = id['TALB'][0]
    if 'TIT2' in id.keys():
        tags['Title'] = id['TIT2'][0]
    if 'TCON' in id.keys():
        tags['Category'] = id['TCON'][0]
    if 'TPE2' in id.keys():
        tags['Album/Artist'] = id['TPE2'][0]
    if 'TPUB' in id.keys():
        tags['Publisher'] = id['TPUB'][0]

    return tags, header
```

Parsing Office metadata – office_parser.py

The last of the plugins, `office_parser.py`, parses DOCX, PPTX, and XLSX files, extracting embedded metadata in XML files. We use the `zipfile` module, which is part of the standard library, to unzip and access the contents of the Office document. This script has two functions, `office_parser()` and `get_tags()`:

```
import zipfile
import os
from time import gmtime, strftime

from lxml import etree
import processors
...
def office_parser():
...
def get_tags():
```

Evaluating the office_parser() function

The `office_parser()` function first checks the input file against the known file signature. All Office documents share the same file signature, `0x504b0304140006000`, and if the input file matches, it's then further processed by the `get_tags()` function, as follows:

```
def office_parser(filename):
    """
    The office_parser function confirms the file type and sends it
    to be processed.
    :param filename: name of the file potentially containing
    embedded metadata.
    :return: A dictionary from get_tags, containing the embedded
    metadata.
    """

    # DOCX, XLSX, and PPTX signatures
    signatures = ['504b030414000600']
    if processors.utility.check_header(
    filename, signatures, 8) == True:
        return get_tags(filename)
    else:
        print(('File signature doesn't match known '
        'signatures.'))
        raise TypeError(('File signature doesn't match '
        'Office objects.'))
```

The get_tags() function for the last time

On line 70, we create the list of headers for our potential dictionary. Line 81 is where the proverbial magic happens. The built-in `zipfile` library is used to read, write, append, and list files in a ZIP archive. On line 81, we create our ZIP file object, allowing us to read the documents contained within it. See the following code:

```
059 def get_tags(filename):
060     """
061     The get_tags function extracts the office metadata from the
062     data object.
063     :param filename: the path and name to the data object.
064     :return: tags and headers, tags is a dictionary containing
065     office metadata and headers are the order of keys for the CSV
066     output.
067     """
068
069     # Set up CSV headers
070     headers = ['Path', 'Name', 'Size', 'Filesystem CTime',
071     'Filesystem MTime', 'Title', 'Author(s)','Create Date',
072     'Modify Date', 'Last Modified By Date', 'Subject', 'Keywords',
073     'Description', 'Category', 'Status', 'Revision',
074     'Edit Time (Min)', 'Page Count', 'Word Count',
075     'Character Count', 'Line Count',
076     'Paragraph Count', 'Slide Count', 'Note Count',
077     'Hidden Slide Count', 'Company', 'Hyperlink Base']
078
079     # Create a ZipFile class from the input object
080     # This allows us to read or write to the 'Zip archive'
081     zf = zipfile.ZipFile(filename)
```

Specifically, on lines 86 and 87, we read the core and app XML files and then convert them into an XML element tree. The `etree.fromstring()` method allows us to build an element tree from a string and is a different method of accomplishing the same task we described earlier in this chapter, which used the `ElementTree.parse()` function:

```
083     # These two XML files contain the embedded metadata of
084     # interest
085     try:
086         core = etree.fromstring(zf.read('docProps/core.xml'))
087         app = etree.fromstring(zf.read('docProps/app.xml'))
088     except KeyError as e:
089         assert Warning(e)
090         return {}, headers
```

As in the previous sections, we create the tags dictionary and populate it with some filesystem metadata:

```
092     tags = {}
093     tags['Path'] = filename
094     tags['Name'] = os.path.basename(filename)
095     tags['Size'] = processors.utility.convert_size(
096         os.path.getsize(filename))
097     tags['Filesystem CTime'] = strftime('%m/%d/%Y %H:%M:%S',
098         gmtime(os.path.getctime(filename)))
099     tags['Filesystem MTime'] = strftime('%m/%d/%Y %H:%M:%S',
100         gmtime(os.path.getmtime(filename)))
```

Starting on line 104, we begin to parse the core XML document by iterating through its children using the `iterchildren()` function. As we iterate through each child, we look for various keywords in the `child.tag` string. If found, the `child.text` string is associated with the appropriate key in the tags dictionary.

These tags in the `core.xml` and `app.xml` files aren't always present and this is the reason we have to first check whether they are there before we can extract them. Some tags, such as the revision tag, are only present in specific Office documents. We'll see much more of that with the `app.xml` file:

```
102     # Core Tags
103
104     for child in core.iterchildren():
105
106         if 'title' in child.tag:
107             tags['Title'] = child.text
108         if 'subject' in child.tag:
109             tags['Subject'] = child.text
110         if 'creator' in child.tag:
111             tags['Author(s)'] = child.text
112         if 'keywords' in child.tag:
113             tags['Keywords'] = child.text
114         if 'description' in child.tag:
115             tags['Description'] = child.text
116         if 'lastModifiedBy' in child.tag:
117             tags['Last Modified By Date'] = child.text
118         if 'created' in child.tag:
119             tags['Create Date'] = child.text
120         if 'modified' in child.tag:
121             tags['Modify Date'] = child.text
122         if 'category' in child.tag:
123             tags['Category'] = child.text
124         if 'contentStatus' in child.tag:
125             tags['Status'] = child.text
```

```
126
127         if (filename.endswith('.docx') or
128         filename.endswith('.pptx')):
129             if 'revision' in child.tag:
130                 tags['Revision'] = child.text
```

The `app.xml` file contains metadata more specific to a given application. On line 133, when we iterate through the children of the element tree, we're only checking tags for specific extensions.

For example, DOCX files contain page and line count metadata that doesn't make sense for PPTX and XLSX files. Therefore, we separate the tags we look for based on the extension of the file. The `TotalTime` tag is particularly insightful and is the time spent editing the document in minutes. See the following code:

```
132     # App Tags
133     for child in app.iterchildren():
134 
135         if filename.endswith('.docx'):
136             if 'TotalTime' in child.tag:
137                 tags['Edit Time (Min)'] = child.text
138             if 'Pages' in child.tag:
139                 tags['Page Count'] = child.text
140             if 'Words' in child.tag:
141                 tags['Word Count'] = child.text
142             if 'Characters' in child.tag:
143                 tags['Character Count'] = child.text
144             if 'Lines' in child.tag:
145                 tags['Line Count'] = child.text
146             if 'Paragraphs' in child.tag:
147                 tags['Paragraph Count'] = child.text
148             if 'Company' in child.tag:
149                 tags['Company'] = child.text
150             if 'HyperlinkBase' in child.tag:
151                 tags['Hyperlink Base'] = child.text
152 
153         elif filename.endswith('.pptx'):
154             if 'TotalTime' in child.tag:
155                 tags['Edit Time (Min)'] = child.text
156             if 'Words' in child.tag:
157                 tags['Word Count'] = child.text
158             if 'Paragraphs' in child.tag:
159                 tags['Paragraph Count'] = child.text
160             if 'Slides' in child.tag:
161                 tags['Slide Count'] = child.text
162             if 'Notes' in child.tag:
163                 tags['Note Count'] = child.text
```

```
            if 'HiddenSlides' in child.tag:
                tags['Hidden Slide Count'] = child.text
            if 'Company' in child.tag:
                tags['Company'] = child.text
            if 'HyperlinkBase' in child.tag:
                tags['Hyperlink Base'] = child.text
        else:
            if 'Company' in child.tag:
                tags['Company'] = child.text
            if 'HyperlinkBase' in child.tag:
                tags['Hyperlink Base'] = child.text

    return tags, headers
```

Moving on to our writers

Within the writers directory, we have two scripts: `csv_writer.py` and `kml_writer.py`. Both of these writers are called depending on the types of data being processed in the `metadata_parser.py` framework.

Writing spreadsheets – csv_writer.py

In this chapter, we'll use `csv.DictWriter` instead of `csv.writer`, just like we did in `Chapter 5`, *Databases in Python*, and `Chapter 6`, *Extracting Artifacts from Binary Files*. As a reminder, the difference is that the `DictWriter` writes dictionary objects to a CSV file and the `csv.writer` function is more suited for writing lists.

The great thing about `csv.DictWriter` is that it requires an argument, `fieldnames`, when creating the writer object. The `fieldnames` argument should be a list that represents the desired order of columns in the output. In addition, all possible keys must be included in the `fieldnames` list. If a key exists that isn't contained in the list, an exception will be raised. On the other hand, if a key isn't present in the dictionary but is in the `fieldnames` list, then that column will simply be skipped for that entry:

```
from __future__ import print_function
import sys
import os
if sys.version_info[0] == 2:
    import unicodecsv as csv
elif sys.version_info[0] == 3:
    import csv
import logging
```

```
...
040 def csv_writer(output_data, headers, output_dir, output_name):
041     """
042     The csv_writer function uses the csv DictWriter module to
043     write the list of dictionaries. The DictWriter can take
044     a fieldnames argument, as a list, which represents the
045     desired order of columns.
046     :param output_data: The list of dictionaries containing
047     embedded metadata.
048     :param headers: A list of keys in the dictionary that
049     represent the desired order of columns in the output.
050     :param output_dir: The folder to write the output CSV to.
051     :param output_name: The name of the output CSV.
052     :return:
053     """
054     msg = 'Writing ' + output_name + ' CSV output.'
055     print('[+]', msg)
056     logging.info(msg)
057
058     out_file = os.path.join(output_dir, output_name)
059
060     if sys.version_info[0] == 2:
061         csvfile = open(out_file, "wb")
062     elif sys.version_info[0] == 3:
063         csvfile = open(out_file, "w", newline='',
064             encoding='utf-8')
```

On line 69, we create our `csv.DictWriter` function, passing in the output file and the headers as a list of `fieldnames` from our plugin function. To write the headers for our CSV file, we can simply call the `writeheader` function, which uses the `fieldnames` list as its list of headers. Finally, we need to iterate through each dictionary in our metadata container list and write them using the `writerow()` function in line 76, as follows:

```
066     with csvfile:
067         # We use DictWriter instead of Writer to write
068         # dictionaries to CSV.
069         writer = csv.DictWriter(csvfile, fieldnames=headers)
070
071         # Writerheader writes the header based on the supplied
072         # headers object
073         writer.writeheader()
074         for dictionary in output_data:
075             if dictionary:
076                 writer.writerow(dictionary)
```

Plotting GPS data with Google Earth – kml_writer.py

The `kml_writer.py` script uses the `simplekml` module (version 1.3.1) to quickly create our KML output. Full documentation for this module can be found at `http://simplekml.com`. This module can be installed with `pip`:

```
pip install simplekml==1.3.1
```

With this module, we can create and add a geotagged point and save KML in three lines of code:

```
001 from __future__ import print_function
002 import os
003 import logging
004
005 import simplekml
...
036 def kml_writer(output_data, output_dir, output_name):
037     """
038     The kml_writer function writes JPEG and TIFF EXIF GPS data to
039     a Google Earth KML file. This file can be opened
040     in Google Earth and will use the GPS coordinates to create
041     'pins' on the map of the taken photo's location.
042     :param output_data: The embedded EXIF metadata to be written
043     :param output_dir: The output directory to write the KML file.
044     :param output_name: The name of the output KML file.
045     :return:
046     """
```

In line 51, we create our KML object using the `simplekml.Kml()` call. This function takes an optional keyword argument name that represents the name of the KML file. Lines 52-71 check whether the original date key is present and prepares our GPS points to be entered into the KML object:

```
047     msg = 'Writing ' + output_name + ' KML output.'
048     print('[+]', msg)
049     logging.info(msg)
050     # Instantiate a Kml object and pass along the output filename
051     kml = simplekml.Kml(name=output_name)
052     for exif in output_data:
053         if ('Latitude' in exif.keys() and
054                 'Latitude Reference' in exif.keys() and
055                 'Longitude Reference' in exif.keys() and
056                 'Longitude' in exif.keys()):
057
```

```
            if 'Original Date' in exif.keys():
                dt = exif['Original Date']
            else:
                dt = 'N/A'

            if exif['Latitude Reference'] == 'S':
                latitude = '-' + exif['Latitude']
            else:
                latitude = exif['Latitude']

            if exif['Longitude Reference'] == 'W':
                longitude = '-' + exif['Longitude']
            else:
                longitude = exif['Longitude']
```

Our GPS coordinates are in decimal format from the `exif_parser.py` script. However, in this script, we didn't account for the reference point. The reference point determines the sign of the GPS coordinate. A south latitude reference makes the latitude negative. Likewise, west makes the longitude negative.

Once that has been accounted for, we can create our geotagged point passing the name, description, and coordinates of the point. The else statement on lines 76 and 77 is executed if the conditional checking of the latitude and longitude EXIF tags that exist return `False`. Although these two lines could be omitted, they should be implemented as a reminder of the implemented logic. Once we've created all of our points, we can save the KML file by calling the `kml.save()` function and passing along the desired output path and the name of the file. The following are lines 73 through 78:

```
073             kml.newpoint(name=exif['Name'],
074             description='Originally Created: ' + dt,
075             coords=[(longitude, latitude)])
076         else:
077             pass
078     kml.save(os.path.join(output_dir, output_name))
```

Supporting our framework with processors

The processors directory contains one script, `utility.py`. This script has some helper functions that are used by all current plugins. Rather than writing the functions for each separate plugin, we gathered them under one script.

Creating framework-wide utility functions – utility.py

This script has two functions, `check_header()` and `convert_size()`. The former performs file signature matching, whereas the latter converts an integer representing the byte size of a file into a human-readable format, as follows:

```
001 import binascii
002 import logging
...
033 def check_header(filename, headers, size):
034     """
035     The check_header function reads a supplied size of the file
036     and checks against known signatures to determine the file
037     type.
038     :param filename: The name of the file.
039     :param headers: A list of known file signatures for the
040     file type(s).
041     :param size: The amount of data to read from the file for
042     signature verification.
043     :return: Boolean, True if the signatures match;
044     otherwise, False.
045     """
```

The `check_header()` function, defined on line 33, takes a filename, list of known signatures, and the amount of data to read from the file as arguments. On line 46, we open the input file and then read the first few bytes based on the value passed in as the size argument. On line 48, we convert the ASCII representation of the data into a hex string. On line 49, we iterate through each known signature and compare it with `hex_header`. If they match, we return `True` and otherwise, we return `False` and log the warning, as follows:

```
046     with open(filename, 'rb') as infile:
047         header = infile.read(size)
048         hex_header = binascii.hexlify(header).decode('utf-8')
049         for signature in headers:
050             if hex_header == signature:
051                 return True
052             else:
053                 pass
054         logging.warn(('The signature for {} ({}) doesn't match '
055             'known signatures: {}').format(
056                 filename, hex_header, headers))
057         return False
```

The `convert_size()` function is a useful utility function that converts byte-size integers into human-readable format. On line 66, we create our list of potential prefixes. Note, we're assuming that the user won't encounter any file requiring more than a `TB` prefix, at least for a few years:

```
059 def convert_size(size):
060     """
061     The convert_size function converts an integer representing
062     bytes into a human-readable format.
063     :param size: The size in bytes of a file
064     :return: The human-readable size.
065     """
066     sizes = ['Bytes', 'KB', 'MB', 'GB', 'TB']
```

We use a `while` loop to continually divide the size by 1024 until it's less than 1024. Every time we make a division, we add one to the index. When the size is less than 1024, the index is the location in the sizes list of the appropriate prefix.

On line 71, we use the string formatting function, `format`, to return our float and prefix in the desired way. `{:.2f}` tells the format function that this first argument is a float and we want to round up to two decimal places:

```
067     index = 0
068     while size > 1024:
069         size /= 1024.
070         index += 1
071     return '{:.2f} {}'.format(size, sizes[index])
```

As seen in the below screenshot, we can run our framework across a directory and gather an output report for our review. In this case, we've run the code against a folder containing an image with geolocation data.

```
(py3.7.1) $ python metadata_parser.py ./ /output
[+] Generating file listing and running plugins.
[+] Writing output to /output
[+] Writing exif_metadata.kml KML output.
[+] Writing exif_metadata.csv CSV output.
[*] Program completed successfully -- exiting..
```

Our output report is shown below, though we've wrapped the columns to ensure it fits on one page.

	A	B	C	D	E	F	G
1	**Path**	**Name**	**Size**	**Filesystem CTime**	**Filesystem MTime**	**Original Date**	**Digitized Date**
2	./img_42.jpg	img_42.jpg	416.51 KB	12/1/18 15:42	12/1/18 15:42	10/10/15 11:11	10/10/15 11:11
3							
4							
5	**Make**	**Model**	**Software**	**Latitude**	**Latitude Reference**	**Longitude**	**Longitude Reference**
6	Nokia	Lumia 635	Windows Phone	40.68291	N	76.19776	W
7							
8							
9	**Exif Version**	**Height**	**Width**	**Flash**			**Scene Type**
10	b'0220'	1456	2592	Flash did not fire, compulsory flash mode			Standard

Our script also generated KML output viewable in Google Earth as shown below:

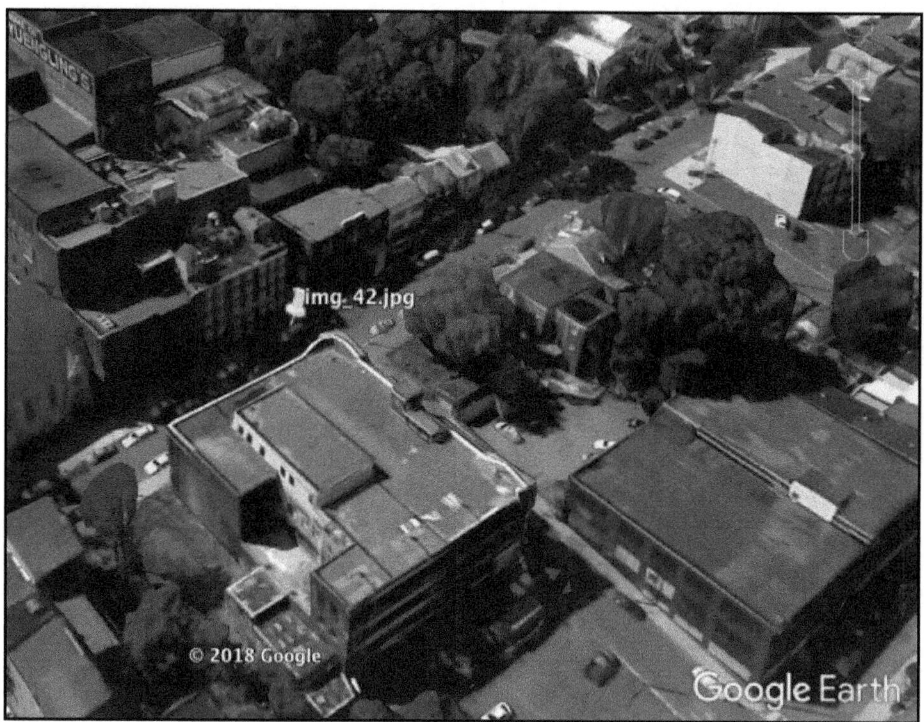

Framework summary

Frameworks are incredibly useful to organize multiple collections of scripts under one roof, so to speak. There are challenges that come with frameworks; mainly keeping standardized operations through the growth of the project. Our `metadata_parser.py` framework is in its first iteration and, if we continue to develop it, we may find that the current setup is only suitable on a smaller level.

For example, as we implement more and more features, we might realize that the efficiency of our framework starts to lag. At that point, we would need to go back to the drawing board and determine whether we're using the correct data type or the best way to write our plugins and writers.

Additional challenges

We had difficulties deciding between two main challenges for this chapter. We could add additional plugins or refine what currently exists. In actual development, your time would be spent balancing these two objectives as the framework continues to grow. For this chapter, we propose a recursive-based challenge.

Remember that, while explaining the post Office 2007 format of documents, we determined that attached media is stored in the media subdirectory of the document. In its current incarnation, when an Office document is encountered, that media subdirectory, which might have copies of files containing embedded metadata themselves, isn't processed. The challenge here is to add the newly discovered files to the current file listing.

We might do that by returning a list of newly discovered files back to `metadata_parser.py`. Another route might be to check the file extensions in the `office_parser.py` script and pass them immediately onto the appropriate plugins. The latter method would be easier to implement but not ideal as it removes some of the control from the `metadata_parser.py` script. Ultimately, it's up to the developer to determine the most efficient and logical method of completing this challenge.

Beyond this, some other efficiency achievements can be made. For example, we don't need to return the headers for the plugin each and every time the plugin is called. Since the headers will always be the same, we only need to have them created/returned once. Alternatively, this framework is limited by the types of writers it supports. Consider adding a writer for Excel spreadsheets to create more useful reports.

Summary

In this chapter, you learned how to handle some of the popular embedded metadata formats, perform basic file signature analysis, and create frameworks in Python. Frameworks become a normal programming solution as programs increase in complexity. The code for this project can be downloaded from GitHub or Packt, as described in the *Preface*.

In the next chapter, you'll learn how to develop a basic graphical user interface, or GUI, in Python using the first-party TkInter module. This GUI will be responsible for converting timestamps of various types into a human-readable format.

9
Uncovering Time

Timestamps are stored in a wide variety of formats unique to the operating system or application responsible for their generation. In forensics, converting these timestamps can be an important aspect of an investigation.

As an example, we may aggregate converted timestamps and create a combined timeline of events to determine a sequence of actions across mediums. This evaluation of time can help us establish whether actions are within a defined scope and provide insights into the relationship between two events.

To decipher these formatted timestamps, we can use tools to interpret the raw values and convert them into human-readable time. Most forensic tools perform this operation silently as they parse known artifact structures (similarly to how our scripts often parse Unix timestamps).

In some cases, we don't have tools that properly or uniformly handle specific timestamps and will have to rely on our ingenuity to decipher the time value.

We'll use common libraries to interpret timestamps from user input and transform them into the desired formats. Using the TkInter library, we'll design a **Graphical User Interface** (**GUI**) that the user will interface with to display date information. We'll use a Python class to better organize our GUI and handle events such as when a user clicks a button on the GUI.

In this chapter, we'll build a graphic interface that converts timestamps between machine- and human-readable formats with the help of the following topics:

- The creation of cross-platform GUIs in Python
- The conversion of common raw timestamp values between machine- and human-readable formats
- The basics of Python class design and implementation, allowing the flexible addition of more time formats

The code for this chapter was developed and tested using Python 2.7.15 and Python 3.7.1

About timestamps

Timestamp formats often boil down to two components: a reference point and a convention or algorithm used to represent the amount of time that has passed from the said reference point. Documentation exists for most timestamps and can help us to determine the best means to convert raw time data into a human-readable timestamp.

As mentioned in the introduction, there is a wide array of timestamp formats, some of which we've already encountered, such as Unix time and Windows FILETIME. This makes the conversion process more difficult as the forensic scripts we develop may need to be prepared to process multiple time formats.

Python has several standard libraries bundled in the distribution that can help us convert timestamps. We've used the `datetime` module before to properly handle time values and store them within a Python object. We'll introduce two new libraries—`time`, which is part of the standard library, and the third-party `dateutil` module.

We can download and install `dateutil` (version 2.7.5) by running `pip install python-dateutil==2.7.5`. This library will be used to parse strings into `datetime` objects. The `parser()` method from the `dateutil` library takes a string as input and attempts to automatically convert it into a `datetime` object. Unlike the `strptime()` method, which requires explicit declaration of the format of the timestamp, the `dateutil.parser` converts timestamps of varying formats without requiring input from the developer.

An example string could be `Tuesday December 8th, 2015 at 6:04 PM` or `12/08/2015 18:04`, and both would be converted by the `parser()` method into the same `datetime` object. The following code block demonstrates this functionality, and works in both Python 2.7.15 and Python 3.7.1:

```
>>> from dateutil import parser as duparser
>>> d = duparser.parse('Tuesday December 8th, 2015 at 6:04 PM')
>>> d.isoformat()
'2015-12-08T18:04:00'
>>> d2 = duparser.parse('12/08/2015 18:04')
>>> d2.isoformat()
'2015-12-08T18:04:00'
```

On the first line of the code block, we import the `dateutil` parser and create an alias, `duparser`, as the function name parser is a generic term that could possibly collide with another variable or function. We then call the `parse()` method and pass a string representing a timestamp. Assigning this parsed value to the variable, `d`, we view its ISO format using the `isoformat()` function. We repeat these steps with a second timestamp in a different format and observe the same end result.

Please refer to the documentation for additional details on the `parse()` method at `http://dateutil.readthedocs.org/en/latest/parser.html`.

What's an epoch?

An *epoch* is a point in time, marked as the origin of time for a given time format, and is usually used as a reference point to track movement through time. While we'll omit any philosophical discussion associated with measuring time, we'll use and reference an epoch as the starting point for a given time format in this chapter.

There're two major epoch times associated with most timestamps: `1970-01-01 00:00:00` and `1601-01-01 00:00:00`. The first, starting in 1970, is traditionally referred to as POSIX time as it's a common timestamp in Unix and Unix-like systems. In most Unix systems, timestamps are measured as seconds elapsed since POSIX time. This carries over to some applications as well, and variations exist that use milliseconds since the same epoch.

The second noted epoch, based in 1601, is commonly found on Windows-based systems and is used because it was the start of the first 400-year cycle of the Gregorian calendar to include leap years. The 400-year cycle starting in 1601 is the first cycle where digital files existed, and so this value became another common epoch. It's common to see Windows system timestamps as a count of 100-nanosecond segments since that epoch. This value will often be stored in hex or as an integer.

The next code block describes the process used to convert timestamps of different epochs. As we've seen in previous chapters, we can use the `datetime` module's `fromtimestamp()` method to convert Unix timestamps because it uses the 1970 epoch. For 1601-based timestamps, we'll need to convert them before using the `fromtimestamp()` function.

To make this conversion easier, let's calculate the constant between these dates and use that constant to convert between the two epochs. On the first line, we import the `datetime` library. Next, we subtract the two timestamps to determine the time delta between `1970-01-01` and `1601-01-01`. This statement produces a `datetime.timedelta` object, which stores the difference in time as a count of days, seconds, and microseconds between the two values.

In this instance, the difference between the 1970 and 1601 timestamps is exactly 134,774 days. We need to convert this into a microsecond timestamp to be able to accurately leverage it in our conversions. Therefore, in the third line, we convert the count of days (`time_diff.days`) into microseconds by multiplying it by `86400000000` (the product of *24 hours x 60 minutes x 60 seconds x 1,000,000 microseconds*) and print the constant value of `11644473600000000`. Take a look at the following code:

```
>>> import datetime
>>> time_diff = datetime.datetime(1970,1,1) - datetime.datetime(1601,1,1)
>>> print (time_diff.days * 86400000000)
11644473600000000
```

With this value, we can convert timestamps between both epochs and properly ingest 1601-based epoch timestamps.

Using a GUI

In this chapter, we'll use a GUI to convert timestamps between raw and human-readable formats. Timestamp conversion is a useful excuse to explore programming GUIs as it offers a solution to a common investigative activity. By using a GUI, we greatly increase the usability of our script among those deterred by the Command Prompt, with all of its arguments and switches.

There are many options for GUI development in Python, though, in this chapter, we'll focus on TkInter. The TkInter library is a cross-platform GUI development library for Python that hooks into the operating system's `Tcl/Tk` library found on Windows, macOS, and several Linux platforms.

This cross-platform framework allows us to build a common interface that's platform-independent. Although TkInter GUIs may not look the most modern, they allow us to rapidly build a functional interface to interact with, in a relatively simple manner.

We'll only be covering the basics of GUI development with TkInter here. Further information can be found online or in books dedicated to the topic that cover the development process and specific features related to developing with TkInter in more detail. The `https://www.python.org/` website has an extensive list of resources for learning and using TkInter at `https://wiki.python.org/moin/TkInter`.

Basics of TkInter objects

We'll use a few different features of TkInter to display our GUI. The first item every TkInter GUI needs is a root window, also known as the master, which acts as the top-level parent to any other items we add to the GUI. Within this window, we'll combine several objects that allow the user to interact with our interface, such as the `Label`, `Entry`, and `Button` items:

- The `Label` object allows us to place text labels that cannot be edited on the interface. This allows us to add titles or provide a description for objects that indicate what should be written to or displayed in the field.
- The `Entry` object allows the user to enter a single line of text as input to the application.
- The `Button` object allows us to execute commands when pressed. In our case, the button will call the appropriate function to convert a timestamp of the specific format and update the interface with the returned value.

Using these three features, we've already introduced all of the GUI elements needed for our interface. There're many more objects available for use and they can be found in greater detail in the TkInter documentation at `https://docs.python.org/3/library/tkinter.html`.

We'll be writing our code in a way that works with both Python 2 and Python 3. For this reason, in Python 2 (for example, version 2.7.15), we'll import `Tkinter` as follows:

```
>>> from Tkinter import *
```

For Python 3, for example, version 3.7.1, we'll instead import it as follows:

```
>>> from tkinter import *
```

To condense this, we can instead use the `sys` module to detect the Python version and import the proper module, as shown here:

```
import sys
if sys.version_info[0] == 2:
    from Tkinter import *
elif sys.version_info[0] == 3:
    from tkinter import *
```

Implementing the TkInter GUI

This section illustrates a simple example of creating a TkInter GUI. In the first seven lines, we import the two modules we'll need to create our interface. This import method, while complex, allows us to import these two modules in a Python 2- or Python 3-specific way.

The first module imports all of the default objects needed for the TkInter GUI design. The `ttk` module imports the themed TkInter pack, which applies additional formatting to the interface depending on the host operating system and is a simple way to improve the overall look of our interface. In the last line, we create our root window.

When typed into a Python interpreter, the execution of the last line should display a blank 200 pixel × 200 pixel square window in the top-left of your screen. The dimensions and location are a default setting that can be modified. See the following code block:

```
>>> import sys
>>> if sys.version_info[0] == 2:
>>>     from Tkinter import *
>>>     import ttk
>>> elif sys.version_info[0] == 3:
>>>     from tkinter import *
>>>     import tkinter.ttk as ttk
>>> root = Tk()
```

The following screenshot displays a TkInter root window created when executing the code block on a macOS system:

With the root window created, we can begin to add items to the interface. A good first item is a label. In the code block mentioned later, we add a label from the themed `ttk` pack to the window:

```
>>> first_label = ttk.Label(root, text="Hello World")
```

The `Label` parameter requires two arguments: the parent window it should be displayed on and the text to display. Additional attributes can be assigned to the label such as fonts and text size.

Note that, after executing the first line of the code block, the window doesn't update. Instead, we must specify how we want to display the object within the window with one of the available geometry managers.

TkInter uses geometry managers to determine the placement of objects within the window. There're three common managers: `grid`, `pack`, and `place`:

- The `grid` geometry manager places elements based on a row and column specification
- The `pack` geometry manager is simpler and will place elements next to each other, either vertically or horizontally depending on a specified configuration
- Finally, the `place` geometry manager uses *x* and *y* coordinates to place elements and requires the most effort to maintain and design

For this example, we chose to use the `pack` method as seen on the second line of the code block. Once we describe which geometry manager to use, our interface is updated with the label:

```
>>> first_label.pack()
```

The following screenshot reflects the addition of the label to our GUI:

As seen in the preceding screenshot, the root window has shrunk to fit the size of its elements. At this point, we can resize the window by dragging the edges to shrink or grow the size of the main window.

Let's add some space around our `Label` object. We can accomplish this by using two different techniques. The first adds padding around the `Label` object, using the `.config()` method. To add padding, we must provide a tuple of padding, in pixels, for the x and y axis.

In the example, we add a 10-pixel padding on both the x and y axes. When the following line is executed, it'll automatically update in the GUI since the geometry manager is already configured:

```
>>> first_label.config(padding=(10,10))
```

The padding is shown in the following screenshot:

This only adds padding around the label itself and not the entirety of the root window. To change the dimensions of the root window, we need to call the `geometry()` method and provide the width, height, position from the left of the screen, and position from the top of the screen.

In the following example, we'll set the dimensions to 200 pixels wide by 100 pixels high with an offset 30 pixels from the left of the screen and 60 pixels from the top of the screen:

```
>>> root.geometry('200x100+30+60')
```

The new resolution of the GUI is displayed in the following screenshot:

Depending on your operating system, the default colors within the GUI may vary due to the available theme packs.

Let's introduce the other two GUI elements we'll use, `Entry` and `Button`. We'll now initialize the `Entry` object, which will allow a user to enter text that we can capture and use in the program. In the first line, we initialize a `StringVar()` variable, which we'll use with the `Entry` object. Unlike prior scripts, we need to set up special variables that can respond to the event-driven nature of GUI interfaces:

```
>>> text = StringVar()
```

TkInter supports a variety of special variables such as the `StringVar()` function for strings, `BooleanVar()` for Booleans, `DoubleVar()` for floats, and `IntVar()` for integers. Each of these objects allows for values to be set using the `set()` method and retrieved using the `get()` method. The preceding code shows the initialization of the `StringVar()`, setting it to a default value, assigning it to a created `Entry` element, and packing it into the root window. Finally, we can gather the input from the user via the `get()` method:

```
>>> text.set("Enter Text Here")
>>> text_entry = ttk.Entry(root, textvariable=text)
>>> text_entry.pack()
>>> text.get()
'Hello World!'
```

The following two consecutive screenshots show the updates to the GUI with the new code block we've implemented:

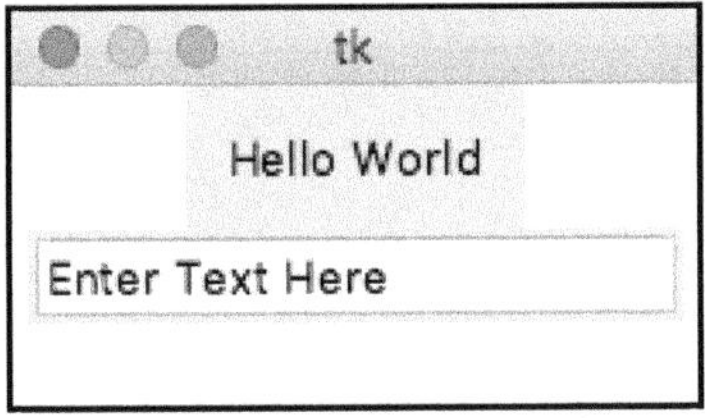

The preceding screenshot shows the default text in the `Entry` box, whereas the following screenshot shows what it looks like with modified values:

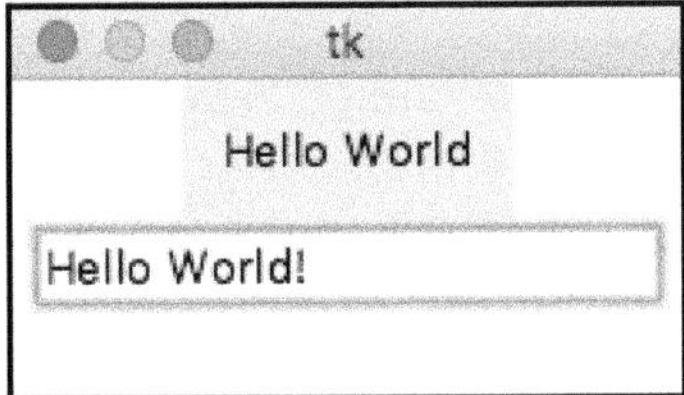

Please note that we wrote `Hello World!` into the `Entry` object before executing the `text.get()` method.

The `Button` object is used to initiate an event when the button is clicked. To set an action into motion, we need a function to call.

In the next example, we define the `clicked()` function, which prints a string as seen in the following code block. After this function, we define the button using the `ttk` theme pack, setting the button text to `Go` and the `command` parameter of the function name. After packing the button into the root window, we can click on it and see the statement printed in the Terminal, as seen on the last line of our following code block. Although this functionality isn't very useful, it demonstrates how a button calls an action. Our script will demonstrate further uses for the `Button` object and its command parameter:

```
>>> def clicked():
...     print "The button was clicked!"
...
>>> go = ttk.Button(root, text="Go", command=clicked)
>>> go.pack()
The button was clicked!
```

The addition of this button is shown in the following screenshot:

Using frame objects

TkInter provides another object we'll use named `frame`. Frames are containers we can place information in and that and provide additional organization. We'll have two frames in our final interface. The first is an input frame containing all of the objects that a user will interact with, and the second is our output frame that will display all of the information processed by the script. In the final code of this chapter, the two `frame` objects will be children to the root window and act as parents to the `Label`, `Entry`, and/or `Button` objects within them.

Another benefit of the `frame` object is that each one can use its own geometry manager. Since each parent object can use only a single geometry manager, this allows us to leverage several different managers within our overall GUI.

In our script, we'll use the `pack()` manager to organize the frames in the root window and the `grid()` manager to organize elements within each frame.

Using classes in TkInter

We're yet to directly use classes in this book; however, it's the preferred way to design a GUI. A class allows us to build an object that can hold functions and attributes. In fact, we've often used classes without knowing it. Objects we're familiar with, such as `datetime` objects, are classes that contain functions and attributes available to them.

Classes, despite not being featured heavily in this book, may confuse new developers but are recommended for more advanced scripts. We'll briefly cover classes in this chapter and recommend further research into classes as your understanding of Python grows. The items we cover with classes are specific to the GUI example in this chapter.

A class is defined with a similar syntax to a function, where we use the `class` keyword in lieu of `def`. Once defined, we nest functions inside the `constructor` class to make these functions callable from a `class` object. These nested functions are called methods and are synonymous with the methods we have called from libraries. A method allows us to execute code just like a function. We have primarily, up to this point, used the terms method and function interchangeably. We apologize; this was done so as to not bore you and ourselves with the same word over and over again.

So far, classes sound like nothing more than a collection of functions. So what gives? The true value of a class is that we can create multiple instances of the same class and assign separate values to each instance. To further extend this, we can run our predefined methods on each instance separately. Say, for example, we have a time class where each time has an associated `datetime` variable. Some of these we may decide to convert into UTC while leaving others in their current time zone. This isolation is what makes designing code within a class valuable.

Classes are great for GUI design because they allow us to pass values across functions without additional duplicative arguments. This is accomplished with the `self` keyword, which allows us to specify values within a class that're portable within the class instance and all of its methods.

In the next example, we create a class, named `SampleClass`, which inherits from the object. This is the basic setup for a class definition, and while there are more parameters available, we'll focus on the basics for this chapter. On line 2, we define our first method named, `__init__()`, which is a special function. You may notice that it has double leading and trailing underscores like the `if __name__ == '__main__'` statements we have created in our scripts. If an `__init__()` method exists within a class, it'll be executed at the initialization of the class.

In the example, we define the `__init__()` method, passing `self` and `init_cost` as arguments. The `self` argument must be the first argument of any method and allows us to reference the values stored under the keyword, `self`. Following this, `init_cost` is a variable that must be set when the class is first called by the user. On line 3, we assign the value of the user-provided `init_cost` to `self.cost`. It's a convention to assign arguments (besides `self`) for class instantiation into class variables. On line 4, we define the second method, `number_of_nickels()`, and pass the `self` value as its only argument. On line 5, we complete the class by returning an integer of `self.cost * 20`, as shown:

```
>>> class SampleClass(object):
...     def __init__(self, init_cost):
...         self.cost = init_cost
...     def number_of_nickels(self):
...         return int(self.cost * 20)
...
```

Next, we initialize `s1` as an instance of our `SampleClass` class with the initial value of `24.60`. Then, we call its value by using the `s1.cost` attribute. The `s1` variable refers to an instance of `SampleClass` and grants us access to the methods and values within the class. We call the `number_of_nickels()` method on `s1` and change its stored value to `15`, which updates the results of the `number_of_nickels()` method. Next, we define `s2` and assign a different value to it. Even though we run the same methods, we're only able to view the data in relation to the specific class instance:

```
>>> s1 = SampleClass(24.60)
>>> s1.cost
24.6
>>> s1.number_of_nickels()
492
>>> s1.cost = 15
>>> s1.number_of_nickels()
300
>>> s2 = SampleClass(10)
>>> s2.number_of_nickels()
200
```

Developing the date decoder GUI – date_decoder.py

This script was tested in both Python 2.7.15 and 3.7.1 and uses the python-dateutil (version 2.7.5) third-party library which can be installed with `pip` like so:

- `pip install python-dateutil==2.7.5`

After this introduction to timestamps, GUI development, and Python classes, let's begin developing our `date_decoder.py` script. We'll design a GUI with two primary functionalities that the end user will interact with.

First, the GUI allows the user to enter a timestamp from an artifact in native format and convert it into a human-readable time. The second feature allows the user to enter a human-readable timestamp and select an option to convert it into the respective machine time. To build this, we'll use an entry box, several labels, and different types of button for the user to interact with the interface.

All dates processed with this code assume local machine time for the time zone. Please ensure you convert all timestamp sources into a uniform time zone to simplify the analysis.

As with our other scripts, this code starts with our import statements followed by authorship details. After importing `datetime` and `logging`, we import TkInter and theme resource modules using our Python 2 and Python 3 conditional. We then import `dateutil`, which, as discussed, will handle date interpretation and conversion operations. We then set up our script license, documentation, and logging values:

```
"""Example usage of Tkinter to convert dates."""
import datetime
import logging
import sys
if sys.version_info[0] == 2:
    from Tkinter import *
    import ttk
elif sys.version_info[0] == 3:
    from tkinter import *
    import tkinter.ttk as ttk
from dateutil import parser as duparser
...
__authors__ = ["Chapin Bryce", "Preston Miller"]
__date__ = 20181027
__description__ = '''This script uses a GUI to show date values
```

```
045     interpreted by common timestamp formats'''
046 logger = logging.getLogger(__name__)
```

We begin by defining the properties of our GUI, such as the dimensions, background, and title of the window, and create the root window. After configuring the base of the GUI, we populate our GUI with the desired widgets we've discussed. Once we've designed the interface, we create methods to handle events, such as converting timestamps and showing the results in the GUI. Instead of our typical `main()` functions, we instead create an instance of this class that'll launch the GUI window when executed.

Our code starts with the declaration of our `DateDecoder` class and its `__init__()` method. This method doesn't require any parameters to be passed by the user since we'll be accepting all of our input values and settings through the GUI. The next function we define will be our `run()` controller on line 74. This controller calls functions that design the GUI and then launches the said GUI:

```
049 class DateDecoder(object):
...
054     def __init__():
...
074     def run():
```

To display the GUI in a structured manner, we need to divide our GUI into functional units. With the methods on lines 84 and 119, we create our input and output frames that make up our GUI. These frames contain widgets pertinent to their action and are governed by their own geometry:

```
084     def build_input_frame():
...
119     def build_output_frame():
```

With the design of our interface established, we can focus on the functions that handle logic operations and events when buttons are clicked. The `convert()` method is used to call timestamp converters to interpret the value as a date.

These converters are specific to each of the supported timestamps and are defined on lines 175, 203, and 239. Our last class method, `output()`, is used to update the interface. This may be misleading as the previous `output()` functions in our scripts have generally created some kind of report. In this case, we'll be using our output function to update the GUI with our results, to display the information to the user in an organized and helpful manner:

```
151     def convert():
...
175     def convert_unix_seconds():
```

```
...
203     def convert_win_filetime_64():
...
239     def convert_chrome_time():
...
183     def output():
```

Unlike in previous chapters, this function has no need to handle command-line arguments. We do, however, still set up logging and then instantiate and run our GUI. In addition, starting on line 202, we initialize a logger using our basic logging convention. We hard-code the path to the log file as no command-line arguments are passed to this script. On lines 211 and 212, the class is initialized and then the `run()` method is called in order for our GUI to be created and displayed to the user, as follows:

```
286 if __name__ == '__main__':
287     """
288     This statement is used to initialize the GUI. No
289     arguments needed as it's a graphic interface
290     """
291     # Initialize Logging
292     log_path = 'date_decoder.log'
293 
294     logger.setLevel(logging.DEBUG)
295     msg_fmt = logging.Formatter("%(asctime)-15s %(funcName)-20s"
296         "%(levelname)-8s %(message)s")
297     fhndl = logging.FileHandler(log_path, mode='a')
298     fhndl.setFormatter(fmt=msg_fmt)
299     logger.addHandler(fhndl)
300 
301     logger.info('Starting Date Decoder v. {}'.format(__date__))
302     logger.debug('System ' + sys.platform)
303     logger.debug('Version ' + sys.version.replace("\n", " "))
304 
305     # Create Instance and run the GUI
306     dd = DateDecoder()
307     dd.run()
```

We've split our flowchart into two screenshots, due to its width. The first screenshot shows the flow for setting up the `DateDecoder` class and the initial `run()` call, which creates our frames:

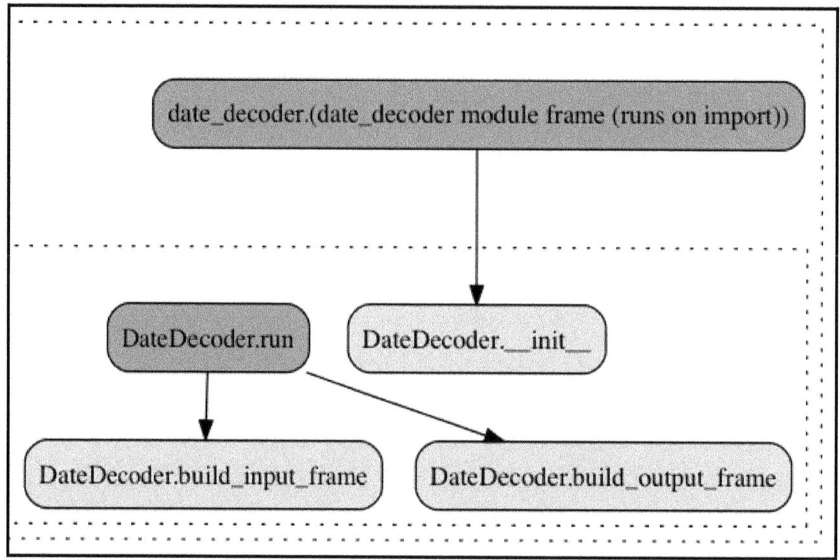

The second screenshot displays the flow for the operational code, where our converter function calls the specific time-converting function and then our `output()` function to display it to the user:

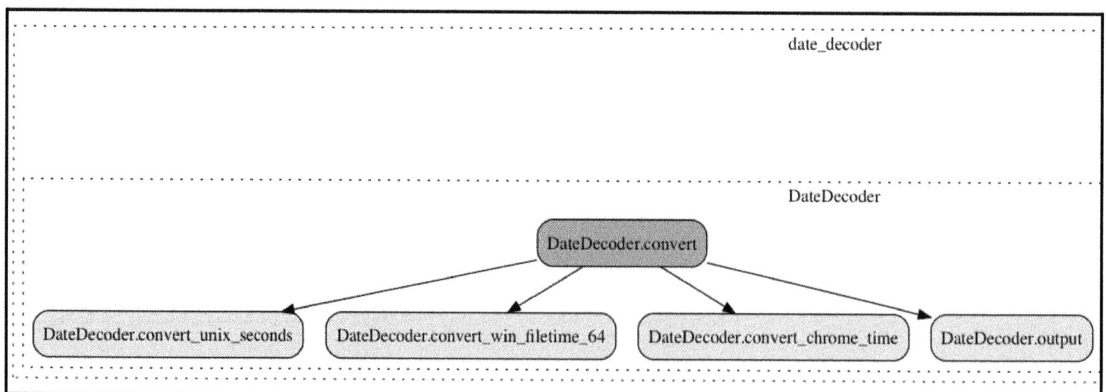

The DateDecoder class setup and __init__() method

We initialize our class using the `class` keyword, followed by the class name, and passing the `object` argument as seen on line 49. It's best practice to name classes using the camelCase convention and methods with underscores to prevent confusion. On line 50, we define the `__init__()` special method described earlier with only the `self` parameter. This class doesn't require any user input at initialization, so we don't need to concern ourselves with adding additional arguments. Take a look at the following code:

```
049 class DateDecoder(object):
050     """
051     The DateDecoder class handles the construction of the GUI
052     and the processing of date & time values
053     """
054     def __init__(self):
055         """
056         The __init__ method initializes the root GUI window and
057         variable used in the script
058         """
```

On line 60, we create the root window of the GUI and assign it to a value within the `self` object. This allows us to reference it and any other object created with `self` in other methods within the class without needing to pass it as an argument, since the `self` parameter stores values for use throughout the class instance. On line 61, we define the size of the window as 500 pixels wide, 180 pixels high, and offset by 40 pixels on both the top and left sides of the screen.

To improve the look of the interface, we've added the background color to reflect the theme shown on macOS, though this can be set to any hexadecimal color as seen on line 62. Finally, we modify the title property of the root, giving it a name that displays on top of the GUI's window:

```
059         # Init root window
060         self.root = Tk()
061         self.root.geometry("500x180+40+40")
062         self.root.config(background = '#ECECEC')
063         self.root.title('Date Decoder')
```

After the initial GUI definition, we need to set the base values for important variables. While this isn't required, it's often best practice to create shared values in the `__init__()` method and define them with default values. After we define three class variables that will store our processed time values, we also define the epoch constants for 1601- and 1970-based timestamps. The code is as follows:

```
        # Init time values
        self.processed_unix_seconds = None
        self.processed_windows_filetime_64 = None
        self.processed_chrome_time = None

        # Set Constant Epoch Offset
        self.epoch_1601 = 11644473600000000
        self.epoch_1970 = datetime.datetime(1970,1,1)
```

The `__init__()` method should be used to initialize of class attributes. In some situations, you may want this class to also run the primary operations of the class, but we'll not be implementing that functionality in our code. We separate the runtime operations into a new method named `run()` to allow us to start operations specific to running the main code. This allows users to change class configuration information before launching GUI.

Executing the run() method

The following method is very short, consisting of function calls to other methods we'll discuss shortly. This includes building the input and output frames for the GUI and starting the main event listener loop. Because the class has already initialized the variables found in the `__init__()` method, we can reference these objects in a safe manner as follows:

```
    def run(self):
        """
        The run method calls appropriate methods to build the
        GUI and set's the event listener loop.
        """
        logger.info('Launching GUI')
        self.build_input_frame()
        self.build_output_frame()
        self.root.mainloop()
```

Implementing the build_input_frame() method

The `build_input_frame()` method is the first instance of the `frame` widget and is defined on lines 90 through 92. In a similar manner to how we defined this element in an earlier example, we call the themed `frame` widget and pass the `self.root` object as the parent window for this frame. On line 91, we add `30` pixels of padding along the *x* axis around the frame before using the `pack()` geometry manager on line 92. Because we can only use one geometry manager per window or frame, we must now use the `pack()` manager on any additional frames or widgets added to the `root` object:

```
084     def build_input_frame(self):
085         """
086         The build_input_frame method builds the interface for
087         the input frame
088         """
089         # Frame Init
090         self.input_frame = ttk.Frame(self.root)
091         self.input_frame.config(padding = (30,0))
092         self.input_frame.pack()
```

After creating the frame, we begin to add widgets to the frame for the user input. On line 95, we create a label using the new `input_frame` as the parent, with the text, `Enter Time Value`. This label is placed on the first row and column of the grid. With the grid manager, the first location will be the top-left location and all other elements will fit around it. Because we don't have any need to call this label at a later point, we don't assign it to a variable and can call the `.grid()` method immediately to add it to our GUI:

```
094         # Input Value
095         ttk.Label(self.input_frame,
096             text="Enter Time Value").grid(row=0, column=0)
```

On line 98, we initialize `StringVar()`, which we use to store the input from the user as a string. We'll need to reference this object and information throughout our code, so we'll want this to be assigned to the object, `self.input_time`.

On line 99 we create another widget, this time `Entry`, and once again will not assign it to a variable since we'll not need to manipulate this element after creation. The information we'll need from this element will be stored in the `self.input_time` variable. To instruct the `Entry` object to store the values in this object, we must pass the object name as the `textvariable` parameter. We also specify the width of the field as 25 characters, add it to the GUI with the `grid()` call, and place it one column over from the label:

```
098         self.input_time = StringVar()
099         ttk.Entry(self.input_frame, textvariable=self.input_time,
100             width=25).grid(row=0, column=1, padx=5)
```

Following the creation of the input area, we must provide the user with options for specifying the input type. This allows the user to select whether the source is a machine-readable or human-readable format. We create another `StringVar()` variable to hold the value of the user's selection.

Since we want the default action to convert raw timestamps into formatted ones, we call the `set()` method on the `self.time_type` variable on line 104 to auto-select the `raw` radio button created on line 106.

On line 106, we create the first radio button, passing the input frame as the parent, the radio button label set to `Raw Value`, and the variable that'll reflect whether the user has selected the radio button or not to `self.time_type`. Finally, we display this button using the grid manager. On line 110, we create the second radio button whose text and value are set to reflect the formatted timestamp input. In addition, we place this radio button on the same row in the adjacent column as the first radio button. Take a look at the following code:

```
102         # Radiobuttons
103         self.time_type = StringVar()
104         self.time_type.set('raw')
105
106         ttk.Radiobutton(self.input_frame, text="Raw Value",
107             variable=self.time_type, value="raw").grid(row=1,
108                 column=0, padx=5)
109
110         ttk.Radiobutton(self.input_frame, text="Formatted Value",
111             variable=self.time_type, value="formatted").grid(
112                 row=1, column=1, padx=5)
```

Finally, we build the button used to submit the data from the `Entry` field for processing. This button setup is similar to the other widgets with the addition of the command keyword, which, when clicked, executes the specified method. We then assign the `convert()` method as the button click action.

This method is started without any additional arguments supplied, as they're stored within the `self` property. We add this element to the interface via the grid manager, using the `columnspan` attribute to have the information spread across two or more columns. We also use the `pady` (pad *y*) attribute to provide some vertical space between the input field and the button:

```
        # Button
        ttk.Button(self.input_frame, text="Run",
            command=self.convert).grid(
                row=2, columnspan=2, pady=5)
```

Creating the build_output_frame() method

The output frame design is similar to that of the input frame. One difference is that we'll need to save the widgets to variables to ensure that we can update them as we process date values. After the definition of the method and docstring, we create `output_frame` and configure the height and width of the frame. Because we used the `pack()` manager for the root, we must continue to use it to add this frame to the root windows of the GUI:

```
    def build_output_frame(self):
        """
        The build_output_frame method builds the interface for
        the output frame
        """
        # Output Frame Init
        self.output_frame = ttk.Frame(self.root)
        self.output_frame.config(height=300, width=500)
        self.output_frame.pack()
```

After initialization, we add various widgets to `output_frame`. All of the output widgets are labels as they allow us to easily display a string value to the user without additional overhead. Another method for accomplishing this task would be to place the output in text entry boxes and mark them as read-only. Alternatively, we could create a single large text area for easy copying by the user. Both of these are challenges specified at the end of this chapter for additional experimentation on your own GUI implementation.

The first label element is titled `Conversion Results`, and is centered using the `pack(fill=X)` method on line 134. This fills the area along the *x* axis and stacks all packed sibling elements vertically. After creating the label on line 131, we configure the font size using the `config()` method and pass a tuple to the `font` keyword. This argument expects the first element to be a font name and the second a font size. By omitting the font name, we leave it as the default and modify only the size:

```
129         # Output Area
130         ## Label for area
131         self.output_label = ttk.Label(self.output_frame,
132             text="Conversion Results")
133         self.output_label.config(font=("", 16))
134         self.output_label.pack(fill=X)
```

The following three labels represent the results for each of the supported timestamps. All three use the output frame as their parent window and set their text to reflect the timestamp type and the default `N/A` value. Finally, each of the labels calls the `pack(fill=X)` method to properly center and stack the values within the frame. We must assign these three labels to variables so we can update their values to reflect the converted timestamps after processing. The labels are set here:

```
        ## For Unix Seconds Timestamps
        self.unix_sec = ttk.Label(self.output_frame,
            text="Unix Seconds: N/A")
        self.unix_sec.pack(fill=X)

        ## For Windows FILETIME 64 Timestamps
        self.win_ft_64 = ttk.Label(self.output_frame,
            text="Windows FILETIME 64: N/A")
        self.win_ft_64.pack(fill=X)

        ## For Chrome Timestamps
        self.google_chrome = ttk.Label(self.output_frame,
            text="Google Chrome: N/A")
        self.google_chrome.pack(fill=X)
```

Building the convert() method

Once the user clicks on the button in the input frame, the `convert()` method is called. This method is responsible for validating the input, calling the converters, and writing the results to the labels built in the previous section. This method, if you will, replaces what would usually be our `main()` method. After the initial definition and docstring, we log the timestamp and format (raw or formatted) provided by the user. This helps keep track of any activity and troubleshoot any errors that may occur:

```
    def convert(self):
        """
        The convert method handles the event when the button is
        pushed. It calls to the converters and updates the
        labels with new output.
        """
        logger.info('Processing Timestamp: {}'.format(
            self.input_time.get()))
        logger.info('Input Time Format: {}'.format(
            self.time_type.get()))
```

First, on lines 163 through 165, we reset the values of the three timestamp variables to `N/A` to clear any residual values when the application is run again. We then call the three methods that handle the timestamp conversion on lines 168 through 170. These methods are independent and will update the values for the three timestamp parameters without us needing to return any values or pass arguments.

As you can see, the `self` keyword really helps to make classes simple by providing access to shared class variables. On line 173, we call the `output()` method to write the newly converted formats to the GUI:

```
162         # Init values every instance
163         self.processed_unix_seconds = 'N/A'
164         self.processed_windows_filetime_64 = 'N/A'
165         self.processed_chrome_time = 'N/A'
166
167         # Use this to call converters
168         self.convert_unix_seconds()
169         self.convert_win_filetime_64()
170         self.convert_chrome_time()
171
172         # Update labels
173         self.output()
```

Defining the convert_unix_seconds() method

The Unix timestamp is the most straightforward of the three timestamps that we'll convert in this chapter. On lines 175 through 179, we define the method and its docstrings before stepping into an `if` statement. The `if` statement on line 180 evaluates whether the value of the radio button described earlier is equal to the `raw` string or `formatted`. If it's set to `raw`, we'll parse the timestamp as a count of seconds since `1970-01-01 00:00:00.0000000`. This is relatively simple because this is the epoch used by the `datetime.datetime.fromtimestamp()` method. In this case, we only have to convert the input into a float as seen on lines 182 and 183 before conversion.

Afterward, on lines 183 and 184, we format the newly formed `datetime` object as a string in the `YYYY-MM-DD HH:MM:SS` format. The logic on line 182 is wrapped in a try-except statement to catch any bugs and report them to the log file and to the user interface in a simplified form. This allows us to test each formula when a date is entered. Line 188 outlines that the conversion error will be displayed when we are unsuccessful in converting the timestamp. This will alert the user that there was an error and allow them to determine whether it's anticipated or not:

```
175     def convert_unix_seconds(self):
176         """
177         The convert_unix_seconds method handles the conversion of
178         timestamps per the Unix seconds format
179         """
180         if self.time_type.get() == 'raw':
181             try:
182                 dt_val = datetime.datetime.fromtimestamp(
183                     float(self.input_time.get())).strftime(
184                         '%Y-%m-%d %H:%M:%S')
185                 self.processed_unix_seconds = dt_val
186             except Exception as e:
187                 logger.error(str(type(e)) + "," + str(e))
188                 self.processed_unix_seconds = str(
189                     type(e).__name__)
```

If the timestamp is a formatted value, we need to first parse the input before attempting to convert it into a Unix timestamp, as it may not follow the intended format. Once converted by `dateutil.parser`, we can use the predefined epoch object to calculate the delta in seconds between the timestamp and epoch on lines 195 through 197. If an error occurs, it will be caught as in the prior `if` statement, logged, and displayed to the user, as follows:

```
191         elif self.time_type.get() == 'formatted':
192             try:
193                 converted_time = duparser.parse(
194                     self.input_time.get())
```

```
            self.processed_unix_seconds = str(
                    (converted_time - self.epoch_1970
                ).total_seconds())
        except Exception as e:
            logger.error(str(type(e)) + "," + str(e))
            self.processed_unix_seconds = str(
                type(e).__name__)
```

Conversion using the convert_win_filetime_64() method

The conversion of Microsoft Windows FILETIME values is a little more complicated as it uses the `1601-01-01 00:00:00` value for epoch and counts time since then in 100-nanosecond blocks. To properly convert this timestamp, we have to take a few extra steps over the previous section.

This method starts the same as the last, including the `if-else` syntax to identify the timestamp type. If it's a raw format, we must convert the input from a hexadecimal string into a base 10 decimal using the `int(value, 16)` typecast seen on lines 210 and 211. This allows us to tell `int()` to convert a base 16 value into decimal (base 10). Base 16 values are often referred to as hexadecimal values.

Once converted, the integer is a count of 100-nanosecond groups since the epoch so all we have to do is convert the microseconds into a `datetime` value then add the epoch `datetime` object. On lines 212 through 214, we use the `datetime.timedelta()` method to generate an object that can be used to add to the epoch `datetime`. Once the conversion is complete, we need to format the `datetime` object as a time string and assign it to the corresponding label. The error handling is the same as the prior converter and will display conversion errors as follows:

```
203     def convert_win_filetime_64(self):
204         """
205         The convert_win_filetime_64 method handles the
206         conversion of timestamps per the Windows FILETIME format
207         """
208         if self.time_type.get() == 'raw':
209             try:
210                 base10_microseconds = int(
211                     self.input_time.get(), 16) / 10
212                 datetime_obj = datetime.datetime(1601,1,1) + \
213                     datetime.timedelta(
214                         microseconds=base10_microseconds)
215                 dt_val = datetime_obj.strftime(
```

```
216                     '%Y-%m-%d %H:%M:%S.%f')
217                 self.processed_windows_filetime_64 = dt_val
218             except Exception as e:
219                 logger.error(str(type(e)) + "," + str(e))
220                 self.processed_windows_filetime_64 = str(
221                     type(e).__name__)
```

If the input timestamp is a formatted value, we need to reverse this conversion. We were able to take some shortcuts before on line 212 using the `datetime.timedelta()` method. When moving in the other direction, we need to manually calculate the microseconds count before converting it into hex.

First, on line 225, we convert the data from a string into a `datetime` object so we can begin to process the values. From here, we subtract the epoch value from the converted time. After subtraction, we convert the `datetime.timedelta` object into microsecond values from the three stored values. We need to multiply the seconds by one million and the days by 86.4 billion to convert each value into microseconds. Finally, on lines 229 through 231, we're almost ready to convert our timestamp after adding all three values together:

```
223         elif self.time_type.get() == 'formatted':
224             try:
225                 converted_time = duparser.parse(
226                     self.input_time.get())
227                 minus_epoch = converted_time - \
228                     datetime.datetime(1601,1,1)
229                 calculated_time = minus_epoch.microseconds + \
230                     (minus_epoch.seconds * 1000000) + \
231                     (minus_epoch.days * 86400000000)
```

On lines 232 and 233, we perform the conversion, by casting the innermost layer, `calculated_time`, into an integer. In the integer state, it's multiplied by 10 to convert into a count of groups of 100 nanoseconds before conversion into hex with the `hex()` typecast. Since the code requires the output to be a string, we cast the hex value to a string as seen in the outside wrap on line 232 before assigning it to the `self.processed_windows_filetime_64` variable.

Similar to the other conversion functions, we add in error handling to the converter on lines 234 through 237:

```
232                 self.processed_windows_filetime_64 = str(
233                     hex(int(calculated_time)*10))
234             except Exception as e:
235                 logger.error(str(type(e)) + "," + str(e))
236                 self.processed_windows_filetime_64 = str(
237                 type(e).__name__)
```

Converting with the convert_chrome_time() method

The last of our showcased timestamps is the Google Chrome timestamp, which is similar to both of the previously mentioned timestamps. This timestamp is the number of microseconds since the `1601-01-01 00:00:00` epoch. We'll leverage the earlier-defined `self.unix_epcoh_offset` value to help in conversion. On line 248, we begin to convert the raw timestamp through a series of functions.

First, we convert the timestamp into a float and subtract the 1601 epoch constant. Next, we divide the value by one million to convert the value from microseconds into seconds so that the `datetime.datetime.fromtimestamp()` method can interpret the value properly. Finally, on line 251, we format `converted_time` to a string using the `strftime()` function. On lines 253 through 255, we handle exceptions that may occur from invalid values as seen in previous sections, as follows:

```
239     def convert_chrome_time(self):
240         """
241         The convert_chrome_time method handles the
242         conversion of timestamps per the Google Chrome
243         timestamp format
244         """
245         # Run Conversion
246         if self.time_type.get() == 'raw':
247             try:
248                 dt_val = datetime.datetime.fromtimestamp(
249                         (float(self.input_time.get()
250                     )-self.epoch_1601)/1000000)
251                 self.processed_chrome_time = dt_val.strftime(
252                     '%Y-%m-%d %H:%M:%S.%f')
253             except Exception as e:
254                 logger.error(str(type(e)) + "," + str(e))
255                 self.processed_chrome_time = str(type(e).__name__)
```

When a formatted value is passed as an input, we must reverse the process. As in our other functions, we convert the input to a `datetime` object from a string using the `duparser.parse()` method. Once converted, we calculate the number of seconds by adding the 1601 epoch constant to the `total_seconds()` method.

This count of seconds is multiplied by one million to convert it into microseconds. Once calculated, we can cast this integer value into a string that will be displayed in our GUI. In the event that any errors arise, we catch them on line 264 through 266 in the same way as with previous methods:

```
257         elif self.time_type.get() == 'formatted':
258             try:
259                 converted_time = duparser.parse(
260                     self.input_time.get())
261                 chrome_time = (converted_time - self.epoch_1970
262                     ).total_seconds()*1000000 + self.epoch_1601
263                 self.processed_chrome_time = str(int(chrome_time))
264             except Exception as e:
265                 logger.error(str(type(e)) + "," + str(e))
266                 self.processed_chrome_time = str(type(e).__name__)
```

Designing the output method

The last method of the class is the `output()` method, and it updates the labels found on the bottom frame of the GUI. This simple construct allows us to evaluate processed values and display them if they're string values. As seen on line 273, following the definition of the method and docstring, we check whether the `self.processed_unix_seconds` value is of the string type.

If it is, then we update the label by calling the `text` attribute as a dictionary key as seen on lines 274 and 275. This could also be accomplished via the use of the `config()` method, though in this instance it's simpler to define it in this manner. When this property is changed, the label is immediately updated as the element has already been set by a geometry manager. This behavior is repeated for each label to be updated, as seen on lines 277 through 283:

```
268     def output(self):
269         """
270         The output method updates the output frame with the
271         latest value.
272         """
273         if isinstance(self.processed_unix_seconds, str):
274             self.unix_sec['text'] = "Unix Seconds: " + \
275                 self.processed_unix_seconds
276 
277         if isinstance(self.processed_windows_filetime_64, str):
278             self.win_ft_64['text'] = "Windows FILETIME 64: " + \
279                 self.processed_windows_filetime_64
280 
```

```
        if isinstance(self.processed_chrome_time, str):
            self.google_chrome['text'] = "Google Chrome: " + \
                self.processed_chrome_time
```

Running the script

With the complete code, we can execute the GUI and begin to convert dates from machine- to human-readable and vice versa. As seen in the following screenshot, the finished GUI reflects our design goal and allows the user to easily interact and process dates:

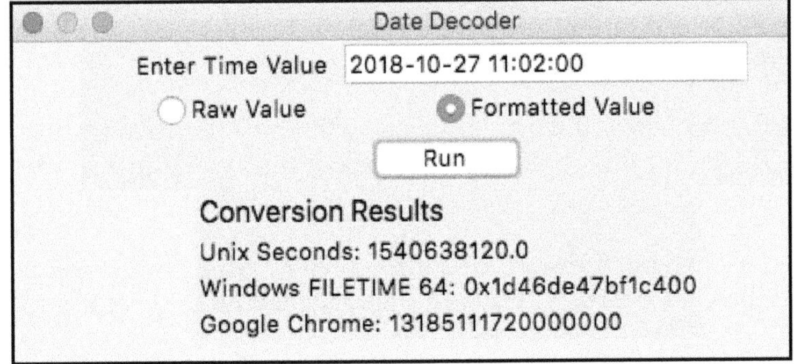

The preceding screenshot also shows us entering a formatted time value and getting all three converted raw timestamps back from our functions. Next, we provide a raw input in the Unix seconds format and can see that our Unix seconds parser returned the correct date:

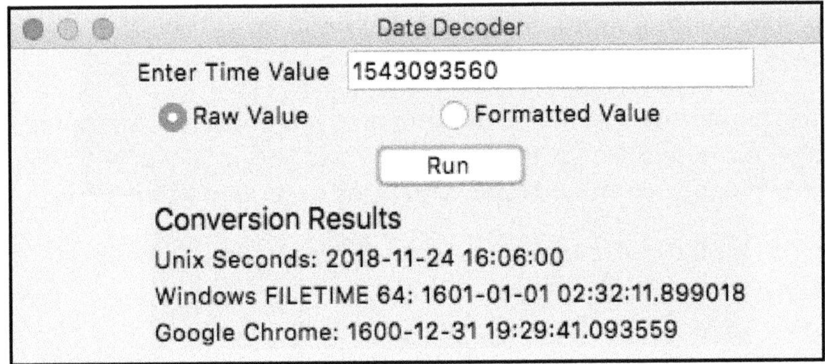

Additional challenges

This script introduced GUIs and some of the methods available to us via the TkInter module for converting timestamps. This script can be extended in many ways. We recommend the following challenges for those wishing to gain a better understanding of GUI development in Python.

As mentioned in this chapter, we only specify the conversion of three formats that're commonly seen in forensics and use several different methods to provide conversion. Try to add support for the FAT directory timestamp entry into the script, providing conversion into and from the raw format. This script is designed such that adding additional formatters is as simple as defining raw and formatted handlers, adding the labels to our output frame, and appending the method name to `convert()`.

In addition, consider replacing the output labels with entry fields so the user can copy and paste the results. A hint for this challenge is to look at the `set()` and `read-only` properties of the `Entry` widget.

The last challenge we present allows the user to specify a time zone, either from the command-line or the GUI interface. The `pytz` library may be of great use for this task.

Summary

In this chapter, we covered how to convert between machine- and human-readable timestamps and display that information in GUI. The primary goal of a forensic developer is to be capable of facilitating rapid design and deployment of tools that provide insight into investigations.

However, in this chapter, we focused a bit more on the end user by spending a little extra time on building a nice interface for the user to operate and interact with. The code for this project can be downloaded from GitHub or Packt, as described in the *Preface*.

In the next chapter, we'll explore triaging systems and how to collect essential live and volatile data from a system using Python.

10
Rapidly Triaging Systems

In today's brave new world, where incidents have a way of rapidly ballooning out of control without a rapid and effective response, it is integral that DFIR professionals are able to query hosts for relevant information, such as the processes and services running on the system, to make informed investigative decisions to quickly contain the incident. While we can often collect this information on a forensic image of a machine, some of this information is volatile or it may be necessary to collect quickly rather than waiting for a forensic image to be created.

In this chapter, we develop a single script that is compatible with modern operating systems and, using various first- and third-party libraries, extract useful information about the system that the script is running on. With some modification, this script could be leveraged in an environment by deploying it to many hosts and collecting basic system information that may be valuable for the investigation. For example, in the case of an incident involving malware, if that malware, as part of its successful infection of a host, creates a new process, one could use this information to quickly determine the universe of hosts infected and, upon further investigation, which machine was likely infected first.

To achieve a script that is compatible across different operating systems, we will rely on a third-party module called `psutil` to obtain information about running processes, while more OS-specific intel, in the case of the Windows operating systems, will be extracted using the **Windows Management Interface** (**WMI**).

In this chapter, we will cover the following topics:

- Extracting OS-agnostic process information using `psutil`
- Interacting with Windows systems by querying the WMI with Python and the `wmi` and `pywin32` modules
- Creating a multi-platform triage artifact collection script

The code for this chapter was developed and tested using Python 2.7.15 and Python 3.7.1.

Understanding the value of system information

Why bother with collecting system information, anyway? Not all investigations revolve around the user and what actions they took on the system, but, rather, what the system is like and how it is behaving. For example, in the previous section, we discussed how running processes and created services can be informative based on indicators of compromise for a given scenario. However, as DFIR professionals well know, sources for system information can also provide insight into user activity, such as what disks are currently attached to the machine or querying the event log for user logins.

In the first edition of this book, this chapter originally showcased a `keylogger` script that we developed, whose purpose was mainly to illustrate how to use operating system APIs. For the second edition, we elected to keep that focus intact, but apply it in a more forensically relevant way. Let's dive in and discuss the third-party libraries. We will need to develop this script starting with `psutil`.

Querying OS-agnostic process information with psutil

The `psutil` module (version 5.4.5) is a cross-platform library capable of gathering various system information from different operating systems, for both 32-bit and 64-bit architectures. While we use this library to extract process information from the host system running the script, be aware that this library is capable of extracting more system information than just running processes.

Let's walk through a few examples, some of which we will not leverage in the script; however, first install the library with `pip`:

```
pip install psutil==5.4.5
```

We can get a list of active process IDs using the `pids()` function and then use a PID to collect additional information about the process. For instance, in the following code block, we select the first PID in the list of PIDs, with PID 62, create a process object for PID 62, and use various functions to display its name, parent PID, and open files.

Note that, for some of these functions, such as the `open_files()` method, you need to run the commands in an elevated Command Prompt:

```
>>> import psutil
>>> pids = psutil.pids()
>>> pids[0]
62
>>> proc = psutil.Process(pids[0])
>>> proc.is_running()
True
>>> proc.name()
syslogd
>>> proc.ppid()
1
>>> proc.parent().name()
launchd
>>> proc.open_files()[0]
popenfile(path='/private/var/run/utmpx', fd=3)
```

While we use this library to print details about processes, we can use it to perform other tasks as well.

For example, we can collect information about connected disks, using the `disk_partitions()` function:

```
>>> for part in psutil.disk_partitions():
...     print("Device: {}, Filesystem: {}, Mount: {},"
...           " Size: {}, Disk Used: {}%".format(
...               part[0], part[2], part[1],
...               psutil.disk_usage(part[1])[0],
...               psutil.disk_usage(part[1])[3]))
...
Device: /dev/disk1s1, Filesystem: apfs, Mount: /, Size: 500068036608, Disk
Used: 82.9%
```

Additionally, we could use the `users()` function to identify user profiles on the system and when the user session started:

```
>>> psutil.users()[0].name
PyForensics
>>> psutil.users()[0].started
1548086912.0
```

```
>>> from datetime import datetime
>>> print(datetime.utcfromtimestamp(psutil.users()[0].started))
2019-01-21 16:08:32
```

You can learn more about this library by reading the documentation page at `https://pypi.org/project/psutil/`.

Using WMI

The `wmi` library, maintained by Tim Golden, is a wrapper for the `pywin32` module, covered in the next section, that allows programmers to interact with the WMI API and provides programmers with a great deal of relevant information about Windows systems. You can even use this library to query other Windows systems on your network.

First, install WMI using `pip` by executing the following at Command Prompt:

```
pip install WMI==1.4.9
```

It should go without saying that the examples that we will discuss here will only work on Windows systems and therefore should be executed on a Windows system. Let's first take a look at querying running services.

We will need to create a WMI object and then use the `query()` method to identify running services:

```
>>> import wmi
>>> conn = wmi.WMI()
>>> for service in conn.query(
...         "SELECT * FROM Win32_Service WHERE State='Running'"):
...     print("Service: {}, Desc: {}, Mode: {}".format(
...          service.Name, service.Description, service.StartMode))
...
Service: PlugPlay, Desc: Enables a computer to recognize and adapt to
hardware changes with little or no user input. Stopping or disabling this
service will result in system instability., Mode: Manual
```

We can, for example, use this module to identify installed printers associated with the system.

A portion of the output, denoted by the string [...], has been sanitized in the following example:

```
>>> for printer in conn.Win32_Printer():
...     print(printer.Name)
...
Microsoft XPS Document Writer
Microsoft Print to PDF
HP[...] (HP ENVY Photo 6200 series)
Fax
```

Lastly, a very useful feature of this library, which we use in this script, allows us to query Windows Event Logs.

In the following example, we query to the `OAlerts.evtx` file, an event log that stores Microsoft Office alerts, and print out each event's message and the time the event was generated. Only one such message is shown here, in order to be succinct:

```
>>> for event in conn.query(
            "SELECT * FROM Win32_NTLogEvent WHERE Logfile='OAlerts'"):
...     print(event.Message, event.TimeGenerated)
...
Microsoft Excel
Want to save your changes to 'logonevent.csv'?
P1: 153042
P2: 15.0.5101.1000
P3:
P4:
20190121031627.589966-000
```

We could discuss many other features of this library; however, we invite you to explore and experiment with its capabilities. We will introduce a few more examples of this library in this chapter's script.

This module requires the `pywin32` library, which is an incredibly powerful library that gives developers access to a number of different Windows APIs and is covered briefly in the next section. Understand that we are only scratching the surface with these libraries and focus on the specific goals of our script. Spend some time reading the documentation for these libraries and experimenting with their capabilities, as you will likely find these libraries useful in any script that interacts with the Windows operating system.

Read more about the `wmi` library and its capabilities on the documentation page at `https://pypi.org/project/WMI/`. Sample cookbook recipes using the `wmi` library can be found here: `http://timgolden.me.uk/python/wmi/cookbook.html`.

What does the pywin32 module do?

One of the most versatile Windows API libraries for Python is `pywin32` (version 224). This project is hosted on GitHub (historically on SourceForge) by Mark Hammond and is an open source project that the community contributes to. There are many different APIs available for Windows through this library. These features allow developers to build GUIs for their applications, leverage built-in authentication methods, and interact with hard drives and other external devices.

The `pywin32` module can be installed with `pip` by executing the following at Command Prompt:

```
pip install pywin32==224
```

Windows defines a **Component Object Model** (**COM**) that allows information to be shared between applications. A COM can be in the form of a **Dynamic Link Library** (**DLL**) or other binary file formats. These modules are designed in such a manner that any programming language can interpret the information. This single set of instructions, for example, allows a C++-based and Java-based program to share a single resource, rather than requiring a separate version for each language. COMs are generally only found on Windows, although they could be ported to a UNIX platform if desired.
The `win32com` library, a part of the `pywin32` library, allows us to interact with COMs in Windows and is used by the `wmi` library to obtain the information we request from it.

The `pywin32` library can be found on GitHub at `https://github.com/mhammond/pywin32`.

Rapidly triaging systems – pysysinfo.py

We are now ready to dive into the focus of this chapter, the `pysysinfo.py` script after having already covered the importance of collecting volatile information and the libraries we will use. This script is composed of a number of functions, most of which have to do with the `psutil` library, but at its heart identifies early on what type of system it is running on and, if that system is using the Windows operating system, runs an additional function using the WMI API, discussed previously. You can see in the following diagram how the various functions interact with each other and make up the code discussed throughout the remainder of this chapter:

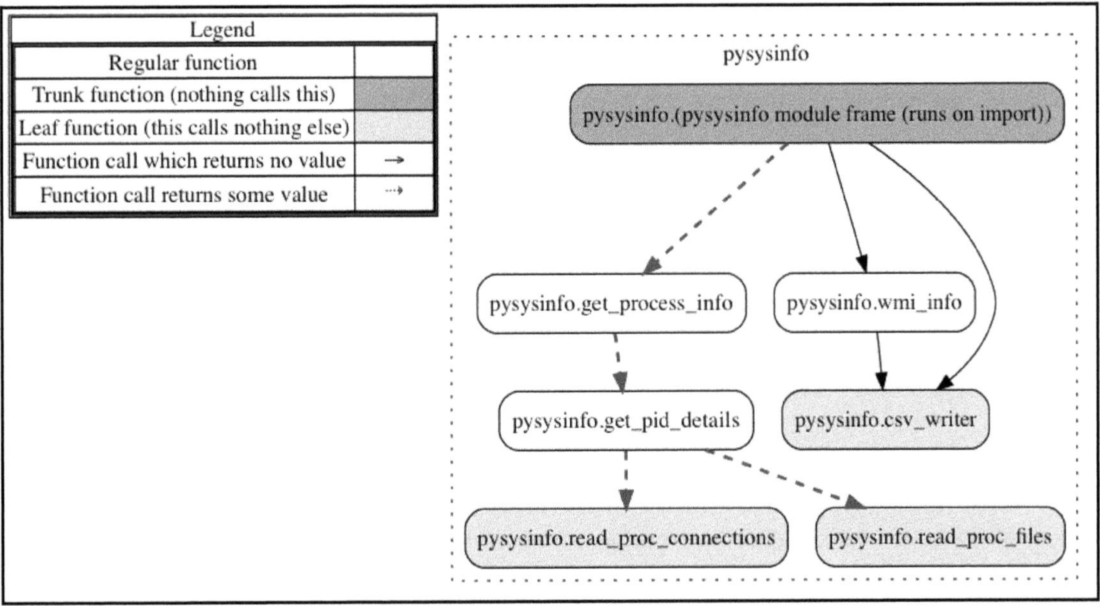

This script was developed and tested on Python 2.7.15 and 3.7.1. As with any script we develop, we must start with the imports necessary to successfully execute the code we've developed. You'll notice a number of the usual imports; however, a few stand out—notably the `platform` module and `psutil` on lines 5 and 8. You may also notice that `wmi` is missing from this set of imports. You will understand why this is imported later in the script in a few paragraphs. This script contains seven different functions, most of which are used to process the data from the `psutil` library.

Note that the `return_none()` function is covered in the following code block instead of in a new section, as it is a one-line function that simply returns `None` to the calling code:

```
002 from __future__ import print_function
003 import argparse
004 import os
005 import platform
006 import sys
007
008 import psutil
009     if sys.version_info[0] == 2:
010 import unicodecsv as csv
011     elif sys.version_info[0] == 3:
012 import csv
...
050 def return_none():
051     """
```

```
    Returns a None value, but is callable.
    :return: None.
    """
    return None
...
def read_proc_connections(proc):
...
def read_proc_files(proc):
...
def get_pid_details(pid):
...
def get_process_info():
...
def wmi_info(outdir):
...
def csv_writer(data, outdir, name, headers, **kwargs):
```

The `platform` module, which we have not touched on previously, is part of the standard library and also provides some information about the system it is running on. In this case, we only use this library to determine the operating system of the host system executing the script.

Learn more about the platform module by reading the documentation page at `https://docs.python.org/3/library/platform.html`.

Moving on to the script setup, we have the argument parser, which is decidedly bland compared to some other chapters, featuring only one positional argument, `OUTPUT_DIR`, the output directory to write the processed data to.

If the desired output directory does not exist, we create it using the `os.makedirs()` function on line 323:

```
313 if __name__ == '__main__':
314     parser = argparse.ArgumentParser(description=__description__,
315                         epilog='Developed by ' +
316                         __author__ + ' on ' +
317                         __date__)
318     parser.add_argument('OUTPUT_DIR',
319     help="Path to output directory. Will create if not found.")
320     args = parser.parse_args()
321
322     if not os.path.exists(args.OUTPUT_DIR):
323         os.makedirs(args.OUTPUT_DIR)
```

Here's where things differ a little from normal. On line 325, using the `platform.system()` function, we check to see if the script is being executed on a Windows system. If so, we try to import the `wmi` module and, if successful, call the `wmi_info()` method. As alluded to earlier, we import the `wmi` library here for a reason. When the `wmi` library is imported, it also loads the `pywin32` module, specifically the `win32com.client` module. On a non-Windows system, where the `pywin32` library won't be installed, this can then cause an `ImportError` exception. For that reason, we do not try importing `wmi` until we know the script is executing on a Windows machine. It's also not a bad idea to only import libraries once they are needed:

```
325     if 'windows' in platform.system().lower():
326         try:
327             import wmi
328         except ImportError:
329             print("Install the wmi and pywin32 modules. "
330             "Exiting...")
331             sys.exit(1)
332         wmi_info(args.OUTPUT_DIR)
```

Regardless of whether the system is Windows or not, we run the code captured in the next code block. On line 336, we call the `get_process_info()` method, which ultimately returns process data in the form of a dictionary. On line 337, we create a list containing the desired column names and keys of our `pid_data` dictionary. Lastly, on line 341, we call the `csv_writer()` method and pass in the data, desired output directory, output name, the `fields` list, and a keyword argument.

We will see what that keyword-argument does in a little bit:

```
334     # Run data gathering function
335     print("[+] Gathering current active processes information")
336     pid_data = get_process_info()
337     fields = ['pid', 'name', 'exe', 'ppid', 'cmdline',
338         'username', 'cwd', 'create_time', '_errors']
339
340     # Generate reports from gathered details
341     csv_writer(pid_data, args.OUTPUT_DIR, 'pid_summary.csv',
342         fields, type='DictWriter')
```

As you may have noticed, we do not have a `main()` function for this script and will, instead, jump right into a review of the `get_process_info()` method. We will cover the Windows-specific function, `wmi_info()`, toward the end of this chapter.

Understanding the get_process_info() function

As far as functions go, the `get_process_info()` function, is relatively straightforward and mainly serves to set up the rest of the code execution. On line 166, we create the `pid_info` dictionary, which is ultimately returned to the calling function on line 336 and contains the extracted process data. Next, using the `psutil.pids()` method as an iterator, which we showed in the demonstration of this library earlier, we pass each process ID to the `get_pid_details()` method and store the returned data in the `pid_info` dictionary, with the PID serving as the dictionary key.

Let's look at the `get_pid_details()` function next:

```
158 def get_process_info():
159     """
160     Gather details on running processes within the system.
161     :return pid_info: A dictionary containing details of
162     running processes.
163     """
164
165     # List of PIDs
166     pid_info = {}
167     for pid in psutil.pids():
168         pid_info[pid] = get_pid_details(pid)
169     return pid_info
```

Learning about the get_pid_details() function

The `get_pid_details()` method starts to gather information about each PID that is passed to it. For each PID, we create a dictionary, `details`, which is pre-populated with relevant keys we can expect to extract values for using the `psutil` library. The dictionary keys are initialized with placeholder values, mostly consisting of empty strings and lists:

```
def get_pid_details(pid):
    """
    Gather details on a specific pid.
    :param pid: an integer value of a pid to query for
    additional details.
    :return details: a dictionary of gathered information
    about the pid.
    """
    details = {'name': '', 'exe': '', 'cmdline': '', 'pid': pid,
               'ppid': 0, 'status': '', 'username': '',
               'terminal': '', 'cwd': '', 'create_time': '',
               'children': [], # list of pid ints
```

```
113                 'threads': [], # list of thread ints
114                 'files': [], # list of open files
115                 'connections': [], # list of network connections
116                 '_errors': []
117     }
```

Next, on line 118, we enter a `try` and `except` block that tries to create a `Process` object for each provided PID. In this case, on lines 120 and 124, we have two different exception clauses to handle situations where there is no process matching the provided PID (perhaps if the process closed immediately after script execution) or if there is an operating system error. In either event, should such exceptions occur, the errors are appended to the `details` dictionary and the dictionary is returned to the calling function.

Rather than crashing or halting the script due to an issue with a given process, the script continues and will provide any such errors as a column in the CSV report that is generated by the script:

```
118     try:
119         proc = psutil.Process(pid)
120     except psutil.NoSuchProcess:
121         details['_errors'].append(
122             (pid, 'Process no longer found'))
123         return details
124     except OSError:
125         details['_errors'].append((pid, 'OSError'))
126         return details
```

If a `Process` object is created for the provided PID, we then iterate through each key in the `details` dictionary on line 128, and if the key is anything other than `pid` or `_errors`, we attempt to get the value associated with the key with the `getattr()` function on line 144. There are a few exceptions to that, however; for instance, we have specific `elif` statements for the `children`, `threads`, `connections`, or `files` keys. In the case of the `children` and `threads` keys, we use list comprehension on lines 134 and 138 to associate the children's PIDs and thread's IDs to the `children` and `threads` keys, respectively.

For both the `connections` and `files` keys, we have developed separate functions to extract the desired information and store the returned data to the appropriate key in the `details` dictionary. Lastly, on lines 145, 148, and 151, we create exceptions that may occur throughout the conditional statements, including handling issues where we lack sufficient privilege, for instance, if the script is running from a non-elevated prompt, or if the process no longer exists, or an operating system error has occurred:

```
128     for key in details:
129         try:
130             if key in ('pid', '_errors'):
```

```
                continue
            elif key == 'children':
                children = proc.children()
                details[key] = [c.pid for c in children]

            elif key == 'threads':
                threads = proc.threads()
                details[key] = [t.id for t in threads]
            elif key == 'connections':
                details[key] = read_proc_connections(proc)
            elif key == 'files':
                details[key] = read_proc_files(proc)
            else:
                details[key] = getattr(proc, key, return_none)()
        except psutil.AccessDenied:
            details[key] = []
            details['_errors'].append((key, 'AccessDenied'))
        except OSError:
            details[key] = []
            details['_errors'].append((key, 'OSError'))
        except psutil.NoSuchProcess:
            details['_errors'].append(
            (pid, 'Process no longer found'))
            break
```

As discussed, for two keys, the `connections` and `files` keys, we called separate functions to handle each of them. Let's now take a look at the first of those.

Extracting process connection properties with the read_proc_connections() function

The `read_proc_connections()` function, defined on line 58, starts by creating an empty list, `conn_details`, which will store the details of each PID connection:

```
058 def read_proc_connections(proc):
059     """
060     Read connection properties from a process.
061     :param proc: An object representing a running process.
062     :return conn_details: A list of process connection
063     properties.
064     """
065     conn_details = []
```

For each connection in the provided process, we create a `conn_items` dictionary, and store within it, the details of each connection, including the status of the connection and the local and remote IP addresses and ports. As seen before, we use the `getattr()` method, querying for named attributes of the specified object and storing the returned value in our dictionary. If the named object does not exist, we use `None` or empty strings as default values defined as the third input of the `getattr()` function.

We then append the dictionary of details for each connection to the `conn_details` list which, after this process has completed for each connection, is itself returned to the calling function:

```
066     for conn in proc.connections():
067         conn_items = {}
068         conn_items['fd'] = getattr(conn, 'fd', None)
069         conn_items['status'] = getattr(conn, 'status', None)
070         conn_items['local_addr'] = "{}:{}".format(
071             getattr(conn.laddr, 'ip', ""), getattr(
072                 conn.laddr, 'port', ""))
073         conn_items['remote_addr'] = "{}:{}".format(
074             getattr(conn.raddr, 'ip', ""), getattr(
075                 conn.raddr, 'port', ""))
076
077         conn_details.append(conn_items)
078     return conn_details
```

Obtaining more process information with the read_proc_files() function

The `read_proc_files()` method, defined on line 81, follows a similar pattern to what was discussed in the preceding section. Essentially, on line 88, we iterate through all of the open files associated with the process and, using the `getattr()` method, attempt to extract information about each open file, such as its path and mode.

We return the `file_details` list after extracting all values for each open file and inserting the data into the `file_details` list:

```
081 def read_proc_files(proc):
082     """
083     Read file properties from a process.
084     :param proc: An object representing a running process.
085     :return file_details: a list containing process details.
086     """
087     file_details = []
```

```
    for handle in proc.open_files():
        handle_items = {}
        handle_items['fd'] = getattr(handle, 'fd', None)
        handle_items['path'] = getattr(handle, 'path', None)
        handle_items['position'] = getattr(
            handle, 'position', None)
        handle_items['mode'] = getattr(handle, 'mode', None)

        file_details.append(handle_items)

    return file_details
```

Extracting Windows system information with the wmi_info() function

The `wmi_info()` function, defined on line 172, starts by defining a dictionary that will store the various types of information we query using the WMI API.

Similarly, on line 185, we create the WMI object and assign it to the variable, `conn`, which is what we will be specifically querying:

```
172 def wmi_info(outdir):
173     """
174     Gather information available through Windows Management
175     Interface. We recommend extending this script by adding
176     support for other WMI modules -- Win32_PrintJob,
177     Win32_NetworkAdapterConfiguration, Win32_Printer,
178     Win32_PnpEntity (USB).
179     :param outdir: The directory to write CSV reports to.
180     :return: Nothing.
181     """
182
183     wmi_dict = {"Users": [], "Shares": [], "Services": [],
184         "Disks": [], "Event Log": []}
185     conn = wmi.WMI()
```

In some of these code blocks, you will notice that we call a specific function of the `conn` object, but in others, we use the `query()` method. Note that either option is viable in some cases. For instance, instead of calling `conn.Win32_UserAccount()`, we could call `conn.query("SELECT * from Win32_UserAccount")`. The `query()` method gives us some additional flexibility, as we can provide additional logic to our query, which will be seen when we query for specific event log entries.

Starting with the `print` statement on line 190, we begin to collect information using the `wmi` library. Iterating through each user profile on line 191, we append various attributes of the user account to the `wmi_dict` users list:

```
187     # See attributes for a given module like so: for user in
188     # conn.Win32_UserAccount(); user._getAttributeNames()
189
190     print("[+] Gathering information on Windows user profiles")
191     for user in conn.Win32_UserAccount():
192         wmi_dict["Users"].append({
193             "Name": user.Name, "SID": user.SID,
194             "Description": user.Description,
195             "InstallDate": user.InstallDate,
196             "Domain": user.Domain,
197             "Local Account": user.LocalAccount,
198             "Password Changeable": user.PasswordChangeable,
199             "Password Required": user.PasswordRequired,
200             "Password Expires": user.PasswordExpires,
201             "Lockout": user.Lockout
202         })
```

We start to use the `query()` method in the following code block to list all (`*`) shares on line 205. For each share, we append various details about it to the appropriate list in the `wmi_dict` dictionary. On line 213, we again use the `query()` method, this time for services, but only capture services that are currently running.

Hopefully, you can appreciate the value of the `query()` method, as it provides the developer with a lot of flexibility on isolating and providing data only matching specified criteria, thereby cutting out a lot of junk:

```
204     print("[+] Gathering information on Windows shares")
205     for share in conn.query("SELECT * from Win32_Share"):
206         wmi_dict["Shares"].append({
207             "Name": share.Name, "Path": share.Path,
208             "Description": share.Description,
209             "Status": share.Status,
210             "Install Date": share.InstallDate})
211
212     print("[+] Gathering information on Windows services")
213     for service in conn.query(
214             "SELECT * FROM Win32_Service WHERE State='Running'"):
215         wmi_dict["Services"].append({
216             "Name": service.Name,
217             "Description": service.Description,
218             "Start Mode": service.StartMode,
219             "State": service.State,
```

```
            "Path": service.PathName,
            "System Name": service.SystemName})
```

On line 224, we begin to collect details on the connected drives by iterating through each drive using the `conn.Win32_DiskDrive()` function. To collect all of the information we want to extract, we need to also iterate through each partition and the logical volume of each disk; hence, the additional `for` loops on lines 225 and 227.

Once we have the `disk`, `partition`, and `logical_disk` objects, we use each and append a dictionary to the appropriate list of the `wmi_dict` dictionary containing the various properties of each disk, partition, and volume:

```
223     print("[+] Gathering information on connected drives")
224     for disk in conn.Win32_DiskDrive():
225         for partition in disk.associators(
226                 "Win32_DiskDriveToDiskPartition"):
227             for logical_disk in partition.associators(
228                     "Win32_LogicalDiskToPartition"):
229                 wmi_dict["Disks"].append({
230                     "Physical Disk Name": disk.Name,
231                     "Bytes Per Sector": disk.BytesPerSector,
232                     "Sectors": disk.TotalSectors,
233                     "Physical S/N": disk.SerialNumber,
234                     "Disk Size": disk.Size,
235                     "Model": disk.Model,
236                     "Manufacturer": disk.Manufacturer,
237                     "Media Type": disk.MediaType,
238                     "Partition Name": partition.Name,
239                     "Partition Desc.": partition.Description,
240                     "Primary Partition": partition.PrimaryPartition,
241                     "Bootable": partition.Bootable,
242                     "Partition Size": partition.Size,
243                     "Logical Name": logical_disk.Name,
244                     "Volume Name": logical_disk.VolumeName,
245                     "Volume S/N": logical_disk.VolumeSerialNumber,
246                     "FileSystem": logical_disk.FileSystem,
247                     "Volume Size": logical_disk.Size,
248                     "Volume Free Space": logical_disk.FreeSpace})
```

Next, on line 253, we create a variable, `wmi_query`, to hold a string that we will use to extract all events with event ID 4624 from the `Security` event log.

Note that it was observed in testing that the script needs to be run from an elevated Command Prompt to be able to extract information from the `Security` event log.

Similar to the other queries, we iterate through the returned results and append various attributes to the appropriate list in the `wmi_dict` dictionary:

```
    # Query for logon events type 4624
    print("[+] Querying the Windows Security Event Log "
    "for Event ID 4624")
    wmi_query = ("SELECT * from Win32_NTLogEvent WHERE Logfile="
        "'Security' AND EventCode='4624'")
    for logon in conn.query(wmi_query):
        wmi_dict["Event Log"].append({
            "Event Category": logon.CategoryString,
            "Event ID": logon.EventIdentifier,
            "Time Generated": logon.TimeGenerated,
            "Message": logon.Message})
```

Lastly, after extracting all of the information and storing it in the `wmi_dict` dictionary, we begin to make calls to the `csv_writer()` function to write a spreadsheet for each type of data to the output directory. Most of the values being passed into the `csv_writer()` are self-explanatory and include the artifact-specific data (that is, **User Profiles** under the `Users` key), the output directory, and the output filename. The last argument is an alphabetically sorted list of keys from the artifact-specific data to serve as column headers for our CSV.

You will also notice that we have a `try` and `except` block to handle writing the event log data. The reason for this, as previously discussed, is that, if the script is not run from an elevated Command Prompt, it is possible that the `Event Log` key will consist of an empty list:

```
    csv_writer(wmi_dict["Users"], outdir, "users.csv",
        sorted(wmi_dict["Users"][0].keys()))
    csv_writer(wmi_dict["Shares"], outdir, "shares.csv",
        sorted(wmi_dict["Shares"][0].keys()))
    csv_writer(wmi_dict["Services"], outdir, "services.csv",
        sorted(wmi_dict["Services"][0].keys()))
    csv_writer(wmi_dict["Disks"], outdir, "disks.csv",
        sorted(wmi_dict["Disks"][0].keys()))
    try:
        csv_writer(wmi_dict["Event Log"],outdir, "logonevent.csv",
                   sorted(wmi_dict["Event Log"][0].keys()))
    except IndexError:
        print("No Security Event Log Logon events (Event ID "
            "4624). Make sure to run the script in an escalated "
            "command prompt")
```

Writing our results with the csv_writer() function

Our `csv_writer()`, defined on line 279, begins normally enough, by creating a `csvfile` file object based on the version of Python being used to execute the script. One thing that is different is the `**kwargs` argument listed in the definition of the function. The `**` component of that argument indicates that this function accepts keyword arguments. In Python, by convention, keyword arguments are referred to as `kwargs`.

We use keyword arguments in this function to differentiate between using the regular `csv.writer()` method and the `csv.DictWriter()` method. This is necessary because the CSV calls from the `wmi_info()` and the `get_process_info()` functions pass in a list and dictionary, respectively.

While using additional logic in the `csv_writer()` method solves our problem, we could also have solved this issue by making both the `wmi_info()` and `get_process_info()` functions return similarly structured objects:

```
279 def csv_writer(data, outdir, name, headers, **kwargs):
280     """
281     The csv_writer function writes WMI or process information
282     to a CSV output file.
283     :param data: The dictionary or list containing the data to
284         write to the CSV file.
285     :param outdir: The directory to write the CSV report to.
286     :param name: the name of the output CSV file.
287     :param headers: the CSV column headers.
288     :return: Nothing.
289     """
290     out_file = os.path.join(outdir, name)
291 
292     if sys.version_info[0] == 2:
293         csvfile = open(out_file, "wb")
294     elif sys.version_info[0] == 3:
295         csvfile = open(out_file, "w", newline='',
296             encoding='utf-8')
```

As you can see on line 298, we check to see if a keyword argument called `type` was passed into the function call. Given that we only do this on the call to this function on line 341,we know what this signifies. We should use the `csv.DictWriter` method. On line 341, you'll note that we assigned the `type` keyword argument to the `DictWriter` string However, in this case, we could have passed any arbitrary string, as we do not use its value at all here. Rather, we need only know that the `type` keyword argument was assigned a value.

For the dictionary from the `get_process_info()` function, we can use list comprehension to write the values of each entry of the dictionary. For the `wmi_info()` function, we need to first iterate through each entry in the provided list and then write the value associated with each of the provided headers to the CSV file:

```
    if 'type' in kwargs:
        with csvfile:
            csvwriter = csv.DictWriter(csvfile, fields,
                extrasaction='ignore')
            csvwriter.writeheader()
            csvwriter.writerows([v for v in data.values()])

    else:
        with csvfile:
            csvwriter = csv.writer(csvfile)
            csvwriter.writerow(headers)
            for row in data:
                csvwriter.writerow([row[x] for x in headers])
```

Executing pysysinfo.py

In the following screenshot, you can see the output printed to the when running this script on a Windows system:

```
(py3.7.1) C:\book\chapters\chapter_10>python pysysinfo.py custodian_desktop
[+] Gathering information on Windows user profiles
[+] Gathering information on Windows shares
[+] Gathering information on Windows services
[+] Gathering information on connected drives
[+] Querying the Windows Security Event Log for Event ID 4624
[+] Gathering current active processes information
```

Additionally, after executing the script on a Windows system, CSV files for connected drives, shares, services, processes, users, and logon events are created in the specified output directory. A screenshot of the contents of one such spreadsheet, the user profile spreadsheet, is captured here:

	A	B	C	D	E	F	G	H	I
1	Description	Domain	InstallDate	Local Account	Lockout	Name	Password Changeable	Password Expires	Password Required
2	Built-in account for administering the computer/domain	HOME-PC		TRUE	FALSE	Administrator	TRUE	FALSE	TRUE
3		HOME-PC		TRUE	FALSE	rastley	TRUE	FALSE	FALSE
4	A user account managed by the system.	HOME-PC		TRUE	FALSE	DefaultAccount	TRUE	TRUE	TRUE
5	Built-in account for guest access to the computer/domain	HOME-PC		TRUE	FALSE	Guest	FALSE	FALSE	FALSE

Challenges

As alluded to in the *Using the WMI* section, consider expanding the script's capabilities by being able to query remote Windows hosts. Similarly, both `wmi` and `psutil` offer access to additional information that is worth collecting. Experiment with these two libraries and collect more information, especially focusing on collecting system information for non-Windows systems, which, in the current iteration of this script, is more fully supported thanks to the `wmi` library.

Lastly, for a more advanced challenge, consider developing a more useful storage repository to collect and query the data. It's all well and good to collect and present data in the way we have for a few systems, but how well would this scale when run across many hundreds of systems? Imagine a scenario where you deploy and run a modified version of this script against many hosts on a network and have that processed information stored in a singular centralized database for storage and, more importantly, as a more efficient means of querying the collected data.

Summary

In this chapter, we confirmed the value of system information and how to extract that information on live systems. Using the `psutil` library, we learned how to extract process information in an OS-agnostic manner. We also briefly touched on how to use the WMI API to obtain even more information from the Windows operating system. The code for this project can be downloaded from GitHub or Packt, as described in the *Preface*.

In the next chapter, we will learn how to process an Outlook archive `.pst` file with Python and create a listing of its contents.

11
Parsing Outlook PST Containers

Electronic mail (**email**) continues to be one of the most common methods of communication in the workplace, surviving the number of new communication services present in today's world. Emails can be sent from computers, websites, and the phones that're in so many pockets across the globe. This medium allows for the transmission of information in the form of text, HTML, attachments, and more in a reliable fashion. It's no wonder, then, that emails can play a large part in investigations, especially for cases involving the workplace. In this chapter, we're going to work with a common email format, **Personal Storage Table** (**PST**), used by Microsoft Outlook to store email content in a single file.

The script we'll develop in this chapter introduces us to a series of operations available through the `libpff` library developed by Joachim Metz. This library allows us to open PST file and explore its contents in a Pythonic manner. Additionally, the code we build demonstrates how to create dynamic, HTML-based, graphics to provide additional context to spreadsheet-based reports. For these reports, we'll leverage the Jinja2 module, introduced in `Chapter 5`, *Databases in Python*, and the D3.js framework to generate our dynamic HTML-based charts.

The D3.js project is a JavaScript framework that allows us to design informative and dynamic charts without much effort. The charts used in this chapter are open source examples of the framework shared with the community at `https://github.com/d3/d3`. Since this book doesn't focus on JavaScript, nor does it introduce the language, we won't cover the implementation details to create these charts. Instead, we'll demonstrate how to add our Python results to a pre-existing template.

Finally, we'll use a sample PST file, which has a large variety of data across time, to test our script. As always, we recommend running any code against test files before using it in casework to validate the logic and feature coverage. The library used in this chapter is in active development and is labeled experimental by the developer.

The following are the topics covered in this chapter:

- Understanding the background of PST files
- Leveraging `libpff` and its Python bindings, `pypff`, to parse PST files
- Creating informative and professional charts using Jinja2 and D3.js

The code for this chapter is developed and tested using Python 2.7.15.

The PST file format

The PST format is a type of **Personal File Format** (**PFF**). Two other types of PFF file include the **Personal Address Book** (**PAB**) for storing contacts and the **Offline Storage Table** (**OST**), which stores offline email, calendars, and tasks. By default, Outlook stores cached email information in OST files, which can be found at the locations specified in the following table. Items in Outlook will be stored in a PST file if archived:

Windows version	Outlook version	OST location
Windows XP	Outlook 2000/2003/2007	`C:\Documents and Settings\USERPROFILE%\Local Settings\Application Data\Microsoft\Outlook`
Windows Vista/7/8	Outlook 2007	`C:\Users\%USERPROFILE%\AppData\Local\Microsoft\Outlook`
Windows XP	Outlook 2010	`C:Documents and Settings\%USERPROFILE%\My Documents\Outlook Files`
Windows Vista/7/8	Outlook 2010/2013	`C:\Users\%USERPROFILE%\Documents\Outlook Files`

From: `https://forensicswiki.org/wiki/Personal_Folder_File_(PAB,_PST,_OST)`. Location of OST files by default.

The `%USERPROFILE%` field is dynamic and replaced with the user account name on the machine. PFF files can be identified through the hex file signature of `0x2142444E` or `!BDN` in ASCII. After the file signature, the type of PFF file is denoted by 2 bytes at offset 8:

Type	Hex signature	ASCII signature
PST	534D	SM

OST	534F	SO
PAB	4142	AB

From http://www.garykessler.net/library/file_sigs.html

The content type (such as 32-bit or 64-bit) is defined at byte offset 10. The structure of the PFF file format has been described in detail by Joachim Metz in several papers that document the technical structure and how to manually parse these files on GitHub at the project's code repository: `https://github.com/libyal/libpff`.

In this chapter, we'll work only with PST files and we can ignore the differences in OST and PAB files. By default, PST archives have a root area containing a series of folders and messages depending on how the archives were created. For example, a user may archive all folders in their view or only a select few. All of the items within the selected content will be exported into the PST file.

In addition to users archiving content, Outlook has an automatic archiving feature that will store items in the PST files after a set time as defined in the following table. Once this expiration period has been reached, the items will be included in the next archive created. The automatic archive stores PSTs by default in `%USERPROFILE%\Documents\Outlook` in Windows 7, `%APPDATA%\Local\Microsoft\Outlook` in Vista, and `%APPDATA%\Local Settings\Microsoft\Outlook` in XP. These defaults could be set by the user or by group policy in a domain environment. This automatic archive functionality provides examiners with a great history of communication information that we can access and interpret in our investigations:

Folder	**Default aging period**
Inbox and Drafts	6 months
Sent Items and Deleted Items	2 months
Outbox	3 months
Calendar	6 months
Tasks	6 months
Notes	6 months
Journal	6 months

Table 11.1: Default aging of Outlook items
(https://support.office.com/en-us/article/Automatically-move-or-delete-older-items-with-AutoArchive-e5ce650b-d129-49c3-898f-9cd517d79f8e)

An introduction to libpff

The libpff library allows us to reference and navigate through PST objects in a programmatic manner. The root_folder() function allows us to reference RootFolder, which is the base of the PST file and the starting point for our recursive analysis of email content. Within RootFolder are folders and messages. The folders can contain other sub-folders or messages. Folders have properties that include the name of the folder, the number of subfolders, and the number of submessages. Messages are objects representing messages and have attributes, including the subject line, the name of all participants, and several timestamps.

How to install libpff and pypff

Installing some third-party libraries is more difficult than running pip install <library_name>. In the case of libpff and the pypff bindings, we need to take a few steps and follow the instructions outlined in the GitHub project repository. The libpff wiki (located at https://github.com/libyal/libpff/wiki/Building) describes the steps we need to take in order to build libpff.

We'll briefly walk through how you would build this library on an Ubuntu 18.04 system. After downloading and installing Ubuntu 18.04 (preferably in a virtual machine), you'll want to install the dependencies by running the following:

```
sudo apt-get update
sudo apt-get install git python-dev python-pip autoconf automake \
    autopoint libtool pkg-config
```

This will install the required packages for both our script and the pypff bindings. We'll then want to download our libpff code by running the following command:

```
git clone https://github.com/libyal/libpff
```

Once the git clone command completes, we'll navigate into the new libpff directory and run the following commands to download additional dependencies, configure, and install the components we need for the library:

```
cd libpff
./synclibs.ps1
./autogen.ps1
./configure --enable-python
make
make install
```

Additional build options are described further on the `libpff` wiki page.

At this point, you should be able to run the following statements and get the same output, though your version may vary:

```
python
>>> import pypff
>>> pypff.get_version()
u'20180812'
```

To make this process easier for you, we've prebuilt the `pypff` bindings and created a Dockerfile to run this entire setup for you. If you're unfamiliar with Docker, it's a virtualization environment that allows us to run virtual machines with minimal effort. While Docker is generally used to host applications, we'll use it more as a traditional virtual machine. What makes this advantageous for us is that we can distribute a configuration file that you can run on your system and generate the same environment that we've tested.

To begin, please follow the instructions to install Docker on your system from `https://docs.docker.com/install/`. Once installed and running, navigate to the `Chapter 11` code folder on your system and run the `docker build` command. This command will generate a system following a series of preconfigured steps:

```
(py3.7.1) $ docker --version
Docker version 18.09.0, build 4d60db4
(py3.7.1) $ docker build --tag lpff-ch11:20181130 .
```

This will create a new image named `lpff-ch11` with the version number **20181130**. An image in Docker is what it sounds like: a base installation that you can use to create running machines. This way you can have multiple machines all based on the same image. Each machine is called a container, and to create a container from this image, we'll use the `docker run` statement:

```
(py3.7.1) $ docker run -it -P --name pst_parser lpff-ch11:20181130
root@3f032bb148ec:/opt/book# service lighttpd start
 * Starting web server lighttpd                                 [ OK ]
root@3f032bb148ec:/opt/book# ls
pst_indexer.py  stats_template.html
root@3f032bb148ec:/opt/book#
```

The `-it` flag in the `docker run` command asks Docker to connect to the bash shell once the container is created. The `-P` parameter asks Docker to provide us with networking to, in our case, the web server running on the container. Lastly, the `--name` argument allows us to assign a familiar name to our container. We then pass in the image name and version and run the command. As you can see, we're provided with a root shell as soon as the Docker instance finishes.

Regarding the previously mentioned web server, we've included `lighttpd` to allow us to serve our HTML-generated report as a web page. This isn't necessary, though we wanted to highlight how these reports could be made accessible on an internal system.

Please don't run this Docker container on a public network as it'll allow anyone with access to your machine's IP address to see your HTML reports.

In the preceding screenshot, we start this web server by running `server lighttpd start` and then list the contents of our current directory. As you can see, we have two files, our `pst_indexer.py` script that we're about to build and the `stats_template.html` that we'll use to generate our sharp report. Let's build our Python script.

Exploring PSTs – pst_indexer.py

In this script, we'll harvest information about the PST file, taking note of the messages in each folder and generating statistics for word usage, frequent senders, and a heat map for all email activity. Using these metrics, we can go beyond the initial collection and reporting of messages and explore trends in the language used or communication patterns with certain individuals. The statistics section highlights examples of how we can utilize the raw data and build informative graphics to assist the examiner. We recommend tailoring the logic to your specific investigation to provide the most informative report possible. For example, for the word count, we'll only be looking at the top ten words that're alphanumeric and longer than four characters, to help reduce common words and symbols. This might not provide the correct information for your investigation and might require tailoring to your specific situation.

An overview

This chapter's script was built to work with Python 2.7.15 and requires the third-party libraries described in the previous section. Please consider using the Docker image alongside this script.

As with our other chapters, this script starts by importing libraries we use at the top. In this chapter, we use two new libraries, one of which is third-party. We've already introduced `pypff`, the Python bindings to the `libpff` library. The `pypff` module specifies the Python bindings that allow us access to the compiled code. On line 8, we introduce `unicodecsv`, a third-party library we've used previously in `Chapter 5`, *Databases in Python*. This library allows us to write Unicode characters to CSV files as the native CSV library doesn't support Unicode characters as nicely.

On line 6, we import a standard library called `collections` that provides a series of useful interfaces including `Counter`. The `Counter` module allows us to provide values to it and it handles the logic of counting and storing objects. In addition to this, the collections library provides `OrderedDict`, which is extremely useful when you need to create a dictionary with keys in a specified order. The `OrderedDict` module isn't leveraged in this book though it does have its place in Python when you wish to use key-value pairs in an ordered list-like fashion:

```
001 """Index and summarize PST files"""
002 import os
003 import sys
004 import argparse
005 import logging
006 from collections import Counter
007
008 import jinja2
009 import pypff
010 import unicodecsv as csv
```

Following our license and script metadata, we'll set up a few global variables. These variables will help us decrease the number of variables we must pass into functions. The first global variable is `output_directory`, defined on line 46, which will store a string path set by the user. The `date_dictionary`, defined on line 47, uses dictionary comprehension to create keys 1 through 24 and map them to the integer 0. We then use list comprehension on line 48 to append seven instances of this dictionary to `date_list`. This list is leveraged to build a heat map to show information about activity within the PST file split within seven days' worth of 24-hour columns:

```
040 __authors__ = ["Chapin Bryce", "Preston Miller"]
041 __date__ = 20181027
```

```
042 __description__ = '''This scripts handles processing and
043     output of PST Email Containers'''
044 logger = logging.getLogger(__name__)
045
046 output_directory = ""
047 date_dict = {x:0 for x in range(1, 25)}
048 date_list = [date_dict.copy() for x in range(7)]
```

This heat map will establish baseline trends and help identify anomalous activity. An example includes the ability to see a spike in activity at midnight on week nights or excessive activity on Wednesdays before the business day starts. The `date_list` has seven dictionaries, one for each day, each of which is identical and contains a key-value pair for the hour of the day with the default value of `0`.

The `date_dict.copy()` call on line 48 is required to ensure that we can update the hours within a single date. If we omit the `copy()` method, every day will be updated. This is because dictionaries are tied together by references to the original object, and we're generating a list of objects without the `copy()` method. When we do use this function, it allows us to create a copy of the values with a new object, so we can create a list of different objects.

With these variables built, we can reference and update their values throughout other functions without needing to pass them again. Global variables are read-only by default and require a special global command in order to be modified by a function.

The following functions outline our script's operation. As usual, we have our `main()` function to control behavior. The following is the `make_path()` function, which is a utility to assist us in gathering full paths for our output files. The `folder_traverse()` and `check_for_msgs()` functions are used to iterate through the available items and start processing:

```
def main():
...
def make_path():
...
def folder_traverse():
...
def check_for_msgs():
```

Our remaining functions focus on processing and reporting data within PSTs. The `process_message()` function reads the message and returns the required attributes for our reports. The first reporting function is the `folder_report()` function. This code creates a CSV output for each folder found within the PST and describes the content found within each.

This function also processes data for the remaining reports by writing message bodies to a single text file, stores each set of dates, and preserves a list of the senders. By caching this information to a text file, the next function is easily able to read the file without a major impact on memory.

Our `word_stats()` function reads and ingests the information into a collection. The `Counter()` object is used in our `word_report()` function. When generating our word count report, we read the collection's. `Counter()` object into a CSV file, which will be read by our JavaScript code. The `sender_report()` and `date_report()` functions also flush data to delimited files for interpretation by JavaScript in the report. Finally, our `html_report()` function opens our report template and writes the custom report information into an HTML file in our output folder:

```
118 def process_msg():
...
138 def folder_report():
...
193 def word_stats():
...
208 def word_report():
...
235 def sender_report():
...
260 def date_report():
...
277 def html_report():
```

As with all of our scripts, we handle our arguments, logs, and the `main()` function call under the `if __name__ == "__main__":` conditional statement on line 302. We define the required arguments, `PST_FILE` and `OUTPUT_DIR`, and the user can specify optional arguments, `--title` and `-l`, for a custom report title and log path:

```
302 if __name__ == "__main__":
303     parser = argparse.ArgumentParser(
304         description=__description__,
305         epilog='Built by {}. Version {}'.format(
306             ", ".join(__authors__), __date__),
307        formatter_class=argparse.ArgumentDefaultsHelpFormatter
308     )
309     parser.add_argument('PST_FILE',
310         help="PST File Format from Microsoft Outlook")
311     parser.add_argument('OUTPUT_DIR',
312         help="Directory of output for temporary and report files.")
313     parser.add_argument('--title', default="PST Report",
314         help='Title of the HTML Report.')
315     parser.add_argument('-l',
```

```
316         help='File path of log file.')
317     args = parser.parse_args()
```

After defining our arguments, we begin processing them so that we can pass them to the `main()` function in a standardized and safe manner. On line 319, we convert the output location into an absolute path so that we can be sure about accessing the correct location throughout the script. Notice how we're calling the `output_directory` global variable and assigning a new value to it. This is only possible because we're not within a function. If we were modifying the global variable within a function, we would need to write `global output_directory` on line 318:

```
319     output_directory = os.path.abspath(args.OUTPUT_DIR)
320
321     if not os.path.exists(output_directory):
322         os.makedirs(output_directory)
```

After we modify the `output_directory` variable, we make sure the path exists (and create it if it doesn't) to avoid errors later in the code. Once complete, we then use our standard logging code snippet to configure logging for this script on lines 331 through 339. On lines 341 through 345, we log debug information on the system executing the script prior to calling the `main()` function. On line 346, we call the `main()` function and pass the `args.PST_FILE` and `args.title` arguments. We don't need to pass the `output_directory` value because we can reference it globally. Once we pass the arguments and the `main()` function completes execution, we log that the script has finished executing on line 347:

```
331     logger.setLevel(logging.DEBUG)
332     msg_fmt = logging.Formatter("%(asctime)-15s %(funcName)-20s"
333         "%(levelname)-8s %(message)s")
334     strhndl = logging.StreamHandler(sys.stderr) # Set to stderr
335     strhndl.setFormatter(fmt=msg_fmt)
336     fhndl = logging.FileHandler(log_path, mode='a')
337     fhndl.setFormatter(fmt=msg_fmt)
338     logger.addHandler(strhndl)
339     logger.addHandler(fhndl)
340
341     logger.info('Starting PST Indexer v. {}'.format(__date__))
342     logger.debug('System ' + sys.platform)
343     logger.debug('Version ' + sys.version.replace("\n", " "))
344
345     logger.info('Starting Script')
346     main(args.PST_FILE, args.title)
347     logger.info('Script Complete')
```

The following flowchart highlights how the functions interact with each other. This flowchart might seem a little complicated but encapsulates the basic structure of our script.

The `main()` function calls the recursive `folder_traverse()` function, which in turn finds, processes, and summarizes messages and folders from the root folder. After this, the `main()` function generates reports with the word, sender, and date reports, which get displayed in one HTML report generated by the `html_report()` function. As a note, the dashed lines represent functions that return a value, while the solid lines represent a function that returns no value:

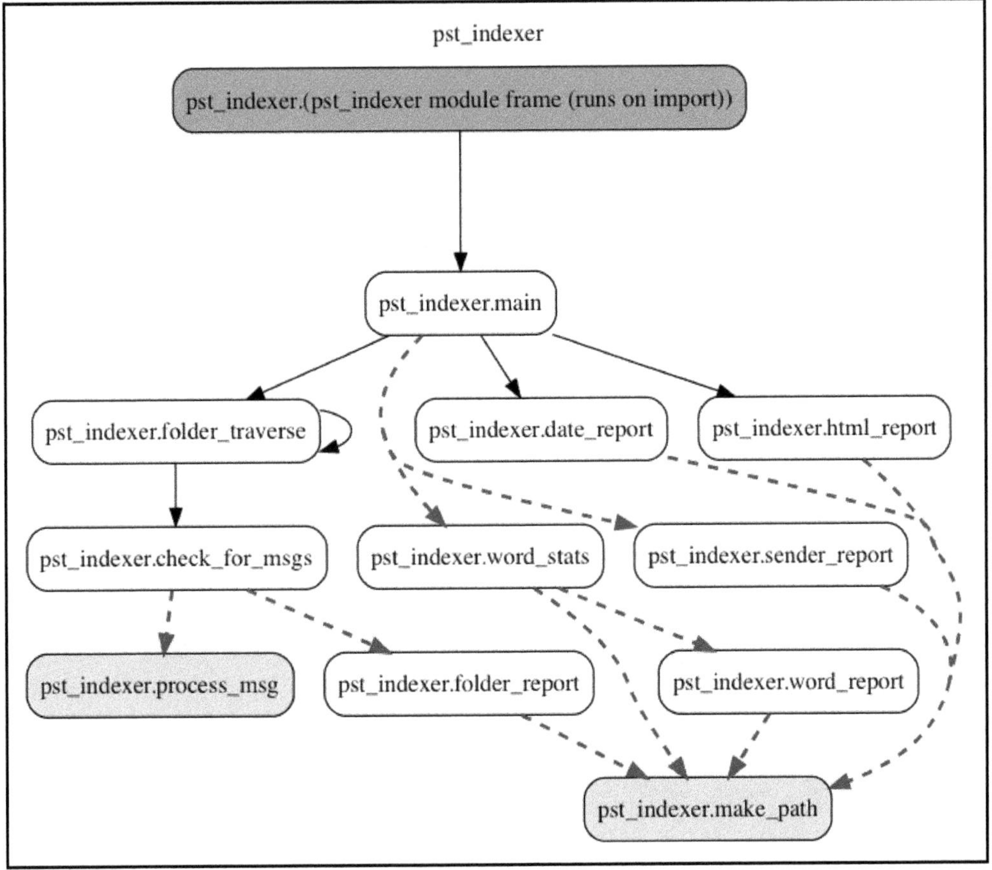

Developing the main() function

The `main()` function controls the primary operations of the script, from opening and initial processing of the file, traversing the PST, to generating our reports. On line 62, we split the name of the PST file from its path using the `os.path` module.

We'll use the `pst_name` variable if a custom title isn't supplied by the user. On the next line, we use the `pypff.open()` function to create a PST object. We use the `get_root_folder()` method to get the PST root folder so we can begin the iteration process and discover items within the folders:

```
051 def main(pst_file, report_name):
052     """
053     The main function opens a PST and calls functions to parse
054     and report data from the PST
055     :param pst_file: A string representing the path to the PST
056     file to analyze
057     :param report_name: Name of the report title
058         (if supplied by the user)
059     :return: None
060     """
061     logger.debug("Opening PST for processing...")
062     pst_name = os.path.split(pst_file)[1]
063     opst = pypff.open(pst_file)
064     root = opst.get_root_folder()
```

With the root folder extracted, we call the `folder_traverse()` function on line 67 to begin traversing the directories within the PST container. We'll cover the nature of this function in the next section. After traversing the folders, we start generating our reports with the `word_stats()`, `sender_report()`, and `date_report()` functions. On line 74, we pass the name of the report, the PST name, and lists containing the most frequent words and senders to provide statistical data for our HTML dashboard, as follows:

```
066     logger.debug("Starting traverse of PST structure...")
067     folder_traverse(root)
068
069     logger.debug("Generating Reports...")
070     top_word_list = word_stats()
071     top_sender_list = sender_report()
072     date_report()
073
074     html_report(report_name, pst_name, top_word_list,
075         top_sender_list)
```

Evaluating the make_path() helper function

To make life simpler, we've developed a helper function, `make_path()`, defined on line 78. Helper functions allow us to reuse code that we might normally write out many times throughout our script in one function call. With this code, we take an input string representing a file name and return the absolute path of where the file should exist within the operating system based on the `output_directory` value supplied by the user. On line 85, two operations take place; first, we join the `file_name` to the `output_directory` value with the correct path delimiters using the `os.path.join()` method.

Next, this value is processed by the `os.path.abspath()` method, which provides the full file path within the operating system environment. We then return this value to the function that originally called it. As we saw in the flow diagram, many functions will make calls to the `make_path()` function:

```
078     def make_path(file_name):
079     """
080     The make_path function provides an absolute path between the
081     output_directory and a file
082     :param file_name: A string representing a file name
083     :return: A string representing the path to a specified file
084     """
085     return os.path.abspath(os.path.join(output_directory,
086         file_name))
```

Iteration with the folder_traverse() function

This function recursively walks through folders to parse message items and indirectly generates summary reports on the folder. This function, initially provided the root directory, is generically developed to be capable of handling any folder item passed to it. This allows us to reuse the function for each discovered subfolder. On line 97, we use a `for` loop to recurse through the `sub_folders` iterator generated from our `pypff.folder` object. On line 98, we check whether the folder object has any additional subfolders and, if it does, call the `folder_traverse()` function again before checking the current folder for any new messages. We only check for messages in the event that there are no new subfolders:

```
089 def folder_traverse(base):
090     """
091     The folder_traverse function walks through the base of the
092     folder and scans for sub-folders and messages
093     :param base: Base folder to scan for new items within
094         the folder.
```

```
    :return: None
    """
    for folder in base.sub_folders:
        if folder.number_of_sub_folders:
            folder_traverse(folder) # Call new folder to traverse
        check_for_msgs(folder)
```

This is a recursive function because we call the same function within itself (a loop of sorts). This loop could potentially run indefinitely, so we must make sure the data input will have an end to it. A PST should have a limited number of folders and will therefore eventually exit the recursive loop. This is essentially our PST specific `os.walk()` function, which iteratively walks through filesystem directories. Since we're working with folders and messages within a file container, we have to create our own recursion. Recursion can be a tricky concept to understand; to guide you through it, please reference the following diagram when reading our explanation in the upcoming paragraphs:

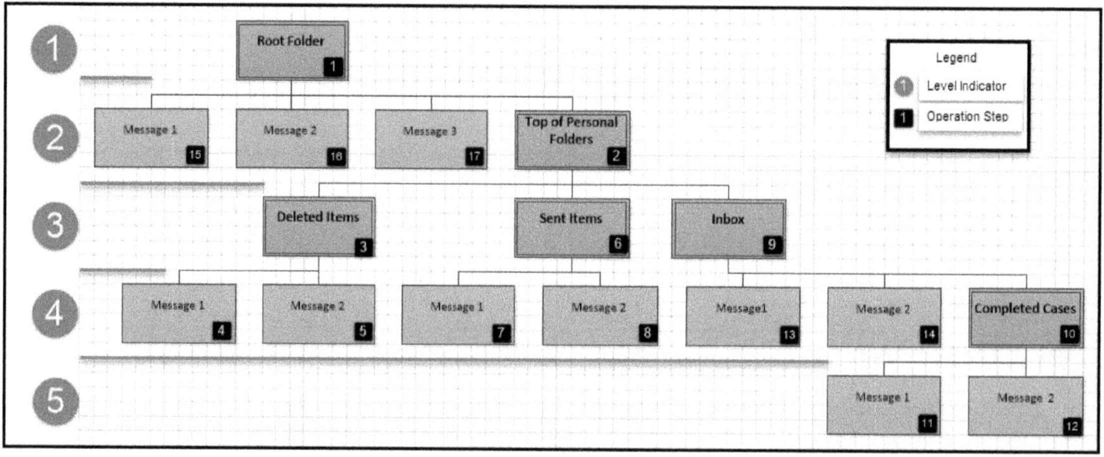

In the preceding diagram, there're five levels in this PST hierarchy, each containing a mixture of blue folders and green messages. On level **1**, we have `Root Folder`, which is the first iteration of the `folder_traverse()` loop. Since this folder has a single subfolder, `Top of Personal Folders`, as you can see on level **2**, we rerun the function before exploring the message contents. When we rerun the function, we now evaluate the `Top of Personal Folders` folder and find that it also has subfolders.

Calling the `folder_traverse()` function again on each of the subfolders, we first process the Deleted Items folder on level **3**. Inside the `Deleted Items` folder on level **4**, we find that we only have messages in this folder and call the `check_for_msgs()` function for the first time.

After the `check_for_msgs()` function returns, we go back to the previous call of the `folder_traverse()` function on level **3** and evaluate the `Sent Items` folder. Since the `Sent Items` folder also doesn't have any subfolders, we process its messages before returning to level **3**.

We then reach the `Inbox` folder on level **3** and call the `folder_traverse()` function on the `Completed Cases` subfolder on level **4**. Now that we're in level **5**, we process the two messages inside the `Completed Cases` folder. With these two messages processed, we step back to level **4** and process the two messages within the `Inbox` folder. Once these messages are processed, we've completed all items in levels **3**, **4**, and **5** and can finally move back to level **2**. Within `Root Folder`, we can process the three message items there before the function execution concludes. Our recursion, in this case, works from the bottom up.

These four lines of code allow us to navigate through the entire PST and call additional processing on every message in every folder. Though this is usually provided to us through methods such as `os.walk()`, some libraries don't natively support recursion and require the developer to do so using the existing functionality within the library.

Identifying messages with the check_for_msgs() function

This function is called for every discovered folder in the `folder_traverse()` function and handles the processing of messages. On line 110, we log the name of the folder to provide a record of what has been processed. Following this, we create a list to append messages on line 111 and begin iterating through the messages in the folder on line 112.

Within this loop, we call the `process_msg()` function to extract the relevant fields into a dictionary. After each message dictionary has been appended to the list, we call the `folder_report()` function, which will create a summary report of all of the messages within the folder:

```
103 def check_for_msgs(folder):
104     """
105     The check_for_msgs function reads folder messages if
106     present and passes them to the report function
107     :param folder: pypff.Folder object
108     :return: None
109     """
110     logger.debug("Processing Folder: " + folder.name)
111     message_list = []
112     for message in folder.sub_messages:
113         message_dict = process_msg(message)
```

```
            message_list.append(message_dict)
        folder_report(message_list, folder.name)
```

Processing messages in the process_msg() function

This function is called the most as it runs for every discovered message. When you're considering how to improve the efficiency of your code base, these are the types of functions to look at. Even a minor efficiency improvement in function that're called frequently can have a large effect on your script.

In this case, the function is simple and exists mainly to remove clutter from another function. Additionally, it compartmentalizes message processing within a single function and will make it easier to troubleshoot bugs associated with message processing.

The return statement on line 126 passes a dictionary to the calling function. This dictionary contains a key-value pair for each of the `pypff.message` object attributes. Note that the `subject`, `sender`, `transport_headers`, and `plain_text_body` attributes are strings. The `creation_time`, `client_submit_time`, and `delivery_time` attributes are Python `datetime.datetime` objects and the `number_of_attachments` attribute is an integer.

The subject attribute contains the subject line found within the message and `sender_name` contains a single string of the name of the sender who sent the message. The sender name might reflect an email address or the contact name depending on whether the recipient resolved the name.

The `transport_headers` contains the email header data transmitted with any message. This data should be read from the bottom up, as new data is added to the top of the header as a message moves between mail servers. We can use this information to possibly track the movement of a message using hostnames and IP addresses. The `plain_text_body` attribute returns the body as plain text, though we could display the message in RTF or HTML format using the `rtf_body` and `html_body` attributes, respectively.

The `creation_times` and `delivery_times` are reflective of the creation of the message and delivery of a received message to the PST being examined. The `client_submit_time` value is the timestamp for when the message was sent. The last attribute shown here is the `number_of_attachments` attribute, which finds additional artifacts for extraction:

```
118 def process_msg(message):
119     """
120     The process_msg function processes multi-field messages
```

```
121     to simplify collection of information
122     :param message: pypff.Message object
123     :return: A dictionary with message fields (values) and
124         their data (keys)
125     """
126     return {
127         "subject": message.subject,
128         "sender": message.sender_name,
129         "header": message.transport_headers,
130         "body": message.plain_text_body,
131         "creation_time": message.creation_time,
132         "submit_time": message.client_submit_time,
133         "delivery_time": message.delivery_time,
134         "attachment_count": message.number_of_attachments,
135     }
```

At this time, the `pypff` module doesn't support interaction with attachments, although the `libpff` library will extract artifacts using its `pffexport` and `pffinfo` tools. To build these tools, we must include the `--enable-static-executables` argument on the command line when running the `./configure` command while building.

Once built with these options, we can run the tools mentioned earlier to export the PST attachments in a structured directory. The developer has stated that he'll include `pypff` support for attachments in a future release. If made available, we'll be able to interface with message attachments and run additional processing on discovered files. If this functionality is needed for analysis, we could add support to call the `pffexport` tool via Python through the `os` or `subprocess` libraries.

Summarizing data in the folder_report() function

At this point, we've collected a fair amount of information about messages and folders. We use this code block to export that data into a simple report for review. To create this report, we require the `message_list` and `folder_name` variables. On line 146, we check whether there're any entries in the `message_list`; if not, we log a warning and return the function to prevent any of the remaining code from running.

If the `message_list` has content, we start to create a CSV report. We first generate the filename in the output directory by passing our desired filename into the `make_path()` function to get the absolute path of the file that we wish to write to. Using this file path, we open the file in `wb` mode to write our CSV file and to prevent a bug that would add an extra line between the rows of our reports on line 152. In the following line, we define the list of headers for the output document.

This list should reflect an ordered list of columns we wish to report. Feel free to modify lines 153 and 154 to reflect a preferred order or additional rows. All of the additional rows must be valid keys from all dictionaries within the `message_list` variable.

Following our headers, we initiate the `csv.DictWriter` class on line 155. If you recall from the start of our script, we imported the `unicodecsv` library to handle Unicode characters when writing to a CSV. During this import, we used the `as` keyword to rename the module from `unicodecsv` to `csv` within our script. This module provides the same methods as the standard library, so we can continue using the familiar function calls we have seen with the `csv` library. In this initialization of `DictWriter()`, we pass along the open file object, the field names, and an argument to tell the class what to do with unused information within the `message_list` dictionaries. Since we're not using all of the keys within the dictionaries in the `message_list` list, we need to tell the `DictWriter()` class that we would like to ignore these values, as follows:

```
138 def folder_report(message_list, folder_name):
139     """
140     The folder_report function generates a report per PST folder
141     :param message_list: A list of messages discovered
142         during scans
143     :folder_name: The name of an Outlook folder within a PST
144     :return: None
145     """
146     if not len(message_list):
147         logger.warning("Empty message not processed")
148         return
149 
150     # CSV Report
151     fout_path = make_path("folder_report_" + folder_name + ".csv")
152     fout = open(fout_path, 'wb')
153     header = ['creation_time', 'submit_time', 'delivery_time',
154         'sender', 'subject', 'attachment_count']
155     csv_fout = csv.DictWriter(fout, fieldnames=header,
156         extrasaction='ignore')
157     csv_fout.writeheader()
158     csv_fout.writerows(message_list)
159     fout.close()
```

With the `csv_fout` variable initialized and configured, we can begin writing our header data using the `writeheaders()` method call on line 157. Next, we write the dictionary fields of interest to the file using the `writerows()` method. Upon writing all the rows, we close the `fout` file to write it to disk and release the handle on the object as seen on line 159.

On lines 119 through 141, we prepare the dictionaries from the `message_list` for use in generating HTML report statistics. We need to invoke the `global` statement as seen on line 162 to allow us to edit the `date_list` global variable. We then open two text files to record a raw list of all of the body content and sender names. These files will be used in a later section to generate our statistics and allow the collection of this data in a manner that doesn't consume large amounts of memory. These two text files, seen on lines 163 and 164, are opened in the `a` mode, which will create the file if it doesn't exist or append the data to the end of the file if it exists.

On line 165, we start a `for` loop to iterate through each message, `m`, in `message_list`. If the message body key has a value, then we write the value to the output file with two line breaks to separate this content. Following this, on lines 168 and 169, we perform a similar process on the sender key and its value. In this instance, we'll only use one line break so that we can iterate through it easier in a later function:

```
162     global date_list # Allow access to edit global variable
163     body_out = open(make_path("message_body.txt"), 'a')
164     senders_out = open(make_path("senders_names.txt"), 'a')
165     for m in message_list:
166         if m['body']:
167             body_out.write(m['body'] + "\n\n")
168         if m['sender']:
169             senders_out.write(m['sender'] + '\n')
```

After collecting the message content and senders, we accumulate the date information. To generate our heat map, we'll combine all three dates of activity into a single count to form a single chart. After checking that a valid date value is available, we gather the day of the week to determine which of the dictionaries within the `date_list` list we wish to update.

The Python `datetime.datetime` library has a `weekday()` method and an `.hour` attribute, which allows us to access the values as integers and handles the messy conversions for us. The `weekday()` method returns an integer from 0 to 6, where 0 represents Monday and 6 represents Sunday. The `.hour` attribute returns an integer between 0 and 23, representing time in a 24-hour fashion, though the JavaScript we're using for the heat map requires an integer between 1 and 24 to process correctly. Because of this, we add 1 to each of the hour values as seen on lines 175, 181, and 187.

We now have the correct weekday and time of day keys we need to update the value in the `date_list`. Upon completing the loop, we can close the two file objects on lines 189 and 190:

```
171         # Creation Time
172         c_time = m['creation_time']
173         if c_time isn't None:
```

```
            day_of_week = c_time.weekday()
            hour_of_day = c_time.hour + 1
            date_list[day_of_week][hour_of_day] += 1
        # Submit Time
        s_time = m['submit_time']
        if s_time isn't None:
            day_of_week = s_time.weekday()
            hour_of_day = s_time.hour + 1
            date_list[day_of_week][hour_of_day] += 1
        # Delivery Time
        d_time = m['delivery_time']
        if d_time isn't None:
            day_of_week = d_time.weekday()
            hour_of_day = d_time.hour + 1
            date_list[day_of_week][hour_of_day] += 1
    body_out.close()
    senders_out.close()
```

Understanding the word_stats() function

With the message content written to a file, we can now use it to calculate a frequency of word usage. We use the `Counter` module we imported from the collections library to generate a word count in an efficient manner.

We initialize the `word_list` as a `Counter()` object, which allows us to call it and assign new words while keeping track of the overall count per word. After initialization, we start a `for` loop on line 200, open the file, and iterate through each line with the `readlines()` method:

```
193 def word_stats(raw_file="message_body.txt"):
194     """
195     The word_stats function reads and counts words from a file
196     :param raw_file: The path to a file to read
197     :return: A list of word frequency counts
198     """
199     word_list = Counter()
200     for line in open(make_path(raw_file), 'r').readlines():
```

At this point, we need to `split()` the line into a list of individual words in order to generate a proper count. By not passing an argument to `split()`, we'll split on all whitespace characters, which, in this case, works to our advantage. Following the split on line 201, we use a conditional statement to ensure only a single word greater than four characters is included in our list, to eliminate common filler words or symbols. This logic may be tailored based on your environment, as you may, for example, wish to include words shorter than four letters or some other filtering criteria.

If the conditional evaluates to true, we add the word to our counter. On line 204, we increment the value of the word in the list by one. After iterating through every line and word of the `message_body.txt` file, we pass this word list to the `word_report()` function:

```
201         for word in line.split():
202             # Prevent too many false positives/common words
203             if word.isalnum() and len(word) > 4:
204                 word_list[word] += 1
205     return word_report(word_list)
```

Creating the word_report() function

Once `word_list` is passed from the `word_stats()` function, we can generate our reports using the supplied data. In order to have more control over how our data is presented, we're going to write a CSV report without the help of the `csv` module. First, on line 216, we need to ensure that `word_list` contains values. If it doesn't, the function logs a warning and returns. On line 220, we open a new file object in `wb` mode to create our CSV report. On line 221, we write our `Count` and `Word` headers onto the first row with a newline character to ensure all other data is written in the rows below:

```
208 def word_report(word_list):
209     """
210     The word_report function counts a list of words and returns
211     results in a CSV format
212     :param word_list: A list of words to iterate through
213     :return: None or html_report_list, a list of word
214         frequency counts
215     """
216     if not word_list:
217         logger.debug('Message body statistics not available')
218         return []
219 
220     fout = open(make_path("frequent_words.csv"), 'wb')
221     fout.write("Count,Word\n")
```

We then use a `for` loop and the `most_common()` method to call out a tuple containing each word and the assigned count value. If the length of the tuple is greater than 1, we write the values into the CSV document in reverse order to properly align the columns with the values, followed by a newline character. After this loop completes, we close the file and flush the results to the disk as seen on line 225:

```
222     for e in word_list.most_common():
223         if len(e) > 1:
224             fout.write(str(e[1]) + "," + str(e[0]) + "\n")
225     fout.close()
```

Following this loop, we then generate a list of the top 10 words. By passing the integer 10 into the `most_common()` method, we select only the top 10 most common entries in `Counter`. We append a dictionary of the results to a temporary list, which is returned to the `word_stats()` function and later used in our HTML report:

```
    html_report_list = []
    for e in word_list.most_common(10):
        html_report_list.append(
            {"word": str(e[0]), "count": str(e[1])})

    return html_report_list
```

Building the sender_report() function

The `sender_report()` functions similarly to `word_report()` and generates a CSV and HTML report for individuals who sent emails. This function showcases another method for reading values into the `Counter()` method. On line 242, we open and read the lines of a file into the `Counter()` method.

We can implement it this way because each line of the input file represents a single sender. Counting the data in this manner simplifies the code and, by extension, saves us a few lines of writing.

This wasn't a feasible option for the `word_stats()` function because we had to break each line into a separate word and then perform additional logic operations prior to counting the words. If we wanted to apply logic to the sender statistics, we would need to create a similar loop to that in `word_stats()`. For example, we might want to exclude all items from Gmail or that contain the word `noreply` in the sender's name or address:

```
235 def sender_report(raw_file="senders_names.txt"):
236     """
237     The sender_report function reports the most frequent_senders
```

```
238     :param raw_file: The file to read raw information
239     :return: html_report_list, a list of the most
240         frequent senders
241     """
242     sender_list = Counter(
243         open(make_path(raw_file), 'r').readlines())
```

After generating the sender count, we can open the CSV report and write our headers to it. At this point, we'll iterate through each of the most common in a `for` loop as seen on line 247, and if the tuple contains more than one element, we'll write it to the file.

This is another location where we could filter the values based on the sender's name. After writing, the file is closed and flushed to the disk. On line 252, we generate statistics for the top five senders for the final report by generating a list of dictionaries containing the tuple values. To access it in our HTML report function, we return this list. See the following code:

```
245     fout = open(make_path("frequent_senders.csv"), 'wb')
246     fout.write("Count,Sender\n")
247     for e in sender_list.most_common():
248         if len(e) > 1:
249             fout.write(str(e[1]) + "," + str(e[0]))
250     fout.close()
251 
252     html_report_list = []
253     for e in sender_list.most_common(5):
254         html_report_list.append(
255             {"label": str(e[0]), "count": str(e[1])})
256 
257     return html_report_list
```

Refining the heat map with the date_report() function

This report provides data to generate the activity heat map. For it to operate properly, it must have the same filename and path specified in the HTML template. The default template for the file is named `heatmap.tsv` and is located in the same directory as the output HTML report.

After opening this file with those defaults on line 267, we write the headers with a tab character delimiting the day, hour, and value columns and ending with a newline character. At this point, we can begin iterating through our list of dictionaries by using two `for` loops to access each list containing dictionaries.

In the first `for` loop, we use the `enumerate()` method to capture the loop iteration number. This number conveniently corresponds to the date we're processing, allowing us to use this value to write the day value:

```
260 def date_report():
261     """
262     The date_report function writes date information in a
263     TSV report. No input args as the filename
264     is static within the HTML dashboard
265     :return: None
266     """
267     csv_out = open(make_path("heatmap.tsv"), 'w')
268     csv_out.write("day\thour\tvalue\n")
269     for date, hours_list in enumerate(date_list):
```

In the second `for` loop, we iterate through each dictionary, gathering both the hour and count values separately by using the `items()` method to extract the key and value as a tuple. With these values, we can now assign the date, hour, and count to a tab-separated string and write it to the file.

On line 271, we add 1 to the date value as the heat map chart uses a 1 through 7 range, whereas our list uses an index of 0 through 6 to count days of the week.

After iterating through the hours, we flush the data to the disk before moving forward to the next dictionary of hours. Once we've iterated through all of the seven days, we can close this document as it's ready to be used with our heat map chart in the `html_report()` function:

```
270         for hour, count in hours_list.items():
271             to_write = "{}\t{}\t{}\n".format(date+1, hour, count)
272             csv_out.write(to_write)
273         csv_out.flush()
274     csv_out.close()
```

Writing the html_report() function

The `html_report()` function is where we tie together all of the pieces of information gathered from the PST into a final report, with much anticipation. To generate this report, we require arguments specifying the report title, PST name, and counts of the top words and senders:

```
277 def html_report(report_title, pst_name, top_words, top_senders):
278     """
279     The html_report function generates the HTML report from a
280         Jinja2 Template
281     :param report_title: A string representing the title of
282         the report
283     :param pst_name: A string representing the file name of
284         the PST
285     :param top_words: A list of the top 10 words
286     :param top_senders: A list of the top 10 senders
287     :return: None
288     """
```

To begin with, we open the template file and read in the contents into a single variable as a string. This value is then passed into our `jinja2.Template` engine to be processed into a template object called `html_template` on line 290.

Next, we create a dictionary of values to pass into the template's placeholders and use the `context` dictionary on line 292 to hold these values. With the dictionary in place, we then render the template on line 295 and provide the `context` dictionary. This rendered data is a string of HTML data, as you expect to see on a web page, with all of our placeholder logic evaluated and turned into a static HTML page.

We write the rendered HTML data to an output file in the user-specified directory as seen on lines 297 through 299. With the HTML report written to the output directory, the report is complete and ready to view in the output folder:

```
289     open_template = open("stats_template.html", 'r').read()
290     html_template = jinja2.Template(open_template)
291
292     context = {"report_title": report_title, "pst_name": pst_name,
293         "word_frequency": top_words,
294         "percentage_by_sender": top_senders}
295     new_html = html_template.render(context)
296
297     html_report_file = open(make_path("pst_report.html"), 'w')
298     html_report_file.write(new_html)
299     html_report_file.close()
```

The HTML template

This book focuses on the use of Python in forensics. Though Python provides many great methods for manipulating and applying logic to data, we still need to lean on other resources to support our scripts. In this chapter, we've built an HTML dashboard to present statistical information about these PST files.

In this section, we'll review sections of HTML, focusing on where our data is inserted into the template versus the intricacies of HTML, JavaScript, and other web languages. For more information in the use and implementation of HTML, JavaScript, D3.js, and other web resources, visit `http://packtpub.com` for pertinent titles or `http://w3schools.com` for introductory tutorials. Since we'll not be delving deeply into HTML, CSS, or other web design aspects, our focus will be primarily on the spaces where our Python script will interact.

This template leverages a couple of common frameworks that allow the rapid design of professional-looking web pages. The first is Bootstrap 3, a CSS styling framework that organizes and styles HTML to look uniform and clean no matter the device used to view the page. The second is the D3.js framework, which is a JavaScript framework for graphic visualizations.

As we've seen before, the template items into which we'll insert our data are contained within double braces, `{{ }}`. We'll insert the report title for our HTML dashboard on line 39 and 44. Additionally, we'll insert the name of the PST file on lines 48, 55, and 62. The `div id` tags on lines 51, 58, and 65 acts as a variable name for the charts that can be inserted by JavaScript in the later section of the template once the code processes the input:

```
...
038   </style>
039   <title>{{ report_title }}</title>
040 </head>
041 <body>
042   <div class="container">
043     <div class="row">
044       <h1>{{ report_title }}</h1>
045     </div>
046     <div class="row">
047         <div class="row">
048           <h3>Top 10 words in {{ pst_name }}</h3>
049         </div>
050         <div class="row">
051           <div id="wordchart">
052           </div>
053         </div>
054         <div class="row">
```

```
055            <h3>Top 5 Senders in {{ pst_name }}</h3>
056          </div>
057          <div class="row">
058            <div id="piechart">
059            </div>
060          </div>
061          <div class="row">
062            <h3>Heatmap of all date activity in {{ pst_name }}</h3>
063          </div>
064          <div class="row">
065            <div id="heatmap"></div>
066          </div>
067        </div>
068      </div>
...
```

After the `div` placeholder elements are in place, the JavaScript on lines 69 through 305 processes the provided data into charts. The first location data is placed on line 92, where the `{{ word_frequency }}` phrase is replaced with the list of dictionaries. For example, this could be replaced with `[{'count': '175', 'word': 'message'}, {'count': '17', 'word': 'iPhone'}]`. This list of dictionaries is translated into chart values to form the vertical bar chart of the HTML report:

```
...
088           .attr("transform", "translate(" + margin.left + "," +
margin.top + ")");
089
090           data = {{ word_frequency }}
091
092         function processData(data) {x.domain(data.map(function(d) {
093           return d;
094         }
...
```

On line 132, we insert the `percentage_by_sender` value from the context dictionary into the JavaScript. This replacement will occur in a similar example to the `word_frequency` insert. With this information, the donut chart generates on the HTML report:

```
...
129       (function(d3) {
130         'use strict';
131
132         var dataset = {{ percentage_by_sender }};
133
134         var width = 960;
...
```

We'll use a new way to insert data for the heat map. By providing the filename discussed in the previous section, we can prompt the code to look for a `heatmap.tsv` file in the same directory as this HTML report. The upside to this is how we're able to generate a report once and use the TSV in a program such as Excel and within our dashboard, though the downside is that this file must travel with the HTML report for it to display properly, as the chart will regenerate on reload.

This chart also has difficulty rendering on some browsers as JavaScript is interpreted differently by each browser. Testing found that Chrome, Firefox, and Safari were OK at viewing the graphic. Ensure that browser add-ons are not interfering with the JavaScript and that your browser doesn't block JavaScript from interacting with local files. If your browser disallows this, consider running the script in the Docker instance, starting the `lighttpd` service, and placing your output in `/var/www/html`. When you visit the IP address of your Docker instance, you'll be able to navigate to the report as the server will provide access to the resources for you:

```
          times = ["1a", "2a", "3a", "4a", "5a", "6a", "7a", "8a", "9a",
"10a", "11a", "12a", "1p", "2p", "3p", "4p", "5p", "6p", "7p", "8p", "9p",
"10p", "11p", "12p"];

        datasets = ["heatmap.tsv"];

        var svg = d3.select("#heatmap").append("svg")
```

The remainder of the template is available in the code repository and can easily be referenced and manipulated if web languages are your strong suit or worth further exploration. The D3.js library allows us to create additional informative graphics and adds another tool to our reporting toolbox that's relatively simple and portable. The following graphics represent examples of data for each of the three charts we've created.

The first chart represents the most used words in the PST file. The frequency is plotted on the y axis and the word on the x axis:

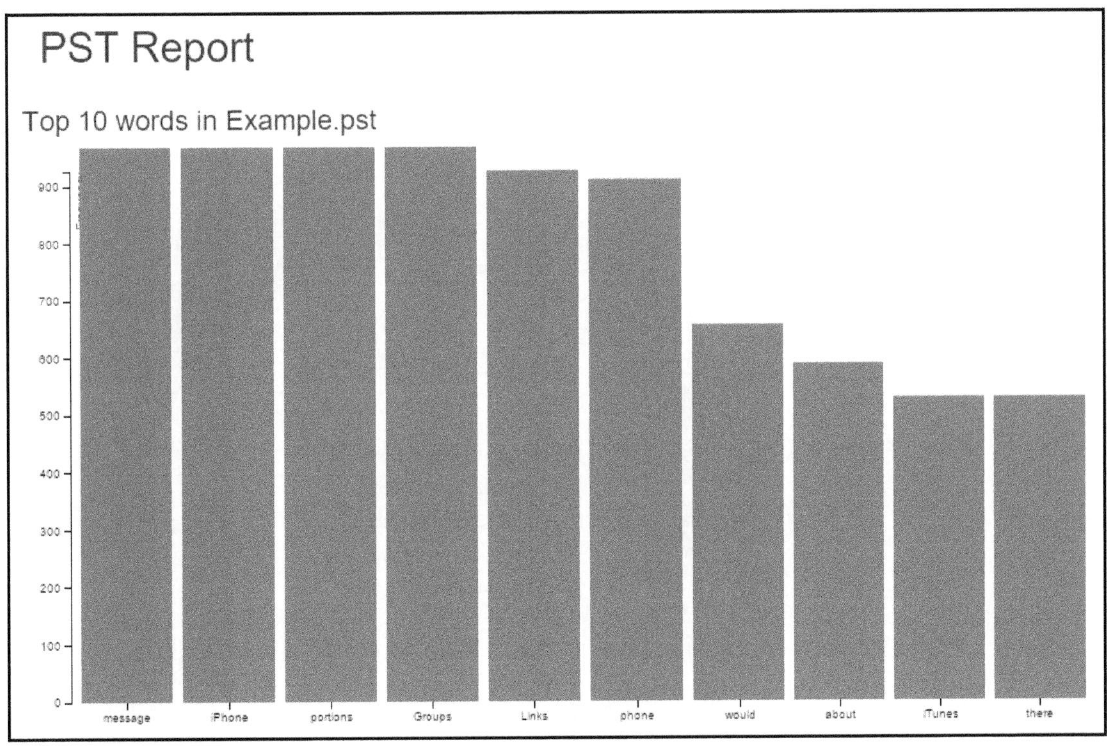

The following chart identifies the top five accounts that have sent an email to the user. Notice how the circle graph helps to identify which participants are most frequent in the dataset. In addition, the text labels provide the name of the address and the number of emails received by that address:

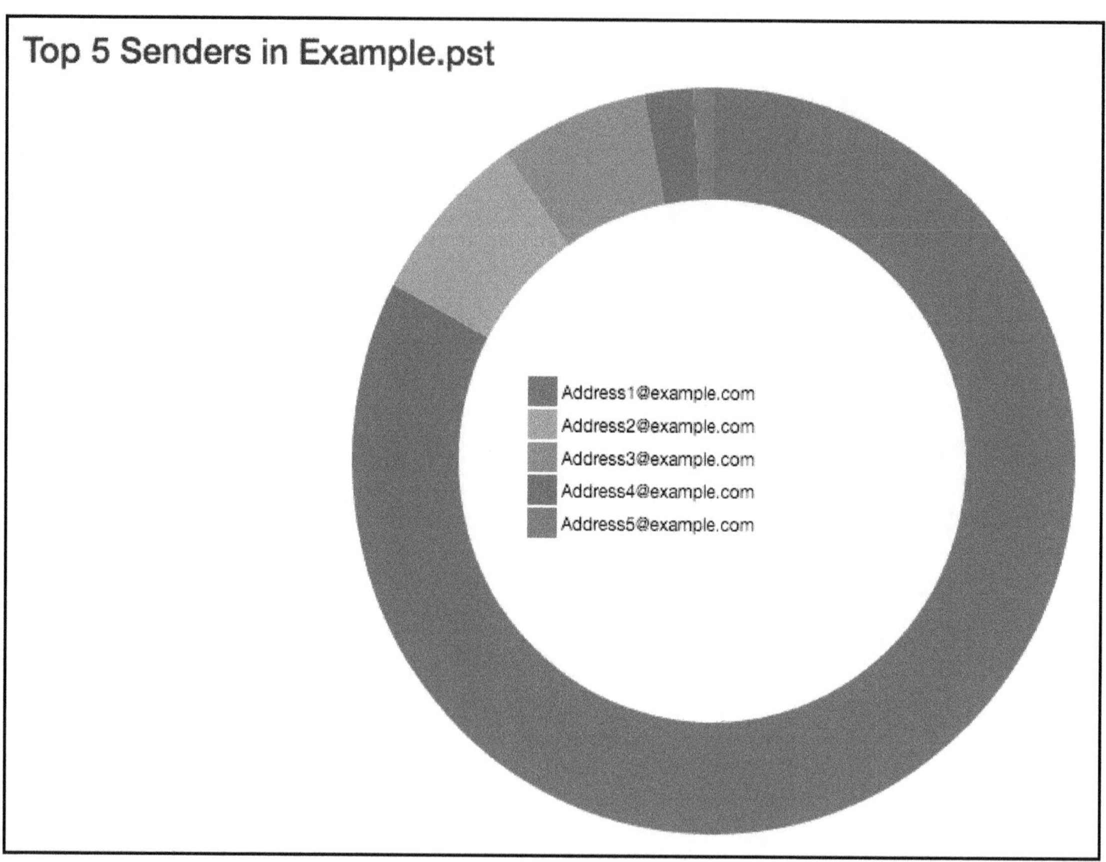

Lastly, the following heat map aggregates all emails into hour-long cells for each day. This is very useful in identifying trends in the dataset.

For example, in this case, we can quickly identify that most emails are sent or received early in the morning and particularly at 6 AM on Tuesdays. The bar at the bottom of the graphic indicates the number of emails. For example, the color of the cell for 6 AM Tuesdays indicates that more than 1,896 emails were sent or received during that time:

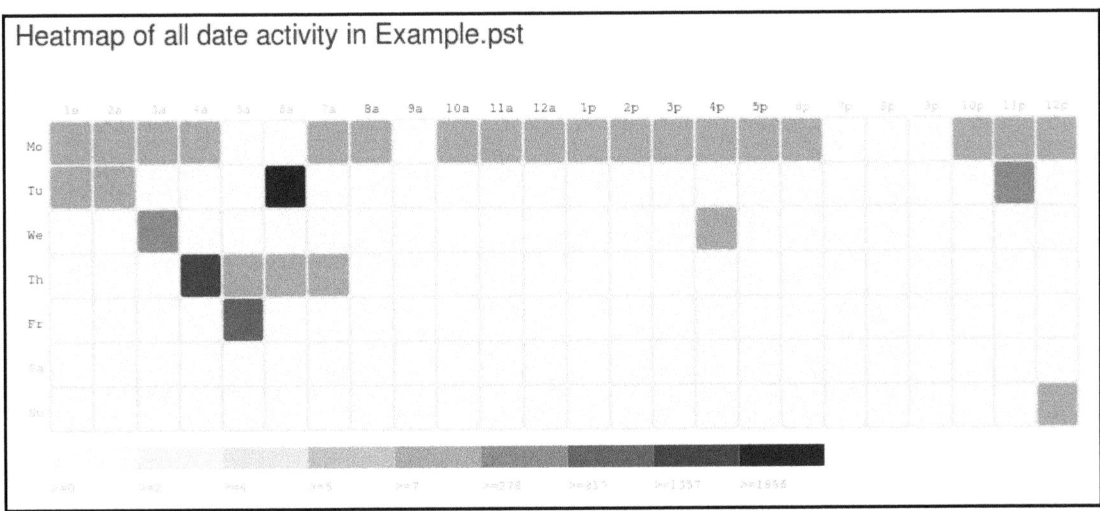

Running the script

With our code complete, both the script and the HTML template, we're ready to execute the code! In our Ubuntu environment, we'll need to run the following command and provide our PST for analysis. If your Ubuntu machine has a configured web server, then the output could be placed in the web directory and served as a website for other users to view when visiting the server.

If you plan on using the Docker container method to run this code, you'll need to copy the PST file into your container using a command such as the one shown in the following. Please note that the following syntax is `docker cp src_file container_name:/path/on/container` and additional functionality is described with `docker cp --help`:

```
$ docker cp sample.pst pst_parser:/opt/book
```

Now that our PST is located within our container; we can run our script as follows:

```
root@4583085379ce:/opt/book# python pst_indexer.py sample.pst /var/www/html
2018-11-30 16:10:01,336 <module>              INFO     Starting PST Indexer v. 20181027
2018-11-30 16:10:01,336 <module>              DEBUG    System linux2
2018-11-30 16:10:01,337 <module>              DEBUG    Version 2.7.15rc1 (default, Nov 1
2 2018, 14:31:15)  [GCC 7.3.0]
2018-11-30 16:10:01,337 <module>              INFO     Starting Script
2018-11-30 16:10:01,337 main                  DEBUG    Opening PST for processing...
2018-11-30 16:10:01,379 main                  DEBUG    Starting traverse of PST structur
e...
2018-11-30 16:10:01,381 check_for_msgs        DEBUG    Processing Folder: SPAM Search Fo
lder 2
2018-11-30 16:10:01,381 folder_report         WARNING  Empty message not processed
2018-11-30 16:10:01,382 check_for_msgs        DEBUG    Processing Folder: Deleted Items
2018-11-30 16:10:01,415 check_for_msgs        DEBUG    Processing Folder: Inbox
2018-11-30 16:10:03,491 check_for_msgs        DEBUG    Processing Folder: Outbox
2018-11-30 16:10:03,491 folder_report         WARNING  Empty message not processed
2018-11-30 16:10:03,492 check_for_msgs        DEBUG    Processing Folder: Sent Items
2018-11-30 16:10:03,497 check_for_msgs        DEBUG    Processing Folder: Calendar
2018-11-30 16:10:03,503 check_for_msgs        DEBUG    Processing Folder: Contacts
2018-11-30 16:10:03,504 folder_report         WARNING  Empty message not processed
2018-11-30 16:10:03,505 check_for_msgs        DEBUG    Processing Folder: Journal
2018-11-30 16:10:03,506 folder_report         WARNING  Empty message not processed
2018-11-30 16:10:03,506 check_for_msgs        DEBUG    Processing Folder: Notes
2018-11-30 16:10:03,507 folder_report         WARNING  Empty message not processed
2018-11-30 16:10:03,508 check_for_msgs        DEBUG    Processing Folder: Tasks
2018-11-30 16:10:03,508 folder_report         WARNING  Empty message not processed
2018-11-30 16:10:03,509 check_for_msgs        DEBUG    Processing Folder: Drafts
2018-11-30 16:10:03,509 folder_report         WARNING  Empty message not processed
2018-11-30 16:10:03,511 check_for_msgs        DEBUG    Processing Folder: Microsoft at H
ome
2018-11-30 16:10:03,525 check_for_msgs        DEBUG    Processing Folder: Microsoft at W
ork
2018-11-30 16:10:03,532 check_for_msgs        DEBUG    Processing Folder: MSNBC News
2018-11-30 16:10:03,595 check_for_msgs        DEBUG    Processing Folder: RSS Feeds
2018-11-30 16:10:03,596 folder_report         WARNING  Empty message not processed
2018-11-30 16:10:03,597 check_for_msgs        DEBUG    Processing Folder: Junk E-mail
2018-11-30 16:10:03,614 check_for_msgs        DEBUG    Processing Folder: Top of Persona
l Folders
2018-11-30 16:10:03,615 folder_report         WARNING  Empty message not processed
2018-11-30 16:10:03,618 check_for_msgs        DEBUG    Processing Folder: All Messages
2018-11-30 16:10:03,618 folder_report         WARNING  Empty message not processed
2018-11-30 16:10:03,619 check_for_msgs        DEBUG    Processing Folder: Search Root
```

The preceding screenshot shows us using `/var/www/html` as our output directory. This means that if we're running the `lighttpd` service on our Docker container, we'll be able to browse to the container's IP address and view the content in a browser on our system. You'll need to run `docker container ls pst_parser` to get the correct port that the web server can be found at.

Additional challenges

For this project, we invite you to implement some improvements that will make our script more versatile. As mentioned earlier in the chapter, `pypff` currently doesn't natively support the extraction or direct interaction with attachments. We can, however, call the `pffexport` and `pffinfo` tools within our Python script to do so. We recommend looking at the subprocess module to accomplish this. To extend this further, how can we connect this with the code covered in previous chapter ? What type of data might become available once we have access to attachments?

Consider methods that would allow a user to provide filtering options to collect specific messages of interest rather than the entire PST. A library that may assist in providing additional configuration options to the user is `ConfigParser` and can be installed with `pip`.

Finally, another challenge would be seeing improvements in the HTML report by adding additional charts and graphs. One example might be to parse `transit_headers` and extract the IP addresses. Using these IP addresses, you could geolocate them and plot them on a map with the D3.js library. This kind of information can increase the usefulness of our reports by squeezing out as much information as possible from all potential data points.

Summary

Email files contain a large amount of valuable information, allowing forensic examiners to gain greater insight into communications and the activity of users over time. Using open source libraries, we're able to explore PST files and extract information about the messages and folders within. We also examined the content and metadata of messages to gather additional information about frequent contacts, common words, and abnormal hot spots of activity. Through this automated process, we can gather a better understanding of the data we review and begin to identify hidden trends. The code for this project can be downloaded from GitHub or Packt, as described in the *Preface*.

Identifying hidden information is very important in all investigations and is one of the many reasons that data recovery is an important cornerstone in the forensic investigation process.

In the next chapter, we'll cover how to recover data from a difficult source, databases. Using several Python libraries, we'll be able to recover data that might otherwise be lost and gain valuable insights into records that're no longer tracked by the database.

12
Recovering Transient Database Records

In this chapter, we will revisit SQLite databases and examine a type of journaling file called a **Write Ahead Log** (**WAL**). Due to the complexity of the underlying structure, parsing a WAL file is a more difficult task than our previous work with SQLite databases. There are no existing modules that we can leverage to directly interact with the WAL file in the same way we used `sqlite3` or `peewee` with SQLite databases. Instead, we'll rely on the struct library and our ability to understand binary files.

Once we've successfully parsed the WAL file, we will leverage the regular expression library, `re`, in Python to identify potentially relevant forensic artifacts. Lastly, we briefly introduce another method of creating progress bars using the third-party `tqdm` library. With a few lines of code, we'll have a functioning progress bar that can provide feedback of program execution to the user.

The WAL file can contain data that's no longer present or not yet been added to the SQLite database. It can also contain previous copies of altered records and give a forensic investigator an idea of how the database changed over time.

We will explore the following topics in this chapter:

- Parsing complex binary files
- Learning about and utilizing regular expressions to locate specified patterns of data
- Creating a simple progress bar in a few lines of code
- Using the built-in Python debugger, `pdb`, to troubleshoot code quickly

The code for this chapter was developed and tested using Python 2.7.15 and Python 3.7.1.

SQLite WAL files

When analyzing SQLite databases, the examiner might come across additional temporary files. There are nine types of temporary SQLite files:

- Rollback journals
- Master journals
- Statement journals
- WAL
- Shared-memory files
- TEMP databases
- Views and subqueries materializations
- Transient indices
- Transient databases

For more details on these files, refer to `https://www.sqlite.org/tempfiles.html`, which describes these files in greater detail. The WAL is one of these temporary files and is involved in the atomic commit and rollback scenarios. Only databases that have set their journaling mode to WAL will use the write ahead log method. The following SQLite command is required to configure a database to use WAL journaling:

```
PRAGMA journal_mode=WAL;
```

The WAL file is created in the same directory as the SQLite database with `-wal` appended to the original SQLite database filename. When a connection is made to the SQLite database, a WAL file is temporarily created. This WAL file will contain any changes made to the database while leaving the original SQLite database unaffected. Advantages of using WAL files include concurrent and speedier read/write operations. Specifics on the WAL file can be read at `https://www.sqlite.org/wal.html`:

Name	Date Modified	Size
Ch11.md	Today, 5:35 PM	3 KB
Code	Today, 3:21 PM	--
Images	Today, 1:14 PM	--
superuser.sqlite	Today, 5:36 PM	45 KB
superuser.sqlite-shm	Today, 5:37 PM	33 KB
superuser.sqlite-wal	Today, 5:37 PM	Zero bytes

By default, records within the WAL file are committed to the original database when either the WAL file reaches 1,000 pages or the last connection to the database closes.

WAL files are forensically relevant for two reasons:

- Reviewing database activity overtime
- Recovering deleted or altered records

The creators of Epilog, an advanced SQLite carving tool, have a well-written article detailing the specific forensic implications of WAL files at `https://digitalinvestigation.wordpress.com/2012/05/04/the-forensic-implications-of-sqlites-write-ahead-log/`. With an understanding of what makes WAL files important, why they are used, and their forensic relevance, let's examine their underlying structure.

WAL format and technical specifications

A WAL file is a collection of frames with embedded B-tree pages that correspond to pages in the actual database. We aren't going to get into the nitty-gritty of how B-trees work. Instead, let's focus on some of the important byte offsets of various structures of interest, so that we can have a better understanding of the code and, in doing so, we'll further exemplify the forensic relevance of WAL files.

The main components of a WAL file include the following:

- WAL header (32 bytes)
- WAL frames (page size)
- Frame header (24 bytes)
- Page header (8 bytes)
- WAL cells (variable length)

Note that the WAL frame size is dictated by the page size, which can be extracted from the WAL header.

The following diagram shows the structure of a WAL file at a high level:

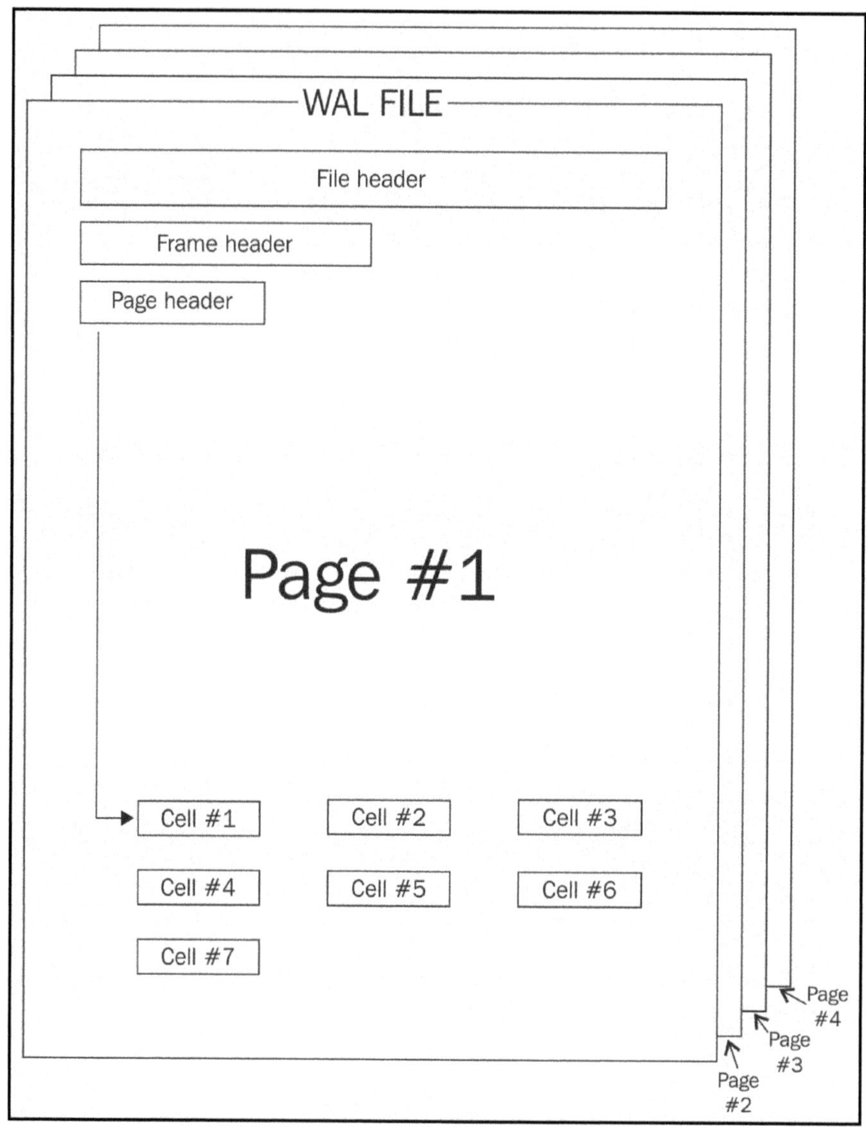

Let's take a look at each of the high-level categories of the WAL file. Some of these structures are described at `https://www.sqlite.org/fileformat2.html`.

The WAL header

The 32-byte WAL header contains properties such as the page size, number of checkpoints, size of the WAL file, and indirectly, number of frames in the WAL file. The following table details the byte offset and description of the 8 big-endian 32-bit integers stored in the header:

Byte offset	Value	Description
0-3	File signature	This is either `0x377F0682` or `0x377F0683`.
4-7	File version	This is the WAL format version, which is currently 3007000.
8-11	Database page size	This is the size of the page within the database, which is usually 1024 or 4096.
12-15	Checkpoint number	This is the number of commits that have occurred.
16-19	Salt-1	This is a random integer that is incremented by one with each commit.
20-23	Salt-2	This is a random integer that changes with each commit.
24-27	Checksum-1	This is the first part of the header checksum.
28-31	Checksum-2	This is the second part of header checksum.

The file signature should always be either `0x377F0682` or `0x377F0683`. The database page size is a very important value as this allows us to calculate how many frames are present in the WAL file. For example, there are 5 frames in a 20,632 byte WAL file using 4,096 byte pages. To calculate the number of frames properly, we need to account for the 32 byte WAL header and the 24-byte WAL frame header in the following equation:

```
(WAL File Size - 32) / (WAL Page Size + 24)
20,600 / 4,120 = 5 frames
```

The checkpoint number indicates how many commits have been triggered, either automatically, or manually by executing PRAGMA `wal_checkpoint`. Now, let's focus on the Salt-1 value. When it comes to creating a timeline of database activity, this is the most important value in the header. The Salt-1 value increments with each commit. In addition to that, each frame stores the current salt values in its own header at the time of the commit. If a record was modified and recommitted, the newer record would have a larger Salt-1 value than the previous version of the record. Therefore, we might have multiple snapshots of a given record in time within the WAL file.

Let's pretend we have a database containing one table, storing data related to employee names, positions, salaries, and so on. Early on, we have an entry for Peter Parker, a 23-year old freelance photographer making $45,000. A few commits later, Parker's salary changes to $150,000 and within the same commit Parker's name is updated to Spiderman:

Frame	Salt-1	Row ID	Employee name	Position	Salary
0	-977652151	123	Spiderman?	Freelance	150,000
1	-977652151	123	Peter Parker	Freelance	150,000
2	-977652150	123	Peter Parker	Freelance	45,000

Because these entries share the same **Row ID**, we know that we're dealing with three different versions of record 123 in the main table. To identify the most recent version of this record, we need to examine the Salt-1 value. Based on our discussion earlier and the Salt-1 values of the records, we know that the records in Frame 0 and 1 are the most recent records and that there have been two commits since the record was first added to the database.

How do we know which of the records in Frames 0 and 1 is the most recent? Dealing with the scenario where we have two records in the same commit, the one in an earlier frame is regarded as the most recent. This is because the WAL file adds new frames to the beginning of the file rather than the end. Therefore, the record in Frame 0 is the most recent and the record in Frame 2 is the oldest.

Note that you can have more than one record per frame. Newer records are found at the beginning of the frame.

In the database, we'll only see the most recent version of the record, but in the WAL file, we can see previous versions. As long as the WAL file exists, we would still see this information, even if the record with Row ID of 123 is deleted from the main database.

The WAL frame

The WAL frame is essentially a B-tree structured page with a frame header. The frame header contains 6 big-endian 32-bit integers:

Byte offset	Value	Description
0-3	Page number	This is the frame or page number in the WAL file.
4-7	Database Size	This is the size of the database in pages for commit records.
8-11	Salt-1	This is copied from the WAL header at the time of writing the frame.
12-15	Salt-2	This is copied from the WAL header at the time of writing the frame.
16-19	Checksum-1	This is the cumulative checksum including this frame.
20-23	Checksum-2	This is the second part of the checksum.

The Salt-1 value is simply the Salt-1 value in the WAL header at the time of creating the frame. We used this value stored in the frame to determine the time of events in the previous example. The page number is an integer starting at zero, where zero is the first frame in the WAL file.

Following the frame header are the contents of a single page in the database, starting with the page header. The page header consists of two 8-bit and three 16-bit big-endian integers:

Byte offset	Value	Description
0	B-Tree flag	This is the type of B-tree node
1-2	Freeblocks	This is the number of freeblocks in the page.
3-4	Cell count	This is the number of cells in the page.
5-6	Cell offset	This is the byte offset to the first cell relative to the start of this header.
7	Fragments	These are the number of fragmented freeblocks in the page.

With this information, we now know how many cells we're dealing with and the offset to the first cell. Following this header are *N* big-endian 16-bit integers specifying the offset for each of the cells. The cell offsets are relative to the start of the page header.

The WAL cell and varints

Each cell is made up of the following components:

- Payload length (varint)
- Row ID (varint)
- Payload header:
    - Payload header length (varint)
    - Array of serial types (varints)
- Payload

The payload length describes the overall length of the cell. The Row ID is the unique key in the actual database corresponding to this record. The serial types array in the payload header contains the length and type of data in the payload. We can subtract the payload length by the payload header length to determine how many bytes of the cell is actually recorded data.

Notice that most of these values are varints, or variable length integers. Varints in SQLite are integers that can be anywhere from 1 to 9 bytes in size based on the first bit of each byte. If the first bit is set, that is, a value of 1, then the next byte is a part of the varint. This continues until you have a 9 byte varint or the first bit of a byte isn't set. The first bit isn't set for all 8-bit integers less than 128. This allows large numbers to be stored flexibly within this file format. More details on varints is available at `https://www.sqlite.org/src4/doc/trunk/www/varint.wiki`.

For example, if the first byte that's processed is `0x03` or `0b00000011`, we know the varint is just one-byte long and has the value of 3. If the first byte that's processed is `0x9A` or `0b10011010`, then the first bit is set and the varint is at least two-bytes long depending on the next byte, using the same decision making process. For our purposes, we will only support varints up to 2 bytes in length. A detailed tutorial on parsing a WAL file can be read at `http://www.forensicsfromthesausagefactory.blogspot.com/2011/05/analysis-of-record-structure-within.html`. It's highly recommended to use a hex editor and parse a page by hand before attempting to develop the code. Handling varints can be a lot easier through examination in a hex editor and helps cement your understanding of the database structure.

Most of the varints are found in the serial types array. This array immediately follows the payload header length and has a value of 1. The resulting table of varint values dictate the size and data type of the cells:

Varint value	Size (bytes)	Data type
0	0	Null
1	1	8-bit integer
2	2	Big-endian 16-bit integer
3	3	Big-endian 24-bit integer
4	4	Big-endian 32-bit integer
5	6	Big-endian 48-bit integer
6	8	Big-endian 64-bit integer
7	8	Big-endian 64-bit float
8	0	Integer constant: 0
9	0	Integer constant: 1
10, 11		Not used
X >= 12 and even	(X-12)/2	BLOB of length (X-12)/2
X >= 13 and odd	(X-13)/2	String of length (X-13)/2

The payload begins immediately following the final serial type. Let's look at how we can use varints to properly parse the contents of the payload properly. For example, if given the following serial types: 0, 2, 6, 8, and 25, we would expect a 16-byte payload containing a `Null` value, a 2-byte 16-bit integer, an 8-byte 64-bit integer, a constant 0, and a 6-byte string. The size of the string is calculated by the equation (25-13) / 2. The following pseudocode highlights this process:

```
Serial Types = 0, 2, 6, 8, and 25
Payload = 0x166400000009C5BA3649737069646572
Split_Payload = N/A , 0x1664, 0x00000009C5BA3649, N/A, 0x737069646572
Converted_Payload = Null, 5732, 163953206, 0, "spider"
```

The preceding example illustrates how the 16-byte payload would be decoded using the known serial types. We will employ this same approach when developing our program. Notice that serial types 0, 8, and 9 don't require any space in the payload as their values are static.

Manipulating large objects in Python

Before developing any script, especially one that deals with a large and complicated structure, it's vital to choose the appropriate data type to work with. For our solution, we will use dictionaries and ordered dictionaries. The difference between a dictionary and an ordered dictionary is that ordered dictionaries preserve the order in which items are added. This feature isn't essential for our script and is merely used as a convenience.

A dictionary allows us to map the structures of the WAL file as key-value pairs. In the end, we'll create a large nested dictionary object, which could easily be saved as a JSON file for use with other programs. Another benefit of this data type is that we can navigate through multiple dictionaries by descriptive keys. This can be used to compartmentalize between different sections of the WAL file and will help keep processed data organized. This covers all of the high-level details we need to know about to write our WAL file parsing script. Before doing so, let's briefly introduce regular expressions and the `tqdm` progress bar module.

Regular expressions in Python

Regular expressions allow us to identify patterns of data by using generic search patterns. For example, searching for all possible phone numbers of the `XXX-XXX-XXXX` type appearing in a document can be easily accomplished by one regular expression. We're going to create a regular expression module that will run a set of default expressions or a user-supplied expression against the processed WAL data. The purpose of the default expressions will be to identify relevant forensic information such as URLs or **Personally Identifiable Information** (**PII**).

While this section is not a primer on regular expression by any means, we'll briefly touch on the basics so that we can understand its advantages and the regular expressions used in the code. In Python, we use the `re` module to run regular expressions against strings. First, we must compile the regular expression and then check whether there are any matches in the string:

```
>>> import re
>>> phone = '214-324-5555'
>>> expression = r'214-324-5555'
>>> re_expression = re.compile(expression)
>>> if re_expression.match(phone): print(True)
...
True
```

Using the identical string as our expression results in a positive match. However, this would not capture other phone numbers. Regular expressions can use a variety of special characters that either represent a subgroup of characters or how the preceding elements are interpreted. We use these special characters to refer to multiple sets of characters and create a generic search pattern.

Square brackets, `[]`, are used to indicate a range of characters such as `0` through `9` or `a` through `z`. Using curly braces, `{n}`, after a regular expression requires that `n` copies of the preceding regular expression must be matched to be considered valid. Using these two special characters, we can create a much more generic search pattern:

```
>>> expression = r'[0-9]{3}-[0-9]{3}-[0-9]{4}'
```

This regular expression matches anything of the `XXX-XXX-XXXX` pattern containing only integers 0 through 9. This wouldn't match phone numbers such as `+1 800.234.5555`. We can build more complicated expressions to include those types of patterns.

Another example we'll take a look at is matching credit card numbers. Fortunately, there exist standard regular expressions for some of the major cards such as Visa, MasterCard, American Express, and so on. The following is the expression we could use for identifying any Visa card. The variable, `expression_1`, matches any number starting with four followed by any 15 digits (0-9). The second expression, `expression_2`, matches any number starting with 4 followed by any 15 digits (0-9) that are optionally separated by a space or dash:

```
>>> expression_1 = r'^4\d{15}$'
>>> expression_2 = r'^4\d{3}([\ \  -]?)\d{4}\1\d{4}\1\d{4}$'
```

For the first expression, we've introduced three new special characters: `^`, `d`, and `$`. The caret (`^`) asserts that the starting position of the string is at the beginning. Likewise, `$` requires that the end position of the pattern is the end of the string or line. Together, this pattern would only match if our credit card is the only element on the line. The `d` character is an alias for [0-9]. This expression could capture a credit card number such as 4111111111111111. Note that, with regular expressions, we use the `r` prefix to create a raw string which ignores backslashes as Python escape characters. Because regular expressions use backslashes as an escape character, we would have to use double backslashes wherever one is present so Python doesn't interpret it as an escape character for itself.

In the second expression, we use parentheses and square brackets to optionally match a space or dash between quartets. Notice the backslash, which acts as an escape for the space, and dash, which are themselves special characters in regular expressions. If we didn't use the backslash here, the interpreter wouldn't realize we meant to use the literal space and dash rather than their special meaning in regular expressions. We can use 1 after we define our pattern in parentheses rather than rewriting it each time. Again, because of `^` and `$`, this pattern will only match if it's the only element on the line or entire string. This expression would capture Visa cards such as 4111-1111-1111-1111 and capture anything `expression_1` would match.

Mastering regular expressions allow a user to create very thorough and comprehensive patterns. For the purpose of this chapter, we'll stick to fairly simple expressions to accomplish our tasks. As with any pattern matching, there's the possibility of generating false positives as a result of throwing large datasets at the pattern.

TQDM – a simpler progress bar

The `tqdm` module (version 4.23.2) can create a progress bar with any Python iterator:

```
C:\>python
Python 3.5.1 (v3.5.1:37a07cee5969, Dec  6 2015, 01:38:48) [MSC v.1900 32 bit (I
ntel)] on win32
Type "help", "copyright", "credits" or "license" for more information.
>>> from tqdm import tqdm
>>> from time import sleep
>>> for x in tqdm(range(100)):
...     sleep(1)
...
  8%|###2                                     | 8/100 [00:08<01:32,  1.00s/it]
```

In the preceding example, we wrapped an iterator that was created by `range(100)` around `tqdm`. That alone creates the progress bar that's displayed in the image. An alternative method, using the `trange()` function, makes our task even simpler. We'll use this module to create a progress bar for processing each WAL frame.

The following code creates the same progress bar, as shown in the previous screenshot. `trange()` is an alias for `tqdm(xrange())` and makes creating a progress bar even simpler:

```
>>> from tqdm import trange
>>> from time import sleep
>>> for x in trange(100):
...     sleep(1)
```

Parsing WAL files – wal_crawler.py

Now that we understand how a WAL file is structured and what data type we'll use to store data, we can begin planning the script. As we're working with a large binary object, we'll make great use of the `struct` library. We first introduced `struct` in `Chapter 6`, *Extracting Artifacts from Binary Files*, and have used it whenever dealing with binary files. Therefore, we won't repeat the basics of `struct` in this chapter.

The goal of our `wal_crawler.py` script is to parse the content of the WAL file, extract and write the cell content to a CSV file, and, optionally, run regular expression modules against the extracted data. This script is considered more advanced due to the complexity of the underlying object we're parsing. However, all we're doing here is applying what we've learned in the previous chapters at a larger scale:

```
002 from __future__ import print_function
003 import argparse
004 import binascii
005 import logging
006 import os
007 import re
008 import struct
009 import sys
010 from collections import namedtuple
011 if sys.version_info[0] == 2:
012     import unicodecsv as csv
013 elif sys.version_info[0] == 3:
014     import csv
015 
016 from tqdm import trange
```

As with any script we've developed, in lines 1-11 we import all modules we'll use for this script. Most of these modules we've encountered before in the previous chapters and are used in the same context. We'll use the following modules:

- `binascii`: This is used to convert data that's read from the WAL file into hexadecimal format
- `tqdm`: This is used to create a simple progress bar
- `namedtuple`: This data structure from the collections module will simply be the process of creating multiple dictionary keys and values when using the `struct.unpack()` function

The `main()` function will validate the WAL file input, parse the WAL file header, and then iterate through each frame and process it with the `frame_parser()` function. After all of the frames have been processed, the `main()` function optionally runs the regular expression `regular_search()` function and writes the processed data to a CSV file with the `csv_writer()` function:

```
def main()
...
def frame_parser():
...
def cell_parser():
...
def dict_helper():
...
def single_varint():
...
def multi_varint():
...
def type_helper():
...
def csv_writer():
...
def regular_search():
```

The `frame_parser()` function parses each frame and executes further validation by identifying the type of B-trees. There are four types of B-trees in a database: `0x0D`, `0x05`, `0x0A`, and `0x02`. In this script, we're only interested in 0x0D type frames and will not process the others. This is because `0x0D` B-trees contain both the Row ID and payload, whereas other tree types contain one or the other. After validating the frame, the `frame_parser()` function processes each cell with the `cell_parser()` function.

The `cell_parser()` function is responsible for processing each cell and all of its components, including the payload length, Row ID, payload header, and payload. Both the `frame_parser()` and `cell_parser()` functions rely on various helper functions to perform their tasks.

The `dict_helper()` helper function returns `OrderedDictionary` from a tuple. This function allows us to process and store struct results in a database on one line. The `single_varint()` and `multi_varint()` functions are used to process single and multiple varints, respectively. Finally, the `type_helper()` function processes the serial type array and interprets the raw data into the appropriate data types:

```
if __name__ == '__main__':

    parser = argparse.ArgumentParser(description=__description__,
```

```
484                     epilog='Developed by ' +
485                     __author__ + ' on ' +
486                     __date__)
487
488     parser.add_argument('WAL', help='SQLite WAL file')
489     parser.add_argument('OUTPUT_DIR', help='Output Directory')
490     parser.add_argument('-r', help='Custom regular expression')
491     parser.add_argument('-m', help='Run regular expression module',
492     action='store_true')
493     parser.add_argument('-l', help='File path of log file')
494     args = parser.parse_args()
```

On line 483, we create our argument parser, specifying the required input values, the WAL file and output directory, and optional input values, executing pre-built or custom regular expressions and log output path. On lines 496 through 508, we perform the same log setup that we used in the previous chapters:

```
496     if args.l:
497         if not os.path.exists(args.l):
498             os.makedirs(args.l)
499         log_path = os.path.join(args.l, 'wal_crawler.log')
500     else:
501         log_path = 'wal_crawler.log'
502     logging.basicConfig(filename=log_path, level=logging.DEBUG,
503                         format=('%(asctime)s | %(levelname)s | '
504                         '%(message)s'), filemode='a')
505
506     logging.info('Starting Wal_Crawler')
507     logging.debug('System ' + sys.platform)
508     logging.debug('Version ' + sys.version)
```

Before executing the `main()` function, we perform some sanity checks and validate the supplied input. On line 510, we check and, optionally, create the output directory if it doesn't exist. Before executing the `main()` function, we validate the input file by checking whether the input actually exists and whether it's a file by using the `os.path.exists()` and `os.path.isfile()` functions. Otherwise, we write an error message to the console and log before exiting the program. Within the `main()` function, we'll further validate the WAL file:

```
510     if not os.path.exists(args.OUTPUT_DIR):
511         os.makedirs(args.OUTPUT_DIR)
512
513     if os.path.exists(args.WAL) and os.path.isfile(args.WAL):
514         main(args.WAL, args.OUTPUT_DIR, r=args.r, m=args.m)
515     else:
516         msg = 'Supplied WAL file does not exist or isn't a file'
517         print('[-]', msg)
```

```
        logging.error(msg)
        sys.exit(1)
```

The following flow diagram highlights the interactions between the different functions and illustrates how our code processes the WAL file:

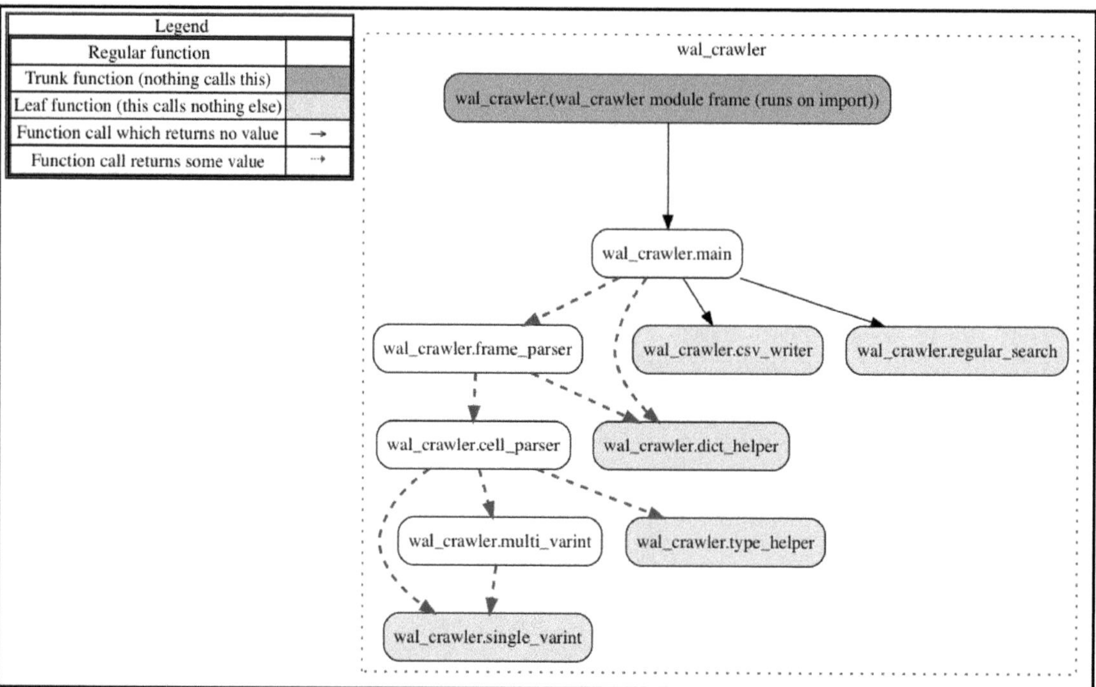

Understanding the main() function

This function is more complicated than our typical `main()` function and starts to parse the WAL file rather than act as a controller for the script. In this function, we will perform file validation, parse the WAL file header, identify the number of frames in the file, and call the function to process those frames:

```
def main(wal_file, output_dir, **kwargs):
    """
    The main function parses the header of the input file and
    identifies the WAL file. It then splits the file into the
    appropriate frames and send them for processing. After
    processing, if applicable, the regular expression modules are
    ran. Finally the raw data output is written to a CSV file.
```

```
062     :param wal_file: The filepath to the WAL file to be processed
063     :param output_dir: The directory to write the CSV report to.
064     :return: Nothing.
065     """
```

On line 70, we create the `wal_attributes` dictionary, which is the dictionary that we'll expand as we parse the WAL file. Initially, it stores the file size, and two empty dictionaries for the file header and the frames. Next, we open the input file in `rb` mode, or read binary mode, and read the first 32 bytes as the file header. On line 79, we try to parse the header and add all of the keys and their values to the header dictionary. This performs another sanity check as struct will throw an error if the file is less than 32 bytes long. We use `>4s7i` as our string to unpack the values pulling out a 4 byte string and seven 32-bit big-endian integers (the endianness is specified by > in the format string):

```
066     msg = 'Identifying and parsing file header'
067     print('[+]', msg)
068     logging.info(msg)
069
070     wal_attributes = {'size': os.path.getsize(wal_file),
071     'header': {}, 'frames': {}}
072     with open(wal_file, 'rb') as wal:
073
074         # Parse 32-byte WAL header.
075         header = wal.read(32)
076
077         # If file is less than 32 bytes long: exit wal_crawler.
078         try:
079             wal_attributes['header'] = dict_helper(header,'>4s7i',
080             namedtuple('struct',
081             'magic format pagesize checkpoint '
082             'salt1 salt2 checksum1 checksum2'))
083         except struct.error as e:
084             logging.error('STRUCT ERROR:', e.message)
085             print('[-]', e.message + '. Exiting..')
086             sys.exit(2)
```

Notice the use of the `dict_helper()` function. We'll explain how exactly this function works in a later section, however, it allows us to parse the data read from the WAL file with struct and return `OrderedDict`, which contain the key-value pairs. This significantly cuts down the amount of code necessary to otherwise add each value in the returned struct tuple to the dictionary.

After parsing the WAL header, we can compare the file magic, or signature, against the known values. We use `binascii.hexlify` to convert the raw data into hex. On line 92, we use an `if` statement to compare the `magic_hex` value. If they don't match, we stop program execution. If they do match, we note it in the log and continue processing the WAL file:

```
088     # Do not proceed in the program if the input file isn't a
089     # WAL file.
090     magic_hex = binascii.hexlify(
091     wal_attributes['header']['magic']).decode('utf-8')
092     if magic_hex != "377f0682" and magic_hex != "377f0683":
093         logging.error(('Magic mismatch, expected 0x377f0682 '
094         'or 0x377f0683 | received {}'.format(magic_hex)))
095         print(('[-] File does not have appropriate signature '
096         'for WAL file. Exiting...'))
097         sys.exit(3)
098
099     logging.info('File signature matched.')
100     logging.info('Processing WAL file.')
```

Using the file size, we can calculate the number of frames on line 103. Note that we need to account for the 32 byte WAL header and the 24-byte frame header in addition to the page size within each frame:

```
102     # Calculate number of frames.
103     frames = int((
104     wal_attributes['size'] - 32) / (
105     wal_attributes['header']['pagesize'] + 24))
106     print('[+] Identified', frames, 'Frames.')
```

On line 111, we create our progress bar using `trange` from `tqdm` and begin processing each frame. We first create an index key, represented by `x`, and an empty dictionary for our frame on line 114. This index will ultimately point to the processed data for the frame. Next, we read the 24-byte frame header. On line 116, we parse the six 32-bit big-endian integers from the header and add the appropriate key-value pairs to the dictionary by calling our `dict_helper()` function:

```
108     # Parse frames in WAL file. Create progress bar using
109     # trange(frames) which is an alias for tqdm(xrange(frames)).
110     print('[+] Processing frames...')
111     for x in trange(frames):
112
113         # Parse 24-byte WAL frame header.
114         wal_attributes['frames'][x] = {}
115         frame_header = wal.read(24)
116         wal_attributes['frames'][x]['header'] = dict_helper(
```

```
117                 frame_header, '>6i', namedtuple('struct',
118                 'pagenumber commit salt1'
119                 ' salt2 checksum1'
120                 ' checksum2'))
```

After parsing the frame header, we read the entire frame from our WAL file on line 122. We then pass this frame to the `frame_parser()` function, along with the `wal_attributes` dictionary and `x`, which represents the index of the current frame:

```
121                 # Parse pagesize WAL frame.
122                 frame = wal.read(wal_attributes['header']['pagesize'])
123                 frame_parser(wal_attributes, x, frame)
```

The `frame_parser()` function calls other functions within it, rather than return data and have `main()` call the next function. Once the parsing of the WAL file has completed parsed, the main function calls the `regular_search()` function if the user supplied the `m` or `r` switch and calls the `csv_writer()` function to write the parsed data out to a CSV file for review:

```
125         # Run regular expression functions.
126         if kwargs['m'] or kwargs['r']:
127             regular_search(wal_attributes, kwargs)
128
129         # Write WAL data to CSV file.
130         csv_writer(wal_attributes, output_dir)
```

Developing the frame_parser() function

The `frame_parser()` function is an intermediate function that continues parsing the frame, identifies the number of cells within the frame, and calls the `cell_parser()` function to finish the job:

```
133 def frame_parser(wal_dict, x, frame):
134     """
135     The frame_parser function processes WAL frames.
136     :param wal_dict: The dictionary containing parsed WAL objects.
137     :param x: An integer specifying the current frame.
138     :param frame: The content within the frame read from the WAL
139     file.
140     :return: Nothing.
141     """
```

As we described previously, the WAL page header is the first 8 bytes after the frame header. The page header contains two 8-bit and three 16-bit big-endian integers. In the struct string, `>b3hb`, `b` will parse the 8-bit integer and `h` parses 16-bit integers. With this header parsed, we now know how many cells are within the page:

```
143     # Parse 8-byte WAL page header
144     page_header = frame[0:8]
145     wal_dict['frames'][x]['page_header'] = dict_helper(
146     page_header, '>b3hb', namedtuple('struct',
147     'type freeblocks cells offset'
148     ' fragments'))
```

On line 150, we check whether the type of the frame is `0x0D` (which, when interpreted as a 16-bit integer, will have the value of 13). If the frame isn't of the appropriate type, we log this information and `pop()` the frame from the dictionary before returning the function. We return the function so that it doesn't continue attempting to process a frame we have no interest in:

```
149     # Only want to parse 0x0D B-Tree Leaf Cells
150     if wal_dict['frames'][x]['page_header']['type'] != 13:
151         logging.info(('Found a non-Leaf Cell in frame {}. Popping '
152         'frame from dictionary').format(x))
153         wal_dict['frames'].pop(x)
154         return
```

Regardless, on line 156, we create a new nested dictionary called cells and use it to keep track of our cells in the exact way we did with our frames. We also print the number of identified cells per frame to provide feedback to the user:

```
155     # Parse offsets for "X" cells
156     cells = wal_dict['frames'][x]['page_header']['cells']
157     wal_dict['frames'][x]['cells'] = {}
158     print('[+] Identified', cells, 'cells in frame', x)
159     print('[+] Processing cells...')
```

Lastly, on line 161, we iterate over each cell and parse their offsets before adding it to the dictionary. We know that *N* 2 byte cell offsets begin immediately following the 8-byte page header. We use the start variable, calculated on line 162 for every cell, to identify the starting offset of the cell offset values:

```
161     for y in range(cells):
162         start = 8 + (y * 2)
163         wal_dict['frames'][x]['cells'][y] = {}
164
165         wal_dict['frames'][x]['cells'][y] = dict_helper(
166         frame[start: start + 2], '>h', namedtuple(
167         'struct', 'offset'))
```

On line 163, we create an index key and empty dictionary for our cell. We then parse the cell offset with the `dict_helper()` function and store the contents in the specific cell dictionary. Once the offset is identified, we call the `cell_parser()` function to process the cell and its contents. We pass along the `wal_attributes` dictionary, the `frame` and cell index, `x` and `y`, respectively, and the frame data:

```
        # Parse cell content
        cell_parser(wal_dict, x, y, frame)
```

Processing cells with the cell_parser() function

The `cell_parser()` function is the heart of our program. It's responsible for actually extracting the data stored within the cells. As we'll see, varints add another wrinkle to the code; however, for the most part, we're still ultimately parsing binary structures using struct and making decisions based on those values:

```
def cell_parser(wal_dict, x, y, frame):
    """
    The cell_parser function processes WAL cells.
    :param wal_dict: The dictionary containing parsed WAL objects.
    :param x: An integer specifying the current frame.
    :param y: An integer specifying the current cell.
    :param frame: The content within the frame read from the WAL
    file.
    :return: Nothing.
    """
```

Before we begin to parse the cells, we instantiate a few variables. The index variable, which we created on line 183, is used to keep track of our current location within the cell. Remember that we're no longer dealing with the entire file itself but a subset of it representing a cell. The frame variable is the page size amount of data read from the database itself. For example, if the page size is 1,024, then the frame variable is 1,024 bytes of data, which correspond to a page in the database. The struct module requires that the data parsed is exactly the length of the data types specified in the struct string. Because of these two facts, we need to use string slicing to provide only the data we want to parse with struct:

```
183     index = 0
```

On line 186, we create `cell_root`, which is essentially a shortcut to the nested cell dictionary within the `wal_attributes` dictionary. This isn't just about being lazy; this helps with code readability and reduce the overall clutter by referring to a variable that points to a nested dictionary rather than typing it out each time. For the same reason, we create the `cell_offset` variable on line 187:

```
184     # Create alias to cell_root to shorten navigating the WAL
185     # dictionary structure.
186     cell_root = wal_dict['frames'][x]['cells'][y]
187     cell_offset = cell_root['offset']
```

Starting on line 191, we encounter our first varint in the cell payload length. This varint will dictate the overall size of the cell. To extract the varint, we call the `single_varint()` helper function supplying it a 9 byte slice of data. This function, which we will explain later, will check whether the first byte is greater than or equal to 128; if so, it processes the second byte. In addition to the varint, the `single_varint()` helper function also returns a count of how many bytes the varint was made up of. This allows us to keep track of our current position in the frame data. We use that returned index to parse the row ID varint in a similar fashion:

```
189     # Parse the payload length and rowID Varints.
190     try:
191         payload_len, index_a = single_varint(
192         frame[cell_offset:cell_offset + 9])
193         row_id, index_b = single_varint(
194         frame[cell_offset + index_a: cell_offset + index_a + 9])
195     except ValueError:
196         logging.warn(('Found a potential three-byte or greater '
197         'varint in cell {} from frame {}').format(y, x))
198         return
```

After processing the first two varints, we add the key-value pair to the `wal_attributes` dictionary. On line 204, we update our index variable to maintain our current position in the frame data. Next, we manually extract the 8-bit payload header length value without the `dict_helper()` function. We do this for two reasons:

- We're only processing one value
- Setting `cell_root` equal to the output of `dict_helper()` was found to erase all other keys in the individual cell nested dictionary described by `cell_root`, which, admittedly, isn't ideal

The following code block shows this functionality:

```
200     # Update the index. Following the payload length and rowID is
201     # the 1-byte header length.
202     cell_root['payloadlength'] = payload_len
203     cell_root['rowid'] = row_id
204     index += index_a + index_b
205     cell_root['headerlength'] = struct.unpack('>b',
206     frame[cell_offset + index: cell_offset + index + 1])[0]
```

After parsing the payload length, row ID, and payload header length, we can now parse the serial types array. As a reminder, the serial types array contains *N* varints that is headerlength, 1 bytes long. On line 210, we update the index by 1 to account for the 1 byte header we parsed on line 205. We then extract all of the varints within the appropriate range by calling the `multi_varint()` function. This function returns a tuple containing the list of serial types and the current index. On lines 218 and 219, we update the `wal_attributes` and `index` objects, respectively:

```
208     # Update the index with the 1-byte header length. Next process
209     # each Varint in "headerlength" - 1 bytes.
210     index += 1
211     try:
212         types, index_a = multi_varint(
213         frame[cell_offset +
index:cell_offset+index+cell_root['headerlength']-1])
214     except ValueError:
215         logging.warn(('Found a potential three-byte or greater '
216             'varint in cell {} from frame {}').format(y, x))
217         return
218     cell_root['types'] = types
219     index += index_a
```

Once the serial types array has been parsed, we can begin to extract the actual data stored in the cell. Recall that the cell payload is the difference between the payload length and payload header length. This value calculated on line 224 is used to pass the remaining contents of the cell to the `type_helper()` helper function, which is responsible for parsing the data:

```
221     # Immediately following the end of the Varint headers begins
222     # the actual data described by the headers. Process them using
223     # the typeHelper function.
224     diff = cell_root['payloadlength'] - cell_root['headerlength']
225     cell_root['data'] = type_helper(cell_root['types'],
226     frame[cell_offset + index: cell_offset + index + diff])
```

Writing the dict_helper() function

The `dict_helper()` function is a one-line function, and is less than six lines of documentation. It utilizes the `named_tuple` data structure, which is passed in as the `keys` variable and calls the `_make()` and `_asdict()` functions to create our ordered dictionary after struct parses the values:

```
def dict_helper(data, format, keys):
    """
    The dict_helper function creates an OrderedDictionary from
    a struct tuple.
    :param data: The data to be processed with struct.
    :param format: The struct format string.
    :param keys: A string of the keys for the values in the struct
    tuple.
    :return: An OrderedDictionary with descriptive keys of
    struct-parsed values.
    """
    return keys._asdict(keys._make(struct.unpack(format, data)))
```

As with most compact one-liners, it's possible to lose the meaning of the function as readability starts to decrease when more functions are called in a single line. We're going to introduce and use the built-in Python debugger to take a look at what is going on.

The Python debugger – pdb

Python is great for a multitude of reasons, which we don't need to rehash now. One excellent feature is a built-in debugging module called `pdb`. This module is simple yet incredibly useful for identifying troublesome bugs or to simply look at variables during execution. If you're using an IDE (highly recommended) to develop your scripts, then chances are that there is already built-in debugging support. However, if you develop your code in a simple text editor, have no fear; you can always use `pdb` to debug your code.

In this instance, we're going to examine each component of `dict_helper()` to fully understand the function. We aren't going to cover all of the uses and commands of `pdb`. Instead, we'll illustrate through example, and for additional information, you can refer to `https://docs.python.org/3/library/pdb.html`.

First, we need to modify the existing code and create a debug point in the code that we want to examine. On line 240, we import `pdb` and call `pdb.set_trace()` in one line:

```
240     import pdb; pdb.set_trace()
241     return keys._asdict(keys._make(struct.unpack(format, data)))
```

Using the semicolon allows us to separate multiple statements on a single line. Normally, we wouldn't use this as it impacts readability. However, this is just for testing and will be removed from the final code.

Now, when we execute the code, we see the `pdb` prompt, as displayed in the following screenshot. The `pdb` prompt is similar to the Python interpreter. We can access current variables within scope, for example, `data`, `format`, and `keys`. We can also create our own variables and execute simple expressions:

```
(py3.7.1) C:\book\chapters\chapter_12>python wal_crawler.py places.sqlite-wal
./wal_output
[+] Identifying and parsing file header
> c:\book\chapters\chapter_12\wal_crawler.py(241)dict_helper()
-> return keys._asdict(keys._make(struct.unpack(format, data)))
(Pdb)
```

The first line of the `pdb` prompt contains the location of the file, the current line within the file, and the current function being executed. The second line is the next line of code that's about to be executed. The `Pdb` prompt has the same significance as the >>> prompt in the Python interpreter, and is where we can enter our own input.

In this example, we're parsing the file header as it's the first time that `dict_helper()` is called. If you recall, the struct string we used was `>4s7i`. As we can see in the following example, `unpack()` returns a tuple of results. However, we want to return a dictionary matching all of the values with their associated keys so that we don't have to perform this task manually:

```
(Pdb) struct.unpack(format, data)
('7x7fx06x82', 3007000, 32768, 9, -977652151, 1343711549, 670940632,
650030285)
```

Notice that `keys._make` creates an object with the appropriate field names set for each value. It does this by associating the field names that were supplied when we created the `keys` variable on line 41 to each value in the struct tuple:

```
(Pdb) keys._make(struct.unpack(format, data))
struct(magic='7x7fx06x82', format=3007000, pagesize=32768, checkpoint=9,
salt1=-977652151, salt2=1343711549, checksum1=670940632,
checksum2=650030285)
```

Finally, we can use `pdb` to verify that the `keys._asdict()` function converts our `namedtuple` into an `OrderedDict`, which is what we return:

```
(Pdb) keys._asdict(keys._make(struct.unpack(format, data)))
OrderedDict([('magic', '7x7fx06x82'), ('format', 3007000), ('pagesize',
32768), ('checkpoint', 9), ('salt1', -977652151), ('salt2', 1343711549),
('checksum1', 670940632), ('checksum2', 650030285)])
```

Using `pdb` in this manner allows us to visualize the current state of variables and execute functions individually. This is incredibly useful when your program encounters an error on a particular function as you can execute line by line and function by function until you identify the issue. We recommend you become familiar with `pdb` as it expedites the debugging process and is much more effective than using print statements for troubleshooting. Press q and *Enter* to exit `pdb` and make sure always to remove debug lines from your final code.

Processing varints with the single_varint() function

The `single_varint` function finds the first varint within the supplied data and uses an index to keep track of its current position. When it finds the varint, it returns the value along with the index. This tells the calling function how many bytes the varint was and is used to update its own index:

```
243 def single_varint(data, index=0):
244     """
245     The single_varint function processes a Varint and returns the
246     length of that Varint.
247     :param data: The data containing the Varint (maximum of 9
248     bytes in length as that is the maximum size of a Varint).
249     :param index: The current index within the data.
250     :return: varint, the processed varint value,
251     and index which is used to identify how long the Varint was.
252     """
```

For this script, we've made a simplifying assumption that varints will never be greater than 2 bytes. This is a simplifying assumption and won't be appropriate in all situations. This leaves two possible scenarios:

- The first byte has a decimal value less than 128
- The first byte is greater than or equal to 128

Based on the outcome, one of the following two things will happen. If the byte is greater than or equal to 128, the varint is 2 bytes long. Otherwise, it's only 1 byte in length. On line 256, we use the `ord()` function to convert the value of the byte into an integer:

```
254     # If the decimal value is => 128 -- then first bit is set and
255     # need to process next byte.
256     if ord(data[index:index+1]) >= 128:
257         # Check if there is a three or more byte varint
258         if ord(data[index + 1: index + 2]) >= 128:
259             raise ValueError
```

If the value is greater than 128, we know that the second byte is also required and must apply the following generic formula, where `x` is the first byte and `y` is the second byte:

```
Varint = ((x - 128) * 128) + y
```

We return this value after incrementing the index by 2:

```
        varint = (ord(data[index:index+1]) - 128) * 128 + ord(
        data[index + 1: index + 2])
        index += 2
        return varint, index
```

If the first byte is less than 128, all we must do is return the byte's integer value and increment the index by 1:

```
    # If the decimal value is < 128 -- then first bit isn't set
    # and is the only byte of the Varint.
    else:
        varint = ord(data[index:index+1])
        index += 1
        return varint, index
```

Processing varints with the multi_varint() function

The `multi_varint()` function is a looping function that repeatedly calls `single_varint()` until there are no more varints in the supplied data. It returns a list of varints and an index to the parent function. On lines 282 and 283, we initialize the list of varints and set our local index variable to zero:

```
273 def multi_varint(data):
274     """
275     The multi_varint function is similar to the single_varint
276     function. The difference is that it takes a range of data
277     and finds all Varints within it.
278     :param data: The data containing the Varints.
279     :return: varints, a list containing the processed varint
280     values, and index which is used to identify how long the
281     Varints were.
282     """
283     varints = []
284     index = 0
```

We use a `while` loop to execute until the length of data is equal to 0. In each loop, we call `single_varint()`, append the resulting varint to the list, update the index, and shorten the data using string slicing. By executing line 293 with the size of the varint returned from the `single_varint()` function, we can progressively shorten data until it has a length of 0. Upon reaching this point, we can be assured that we've extracted all varints in the string:

```
286     # Loop forever until all Varints are found by repeatedly
287     # calling singleVarint.
288     while len(data) != 0:
289         varint, index_a = single_varint(data)
290         varints.append(varint)
291         index += index_a
292         # Shorten data to exclude the most recent Varint.
293         data = data[index_a:]
294
295     return varints, index
```

Converting serial types with the type_helper() function

The `type_helper()` function is responsible for extracting the payload based on the types of values in the data. While consisting of many lines of code, it's really no more than a series of conditional statements that, if one is `True`, dictates how the data is processed:

```
298 def type_helper(types, data):
299     """
300     The type_helper function decodes the serial type of the
301     Varints in the WAL file.
302     :param types: The processed values of the Varints.
303     :param data: The raw data in the cell that needs to be
304     properly decoded via its varint values.
305     :return: cell_data, a list of the processed data.
306     """
```

On lines 307 and 308, we create the list that will store the extracted payload data and the index. The index is used to denote the current position within the data. On line 313, we begin iterating over each serial type to check how each should be processed:

```
307     cell_data = []
308     index = 0
```

The first ten types are fairly straightforward. We're using the serial types table to identify the type of data and then using struct to unpack it. Some of the types, such as 0, 8, and 9 are static and don't require us to parse the data or update our index value. Types 3 and 5 are data types that are not supported by struct and require a different method of extraction. Let's take a look at both struct supported and unsupported types to ensure we understand what's happening:

```
310     # Value of type dictates how the data should be processed.
311     # See serial type table in chapter for list of possible
312     # values.
313     for type in types:
314
315         if type == 0:
316             cell_data.append('NULL (RowId?)')
317         elif type == 1:
318             cell_data.append(struct.unpack('>b',
319                 data[index:index + 1])[0])
320             index += 1
321         elif type == 2:
322             cell_data.append(struct.unpack('>h',
323                 data[index:index + 2])[0])
324             index += 2
325         elif type == 3:
326             # Struct does not support 24-bit integer
327             cell_data.append(int(binascii.hexlify(
328                 data[index:index + 3]).decode('utf-8'), 16))
329             index += 3
330         elif type == 4:
331             cell_data.append(struct.unpack(
332                 '>i', data[index:index + 4])[0])
333             index += 4
334         elif type == 5:
335             # Struct does not support 48-bit integer
336             cell_data.append(int(binascii.hexlify(
337                 data[index:index + 6]).decode('utf-8'), 16))
338             index += 6
```

We know from the serial types table that type 6 (on line 339) is a 64-bit big-endian integer. The `q` character in struct parses 64-bit integers making our job relatively simple. We must make sure to supply struct only with the data that makes up the 64-bit integer. We can do this by string slicing with the current index and stopping after 8 bytes. Afterwards, we need to increment the index by 8, so the next type is at the correct starting point.

If struct doesn't support the type of variable, such as is the case for type 3, a 24-bit integer, we need to extract the data in a more round-about fashion. This requires us to use the `binascii.hexlify()` function to convert our data string into hex. We then simply wrap the `int()` object constructor around the hex to convert to its integer value. Notice that we need to specifically tell the `int` function the base of the value being converted, which in this case is base 16 as the value is in hexadecimal:

```
339         elif type == 6:
340             cell_data.append(struct.unpack(
341                 '>q', data[index:index + 8])[0])
342             index += 8
343         elif type == 7:
344             cell_data.append(struct.unpack(
345                 '>d', data[index:index + 8])[0])
346             index += 8
347         # Type 8 == Constant 0 and Type 9 == Constant 1. Neither of
these take up space in the actual data.
348         elif type == 8:
349             cell_data.append(0)
350         elif type == 9:
351             cell_data.append(1)
352         # Types 10 and 11 are reserved and currently not implemented.
```

For types 12 and 13, we must first identify the actual length of the value by applying the appropriate equation. Next, we can simply append the extracted string right into the `cell_data` list. We also need to increment the index by the size of the calculated string:

```
353         elif type > 12 and type % 2 == 0:
354             b_length = int((type - 12) / 2)
355             cell_data.append(data[index:index + b_length])
356             index += b_length
357         elif type > 13 and type % 2 == 1:
358             s_length = int((type - 13) / 2)
359             cell_data.append(
360                 data[index:index + s_length].decode('utf-8'))
361             index += s_length
```

On line 363, we create an else case to catch any unexpected serial types and print and log the error. After all types are processed, the `cell_data` list is returned on line 368:

```
363         else:
364             msg = 'Unexpected serial type: {}'.format(type)
365             print('[-]', msg)
366             logging.error(msg)
367
368     return cell_data
```

Writing output with the csv_writer() function

The `csv_writer()` function is similar to most of our previous CSV writers. A few special considerations need to be made due to the complexity of the data being written to the file. Additionally, we're only writing some of the data out to a file and discarding everything else. Dumping the data out to a serialized data structure, such as JSON, is left to the reader as a challenge. As with any `csv_writer`, we create a list of our headers, open `csvfile`, create our writer object, and write the headers to the first row:

```
def csv_writer(data, output_dir):
    """
    The csv_writer function writes frame, cell, and data to a CSV
    output file.
    :param data: The dictionary containing the parsed WAL file.
    :param output_dir: The directory to write the CSV report to.
    :return: Nothing.
    """
    headers = ['Frame', 'Salt-1', 'Salt-2', 'Frame Offset',
        'Cell', 'Cell Offset', 'ROWID', 'Data']

    out_file = os.path.join(output_dir, 'wal_crawler.csv')

    if sys.version_info[0] == 2:
        csvfile = open(out_file, "wb")
    elif sys.version_info[0] == 3:
        csvfile = open(out_file, "w", newline='',
            encoding='utf-8')

    with csvfile:
        writer = csv.writer(csvfile)
        writer.writerow(headers)
```

Because of our nested structure, we need to create two `for` loops to iterate through the structure. On line 399, we check to see whether the cell actually contained any data. We noticed during development that sometimes empty cells would be generated and are discarded in the output. However, it might be relevant in a particular investigation to include empty cells, in which case we'd remove the conditional statements:

```
394         for frame in data['frames']:
395
396             for cell in data['frames'][frame]['cells']:
397
398             # Only write entries for cells that have data.
399             if ('data' in data['frames'][frame]['cells'][cell].keys()
and
400             len(data['frames'][frame]['cells'][cell]['data']) > 0):
```

If there is data, we calculate the `frame_offset` and `cell_offset` relative to the beginning of the file. The offsets we parsed before were relative to the current position within the file. This relative value wouldn't be very helpful to an examiner who would have to backtrack to find where the relative offset position starts.

For our frame offset, we need to add the file header size (32 bytes), the total page size (frames * page size), and the total frame header size (frames * 24 bytes). The cell offset is a little simpler and is the frame offset plus the frame header size, and the parsed cell offset from the `wal_attributes` dictionary:

```
401                     # Convert relative frame and cell offsets to
402                     # file offsets.
403                     frame_offset = 32 + (
404                         frame * data['header']['pagesize']) + (
405                         frame * 24)
406                         cell_offset = frame_offset + 24 +
data['frames'][frame]['cells'][cell]['offset']
```

Next, we create a list, `cell_identifiers`, on line 411, which will store the row data to write. This list contains the frame number, `salt-1`, `salt-2`, `frame offset`, cell number, `cell offset`, and the row ID:

```
408                     # Cell identifiers include the frame #,
409                     # salt-1, salt-2, frame offset,
410                     # cell #, cell offset, and cell rowID.
411                     cell_identifiers = [frame,
data['frames'][frame]['header']['salt1'],
412                         data['frames'][frame]['header']['salt2'],
413                         frame_offset, cell, cell_offset,
414                         data['frames'][frame]['cells'][cell]['rowid']]
```

Finally, on line 418, we write the row along with the payload data to CSV file writer:

```
416                     # Write the cell_identifiers and actual data
417                     # within the cell
418                     writer.writerow(
419                         cell_identifiers +
data['frames'][frame]['cells'][cell]['data'])
```

If the cell had no payload, then the continue block is executed and we proceed to the next cell. Once the outer for loop finishes executing, that is, all frames are written to the CSV, we flush any remaining buffered content to the CSV and close the handle on the file:

```
                else:
                    continue

        csvfile.flush()
        csvfile.close()
```

An example of the CSV output that might be generated from a WAL file is captured in the following screenshot:

	A	B	C	D	E	F	G	H	I
1	Frame	Salt-1	Salt-2	Frame Offset	Cell	Cell Offset	ROWID	Data	
2	0	-9.78E+08	1.344E+09	32	0	32293	3	NULL (RowId?)	https://www.mozilla.org/en-US/firefox/central/
3	0	-9.78E+08	1.344E+09	32	1	32204	4	NULL (RowId?)	https://www.mozilla.org/en-US/firefox/help/
4	0	-9.78E+08	1.344E+09	32	2	32110	5	NULL (RowId?)	https://www.mozilla.org/en-US/firefox/customize/
5	0	-9.78E+08	1.344E+09	32	3	32023	6	NULL (RowId?)	https://www.mozilla.org/en-US/contribute/
6	0	-9.78E+08	1.344E+09	32	4	31941	7	NULL (RowId?)	https://www.mozilla.org/en-US/about/
7	0	-9.78E+08	1.344E+09	32	5	31887	8	NULL (RowId?)	place:sort=8&maxResults=10
8	0	-9.78E+08	1.344E+09	32	6	31739	9	NULL (RowId?)	place:folder=BOOKMARKS_MENU&folder=UNFILED_B
9	0	-9.78E+08	1.344E+09	32	7	31677	10	NULL (RowId?)	place:type=6&sort=14&maxResults=10

Using regular expression in the regular_search() function

The `regular_search()` function is an optional function. If the user supplies the `-m` or `-r` switches, the function is executed. This function uses regular expressions to identify relevant information within the WAL file and, if identified, print the data to the Terminal:

```
def regular_search(data, options):
    """
    The regular_search function performs either default regular
    expression searches for personal information or custom
    searches based on a supplied regular expression string.
    :param data: The dictionary containing the parsed WAL file.
    :param options: The options dictionary contains custom or
    pre-determined regular expression searching
    :return: Nothing.
    """
```

We'll use a dictionary that contains the regular expression patterns to run. This will make it easy to identify what category of expression, that is, URL or phone number, had a match and print that with the data to provide context.

First, we must identify which switches were specified by the user. If only `args.r` was specified, then we only need to create the regexp dictionary with the supplied custom regular expression. Because either `args.r` or `args.m` were supplied to even reach this function, we know that if the first `if` is `False`, then at least `args.m` must have been supplied:

```
438     msg = 'Initializing regular expression module.'
439     print('\n{}\n[+]'.format('='*20), msg)
440     logging.info(msg)
441     if options['r'] and not options['m']:
442         regexp = {'Custom': options['r']}
443     else:
444         # Default regular expression modules include: Credit card
445         # numbers, SSNs, Phone numbers, URLs, IP Addresses.
446         regexp = {'Visa Credit Card': r'^4\d{3}([\ \-
]?)\d{4}\1\d{4}\1\d{4}$',
447                   'SSN': r'^\d{3}-\d{2}-\d{4}$',
448                   'Phone Number': r'^\d{3}([\ \. \-]?)\d{3}\1\d{4}$',
449                   'URL':
r"(http[s]?://)|(www.)(?:[a-zA-Z]|[0-9]|[$-_@.&+]|[!*\(\),]|(?:%[0-9a-fA-F]
[0-9a-fA-F]))+",
450               'IP Address': r'^\d{1,3}.\d{1,3}.\d{1,3}.\d{1,3}$'}
```

If that's the case, we need to build our regexp dictionary containing our regular expression patterns. By default, we have included our credit card and phone number examples from before, along with the patterns for SSNs, URLs, and IP addresses. Additionally, on line 452, we need to check for the scenario where both `args.r` and `args.m` were passed. If they were, we add the custom expression to our dictionary, which already contains the `args.m` expressions:

```
452         if options['r']:
453             regexp['Custom'] = options['r']
```

For each expression in our dictionary, we need to compile it before we can use the match function. As we compile each expression, we use several more loops to walk through the `wal_attributes` dictionary and check each cell for any matches:

```
455     # Must compile each regular expression before seeing if any
456     # data "matches" it.
457     for exp in regexp.keys():
458         reg_exp = re.compile(regexp[exp])
```

Starting with lines 457, we create a triple `for` loop to get at each individual piece of data. In `csv_writer()`, we only used two `for` loops because we didn't need to interact with each data point. However, in this case, we need to do this to successfully identify matches using regular expressions.

Notice the try and except wrapped around the match function. The match function expects a string or buffer. It will error out if it tries to match the expression to an integer. So, we decided to catch the error and, if encountered, skip to the next piece of data. We could have also solved the issue by casting the datum as a string using the `str()` function:

```
460         for frame in data['frames']:
461
462             for cell in data['frames'][frame]['cells']:
463
464                 for datum in range(len(
465                 data['frames'][frame]['cells'][cell]['data'])):
466                     # TypeError will occur for non-string objects
467                     # such as integers.
468                     try:
469                         match = reg_exp.match(
470
data['frames'][frame]['cells'][cell]['data'][datum])
471                     except TypeError:
472                         continue
473                     # Print any successful match to user.
474                     if match:
475                         msg = '{}: {}'.format(exp,
476
data['frames'][frame]['cells'][cell]['data'][datum])
477                         print('[*]', msg)
478     print('='*20)
```

Executing wal_crawler.py

Now that we've written the script, it's time to actually run it. The simplest way of doing so is to supply the input WAL file and output directory:

```
(py3.7.1) C:\book\chapters\chapter_12>python wal_crawler.py places.sqlite-wal
./wal_output
[+] Identifying and parsing file header
[+] Identified 3 Frames.
[+] Processing frames...
  0%|                                                        | 0/3 [00:00<?, ?it/s][
+] Identified 15 cells in frame 0
[+] Processing cells...
[+] Identified 15 cells in frame 1
[+] Processing cells...
100%|████████████████████████████████████████| 3/3 [00:00<00:00, 602.49it/s]
```

Optionally, we can use the `-m` or `-r` switches to engage the regular expression module. The following screenshot shows an example of what the regular expression output looks like:

```
(py3.7.1) C:\book\chapters\chapter_12>python wal_crawler.py places.sqlite-wal
./wal_output -m
[+] Identifying and parsing file header
[+] Identified 3 Frames.
[+] Processing frames...
  0%|                                                        | 0/3 [00:00<?, ?it/s][
+] Identified 15 cells in frame 0
[+] Processing cells...
[+] Identified 15 cells in frame 1
[+] Processing cells...
100%|████████████████████████████████████████| 3/3 [00:00<00:00, 600.53it/s]

====================
[+] Initializing regular expression module.
[*] URL: https://www.mozilla.org/en-US/firefox/central/
[*] URL: https://www.mozilla.org/en-US/firefox/help/
[*] URL: https://www.mozilla.org/en-US/firefox/customize/
[*] URL: https://www.mozilla.org/en-US/contribute/
[*] URL: https://www.mozilla.org/en-US/about/
```

Note that, when supplying a custom regular expression to run with the `-r` switch, surround the expression with double quotes. If you fail to do so, you might encounter an error due to havoc that was wreaked by the special characters in the regular expression.

Challenge

There are a few directions in which we could take this script. As we've already mentioned, there's a great deal of potentially useful data that we aren't writing out to a file. It might be useful to store the entire dictionary structure in a JSON file so that others can easily import and manipulate the data. This would allow us to utilize the parsed structure in a separate program and create additional reports from it.

Another useful feature we could develop is a timeline report or graphic for the user. This report would list the current contents of each record and then show a progression from the current contents of the records to their older versions or even non-existing records. A tree-diagram or flowchart might be a good means of visualizing change for a particular database record.

Finally, add in a function that supports processing of varint that can be greater than 2 bytes. In our script, we made a simplifying assumption that we were unlikely to encounter a varint greater than 2 bytes. However, it isn't impossible to encounter a larger varint and so it may be worthwhile adding in this functionality.

Summary

In this chapter, we learned the forensic significance of a WAL file and how to parse it. We also briefly touched on how to use regular expressions in Python with the `re` module to create generic search patterns. Lastly, we utilized the `tqdm` module to create a progress bar in one line of code. The code for this project can be downloaded from GitHub or Packt, as described in the *Preface*.

In the next chapter, we'll be combining our knowledge from this entire book into a single framework. We'll design a framework that allows for basic pre-processing of common artifacts that we've covered. We'll demonstrate the framework design and development process and reveal the framework you've been secretly building throughout this book.

13
Coming Full Circle

In this chapter, we will revisit the scripts we've built in the previous chapters to create a prototype forensic framework. This framework will accept an input directory, such as the root folder of a mounted image, and run our plugins against the files to return a series of spreadsheet reports for each plugin.

Up to this point, we've developed standalone scripts in each chapter, never building upon the work in the previous chapters. By developing a framework, we will illustrate how to bring these scripts together and execute them in one context.

In `Chapter 8`, *The Media Age*, we created a miniature framework for parsing various types of embedded metadata. We will borrow from that design and add object-oriented programming to it. Using classes simplifies our framework by creating an abstract object for plugins and writers.

Additionally, in our framework, we will showcase the use of a few external libraries that serve an aesthetic purpose rather than functional. These are colorama and FIGlet, which allow us to easily print colored text to standard out and create ASCII art, respectively. In addition, our framework requires all of the third-party modules that we used in the previous chapters.

The following topics will be discussed in this chapter:

- Framework fundamentals, challenges, and structure
- Adding aesthetic touches to our programs with Colorama and FIGlet

The code for this chapter was developed and tested using Python 2.7.15 and Python 3.7.1.

Frameworks

Why build a framework? The question could be, why develop a script at all? Frequently, we perform the same series of steps for a given piece of evidence. For example, we commonly prepare reports for LNK, prefetch, and jumplist files, examine registry keys, and establish external device and network activity to answer forensic questions. As we've seen, we can develop a script to parse these artifacts for us and display the data in a format that's conducive for rapid analysis. Why not write a series of scripts, each responsible for one artifact, and then control them with a singular script, to execute all at once and hence further automate our analysis?

A framework can be developed to run a series of scripts and parse multiple artifacts at once. The output of such a framework could be a series of analysis-ready spreadsheets. This allows the examiner to skip the same tedious series of steps and start answering meaningful questions about the evidence.

Frameworks typically have three main components:

- A main controller
- Plugins
- Writers

The main controller isn't very different from our `main()` functions and essentially calls a series of plugins on some input, which parse specific artifacts, store the returned results, and then send the results to a writer for output. Our plugins are scripts that perform a specific task, for example, a script that parses `UserAssist` artifacts. Writers, similar to our `csv_writer()` functions, take the output from our plugins and write it out to disk. While this seems like a fairly straightforward process, developing frameworks is more complex than developing a single script. This is because we have to worry about building a simple yet efficient structure and keeping data standardized between plugins.

Building a framework to last

A challenge when developing frameworks is how to keep the code simple and efficient while continuously adding more functionality to the framework. You might find that while the structure of the framework made sense initially, it doesn't support the needs of your increasingly complex framework, requiring you to rethink and rebuild the internals of the framework. Unfortunately, there's no magical way to future-proof your framework and will likely require multiple revisions during its development cycle.

This is no different from normal script development. In the early chapters of this book, we iterated through multiple versions of a script. We did this to illustrate the iterative build process you'll discover during development. This same iterative process can be applied at a larger scale for frameworks. While we are not highlighting that process in this chapter, keep in mind that you may need to rewrite the framework developed here might need to be rewritten if more plugins are later added and efficiency starts to lag. Development by iteration allows us to continuously improve on our original design to create a stable and efficient program.

Data standardization

One of the biggest challenges when developing a framework is data standardization. What that means is standardizing the input and output data for each plugin to keep things simple. For example, imagine one plugin that returns a list of dictionaries and another that returns just a list. To process these results correctly, you would need to include logic in your writers to handle both scenarios. It pays to implement each plugin in such a way that they return the same data structures. This helps keep your code simple by minimizing additional logic for a variety of special cases.

That said, there may very well be special scenarios you need to consider for each plugin. In our framework, for example, we'll see that some plugins return a list of dictionaries, whereas others return a single dictionary. Consider `setupapi_parser.py` from `Chapter 3`, *Parsing Text Files*—for a moment, it can identify multiple distinct USB devices and generate a dictionary for each one, whereas our `exif_parser.py` only returns one dictionary containing the embedded metadata within a single file. In this case, rather than trying to rewrite the plugins to comply with our rule, we leverage logic to handle additional recursion.

Forensic frameworks

There are a lot of forensic frameworks and plenty of these are open source, allowing anyone to contribute to their development. These frameworks are great, not only to contribute to, but to see how experienced developers structure their frameworks. Some popular open source forensic frameworks include the following:

- **Volatility**: A memory forensic framework (`http://github.com/volatilityfoundation/volatility`)
- **Plaso**: A artifact timelining tool (`http://github.com/log2timeline/plaso`)

- **GRR (short for Google Rapid Response)**: An agent-based analysis and response framework for remote forensic analysis (`http://github.com/google/grr`)

Contributing on an actively developing project, whether it's a framework or not, is a great way of actively learning good programming techniques and developing connections for collaboration on future projects.

Make sure to read contribution rules before developing for any project.

Enough has been said about frameworks: let's discuss the third-party modules we'll use to enhance the aesthetics of our framework.

Colorama

The `colorama` module (version 0.4.1) allows us to easily create colored Terminal text. We're going to use this to highlight good and bad events to the user. For example, when a plugin completes without errors, we display that with a green font. Similarly, we will print encountered errors in red. The colorama module can be installed with pip:

```
pip install colorama==0.4.1
```

Traditionally, printing colored text to the Terminal is achieved by a series of escape characters on Linux or macOS systems. This, however, won't work for Windows operating systems. The following are examples of ANSI escape characters being used to create colored text in Linux or macOS Terminals:

```
>>> print '\033[31m' + '31 is the ANSI color code for red'
31 is the ANSI color code for red
>>> print '\033[39m' + '39 will reset our foreground color to default'
39 will reset our foreground color to default
>>> print '\033[47; 31m' + 'We can supply multiple options by separating them with the semicolon. The last option must be immediately followed by "m"'
We can supply multiple options by separating them with the semicolon. The last option must be immediately followed by "m"
```

The color format is the escape character, `\033`, followed by an open bracket and then the desired color code. We can change the background color in addition to the foreground color and even do both at the same time by separating the codes with a semicolon. The color code, `31m`, sets the foreground text to red. The color code, `47m`, sets the background to white. Notice in the second example, in the preceding screenshot, `m` designates the end of the color codes and should therefore only follow the final color code.

We can use the `colorama` and `call` built-in variables, which are aliases for the desired ANSI codes. This makes our code more readable and best of all works with Windows Command Prompts after calling `colorama.init()` at the beginning of your script:

```
>>> import colorama
>>> print colorama.Fore.RED + 'Red foreground text'
Red foreground text
>>> print colorama.Fore.RED + colorama.Back.GREEN + 'Red foreground text and gre
en background'
Red foreground text and green background
>>> print colorama.Style.RESET_ALL

>>> print 'Back to defaults'
Back to defaults
```

The `colorama` module has three main formatting options: `Fore`, `Back`, and `Style`. These allow us to make changes to the foreground or background text color and its style, respectively. The colors available for the foreground and background include: black, red, green, yellow, blue, magenta, cyan, and white.

It's possible to change other text properties using ANSI escape characters, such as if we wanted to make the text dimmer or brighter. ANSI color codes and other information on the `colorama` library is available at `https://pypi.python.org/pypi/colorama`.

FIGlet

FIGlet, and its Python extension, `pyfiglet` (version 0.8.post0), is a simple way of generating ASCII art. All we need to do is supply FIGlet with a string of our choice and a font style, which dictates the design of our text. We'll use this module to print the title of our framework at the beginning of the program's execution to give it some personality. We can use pip to install pyfiglet:

```
pip install pyfiglet==0.8.post0
```

To use FIGlet, we need to create a FIGlet object and specify the type of font we would like to use. We then call the object's `renderText` method, along with the string to style. A full list of fonts is available at `http://www.figlet.org/examples.html`:

```
>>> from pyfiglet import Figlet
>>> f = Figlet(font='banner')
>>> print(f.renderText('Forensics'))
#######
#        ####  #####  ###### #    #  ####  #  ####   ####
#       #    # #    # #      ##   # #      # #    # #
#####   #    # #    # #####  # #  #  ####  # #       ####
#       #    # #####  #      #  # #      # # #            #
#       #    # #   #  #      #   ## #    # # #    # #    #
#        ####  #    # ###### #    #  ####  #  ####   ####
```

With the necessary third-party modules introduced, let's start walking through the framework code itself.

Exploring the framework – framework.py

Our framework takes some input directory, recursively indexes all of its files, runs a series of plugins to identify forensic artifacts, and then writes a series of reports into a specified output directory. The idea is that the examiner could mount a `.E01` or `.dd` file using a tool such as FTK Imager and then run the framework against the mounted directory.

The layout of a framework is an important first step in achieving a simplistic design. We recommend placing writers and plugins in appropriately labeled subdirectories under the framework controller. Our framework is laid out in the following manner:

```
|-- framework.py
|-- requirements.txt
|-- plugins
    |-- __init__.py
    |-- exif.py
    |-- id3.py
    |-- office.py
    |-- pst_indexer.py
    |-- setupapi.py
    |-- userassist.py
    |-- wal_crawler.py
    |-- helper
        |-- __init__.py
        |-- utility.py
        |-- usb_lookup.py
```

```
|-- writers
    |-- __init__.py
    |-- csv_writer.py
    |-- xlsx_writer.py
    |-- kml_writer.py
```

Our `framework.py` script contains the main logic of our framework-handling the input and output values for all of our plugins. The `requirements.txt` file contains one third-party module on each line used by the framework. In this format, we can use this file with `pip` to install all of the listed modules. `pip` will attempts to install the latest version of the module unless a version is specified immediately following the module name and two equal to signs (that is, `colorama==0.4.1`). We can install third-party modules from our `requirements.txt` file using the following code:

```
pip install -r requirements.txt
```

The plugins and writers are stored in their own respective directories with an `__init__.py` file to ensure that Python can find the directory. Within the plugins directory are seven initial plugins our framework will support. The plugins we'll include are as follows:

- The EXIF, ID3, and Office embedded metadata parsers from `Chapter 8`, *The Media Age*
- The PST parser from `Chapter 11`, *Parsing Outlook PST Containers*
- The Setupapi parser from `Chapter 3`, *Parsing Text Files*
- The UserAssist parser from `Chapter 6`, *Extracting Artifacts from Binary Files*
- The WAL file parser from `Chapter 12`, *Recovering Transient Database Records*

There's also a `helper` directory containing some helper scripts that are required by some of the plugins. There are currently three supported output formats for our framework: CSV, XLSX, and KML. Only the `exif` plugin will make use of `kml_writer` to create a Google Earth map with plotted EXIF GPS data, as we saw in `Chapter 8`, *The Media Age.*

Now that we understand the how, why, and layout of our framework, let's dig into some code. On lines 2 through 11, we import the modules we plan to use. Note that this is only the list of modules that are required in this immediate script. It doesn't include the dependencies required by the various plugins. Plugin-specific imports are made in their respective scripts.

Most of these imports should look familiar from the previous chapters, with the exception of the new additions of `colorama` and `pyfiglet`. On lines 7 and 8, we import our plugins and writers subdirectories, which contain the scripts for our plugins and writers. The `colorama.init()` call on line 13 is a prerequisite that allows us to print colored text to the Windows Command Prompt:

```
002 from __future__ import print_function
003 import os
004 import sys
005 import logging
006 import argparse
007 import plugins
008 import writers
009 import colorama
010 from datetime import datetime
011 from pyfiglet import Figlet
012
013 colorama.init()
```

On line 49, we define our `Framework` class. This class will contain a variety of methods, all of which handle the initialization and execution of the framework. The `run()` method acts as our typical main function and calls the `_list_files()` and `_run_plugins()` methods. The `_list_files()` method walks through files in the user-supplied directory and, based upon the name or extension, adds the file to a plugin-specific processing list. Then, the `_run_plugins()` method takes these lists and executes each plugin, stores the results, and calls the appropriate writer:

```
049 class Framework(object):
...
051     def __init__():
...
061     def run():
...
074     def _list_files():
...
115     def _run_plugins():
```

Within the `Framework` class are two subclasses: `Plugin` and `Writer`. The `Plugin` class is responsible for actually running the plugin, logging when it completes, and sending data to be written. The `run()` method repeatedly executes each function for every file in the plugin's processing list. It appends the returned data to a list, mapped to the key in a dictionary. This dictionary also stores the desired field names for the spreadsheet. The `write()` method creates the plugin specific output directory and, based on the type of output specified, makes appropriate calls to the `Writer` class:

```
    class Plugin(object):
...
        def __init__():
...
        def run():
...
        def write():
```

The `Writer` class is the simplest class of the three. Its `run()` method simply executes the desired writers with the correct input:

```
    class Writer(object):
...
        def __init__():
...
        def run():
```

As with all of our scripts, we use `argparse` to handle command-line switches. On lines 285 and 287, we create two positional arguments for our input and output directories. The two optional arguments on lines 288 and 290 specify XLSX output and the desired log path, respectively:

```
279 if __name__ == '__main__':
280
281     parser = argparse.ArgumentParser(description=__description__,
282                                      epilog='Developed by ' +
283                                      __author__ + ' on ' +
284                                      __date__)
285     parser.add_argument('INPUT_DIR',
286         help='Base directory to process.')
287     parser.add_argument('OUTPUT_DIR', help='Output directory.')
288     parser.add_argument('-x', help='Excel output (Default CSV)',
289         action='store_true')
290     parser.add_argument('-l',
291         help='File path and name of log file.')
292     args = parser.parse_args()
```

We can see our first use of the `colorama` library on line 297. If the supplied input and output directories are files, we print a red error message to the console. For the rest of our framework, we use error messages displayed in red text and success messages in green:

```
294     if(os.path.isfile(args.INPUT_DIR) or
295             os.path.isfile(args.OUTPUT_DIR)):
296         msg = 'Input and Output arguments must be directories.'
297         print(colorama.Fore.RED + '[-]', msg)
298         sys.exit(1)
```

On line 300, we check whether the optional directory path was supplied for the log file. If so, we create these directories (if they don't exist), and store the filename for the log in the `log_path` variable:

```
300     if args.l:
301         if not os.path.exists(args.l):
302             os.makedirs(args.l) # create log directory path
303         log_path = os.path.join(args.l, 'framework.log')
304     else:
305         log_path = 'framework.log'
```

On lines 307 and 309, we create our `Framework` object and then call its `run()` method. We pass the following arguments into the `Framework` constructor to instantiate the object: `INPUT_DIR`, `OUTPUT_DIR`, `log_path`, and `excel`. In the next section, we inspect the `Framework` class in greater detail:

```
307     framework = Framework(args.INPUT_DIR, args.OUTPUT_DIR,
308     log_path, excel=args.x)
309     framework.run()
```

The following flow chart highlights how the different methods in the `framework.py` script interact. Keep in mind that this flow chart only shows interactions within the immediate script and doesn't account for the various plugin, writer, and utility scripts:

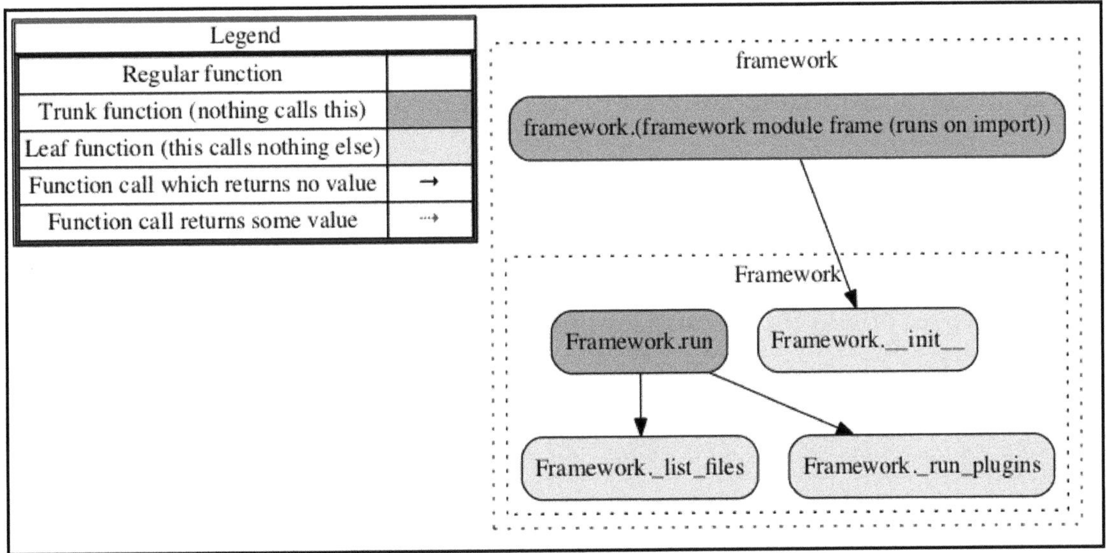

Exploring the Framework object

We developed our framework with an object-oriented programming design in mind. This allows us to create compartmentalized and reusable objects. Within our `Framework` object are the `Plugin` and `Writer` objects, which we explored in the proceeding sections. The `Framework` class is defined on line 49 and extends the `object` class. In Python 2.X, inheriting from an object that replaces the previous tradition of inheriting nothing has become standard in Python 3.X:

```
049 class Framework(object):
```

Understanding the Framework __init__() constructor

The `__init__()` method for the framework is defined on line 51. In this constructor, we assign the arguments passed to the constructor as instance variables. We also configure the logging module on line 55. Let's look at the `run()` method, which, as we saw, is called immediately after the `Framework` object is instantiated:

```
051     def __init__(self, input_directory, output_directory, log,
052     **kwargs):
053         self.input = input_directory
054         self.output = output_directory
055         logging.basicConfig(filename=log, level=logging.DEBUG,
```

```
                        format=('%(asctime)s | %(levelname)s | '
                        '%(message)s'), filemode='a')
        self.log = logging.getLogger(log)
        self.kwargs = kwargs
```

Creating the Framework run() method

The `run()` method, defined on line 61, executes the entire logic of our framework in a few lines of code. Lines 62 through 68 simply print and log startup information for debugging purposes. Notice the use of `Figlet` on lines 65 and 66 to print our framework's title to the console:

```
061     def run(self):
062         msg = 'Initializing framework'
063         print('[+]', msg)
064         self.log.info(msg)
065         f = Figlet(font='doom')
066         print(f.renderText('Framework'))
067         self.log.debug('System ' + sys.platform)
068         self.log.debug('Version ' + sys.version)
```

On line 69, we check to see whether the output directory exists. If it doesn't, we create it using the `os.makedirs()` method. Finally, on lines 71 and 72, we call the `_list_files()` and `_run_plugins()` methods to index the input directory files and run our plugins against them:

```
069         if not os.path.exists(self.output):
070             os.makedirs(self.output)
071         self._list_files()
072         self._run_plugins()
```

Iterating through files with the Framework _list_files() method

The `_list_files()` method is used to iterate through each file in the input directory recursively. It stores the files into a processing list for a plugin based on the file's name or extension. One drawback to this approach is that we're relying on file extensions to be correct rather than using the file signatures themselves. We could implement this functionality into the framework by using struct to check each file's signature, as we've done in the previous chapters.

Notice that the `_list_files()` method has a single leading underscore. This is Python's way of declaring an internal method. What it means here is that we're declaring that the `_list_files()` method shouldn't be imported and, generally, shouldn't be directly called by the user. For instance, we should not call `Framework._list_files()` on our `Framework` object after we instantiated it on line 309. Instead, we can call the `run()` method, which in turn calls the `_list_files()` method.

The `_list_files()` method is defined on line 74 and prints and logs the current execution status. On lines 79 through 85, we create a series of lists specific to each plugin. These lists are used to store any file identified as compatible with a plugin for later processing:

```
074     def _list_files(self):
075         msg = 'Indexing {}'.format(self.input)
076         print('[+]', msg)
077         logging.info(msg)
078
079         self.wal_files = []
080         self.setupapi_files = []
081         self.userassist_files = []
082         self.exif_metadata = []
083         self.office_metadata = []
084         self.id3_metadata = []
085         self.pst_files = []
```

Starting on line 87, we use the `os.walk()` method that we used in the previous chapters to iterate over the input directory. For each file, we create two variables, one for the name of the current file and another for the extension of the current file:

```
087         for root, subdir, files in os.walk(self.input,
088         topdown=True):
089             for file_name in files:
090                 current_file = os.path.join(root, file_name)
091                 if not os.path.isfile(current_file):
092                     logging.warning((u'Could not parse file {}...'
093                     ' Skipping...').format((current_file)))
094                     continue
095                 ext = os.path.splitext(current_file)[1].lower()
```

Using our `current_file` and `ext` variables, we use a series of conditional statements to identify files for our plugins. For example, on line 96, we check whether the file contains `ntuser.dat` in its name as this most likely identifies it as a user's registry hive and is appended to our `userassist_files` list.

Similarly, on line 100, anything ending in `.jpeg` or `.jpg` is most likely a photo with EXIF embedded metadata and is appended to our `exif_metadata` list. If the current file doesn't meet any of our requirements, then we can't parse it with our current plugins, and we use `continue` to start the next loop:

```
096             if current_file.lower().endswith('ntuser.dat'):
097                 self.userassist_files.append(current_file)
098             elif 'setupapi.dev.log' in current_file.lower():
099                 self.setupapi_files.append(current_file)
100             elif ext == '.jpeg' or ext == '.jpg':
101                 self.exif_metadata.append(current_file)
102             elif(ext == '.docx' or
103                     ext == '.pptx' or
104                     ext == '.xlsx'):
105                 self.office_metadata.append(current_file)
106             elif ext == '.mp3':
107                 self.id3_metadata.append(current_file)
108             elif ext == '.pst' or ext == '.ost':
109                 self.pst_files.append(current_file)
110             elif ext.endswith('-wal'):
111                 self.wal_files.append(current_file)
112             else:
113                 continue
```

Developing the Framework _run_plugins() method

The `_run_plugins()` is another internal method and handles the logic for calling each plugin and then sending the returned results to the appropriate writer. There are two twists in handling each plugin. We highlight these different twists for two plugins. We won't cover the other five plugins to cut down on explaining the same code.

The first plugin example is the `wal_crawler` plugin. On line 117, we check whether we need to create a `Plugin` object for the `wal_crawler` at all because if the `wal_files` list is empty, there'll be nothing to run the plugin against. If it isn't empty, we create a `Plugin` object on line 118.

Next, we create `wal_output`, which stores our plugin's output directory. On line 121, we call the `run()` method of the `Plugin` class and then, based on whether the `excel` output option is specified, `write()` the results of the plugin, passing along the `excel` keyword argument, if necessary.

Recall that the `wal_crawler` script returns a list of dictionaries where each dictionary contains a cells worth of data. When we call the plugin, we put the results in yet another list. By default, the writers expect just a list of dictionaries to iterate over and write the appropriate report. Because we append a list of dictionaries to yet another list, we need to tell the writer that it needs another `for` loop to access the list of dictionaries. We do this by passing the recursion keyword argument to the plugin's `write()` method. We set the `recursion` value to `1`, to mark it as enabled:

```
    def _run_plugins(self):
        # Run Wal Crawler
        if len(self.wal_files) > 0:
            wal_plugin = Framework.Plugin('wal_crawler',
            self.wal_files, self.log)
            wal_output = os.path.join(self.output, 'wal')
            wal_plugin.run(plugins.wal_crawler.main)
            if self.kwargs['excel'] is True:
                wal_plugin.write(wal_output, recursion=1, excel=1)
            else:
                wal_plugin.write(wal_output, recursion=1)
```

Unlike in the previous example, our ID3 metadata script returns a single dictionary, which is appended to a list. In these scenarios, we don't need to specify the `recursion` keyword argument, as seen on lines 190 and 193. Beyond this single difference, the plugin is handled in the same fashion as the previous plugin.

Remember one goal of our framework is to be able to disable or add a new plugin in as few lines of code as possible.

This increases the simplicity of the framework, making it far easier to maintain. We've tried to maintain that here by keeping the logic consistent and using keyword arguments to handle slight variations:

```
182         # Run ID3 metadata parser
183         if len(self.id3_metadata) > 0:
184             id3_metadata_plugin = Framework.Plugin('id3_metadata',
185             self.id3_metadata, self.log)
186             id3_metadata_output = os.path.join(self.output,
187                 'metadata')
188             id3_metadata_plugin.run(plugins.id3.main)
189             if self.kwargs['excel'] is True:
190                 id3_metadata_plugin.write(id3_metadata_output,
191                     excel=1)
192             else:
193                 id3_metadata_plugin.write(id3_metadata_output)
```

Exploring the Plugin object

On line 207, we have the beginning of the `Plugin` subclass. This class contains the `run()` and `write()` methods, which are used to handle the execution of each plugin as well as the calls to the writers:

```
207     class Plugin(object):
```

Understanding the Plugin __init__() constructor

The `Plugin` constructor method is fairly straightforward. We create instance variables for the plugin name, the files to process, the log, and a dictionary containing the results of the plugin. The results dictionary contains a data list, which stores the actual results returned from each plugin call. The headers key will eventually have a list storing the field names to use in the writers:

```
209         def __init__(self, plugin, files, log):
210             self.plugin = plugin
211             self.files = files
212             self.log = log
213             self.results = {'data': [], 'headers': None}
```

Working with the Plugin run() method

The `run()` method defined on line 215 is responsible for executing the plugin against each file stored in the plugin's list. In addition, this method prints out various status messages pertaining to the execution of the plugin.

The function argument passed into the `run()` method is the name of the entry-point method in the plugin. We call this entry-point for each file in the plugin's file list. For example, the `wal_crawler` plugin's entry-point method is `plugins.wal_crawler.main`:

```
215         def run(self, function):
216             msg = 'Executing {} plugin'.format(self.plugin)
217             print(colorama.Fore.RESET + '[+]', msg)
218             self.log.info(msg)
```

On line 220, we begin to iterate through each file in the plugin's file list. On line 222, we call the function variable and supply it with the file to process. This restricts all of our plugins to comply with a single file as its input. Some of the modifications we made to our existing plugins involved modifying their required arguments to work within the bounds of the framework. For example, in the previous chapters, we may have passed in an output file or directory as one of the script's arguments. However, now, the writers, a separate part of the framework, handle the output and so the plugins only need to focus on processing and returning the data to the framework.

Notice that the function call is wrapped around try and except. In the plugins themselves, you can see that we raise `TypeError` when we encounter an error in the plugin; in the case of an error, the plugin logs the actual error while the framework continues to process the next file.

On lines 223 and 224, we append the returned results from the plugin to the data list and set the headers for the plugin. The returned headers list is a constant list of field names that's set whenever the plugin returns successfully:

```
220             for f in self.files:
221                 try:
222                     data, headers = function(f)
223                     self.results['data'].append(data)
224                     self.results['headers'] = headers
225
226                 except TypeError:
227                     self.log.error(('Issue processing {}. '
228                         'Skipping...').format(f))
229                     continue
```

Finally, on lines 231 through 234, we print out and log the successful completion of the plugin, including the current time to the user:

```
231             msg = 'Plugin {} completed at {}'.format(self.plugin,
232             datetime.now().strftime('%m/%d/%Y %H:%M:%S'))
233             print(colorama.Fore.GREEN + '[*]', msg)
234             self.log.info(msg)
```

Handling output with the Plugin write() method

The `write()` method is first defined on line 236. This method creates the plugin-specific output directory and call the appropriate writer to create the plugin report. On lines 241 and 242, after printing out a status message to the user, we create the plugin output directory if it doesn't already exist:

```
236     def write(self, output, **kwargs):
237         msg = 'Writing results of {} plugin'.format(
238         self.plugin)
239         print(colorama.Fore.RESET + '[+]', msg)
240         self.log.info(msg)
241         if not os.path.exists(output):
242             os.makedirs(output)
```

On line 243, we check to see whether the `excel` keyword argument was specified in the function call. If it was, we call `xlsx_writer` and pass the output directory, the desired filename, field names, and the data to write.

If the `excel` keyword argument isn't supplied, the default `csv_writer` is called instead. This function takes the same arguments as `xlsx_writer`. On line 253, we check whether the plugin name is `exif_metadata`. If so, we call `kml_writer` to plot the Google Earth GPS data:

```
243         if 'excel' in kwargs.keys():
244             Framework.Writer(writers.xlsx_writer.writer,
245                 output, self.plugin + '.xlsx',
246                 self.results['headers'],
247                 self.results['data'], **kwargs)
248         else:
249             Framework.Writer(writers.csv_writer.writer,
250                 output, self.plugin + '.csv',
251                 self.results['headers'],
252                 self.results['data'], **kwargs)
253         if self.plugin == 'exif_metadata':
254             Framework.Writer(writers.kml_writer.writer,
255                 output, '', self.plugin + '.kml',
256                 self.results['data'])
```

Exploring the Writer object

The `Writer` object is defined on line 258. This class is responsible for creating the report for each plugin. The class has one main method, `run()`, which simply calls the writer that was described in the `plugin.write` method:

```
258     class Writer(object):
```

Understanding the Writer __init__() constructor

The constructor method instantiates session variables, including the output filename of the report, the header, and the data to be written. If the `recursion` keyword argument is present, we set the session variable before calling the `run()` method:

```
260         def __init__(self, writer, output, name, header, data,
261         **kwargs):
262             self.writer = writer
263             self.output = os.path.join(output, name)
264             self.header = header
265             self.data = data
266             self.recursion = None
267             if 'recursion' in kwargs.keys():
268                 self.recursion = kwargs['recursion']
269             self.run()
```

Understanding the Writer run() method

The `run()` method is very straightforward. Based on whether recursion was specified, we call the specified writer, passing along the `recursion` keyword argument:

```
271         def run(self):
272             if self.recursion:
273                 self.writer(self.output, self.header, self.data,
274                     recursion=self.recursion)
275             else:
276                 self.writer(self.output, self.header, self.data)
```

Our Final CSV writer – csv_writer.py

Each writer essentially works in the same manner. Let's briefly discuss the `csv_writer` method before discussing the more complex `xlsx_writer` script. Depending on whether the framework is run with Python 2.X or 3.X, we import the native `csv` or `unicodecsv` modules to handle Unicode strings. The `unicodecsv` module was first introduced in `Chapter 5`, *Databases in Python*:

```
from __future__ import print_function
import sys
import os
if sys.version_info[0] == 2:
    import unicodecsv as csv
elif sys.version_info[0] == 3:
    import csv
```

Our writer is very simple. On line 61, we create a `csv.DictWriter` object and pass it the output filename and headers list. As always, we indicate to the writer to ignore the case where they are keys that are not specified in the supplied headers:

```
038 def writer(output, headers, output_data, **kwargs):
039     """
040     The writer function uses the csv.DictWriter module to write
041     list(s) of dictionaries. The DictWriter can take a fieldnames
042     argument, as a list, which represents the desired order of
043     columns.
044     :param output: The name of the output CSV.
045     :param headers: A list of keys in the dictionary that
046     represent the desired order of columns in the output.
047     :param output_data: The list of dictionaries containing
048     embedded metadata.
049     :return: None
050     """
051 
052     if sys.version_info[0] == 2:
053         csvfile = open(output, "wb")
054     elif sys.version_info[0] == 3:
055         csvfile = open(output, "w", newline='',
056             encoding='utf-8')
057 
058     with csvfile:
059         # We use DictWriter instead of writer to write
060         # dictionaries to CSV.
061         w = csv.DictWriter(csvfile, fieldnames=headers,
062             extrasaction='ignore')
```

With the `DictWriter` object created, we can use the built-in `writerheader()` method to write our field names as the first row of the spreadsheet. Notice that we wrap this in a try and except, something we haven't done in the past. Imagine a scenario where there's only one file for a plugin to process and it encounters and error and returns prematurely. In this case, the headers list will be none, which will cause an error. This last check allows us to exit writing invalid output files for this scenario:

```
064         # Writerheader writes the header based on the supplied
065         # headers object
066         try:
067             w.writeheader()
068         except TypeError:
069             print(('[-] Received empty headers...\n'
070                 '[-] Skipping writing output.'))
071             return
```

Next, on line 73, if the `recursion` keyword argument was supplied, we use two `for` loops before calling the `writerow` method on the dictionaries. Otherwise, on line 79, we only need to use one `for` loop to access the data to write:

```
073         if 'recursion' in kwargs.keys():
074             for l in output_data:
075                 for data in l:
076                     if data:
077                         w.writerow(data)
078         else:
079             for data in output_data:
080                 if data:
081                     w.writerow(data)
```

The writer – xlsx_writer.py

The `xlsx_writer` function is a slightly modified version of `xlsx_writer`, which we created in `Chapter 6`, *Extracting Artifacts from Binary Files*. We use the same `xlsxwriter` third-party module to handle the excel output. On line 32, we use list comprehension to create a list of capitalized alphabetical characters from `A` to `Z`. We're going to use this list to designate the column letter based on the supplied headers length. This method works as long as there are less than 26 field names, which for the current set of plugins is true:

```
001 from __future__ import print_function
002 import xlsxwriter
...
032 ALPHABET = [chr(i) for i in range(ord('A'), ord('Z') + 1)]
```

On line 44, we create the `xlsxwriter` workbook and supply the output filename to save it as. Before going any further, we check whether the supplied headers are equal to none. This check is necessary, just as in `csv_writer`, to avoid writing invalid data from a bad call to the writer. On line 52, we set `title_length` equal to the letter that the right-most column will be, in case there are more than 26 columns. We've currently set the right-most value to be `Z`:

```
035 def writer(output, headers, output_data, **kwargs):
036     """
037     The writer function writes excel output for the framework
038     :param output: the output filename for the excel spreadsheet
039     :param headers: the name of the spreadsheet columns
040     :param output_data: the data to be written to the excel
041     spreadsheet
042     :return: Nothing
043     """
044     wb = xlsxwriter.Workbook(output)
045 
046     if headers is None:
047         print('[-] Received empty headers... \n'
048             '[-] Skipping writing output.')
049         return
050 
051     if len(headers) <= 26:
052         title_length = ALPHABET[len(headers) - 1]
053     else:
054         title_length = 'Z'
```

Next, on line 56, we create our worksheet. In a similar fashion to the `csv_writer` function, if recursion is specified, we loop through the list, adding a worksheet for each additional list to prevent them from writing over each other. We then use list comprehension to quickly order the dictionary values based on the order of the field names. In `csv_writer`, the `writerow` method from the `DictWriter` object orders the data automatically. For `xlsx_writer`, we need to use list comprehension to recreate that same effect:

```
056     ws = add_worksheet(wb, title_length)
057 
058     if 'recursion' in kwargs.keys():
059         for i, data in enumerate(output_data):
060             if i > 0:
061                 ws = add_worksheet(wb, title_length)
062             cell_length = len(data)
063             tmp = []
064             for dictionary in data:
065                 tmp.append(
066                 [str(dictionary[x]) if x in dictionary.keys() else ''
```

```
for x in headers]
067                 )
```

On line 69, we create a table from `A3` to `XY`, where `X` is the alphabet character representing the length of the field names list and `Y` is the length of the `output_data` list. For example, if we have a dataset that has six field names and 10 entries, we want our table to span from `A3` to `F13`. In addition, we pass along the ordered data and specify each column using list comprehension once again to specify a dictionary with one key-value pair for each header:

```
069             ws.add_table(
070                 'A3:' + title_length + str(3 + cell_length),
071                 {'data': tmp,
072                 'columns': [{'header': x} for x in headers]})
```

On line 74, we handle the scenario where we don't supply the `recursion` keyword argument. In this case, we handle the same execution minus the additional `for` loop. Lastly, on line 84, we close the workbook:

```
074     else:
075         cell_length = len(output_data)
076         tmp = []
077         for data in output_data:
078             tmp.append([str(data[x]) if x in data.keys() else '' for x
in headers])
079         ws.add_table(
080             'A3:' + title_length + str(3 + cell_length),
081             {'data': tmp,
082             'columns': [{'header': x} for x in headers]})
083
084     wb.close()
```

The `add_worksheet()` method is called on lines 56 and 61. This function is used to create the worksheet and writes the first two rows of the spreadsheet. On line 96, we create the `title_format` style, which contains the text properties we want for our two title rows. On lines 101 and 103, we create both of our title rows. Currently, the values of these title rows are hardcoded but could be programmed into the framework by adding them as optional switches in `argparse`:

```
087 def add_worksheet(wb, length, name=None):
088     """
089     The add_worksheet function creates a new formatted worksheet
090     in the workbook
091     :param wb: The workbook object
092     :param length: The range of rows to merge
093     :param name: The name of the worksheet
094     :return: ws, the worksheet
```

```
    """
    title_format = wb.add_format({'bold': True,
    'font_color': 'black', 'bg_color': 'white', 'font_size': 30,
    'font_name': 'Arial', 'align': 'center'})
    ws = wb.add_worksheet(name)

    ws.merge_range('A1:' + length + '1', 'XYZ Corp',
        title_format)
    ws.merge_range('A2:' + length + '2', 'Case ####',
        title_format)
    return ws
```

Changes made to plugins

We've discussed the framework, its subclasses, and the two main writer scripts. What about the changes we had to make to the plugin scripts from previous chapters? For the most part, their core functionality is unchanged. Modifications we made include removing printing and logging statements, deleting the `argparse` and log setup sections, and removing unnecessary functions such as the script's output writer (since the framework handles that).

Instead of walking through each plugin, we invite you to view the source files yourself and compare. You'll see that these files are mostly the same from the previous scripts. Keep in mind that when we originally wrote these scripts, we had it in the back of our minds that they would eventually be added to a framework. While the similarity between the framework and non-framework versions of the scripts was intentional, it was necessary to still make modifications to get everything working correctly.

Executing the framework

To run the framework, at a minimum, we need to supply an input and output directory. Optionally, we can provide arguments for the desired log output path and enable XLSX output rather than the default CSV. The first example and the following screenshot highlight the minimum arguments to run the framework. The second example shows the additional switches we can call with our framework:

```
python framework.py /mnt/evidence ~/Desktop/framework_output
python framework.py /mnt/evidence ~/Desktop/framework_output -l
~/Desktop/logs -x
```

Upon running the framework, the user will be presented with a variety of output text detailing the execution status of the framework:

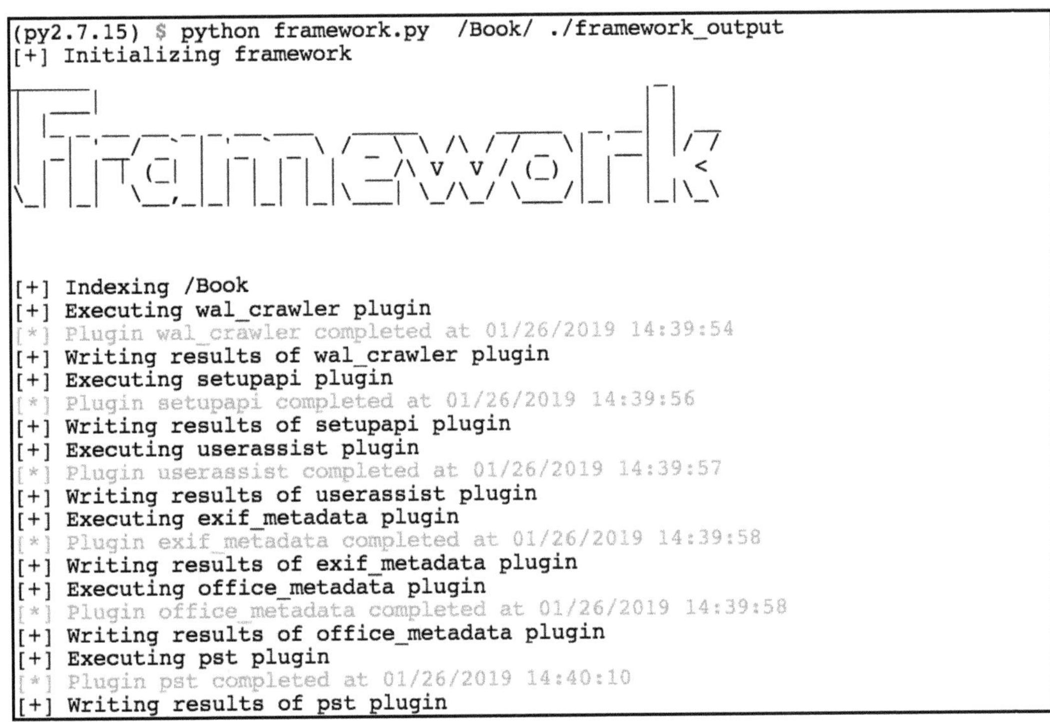

(py2.7.15) $ python framework.py /Book/ ./framework_output
[+] Initializing framework
[+] Indexing /Book
[+] Executing wal_crawler plugin
[*] Plugin wal_crawler completed at 01/26/2019 14:39:54
[+] Writing results of wal_crawler plugin
[+] Executing setupapi plugin
[*] Plugin setupapi completed at 01/26/2019 14:39:56
[+] Writing results of setupapi plugin
[+] Executing userassist plugin
[*] Plugin userassist completed at 01/26/2019 14:39:57
[+] Writing results of userassist plugin
[+] Executing exif_metadata plugin
[*] Plugin exif_metadata completed at 01/26/2019 14:39:58
[+] Writing results of exif_metadata plugin
[+] Executing office_metadata plugin
[*] Plugin office_metadata completed at 01/26/2019 14:39:58
[+] Writing results of office_metadata plugin
[+] Executing pst plugin
[*] Plugin pst completed at 01/26/2019 14:40:10
[+] Writing results of pst plugin

As each plugin successfully processes, a report is generated in the plugin's output folder. We decided to organize the output by storing each plugin report in a separate folder to allow the examiner to drill down to their plugin of interest easily:

Name	Size	Date Modified
metadata	--	Today, 2:41 PM
exif_metadata.csv	40 KB	Today, 2:40 PM
exif_metadata.kml	3 KB	Today, 2:40 PM
office_metadata.csv	7 KB	Today, 2:40 PM
setupapi	--	Today, 2:41 PM
setupapi.csv	962 bytes	Today, 2:40 PM
userassist	--	Today, 2:41 PM
userassist.csv	77 KB	Today, 2:40 PM
wal	--	Today, 2:41 PM
wal_crawler.csv	307 KB	Today, 2:40 PM

Additional challenges

There are a lot of potential opportunities for improvement with our framework. Obviously, we could continue to add more plugins and writers to the framework. For example, while we have the beginning of USB device artifacts with the `Setupapi` plugin, it could be expanded by parsing various USB pertinent registry keys using the `Registry` module from `Chapter 6`, *Extracting Artifacts from Binary Files*. Alternatively, consider adding other scripts we've already created. For instance, it might be useful to generate an active file listing using the script from `Chapter 5`, *Databases in Python*. This would allow us to monitor what files have been processed by the framework.

Additionally, adding novel sources of user activity artifacts, such as a prefetch parser would enhance the intrinsic value of the framework. The file format for prefetch files is described at `http://forensicswiki.org/wiki/Windows_Prefetch_File_Format`. As with any binary file, we recommend using the struct module to parse the file.

Finally, for those looking for a challenge, consider adding `E01` and `dd` support by using `libewf` (`https://github.com/libyal/libewf`) or `libtsk` (`https://github.com/py4n6/pytsk`). This would get rid of the need to mount the image file before running the framework against it. This would be more of an undertaking and will likely require a rewrite of the framework. However, the harder the challenge, the more you'll get out of it once complete.

An example of this implementation is available in the Python Digital Forensics Cookbook by Packt, which is available at `https://www.packtpub.com/networking-and-servers/python-digital-forensics-cookbook`.

Summary

This is the final chapter, where we learned how to develop our own forensic framework using scripts we've previously built. This is the first step to building your very own automated forensic solution, greatly increasing your lunch break, or for the more serious, efficiency. We've learned how to balance code complexity with efficiency to develop a sustainable framework to help us to answer investigative questions. The code for this project can be downloaded from GitHub or Packt, as described in the *Preface*.

At the outset of this book, we wanted to teach investigators the advantages of Python by showing increasingly complex scripts. Throughout this process, we've introduced common techniques, best practices, and a myriad of first and third-party modules. We hope that, at this point, you're comfortable with developing your own scripts and understand the fundamentals of Python and are well on your way to becoming a forensic developer.

As we close out of this book, we wanted to list a few recommendations. If you haven't done so, please attempt to solve the various challenges. Some are fairly straightforward while others are more difficult, but in any case, they will help you develop your skills further. Additionally, go beyond just following along with the code provided with this book. Find a problem or task that's frequently encountered and script it from scratch. And, as always, ask friends, use the internet, read additional books, and collaborate with others to continue learning. Our capacity to learn is only waylaid by our lack of effort to pursue it.

Other Books You May Enjoy

If you enjoyed this book, you may be interested in these other books by Packt:

Mastering Reverse Engineering
Reginald Wong

ISBN: 9781788838849

- Learn core reverse engineering
- Identify and extract malware components
- Explore the tools used for reverse engineering
- Run programs under non-native operating systems
- Understand binary obfuscation techniques
- Identify and analyze anti-debugging and anti-analysis tricks

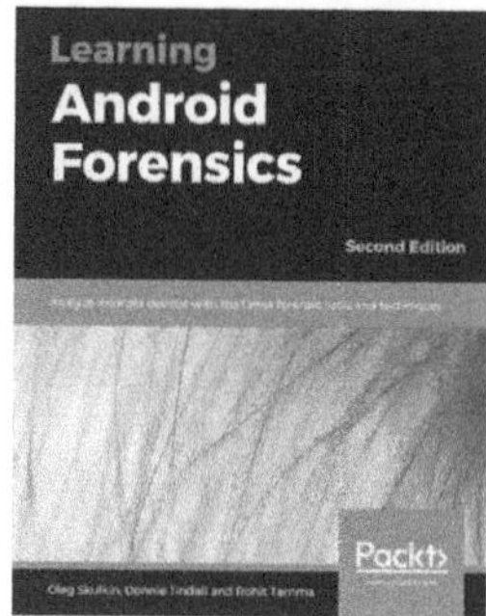

Learning Android Forensics - Second Edition
Oleg Skulkin, Donnie Tindall, Rohit Tamma

ISBN: 9781789131017

- Understand Android OS and architecture
- Set up a forensics environment for Android analysis
- Perform logical and physical data extractions
- Learn to recover deleted data
- Explore how to analyze application data
- Identify malware on Android devices
- Analyze Android malware

Leave a review - let other readers know what you think

Please share your thoughts on this book with others by leaving a review on the site that you bought it from. If you purchased the book from Amazon, please leave us an honest review on this book's Amazon page. This is vital so that other potential readers can see and use your unbiased opinion to make purchasing decisions, we can understand what our customers think about our products, and our authors can see your feedback on the title that they have worked with Packt to create. It will only take a few minutes of your time, but is valuable to other potential customers, our authors, and Packt. Thank you!

Index

A

B

C

D

E

F

T

U

V

CPSIA information can be obtained
at www.ICGtesting.com
Printed in the USA
LVHW021942150122
708348LV00003B/13

9 781789 341690